HEMANT

The TUXEDO System

The TUXEDO System: Software for Constructing and Managing Distributed Business Applications

Juan M. Andrade

Mark T. Carges

Terence J. Dwyer

Stephen D. Felts

▲▼▲
Addison-Wesley Publishing Company
Reading, Massachusetts   Menlo Park, California   New York
Don Mills, Ontario   Wokingham, England   Amsterdam   Bonn
Sydney   Singapore   Tokyo   Madrid   San Juan
Seoul   Milan   Mexico City   Taipei

The publisher offers discounts on this book when ordered in quantity for special sales.

For more information, please contact:

Corporate & Professional Publishing Group
Addison-Wesley Publishing Company
One Jacob Way
Reading, Massachusetts 01867

Library of Congress Cataloging-in-Publication Data

The TUXEDO System : software for constructing and managing distributed
   business applications / Juan M. Andrade . . . [et al.].
        p. cm.
     Includes bibliographical references and index.
     ISBN 0-201-63493-7 (acid-free paper)
     1. Transaction systems (Computer systems) 2. TUXEDO Systems.
   3. Electronic data processing—Distributed processing. 4. Business—
Data processing. I. Andrade, Juan M., 1951–
QA76.545.T845   1996
005.75'8—dc20   96-22121
                                                               CIP

ISBN 0-201-63493-7

Text printed on recycled and acid-free paper.

1 2 3 4 5 6 7 8 9 10 - MA - 99989796

First Printing, July 1996.

To my wife, Ana Maria, for her support, understanding, and encourgement, and my children, Patricia and Roberto, who endured a longer-than-planned project.

—Juan Andrade

To my wife, Carol, for her enduring support of my work on the TUXEDO Project and, especially, on this book.

—Mark Carges

To Jane Dwyer, my wife and best friend, for all of her support and encouragement during my work on the TUXEDO Project.

—Terence Dwyer

Dedicated to my wife, Helen, and children, Christina and Rebekah, for putting up with the many hours spent writing and printing this book.

—Stephen Felts

Contents

Part I

Setting the Stage for Understanding the TUXEDO System 1

Part II

Part III

Part IV

Figures

Listings

Tables

Preface

About This Book

This introductory book on the TUXEDO System was written by its principal inventors and architects. The intended audience for the book includes managers of software teams, software architects, and software designers and developers who wish to understand issues in constructing distributed business applications and who wish to see how the TUXEDO System can help them do their jobs. The purpose of this book is to give an overview of, and motivation for, the facilities found within the TUXEDO System. Although this book is neither a reference manual nor a programming guide for the TUXEDO System, the epilogue tells you how to obtain these manuals [TUXEDO], as well as providing additional sources of information, for example, case studies, regarding the use of the TUXEDO System.

The software which comprises the TUXEDO System derives from a number of computer science disciplines, including networking, database and transaction processing systems, operating systems, and language theory. It is not the intent of this book to explain the theory of these subject areas with any rigor. Rather, topics from them will be cursorily introduced as they relate to the facilities provided by the TUXEDO System. For a comprehensive text that covers much of the theory referenced in this book, we suggest that you read [Gray–Reuter].

Our book contains interface descriptions, programming fragments, and a complete example. As an introductory book, the intent of these descriptions and programming fragments is to give you a concrete visualization of how the programming facilities of the TUXEDO System may be used. This book is not intended to be a substitute for the TUXEDO System product documentation.

A Brief History of the TUXEDO System

The TUXEDO System is a set of software modules that enables the construction, execution, and administration of high performance, distributed business applications. Originally planned as a framework for building such applications atop the UNIX Operating System, the TUXEDO System has widened its scope to enable the construction of distributed business systems which integrate a variety of desktop and server operating systems.

Construction of the TUXEDO System began in 1983 as an applied, forward-looking work project, at the time called The UNIX Transaction System (UNITS), within the Bell Laboratories division of AT&T. The target applications for UNITS were UNIX-based operations support systems within AT&T. Many of the ideas found within the UNITS System can be traced to the system software components of the LMOS Project [LMOS], an application which tracked repair incidents in telephone circuits and which was one of the first successful UNIX-based "down-sized" applications.

During the development of LMOS, no substantial commercial database technology was offered on the UNIX Operating System. Thus, UNITS research initially focused on database technology and produced a database system codenamed DUX (Database for UNIX). DUX was used on projects internal to AT&T, but was never sold commercially. To provide for applications requiring a large number of users, UNITS research also began an investigation into *client-server*-based application technology, and produced a client-server framework codenamed TUX (Transactions for UNIX). Like DUX, TUX was used on internal AT&T projects, but was never sold commercially. Ideas from the DUX and TUX efforts were subsequently combined into a transaction-enabled, client-server communications framework. When this framework was first distributed onto AT&T 3B4000 computers in Release 3.0, Tom Bishop, a principal architect of the 3B4000, coined the term "TUXEDO" when he quipped that "TUX has been Extended for Distributed Operation!"

In 1989, the UNITS project was transferred to the UNIX System Laboratories (USL) division of AT&T, and its client-server framework was offered as a commercial product under the name "The TUXEDO System." The TUXEDO System was transferred to Novell, Inc. when it acquired USL in 1993. In 1996, BEA, Inc. entered into an exclusive agreement with Novell to distribute and continue development of the TUXEDO System on a variety of computer platforms. In the meantime, numerous AT&T applications, which had adopted UNITS as an application framework, "graduated" to the TUXEDO System. By 1995, the TUXEDO System had found wide applicability to a large variety of uses in numerous industries.

Release 1.0 of the TUXEDO System, available in 1984 and depicted in Figure P.1, provided client-server facilities within a single random access memory computer—you can think of it as "Client Server in a Box," as shown in Figure P.1. Release 1.0 allowed an application to be partitioned into a set of cooperating client and server processes and provided a rudimentary *Application Programming Interface (API)* that supported *request/response* interactions among them. Clients located and sent their requests to servers via a high-speed name server called the *Bulletin Board (BB)*.

Release 2.0 became available in 1986 and contained the system's first facility to supply high availability applications. This took the form of a system monitor which restarted failed application servers. The high availability facilities have increased over subsequent releases in the form of various "buddy systems," "heartbeat monitors," and "self-healing" functions for system and application software components.

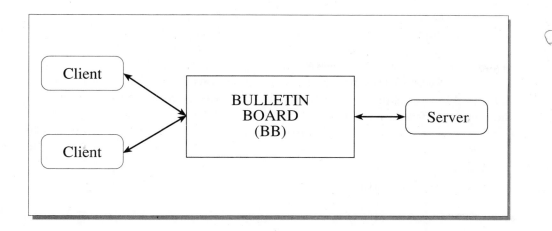

Figure P.1   P.1 Release 1.0, "Client-Server in a box

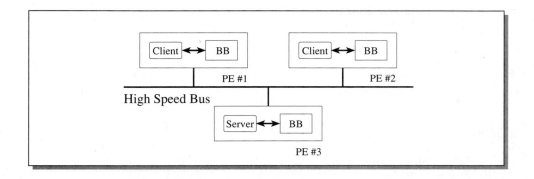

Figure P.2   Release 3.0 "LAN in a Box"

Release 3.0, available in 1987 and depicted in Figure P.2, provided client-server facilities within a single computer, AT&T's 3B4000, that had individual Processing Elements (PEs), each consisting of a CPU and private memory. The PEs were connected by a high-speed bus. The concept was essentially a small "LAN in a Box." Release 3.0 provided the first distribution of clients and servers onto separate memories and maintained Release 1.0's request/response API. A key to the implementation of Release 3.0 was the replication of the Bulletin Board in the memory of each PE. Release 3.0 also introduced a central configuration file for an application and provided boot, shutdown, and administration commands for an application.

Release 4.0, available in 1989 and depicted in Figure P.3, provided client-server facilities across a set of heterogeneous computers connected via a *Local Area*

Network (LAN). Figure P.3 shows an application spread across computers from the IBM, HP, and SUN companies. Release 4.0 drew some technology from Release 3.0, in particular, the distribution of the Bulletin Board, while introducing *transaction support* and the Application-to-Transaction Monitor interface (ATMI) into the TUXEDO System. The introduction of transactions led to the invention of the *XA* interface to support the transactional control of heterogeneous databases, and the requirement to use a common library interface to support the transmission of different types of data among heterogeneous computers led to the invention of *typed buffers*. Release 4.0 was the first commercially licensed release of the TUXEDO System.

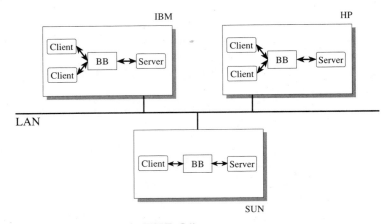

Figure P.3   **Release 4.0 "LAN TUXEDO"**

Release 4.2, available in 1993 and depicted in Figure P.4, provided for the inclusion of personal computers and workstations as client devices for the TUXEDO System. Release 4.2 also included support for communications to mainframes, thus enabling enterprise connectivity from desktop to mainframe. Support for *conversational* and *queued* communication paradigms was also introduced into ATMI in this release.

Release 5.0, available in 1994 and depicted in Figure P.5, provided for the federation of TUXEDO applications through a facility called *Domains*. In Figure P.5, each shape depicts the logical equivalent of an entire system depicted in Figure P.4. Application A, which itself may be a distributed application, interacts with applications B and C; application C interacts with Application D. Release 5.0 also provided for the inclusion of *Transactional Remote Procedure Call (TxRPC)* as a syntax for request/response communication and provided for gateways to the Open Software Foundation's (OSF) Distributed Computing Environment (DCE)-based applications. The result was the enablement of very large enterprise configurations, as well as *inter-enterprise transaction processing*.

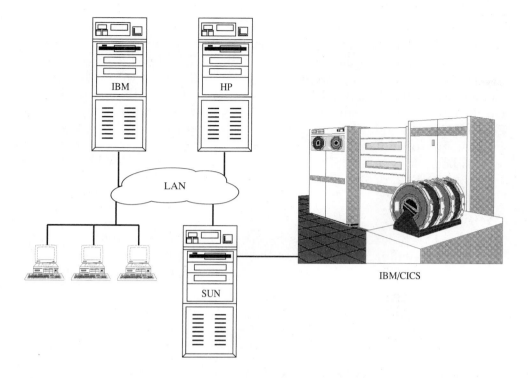

Figure P.4   Release 4.2 "Enterprise TUXEDO"

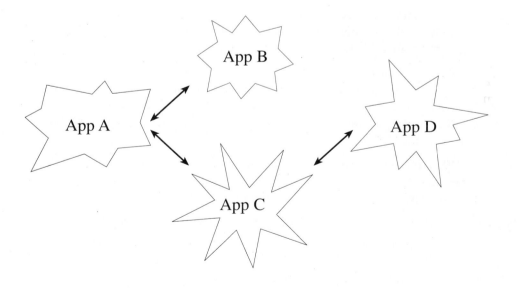

Figure P.5   Release 5.0 "Domains TUXEDO"

Release 6.1, available in 1995, provided a comprehensive architecture for administering TUXEDO System based applications. This architecture includes a published classification, called the *TMIB*, of the TUXEDO System's administrative data, a programming interface called *TMIB API* to the TMIB, and a Graphical User Interface (GUI) to access and modify the TMIB. Release 6.1 also saw the introduction of additional security controls in the form of Access Control Lists (ACLs). In addition, another communication paradigm, called *brokered events*, was introduced into ATMI in this release.

This book describes the TUXEDO System as of April, 1996. This includes work through Release 6.1, as well as a number of add-on products.

Neat Stuff

Substantial technical innovations have been made by the engineers of the TUXEDO System in the years since the start of the UNITS forward-looking work project, including:

- *ATMI* [ATMI], an interface for distributed application communication. A subset of this interface has since been adopted by the X/Open Company under the name *XATMI* [X/Open-XATMI];

- *Typed buffers*, a patented technology for identifying data collections that need to be transformed when they are communicated among computers with differing data representations. Typed buffers are the application message containers used in ATMI;

- *FML*, a data structure and associated access methods for communicating a variable number of typed parameters among cooperating application programs. FML is a built-in typed buffer;

- *XA*, an interface for communication between an external *Transaction Manager* (*TM*) and software components, called *Resources Managers* (*RMs*), which provide transaction semantics. The TUXEDO System XA interface became the basis of an X/Open Company interface of the same name [X/Open-XA];

- */WS*, an implementation of the client-side calls of ATMI, intended to be run on desktop computers running operating systems such as Windows, Mac OS, OS/2, DOS and the UNIX Operating System;

- */Q*, a transactionally enabled, XA compliant, Application Queuing System incorporating typed buffers. /Q provides for time-independent communication among software modules;

- */HOST* and *SNA Domains*, subsystems providing ATMI interfaces for interoperability with IBM's CICS transaction system;

▌ */OSI-TP*, the first commercial implementation of the ISO standard TP protocol;

▌ *The EventBroker*™, a post-and-subscribe communications system with transaction semantics. The use of transactions for the anonymous style of communication found in the EventBroker is the subject of a pending patent;

▌ The *TMIB API*, a programming interface which, through its use of FML, provides an easy way to access the TMIB.

Organization of This Book

This book is divided into four parts, comprising 18 chapters. It proceeds from the general to the specific and visits the main concepts and facilities found in the TUXEDO System at progressively more detailed levels. The initial treatment of a facility is at the conceptual level. The concept is next discussed in a TUXEDO setting, and finally, the specific usage of the concept is presented. For example, the notion of a transaction is introduced in Part I Chapter 3, the relationship of transactions to facilities found within a TUXEDO application is discussed in Part II Chapter 4, the specifics for programmatic use within a TUXEDO application are presented in Part III Chapter 14, and administration of transactions is discussed in Part IV Chapter 15. An example showing the use of transactions is given in Appendix A.

Part I of this book, "Setting the Stage for Understanding the TUXEDO System," provides background and motivation for the facilities found in the TUXEDO System and for the application architectures enabled by these facilities. This part gives an overview of the technologies involved in distributed business applications and will be understood by those with a basic familiarity with computerized business systems. Project managers and Information Technology (IT) managers will find Part I particularly useful.

Chapter 1, "Opportunities and Challenges in Distributing Business Applications," describes the forces in the computer industry that require the distribution of business applications. It goes on to describe the business requirements that distributed application frameworks need to satisfy.

Chapter 2, "Distributing Data and Logic," gives an overview of popular techniques for distributing data and processing in business applications and describes *Application Function Shipping* as the programming method encouraged by the TUXEDO System.

The TUXEDO System provides easy to use, yet sophisticated, communications interfaces for programmers and a comprehensive and programmable administrative system for administrators. The concepts behind these interfaces are introduced in Chapter 3, "Communication and Administration Paradigms for Distributed Business Applications."

Part II of this book, "Overview of the TUXEDO System," describes the programming and administration interfaces and facilities provided in the TUXEDO System. Application architects and software designers will find this part of the book very useful. IT managers may wish to skim these chapters.

Chapter 4, "Application Development—Overview," concentrates on application programming facilities, with emphasis on the TUXEDO System concepts of clients, servers, queues, events, and transactions. The role, construction method, and use of these facilities within a TUXEDO-based application are described.

Chapter 5, "Application Administration—Overview," relates the administrative concepts introduced in Chapter 3 to administrative functionality provided in the TUXEDO System. It indicates the major system entities that are to be administered and provides an overview of the programming and graphical facilities used to create and monitor a TUXEDO-based application. Chapter 5 also introduces the concept of a *Domain*, which identifies the administration boundary of a TUXEDO-based application.

Chapter 6, "The Anatomy of a TUXEDO Application," provides an overall architectural view of a TUXEDO System-based application. It identifies the system software that supports application logic and shows the flow of application calls. This chapter is ideal for architects, designers, and administrators trying to understand what a distributed TUXEDO application "really looks like."

Part III of this book, "Development of a TUXEDO Application," provides a tour through the development facilities provided by the TUXEDO System. It is intended for potential developers of TUXEDO-based applications and assumes a fluency with the C or COBOL programming languages. IT managers may wish to skim this part of the book.

Chapter 7, "Introduction to the Application Programming Interface," provides an introduction to the design of the TUXEDO System Application Programming Interfaces (APIs), the language bindings supported by the system, and indicates the methods used to create application modules.

Chapter 8, "Typed Buffers," deals with the problem of the representation of data elements passed between communicating programs on different computer types. It describes TUXEDO's built-in facilities for data representation and automatic data conversion, including FML, a unique data representation found within the TUXEDO System. FML is one of the TUXEDO System's most popular features and enables applications to pass variable numbers of variable length fields among communicating modules.

Chapter 9, "Joining and Leaving the Application," describes the interfaces used by client and server programs to join and leave a running application. For clients, this includes the presentation of any required security information. For server modules, it includes the functions used to advertise and withdraw advertisements of "services" within a domain.

Chapter 10, "Request/Response Communication," provides details on the request/response facilities provided by the system, including library-based ATMI calls, and *Transactional Remote Procedure Calls* (*TxRPCs*). The chapter describes synchronous and parallel constructs for request/response interactions and details several constructs unique to the TUXEDO System, including *fan-out* and *pipelined parallelism*.

Chapter 11, "Conversational Communication," presents the TUXEDO System's *conversational* programming interface. This interface is used when communicating modules need to conduct their business over a sequence of communications.

Chapter 12, "Application Queues," gives details on the *Application Queuing System* offered by the TUXEDO System. Application Queues allow modules to communicate in a time-independent manner. This software may be used to perform deferred actions, implement work-flow systems, and buffer communications to systems where the rate of input exceeds processing capacity.

Chapter 13, "Event-Based Communication," covers the TUXEDO System's APIs for direct and brokered event communication, including the methods used to generate an event and the facilities to receive and act on events. Transactional brokered events are unique to the TUXEDO system and provide a novel tool to be used in the programming of TUXEDO-based applications.

Chapter 14, "Transactions in the TUXEDO System," provides an introduction to the use of transactions within a TUXEDO application, including the programmatic initiation and termination of transactions, and *transactional infection* and *transactional isolation* across communications boundaries.

Part IV of this book, "Administration of a TUXEDO Application," concentrates on the administration facilities provided by the system. This chapter should be of interest not only to those who might become the administrators and operators of TUXEDO-based applications, but also for the application architects who may wish to design their application with the needs of the administrator in mind. Indeed, as pointed out in this part of the book, close cooperation between application designers and administrators is essential to having a distributed application successfully deployed.

Chapter 15, "Application Administration and Monitoring," begins a task-oriented view of the administrator's job and indicates the various facilities provided to help make the administration of an application as easy as its creation.

Failures are the parts most often ignored in application design. However, it is precisely at the height of a failure scenario that the system needs to provide the right tools to help analyze and repair the problem. Chapter 16, "Failure Handling," describes the TUXEDO System approach to the handling of failures in a distributed application.

Chapter 17, "A Tour of the TUXEDO Management Information Base," provides in-depth coverage of the TUXEDO System's Management Information Base (TMIB). Understanding the TMIB is a great way to understand the essentials of the TUXEDO System.

The *Domains* subsystem of the TUXEDO System allows multiple TUXEDO-based applications to work together, forming "super applications." Moreover,

Domains provides a good way to interoperate with non-TUXEDO distributed applications, including a variety of proprietary TP monitors and other distributed systems frameworks, such as the Object Management Group's (OMG) Common Object Request Broker Architecture (CORBA). Chapter 18, "Getting Applications to Work Together," provides an introduction to the Domains subsystem.

The Epilogue of this book provides a retrospective on what you have just read and additional information sources on the TUXEDO System.

Appendix A provides a complete example of the construction of a TUXEDO-based application. Appendix B provides a comprehensive glossary for terms introduced in this book. Appendix C provides a list of references used throughout the book.

Conventions

Throughout this book, when new terms are introduced, they appear in an *italic* typeface. A definition of such terms may be found in the glossary. The terms function, procedure, primitive, and routine are used interchangeably throughout the book. Function names and system variables appear in a **bold** typeface. Throughout the book, code fragments are presented as examples of programming interface usage. Such fragments often omit error checking. This is intentional and is done so the reader can concentrate on the construct being described.

Related Information

The Epilogue of this book contains references where you may obtain additional information on the TUXEDO System.

Acknowledgments

Our thanks go to Steve Pendergrast for his persistent suggestions that we write this book. We also express our gratitude to Steve, Ed Felt, and Randy MacBlane for consultations they provided on certain technical aspects of the book. We wish to thank Novell for its permission to use its computing facilities to test examples found within this book and to create, capture, and reproduce renditions of the TUXEDO System's Graphical User Interface. We also thank the staff of Addison-Wesley, particularly, Katie Duffy, Avanda Peters, and Mike Hendrickson for the assistance and understanding they have provided during this project. Thanks go to LMY Studios for their work in re-rendering our figures. We commend Kenneth Ingham, Lynn Kubeck, Laura Michaels, Neil Ostrove, Steve Pendergrast, and Christopher Youngworth for their thoughtful reviews of an early draft of the book.

We wish to provide special acknowledgment for members of the TUXEDO project, past and present. Our fellow engineers, including engineers from other companies, and technical writers have contributed enormously to the conception and high-quality implementation of the software and documentation described in this book. Our marketing and product management organizations have helped popularize and promote the TUXEDO System throughout the world. The salespeople of our company and our licensees and distributors have brought the TUXEDO System to numerous satisfied customers.

We wish to recognize the contributions of our customers, who have continually supported our efforts, demanded excellence, and challenged our creativity.

Finally, we wish to acknowledge the management of AT&T, USL, Novell, and BEA for their continued support and encouragement during the course of the TUXEDO project.

I

Setting the Stage for Understanding the TUXEDO System

In Part I of this book we discuss the evolution of business computing toward distributed applications. This part of the book contains background to understand the TUXEDO System, but contains little information on the TUXEDO System per se. Those readers who are familiar with the concepts and practice of distributed systems may wish to skim Part I or go directly to Part II of this book.

In the opening chapter of Part I, we briefly discuss the hardware and software advances enabling application distribution, and we tell you why it is important for you to consider distributed applications in your business. In the second chapter, we discuss common methods used to distribute applications. We describe the difference between distributed data and distributed processing and explain the role of database systems and *Service Request Brokers*, such as the TUXEDO System, in enabling distributed applications. In the third and final chapter of Part I, we introduce concepts which form the basis for programming and managing distributed applications.

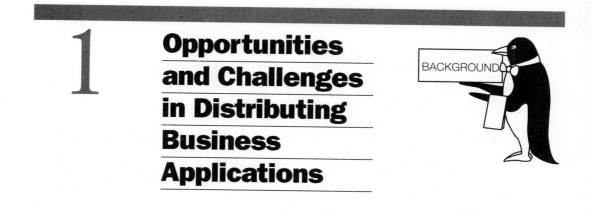

1 Opportunities and Challenges in Distributing Business Applications

In this opening chapter, we explore the advances in the computing industry that require businesses to distribute their applications. The opportunity for your company is to have its business applications provide you with a competitive advantage. The challenge is primarily one of software—it must be possible to design, program, and administer highly available and secure, distributed applications in a cost-effective manner.

1.1   Mainframes—"Once Upon a Time . . ."

In the past, most business applications were developed on high-capacity mainframe computers. These machines were characterized by a single central processing unit, a single random-access memory, directly attached secondary storage devices, locally attached card, paper-tape, terminal and printer devices—and a large monthly payment to the mainframe company! Initially *batch-oriented*, mainframe use in business operations evolved over three decades to give *on-line access* to business processing [IBM-CICS].

Techniques to distribute computing among mainframes have been the subject of much engineering work. Early efforts centered on the interchange of information between mainframe computers using batch techniques, such as file or record transfer with tape devices. Subsequently, the invention of remote peripheral input and output devices—particularly terminals and printers made mainframe computers and the information they held more accessible to corporate users.

Overall, business applications created for mainframe computers tended to be monolithic. Human interfaces, business logic, and data access were usually bound together into the same application program. The data was kept in record-oriented sequential or random-access files, with much of the data replicated, and little control over its access. Some attempts at providing distribution facilities for applications [IBM-LU6.2] and data [IBM-R*] were eventually made possible.

1.2   Minicomputers—Davids Take on Goliath

The advent of the minicomputer brought computing to the laboratory, the factory, and the department. For businesses, this enabled new types of applications to be developed and for computing functions to move closer to the business operations requiring them. In addition, it allowed business processing to begin a movement away from centralized mainframe computers toward smaller, less expensive, minicomputers. The introduction of *Local Area Network* (*LAN*) hardware, and communications software such as the *Transmission Control Protocol* (*TCP*), allowed the interconnection of minicomputers and the applications running on them. The movement to minicomputers and their workstation replacements accelerated through the 1990s, with Intel and RISC-based processors and commodity memory, and disk technology driving down the cost of business computing.

The software environment of the minicomputer encouraged networking and distributed applications. The operating systems for minicomputers shifted in the early 1980s from proprietary systems to the portable UNIX Operating System. The availability and portability of the UNIX System, in turn, accelerated the introduction of new minicomputers, because hardware vendors no longer needed to invest large sums in writing their own operating systems. Typically, such systems were interconnected via LANs and dial up modems. Mail applications, file copy, and remote command execution allowed such systems to cooperate in performing business operations. Some early attempts at distributed on-line business applications on minicomputers also proved successful [LMOS]. By the late 1980s, software tools such as the TUXEDO System, whose purpose is to enable distributed business systems, in combination with high-performance relational databases, allowed UNIX-based servers to provide price performance for business applications substantially better than mainframes.

1.3   PCs—David Becomes Goliath!

The advent of the Personal Computer (PC) in the 1980s brought computing to the desktop, the home, the classroom, and the individual. Initially, PCs tended to be isolated—but, as shown in Figure 1.1, software and hardware advances soon enabled people to share storage and printing devices among their PCs. PC operating systems evolved into client-side operating systems, such as MacOS, DOS, and Windows, and server-side operating systems, such as NetWare, Windows NT, and UNIX.

Although early uses of PCs by businesses tended to be for word processing and spreadsheet processing, the subsequent availability of networking and database

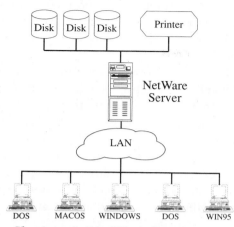

Figure 1.1   **Device Sharing via NetWare Server**

software brought them into use for workgroup applications. In addition, application designers began using PCs as interface devices for on-line business systems, including access to mainframe and minicomputer-based applications. Just as minicomputers off-loaded processing from the mainframe, so too, groups of PCs began to "downsize" the minicomputer. The software environments which allowed PCs to be part of business processing included standardized interfaces for access to networks, remote databases, access software to mainframe transaction processing systems, and *client-server* programming interfaces such as the TUXEDO System's *ATMI* interface.

A new class of software has allowed PCs to be used by consumers to send each other electronic mail (E-mail), to transact business with banks, and to do "electronic shopping," all from home. The once isolated PC has become a computing device capable of communicating with thousands of businesses, and millions of other PCs.

1.4   The Effect of Mobile Computing— There Is No Escaping the System

By the mid-1990s, technology enabling distribution and interconnection of computing devices reached new heights. Advances in processing and memory devices enabled portable, "notebook," "palmtop," and embedded devices. Inexpensive and compact modems enabled relatively cheap connectivity through the telephone network. Mobile telephones extended the phone network nearly everywhere, thus allowing computing devices to "connect," or be "connected to," from virtually anywhere. Enhancements to communication protocols to include a variety suitable for reliable access to systems via dial-up lines have removed the constraint of hard-wired terminals. Access to corporate business systems can now be achieved from virtually anywhere.

We give two examples of how mobile computing is affecting corporate work. Service workers, such as telephone repair people, now commonly carry computers with them. When completing a service call, they dial up a dispatching application which assigns them their next service call. The dispatching application can assign them jobs in response to urgency of call, promised commitments to customers, and optimization of travel time. The result is more efficient use of resources to meet customer needs. In another example, managers traveling on business can "call in" to process their E-mail. This allows them to stay in touch with daily activities at the office even when they are on the road. The result is increased productivity of such managers.

1.5 Improved Networking—Hardware and Software

Not only has computer hardware advanced at a rapid rate, but the hardware systems to interconnect computers have made great strides as well. High-speed modems, routers, hubs, and the like are enabling the data equivalent of telephone networks. Indeed, speech and video are now all carried over the same digital networks.

Important steps in allowing networked applications to be constructed have also taken place. Database systems allow distribution of their data, as well as remote access to it. Frameworks to support distributed application processing, such as the TUXEDO System, have emerged. LANs have become interconnected via the Internet. Hypertext-oriented applications, such as the World Wide Web, allow Internet users to share information across continents.

1.6 The Benefits of Distributing Your Business Applications

The availability of mini and micro devices at low cost and the ability to connect them to powerful server computers provides new opportunities for businesses to reduce their costs, to provide enhanced services to their customers, and to cooperate with their partners.

1.6.1 The Virtual Corporation—Brought to You by the Network

More and more companies are using computers to run their business operations. Moreover, the proliferation of networking is enabling the operations to be distributed and interconnected. For example, when you call to order merchandise from a catalog company, it is difficult to predict where the operator you talk to works. He or she may be in a part of the country entirely different than you associate with the company. In fact, the workers you talk to may even be working at home! Your order is taken, records are updated, the shipping department is notified, and your bill is prepared. Such distribution and interconnection are leading to virtual corporations that are tied together by their telecommunications and data networks. Order takers at home, sales people connected from their hotel rooms, executives in touch via E-mail—the centralized company is going the way of the centralized computer.

However, as various departments within the corporation turn to distributed computing, the result is that often the systems they create cannot communicate with each other. Although each department may have increased its efficiency locally, the result for the entire corporation could be even greater productivity if the systems could only "speak" to each other. For example, sales forecasting systems could send directives to the factory to gear up (or down) for a production change. Shipping systems can provide data to the sales forecasting system to refine forecasts.

When creating a departmental application, a business needs to keep several things in mind:

■ The application should be usable by other departments within the company. Such applications, therefore, will need well-defined interfaces. Moreover, as applications become interdependent, their "care and feeding" become very important.

■ Companies need to cultivate interapplication architects. These are people who understand the scope of the business and how to tie together its various departmental applications to provide the company with the maximum benefit from its computing systems.

■ The users of a system may go beyond the employees of the company. In the next section, we discuss direct consumer access to a company's applications. The design of the system's interfaces needs to protect the privacy and security of the company's data, including records of other customers.

1.6.2 Electronic Customers—"Beam Me over to the Mall!"

In the previous section, we discussed the scenario of a customer calling a company to order merchandise. Just as Automated Teller Machines in the banking industry have removed the need for many human tellers, other forms of customer interactions with a company will also be via computers. Increasingly, companies are allowing their customers direct access to computer applications to order merchandise or modify their accounts. For example, banking and bill paying are commonly done from home.

In fact, the definition of a customer is changing. For many companies, a new type of customer is anyone with a computer and a credit card. Such customers are initially unknown to the business—but instantly they can become users of its ordering system! The ordering system needs to verify their identities, accept their requests, and create customer records for them. Of course, communication to other systems within the company is highly desirable. The sales department may want to put electronic customers on a list for "special offers," the marketing department might want to send these new customers a welcome gift, and the accounting department might need to send a bill to the customer's credit card company.

1.6.3 Cooperation with Other Businesses—
Suppliers, Partners, and Perhaps Competitors!

In addition to their own customers, businesses deal with other businesses, and, perhaps, the customers of those businesses. For example, inventory systems can automatically place orders for restocking with suppliers' systems, referrals for service can be automatically made to partner companies, customer satisfaction and confidence can be gained by providing information on competitors' products. In the previous section, we saw an example of interbusiness commerce: the catalog company sent a bill to the customer's credit card company for the merchandise that the customer ordered. In effect, when the catalog company's system talks to the credit card company's system, they are each parts of a larger distributed application. Interenterprise cooperation means that your company's computer applications need to "talk" to your partner-companies' applications.

The cooperation of such systems is basically the same problem as described for cooperation of departmental level systems within a company. Systems need to be designed as if they will be accessed by other companies, and intercompany application architects need to design the interconnect strategies.

When applications "talk" across enterprises, they have to have an agreement on what information they will exchange and how they will exchange it. Thus, they need well-defined *protocols* for their interoperation.

Figure 1.2 depicts such a scenario. Here, companies A and B are attempting to interoperate. While each company administers its own computers separately, the systems interoperate via messages they send to each other. The set of valid messages, that can be exchanged between systems, and the sequence in which they

Figure 1.2   **Inter-Enterprise Communication**

may be sent, is called a *protocol*. We'll discuss more about protocols in the following chapters. Of course, such an interoperating system may not have been originally designed as one large system. Perhaps A and B only became involved after their systems were in existence. In effect the larger system becomes a federation of both the A and the B systems. Note also, that A and B need not be separate companies—they may be divisions within the same company.

1.7   The Costs of Distributing Your Business Applications

The tasks in converting a business function to a computer application include

- creating the application (including analysis, design, implementation, and testing it)
- administering the application (installing, configuring, securing, and operating it)
- maintaining the application (correcting its faults, porting it to new computers, etc.)
- extending the application to provide new features
- training users in accessing and manipulating the application

The costs of these tasks include the labor to perform them (e.g., the salaries of the programmers and operators of the system), the purchasing (or leasing) of the hardware and software to run and access them, and the training of its users. Although some business applications require the use of specialized hardware, the vast majority can use relatively inexpensive off-the-shelf hardware. Thus, the main costs of distributed applications become those associated with software creation and operation. Sometimes, off-the-shelf software packages are suitable for distributed applications. Such packages may require only minor modification or some customization to implement the business function. But these packages need to be created and maintained by someone, and their creators and users will be looking for the same economies as if the package had been built only for custom use. Therefore, an important requirement to enable you to construct distributed applications is the availability of software which will reduce the costs associated with the tasks just listed.

1.8   Summary—"Should You Choose to Accept This Assignment . . ."

Those companies that can capitalize on the types of efficiencies and innovations described in this chapter will dominate their competitors. If you're wondering *when* you should start to distribute your applications, the answer will probably be given to you by some of your competitors who are *already* deploying such systems! If you are wondering *how* to create applications which are distributed, *read on!* We will describe the essential problems that need to be addressed and how the TUXEDO System helps you to solve them.

2 Distributing Data and Logic

Data manipulations form the basis of business computing. To perform distributed business computing, either the data, the processing of the data, or both the data and its processing are spread across a set of computers. In this chapter, we discuss several common approaches that application architects use to distribute data and its processing within business systems. We indicate the advantages and disadvantages of each approach, and highlight *application function shipping* as the method encouraged by the TUXEDO System.

2.1 Monolithic Applications—All Your Instructions in One Basket

Before discussing distribution methods, we should first discuss the nondistributed approach. As described in Chapter 1, early computerized business applications were built as monolithic programs running on stand-alone mainframe computers. Such a program, depicted in Figure 2.1, typically contains logic to handle an external interface interaction, for example, that from a terminal device, business logic, and data access. Any distribution of function was at the hardware level, for example, by having remote terminals. One of the main advantages of these applications

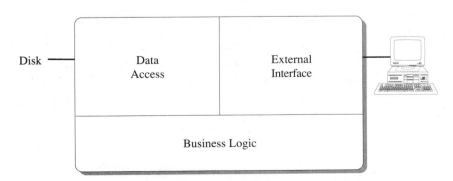

Figure 2.1   Monolithic Application Program

is that all computing is done in one place. If the application or computer stops working, the entire application stops. One does not have to worry about some modules of an application "being down" while others are "up." One of the difficulties of distributed systems, a lack of global knowledge of the application, is solved by restricting "the globe" to whatever could be processed by applications that executed and stored data on one computer. The main disadvantages of this style of computing are that all work and data must be brought to the computer for processing, and all of the business' "processing eggs" are in one "computer basket."

2.2   Distributing Data—The Easy Choice

Any nontrivial business application must store information on permanent devices, so that, should the hardware stop operation, the application can be restarted without amnesia. The stored information represents the permanent state of the application and the business. The information may be organized by various techniques, including file systems and database management systems. The data accessed by an application may be regarded as one logical unit, that is, as one database, or may comprise multiple independent, but somehow related, units. Any one of these units may reside totally on the storage devices of one computer or may be distributed across the storage devices of multiple computers.

2.2.1   Applications Built on Sharing of Files

The sum of the executable code of any nontrivial business application will be contained in multiple, independently executable units, which we'll call executable programs, or simply *executables*. That is, the business logic is not literally in one executable; it is distributed across multiple executables. The architecture and implementation of the application may require that the executables be run on one single computer or on multiple computers. Moreover, the executables comprising the logic of the application may be executing concurrently or serially. Executables can communicate in a number of ways, for example, by using persistent data stored in a file or database system. Figure 2.2 depicts two executables cooperating via the PENDING ORDER FILE (POF). The ORDER ENTRY executable interacts with a terminal device to accept order information, applies business specific validations to it, and inserts correct orders in the POF (flow 1). The ORDER PROCESSING executable reads the POF (flow 2) and prepares inventory requests and directives to the billing system. After processing each item, ORDER PROCESSING archives it and deletes it from the POF (flow 3).

When one executable retrieves permanent data stored by another executable, the two executables have cooperated via shared data. This type of cooperation is indirect, essentially time-independent, and through the side effect of file update. In order for the data to make any sense to the retrieving executable, it must have

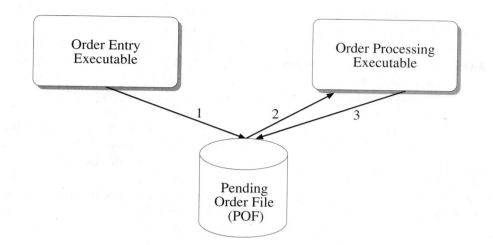

Figure 2.2   **Executables Cooperating via Shared Data**

some "agreement" with the storing executable on the format, content, and meaning of the data. This agreement is a *protocol* between the two executables based on the data. The POF of Figure 2.2 has a format known both to the ORDER ENTRY and ORDER PROCESSING executables. Ultimately, any such nontrivial business system must have such protocols. The protocols may be implicit in the storage/access routines of the executables or may be explicit via catalogs and dictionaries of the storage system. The cooperation of executables through data is essentially time-independent. The storage of data does not itself cause the execution of an executable. The data are passive entities, written and read by processing programs. In Figure 2.2, ORDER PROCESSING processes the POF at fixed intervals, say, once a day at midnight.

2.2.2 Applications Built on Sharing of Distributed Files

One way to distribute applications is to permit remote access to files. This would allow the executables shown in Figure 2.2 to reside on different computers. They would still communicate indirectly via the POF, but they could do so from different computers. We will discuss this type of application distribution in this section.

File systems are organizational units used to store permanent data items on secondary storage devices, such as disks. File systems contain files, which are collections of related records or bytes. Files are read and written by executing programs. Distributed file systems allow programs to access files remotely. That is, the program reading or writing a file may be executing on one computer, whereas the file itself is located on disks attached to another computer. The most notable examples of distributed file systems include the NFS system [NFS] and the NetWare system [NetWare].

When a program reads a remote file, the file system software accepts the read request on the machine where the request is made, and forwards the read request to file system software running on the machine where the file resides. The remote file system software performs the read and returns the requested portion of the file to the application. If the application wishes to write the file, the flow is in the opposite direction. Figure 2.3 depicts an application on computer A accessing files that are local to A, and accessing files that are on computer B. Note that the distribution is logically at the file system level. In fact, the data itself is stored on physical media, such as disks, with physical access. Such access may in turn be distributed at its own level. That is, the disks that the file system software is reading or writing may be physically remote from the place the file system issues its access calls. The point here is that data access itself is a layered process, analogous to communications software.

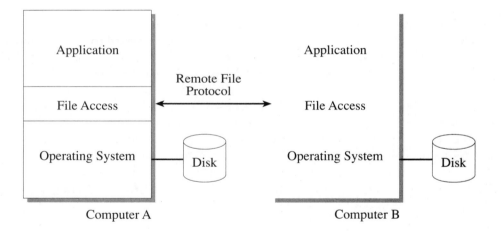

Figure 2.3   **Remote File Access via Distributed File System**

We have begun an implicit discussion of *data shipping* and *function shipping*. When data and the executable code that manipulates that data reside on separate computers, there are two choices to bring them together into the same memory so that code manipulation of the data can proceed. In data shipping, the data is sent to the computer where the code is located. It is then manipulated by the code and sent back to the computer where it is stored. In function shipping, the code that manipulates the data is sent to the computer where the data resides. There it accesses the data, manipulates it, and stores it. If the manipulation function is used often on the computer with the data, it can be prepositioned, permanently reside on that computer, and be invoked remotely. In this latter case, it is not the logic of the function which is shipped, but the inputs to and outputs from the execution of the logic that are shipped.

During data shipping, of course, the data does not ship itself. Some instructions need to be executed to fetch, transport, and restore the data. At the macro level, applications which use distributed file systems perform data shipping. That is, data from remote files is shipped to the computer where the application executes. To actually ship the data, the distributed file system uses function shipping. Typically, this is done by function shipping the file system's access routines, which are being invoked locally by the application, to the computers where the "real" file access operations are performed. At its own level, the file system is a distributed application.

Although early versions of distributed file systems employed a special syntax for remote file access and were not on-line (file access requests were queued) [uucp], current distributed file systems access remote files on-line in a *location transparent* manner. This is done by allowing applications to use the same syntax for all file access and by function shipping to remote locations for immediate file access. The term location transparency means that access to an object, for example, reading a file or invoking a procedure, has a syntax that contains no information as to the location of the object. All references to the object are constructed as if the object were local to the code making the reference. With regard to data shipping, location transparency means that access functions that an application uses for remote data are identical to those it uses for local data. With regard to function shipping, location transparency means that the invocation of a function has the same syntax whether or not the code for the function is executed locally or is actually executed on a remote computer.

The main advantage of distributed file systems is that, because of their location transparency, they can easily be used by a wide variety of software to cooperate in a distributed system through file sharing. In doing so, applications do not need to be aware of other programs—they just read and write files. Access to remote files is easy, because location transparency means that the remoteness of the files is totally hidden from the accessors. Virtually any file read or write can be intercepted locally, and performed remotely.

The main disadvantage of distributed file systems, particularly for *byte stream files*, where the contents of the file are totally uninterpreted by the file system, is that many blocks of data may need to be transmitted across the network to complete a business operation. For example, many *Relational Database Management Systems (RDBMS)* provide record structure atop byte stream file systems. The RDBMS accepts database queries in the form of *Structured Query Language (SQL)* [Date2] commands, and issues reads and writes to the file system to get records into memory. A query to access an indexed record would read the index and then read the block containing the data record. The access to the index might require several reads, say, in the case of a btree, and the read of the record might take an additional read. Thus, the operation that returned a single record may involve multiple file system reads. An update of the record might require multiple writes if the index has to be changed. When the index and base files are remote from the SQL access to them, the data for each of these accesses must be transmitted over the network.

Similarly, a query that scans an entire relation, say, an unindexed query looking for a specific record, means that not only does the entire file need to be read from disk, but it needs to be transmitted across the network. In such cases, it is often better to do the SQL processing on the computer where the data is located, rather than ship the uninterpreted file data to the SQL processing software in the requestor.

Applications that are distributed by virtue of distributed file systems are sometimes called *fat-client/skinny-server* systems. The term is used because the client contains all of the application logic, and the server is relegated to simple file serving.

2.2.3 Applications Built on Distributed Databases

Because of the inefficiency of remote file systems for distributed database processing, many distributed database systems function ship database accesses across the network. For example, in a distributed RDBMS, SQL operations are function shipped to a remote computer for execution. Figure 2.4 shows this scenario. One large benefit is that, if multiple file system accesses need to be done in computer B to satisfy an SQL statement issued on computer A, those accesses need only be done on B. Only the results of the processing, for example, an extracted record, need to be sent back across the network to A. The actual file system blocks need not be sent.

Note that Figure 2.4 is remarkably similar to Figure 2.3. In effect, distributed relational database systems are distributed applications in their own right. They consist of cooperating software modules running concurrently on multiple computers, and they ship SQL requests and replies among themselves. The application is doing data shipping via the RDBMS' function shipping. The use of SQL allows a higher level of access to the data by the application. That is, the RDBMS has

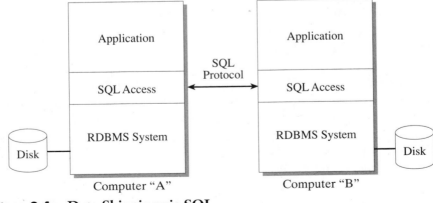

Figure 2.4   Data Shipping via SQL

organized the data into relations, tuples, etc., and allows a higher level expression of data access than just file system access. The RDBMS sends the results of SQL execution and not the raw file data back across the network. Using an RDBMS, applications can cooperate indirectly via the data stored in the database. The concept is similar to the indirect cooperation afforded by file systems.

Even though RDBMS send less data over the network than distributed file systems, SQL traffic can still easily saturate networks. Often, applications do not issue a single SQL request to perform a business function. Instead, they issue multiple requests for data from various parts of the data store.

For example, the transfer of data from one account to another may involve the SQL statements shown in Listing 2.1. There are eight SQL statements whose purpose is to cause the amount "xfer_amt" to be transferred from the account with id "debacctid" to the account with id "credacctid." Each of the SQL fetch and SQL update statements requires a request and response message to be sent over the network. The result is that at least eight network messages are required to

```
        /* create a cursor for access to debited account */
EXEC SQL declare acctcur cursor for
    select BALANCE from ACCOUNT
    where ACCT_ID = :debacctid;
EXEC SQL open acctcur;
        /* fetch the debited account's  record */
EXEC SQL fetch acctcur into :acct_bal;   /* generates 2 network messages*/
        /* decrement the balance field */
acct_bal = acct_bal - xfer_amt;
        /* update the account being debited */
EXEC SQL update ACCOUNT set BALANCE = acct_bal
    where current of acctcur;              /* generates 2 network messages*/


        /* create a cursor for access to credited account */
EXEC SQL declare acctcur2 cursor for
    select BALANCE from ACCOUNT
     where ACCT_ID = :credacctid;
EXEC SQL open acctcur2;
        /* fetch the credit account's  record */
EXEC SQL fetch acctcur2 into :acct_bal; /* generates 2 network messages*/
        /* increment the balance field */
acct_bal_bal = acct_bal + xfer_amt;
        /* update the account being creditted */
EXEC SQL update ACCOUNT set BALANCE = acct_bal
     where current of acctcur2;            /*generates 2 network messages*/
```

Listing 2.1   *SQL Statements to Effect Transfer*

perform a simple task. Other applications may retrieve many records for analysis to generate a simple result (e.g., "yes" or "no"). Each of these requires substantial traffic on the network.

To alleviate such traffic, RDBMS systems offer the ability to define sets of SQL commands, called *stored procedures*, inside the database, and allow programs to invoke the stored procedures remotely. Here, the parameters to the stored procedure are supplied by the application via the stored procedure access functions, the parameters are function shipped to the remote RDBMS site, the stored procedure is executed on the remote site, and the results of the entire procedure are returned. This scenario is depicted in Figure 2.5. This saves SQL traffic on the network. If the SQL statement of Listing 2.1 were kept in a stored procedure, there would only need to be two network messages used—one to send the stored procedure arguments (xfer_amt, debacctid, and credacctid) to the database, and one to get a reply.

Note that Figure 2.5 is similar to Figure 2.4, which we previously noted was similar to Figure 2.3 In fact, all three figures depict the access of data on remote devices via function shipping. The difference is that different levels of data access are afforded by the different systems. In the progression from file systems to databases to database stored procedures, the storage system becomes more abstract and offers higher level services. As less work is actually done in the client, the system evolves from a fat-client/skinny-server system toward a *skinny-client/ fat-server* system. At the stored procedure level, the application programmer actually need not know the details of the SQL statements contained within the procedure. All that need be known are the inputs and the outputs from the stored procedure. Moreover, the higher the level of access, the less unused data is sent over the network.

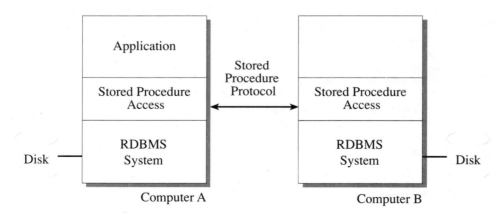

Figure 2.5   **Stored Procedure Invocation**

2.3 Distributing Logic—The Right Choice

Partitioning an application is a good thing. The application's logic is broken down into software modules which work together. Each module should perform a well-defined task and should be easier to build, understand and maintain than the entire application itself. The modules become the application's units which may be considered for distribution onto different computers. Such "divide-and-conquer" techniques to application construction demand a design, which becomes the architectural underpinnings for the application. Note that, although application partitioning is absolutely required for distributed applications, application partitioning is a good thing even for applications which operate within a single computer. Such an application has the same economic advantages in its conception, implementation, extension, comprehensibility, and maintainability that a distributed application has. Moreover, such an application might later be distributed onto multiple computers, even though the original requirement was that it would run on a single computer "forever."

When partitioning an application into communicating parts, it must be clearly understood what the parts will "say" to each other. What applications "say to each other" and how they say it is called an *application protocol*. Figure 2.6 shows two application modules and their associated application protocol. In the discussion of file sharing earlier in this chapter, we encountered the term *protocol* in connection with the indirect cooperation of executables via files. The use of the term in both contexts is similar. Whether the cooperation is direct via function shipping messages sent between concurrently running executables or indirect via file sharing, the cooperating modules must understand the format of the information they are sharing and any rules governing its exchange.

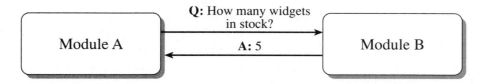

Figure 2.6   Simple Application Request / Response Protocol

2.3.1 Application Function Shipping

In the previous sections of this chapter, we have described various techniques to distribute an application's data. The manipulation of that data, that is, the implementation of the business' rules via the execution of stored program logic, may also be distributed. Figure 2.7 depicts the distribution of a merchandise company's order entry application logic across multiple executables, possibly executing on separate computers. These executables cooperate by application level communication—they use function shipping to communicate. Basically, these modules request each other to perform tasks and produce results. For example, the PROCESS ORDER executable asks the SHIP ORDER executable to prepare the shipping ticket and asks the SEND BILL executable to prepare a bill for the customer. Note that the SHIP ORDER executable need not even be running on a computer owned by the company selling this merchandise! It could be executing on a computer owned by the shipping company that partners with the merchandise company. We call such distribution *Application Function Shipping* because requests to perform application level functionality are shipped to a computer capable of performing the function. This, of course, allows arbitrary application modules to communicate, not just those that include file system or database accesses within them. The implementations of the functions are contained within the application modules and are hidden from the function invokers.

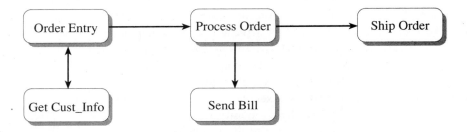

Figure 2.7 **Application Function Shipping**

Those modules that do use database access to implement their task completely hide this database access. In effect, they provide higher level value to data access than stored procedures by providing additional business logic to manipulate the data before returning it to the application module that requested it, or prior to inserting it in the database. Because application server modules provide higher level value than stored procedures, they are correspondingly "fatter," and the clients that access them are somewhat "skinnier" than applications that use SQL or stored procedures. The business logic that surrounds the data access moves from the client to the server with the following benefits:

■ Application modularity is encouraged. As previously discussed, this has substantial economic benefits in terms of extensibility and maintainability of the application. A key to modularity is *information hiding*—keeping the details of an implementation known only to the implementation. Raw database access, for example via SQL, requires the publishing of a database's organizational structure, called its *schema*. Publishing the schema reveals the implementation of the enterprise's data and breaks down information hiding. The database cannot be changed because everyone to whom it is published knows it. At the macro level, the database schema corresponds to global variables within a program. The more there are, the less modularity there is.

■ It is not required to reveal the structure of the data to those without a need to know, including programmers from other enterprises, or even *federated applications* from the same enterprise. In effect, the data is guarded by application functions which provide controlled access to it.

■ The structure of the data can be reimplemented without affecting remote parts of the application. So long as the application modules maintain their interfaces with each other, they can be reimplemented to give better performance and perform enhanced versions of their tasks.

■ The amount of unused data transmitted across the network can be reduced, because a higher level request can be sent to an application function than to a stored procedure.

■ The need for programmers who understand specialized database retrieval languages, such as SQL, is reduced.

2.3.2 Application Partitioning—Consider the Parts

Partitioning an application means breaking it into well-defined modules that co-operate to perform the tasks of a business application. Once the modules have been identified, they become the executables subject to distribution across multiple computers. Although it is not the intent of this book to provide an exposition on modular design and programming, we make the following observations gained from our experience with distributed business systems:

■ In trying to define application modules, examine the business processes to be implemented, and look for commonality in application-oriented tasks that comprise them. Make these common tasks the reusable modules of your system. Just as a database system needs a design, so, too, does the creation of modules for an application.

■ The downside of creating modules is that, in general, there is a performance penalty in invoking a module. The invocation of remote modules is even more expensive. Don't do trivial tasks in modules. Instead, look for medium- or coarse-grained tasks as good candidates for modules. Such modularization will promote reuse and provide efficient applications.

■ When designing an application and when actually distributing an application, do processing close to resources needed for the processing. In fact, resources are natural items around which to construct modules. The "weight" of your clients and servers should be governed by this principle.

The reason for this is that utilization of the resource will itself take communication if the resource is remote from its access point. For example, modules responsible for controlling PCs should be run as close to the PCs as possible. Remember that PCs are computers! Their cycles are excellent for screen control and syntactic checking of input data. Consider running the human interface on them. Along the same line, modules that access database resources should be run on computers that contain the database. You need to understand the trade-offs in shipping the data to the application versus shipping the processing to the data. Ensure that only the data actually needed is what is shipped across the network.

▪ Creating an application is only one step in a product's life cycle. The operating and maintenance costs of the software may far exceed its creation costs. Application module design needs to take account of its operation, maintenance, and extension. A certain car manufacturer once designed a car which required the removal of the engine from the car to change its spark plugs. It would be nice if you didn't have to take your entire application apart when you need to service one of its "spark plugs!" Consider support interfaces to modules so that they might respond to application level requests for tracing, debugging, or to provide other information to help isolate problems.

▪ The interfaces to modules need careful design. They become the *contracts* between application modules and, in general, need interoperability across software releases. Various communication methods employed among cooperating modules, as well as the format of data they exchange, are explored in Chapter 3. Chapter 8 describes *FML*, a facility provided in the TUXEDO System, that enables interfaces among modules to be extended in an interoperable fashion.

2.3.3 Why a Distributed Database Does Not Suffice for a Distributed Application

As discussed previously in this chapter, permanent storage is a requirement for a business application. A number of models for organization, storage, and retrieval of business data have been used to construct databases, with distributed relational products currently dominating the market. The fact that these products provide for distribution enables parallelism, redundancy, and remote access to data. A number of such products have provided procedural languages to manipulate database entities. An often asked question is, "Why do I need anything other than a distributed database system to implement a distributed business application?"

The use of database management systems should be to manage data. Applications, however, consist of more than data management. They include functions to

- interface to external devices, such as PCs, printers, speech recognition devices, etc.
- perform business calculations, validate business rules, etc.
- interface and route requests to other systems; these may be either intra-company systems or intercompany systems; such systems may be "current" systems or "legacy" systems
- integrate multiple data sources
- manage the application's processing, not just its data
- manage security into, within, and out of an application
- be managed entities in larger scale management frameworks

In short, applications need application management, not just data management. Database systems should provide access to, and management of, centralized or distributed data. Stored procedures as parameterized data access functions provide a good performance alternative to embedded SQL. However, they should not substitute for conventional programming languages because

- As interpreted languages, performance for complex business functions will suffer.
- Their expressive power is inferior to that of conventional programming languages.
- Their definition is nonstandard.
- They represent yet another language whose syntax, debugging tools, etc. must be learned.
- They are data centric and may not cover an application's total processing needs, as previously described.

2.4   Integrating Data and Processing—The World of Brokers

Throughout this chapter we have discussed data and logic distribution. Data and its manipulation are unified through the concepts of Objects. An *object* is a data item and the functions used to manipulate it. The data item of an object might be as simple as a primitive data type, for example, an integer, or as complex as an entire database system. The manipulation functions of an object are called its *methods*. An object and its methods are inseparable. An object may invoke another object's methods. As will be discussed in Chapter 3, function invocation is a form of request/response communication. Thus, objects perform request/response communication by invoking each others' methods. *Distributed objects* are objects that reside on separate computers and that communicate across a network. An *Object Request Broker (ORB)* is a software system that enables distributed objects to communicate. The *Common Object Request Broker Architecture (CORBA)*[CORBA] is a specification of the Object Management Group of the functionality and interfaces required of an ORB and ORB-related software.

"What does this have to do with the TUXEDO System?" you ask. As we will explain in more detail in Chapter 6, the TUXEDO System is fundamentally a *Service Request Broker (SRB)* and performs many functions analogous to an ORB. In the TUXEDO System, *service calls* correspond to method invocations. Unlike CORBA, *object references* are not explicitly used in TUXEDO applications. All objects are implicitly accessed via application function shipping in the form of service calls. In a TUXEDO application, objects may communicate via any of the communications paradigms offered by the TUXEDO System. Thus, for example, objects may "converse" by using TUXEDO's conversation functions. We will discuss such communications paradigms in the next chapter. Similarly, the CORBA specification for transaction control, called the *Object Transaction Service (OTS)*, has an analog in the TUXEDO System's transaction control facility. Both systems enable the effects of distributed method invocation to be bound into an atomic unit called a *transaction*. We'll also introduce transactions in the next chapter.

2.5 Summary

Applications consist of data and data manipulation. Distribution alternatives for applications include data shipping at progressively higher levels, from distributed file systems to stored procedures. As we'll explore in Parts II and III of this book, the TUXEDO System provides facilities to perform application function shipping. This approach to application construction advocates the decomposition of an application into modules which intercommunicate via well-defined interfaces. A variety of communication techniques, as introduced in Chapter 3 and expanded upon in Chapters 7 through 14, enable such communication. Application function shipping is encouraged for the following reasons:

- It creates modular applications which are extensible, maintainable, and manageable.

- Such systems can be distributed easily by running the modules on separate computers.

- Such systems provide information hiding, allowing reimplementation of business functions.

- Such systems provide better economy of operation by performing functions close to the resources they need, and thus reduce network traffic.

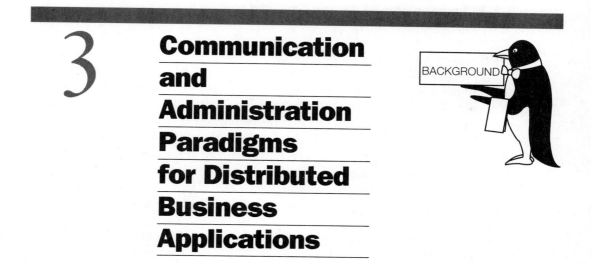

3 Communication and Administration Paradigms for Distributed Business Applications

BACKGROUND

This chapter explores a number of techniques used by distributed application components to cooperate. Components cannot cooperate unless they communicate—their communication occurs via the messages they exchange. Such message exchanges can be performed for a number of reasons and in a variety of ways.

This chapter starts by defining some terminology and proceeds through the most common communication techniques. It also describes techniques for structuring data that is passed among application modules residing on computers with different binary data representations. The handling of errors is one of the most difficult parts of programming distributed applications, and this chapter also describes techniques, such as *time-outs* and *transactions*, that ease the programmer's burden in the face of error conditions.

The orderly execution of a distributed business application is as important to its success as its creation. The second part of this chapter introduces administrative terminology and describes techniques for the construction of administrative software for distributed business applications. One specialized part of the administration task of an application is the configuration and monitoring of its security system. This chapter concludes with an introduction to the security terminology relevant to distributed business applications.

3.1   Application Communication

Effective cooperation among software modules requires precise communication among them. In this section, we introduce some of the concepts used in intermodule communication and describe interface design principles used to prevent miscommunication.

3.1.1 Terminology—Can You Say Protocol?

Application software consists of application code, and application code consists of sequences of statements manipulating variables, logic constructs (conditional tests, loops, etc.), and calls to prepackaged chunks of software. Prepackaged chunks are variously called *subroutines*, *routines*, *functions*, *primitives*, or *procedures*. In this book, we'll use them interchangeably. Sometimes, a set of procedures is used to perform an overall task, such as providing access to a file system. An *application programming interface (API)* is the definition of the calling formats to a set of procedures that perform a set of related tasks. An API specifies the inputs, outputs, and rules governing calls to its procedures. For example, access to a file system often involves procedures to open and close files, to read data from them, and to write data into them. Such procedures form the file system's API.

A *communications API* is an interface to a set of procedures that may be used to communicate with other software modules. The software that implements the communications API is often called a *communications stack*. This term derives from the Open Systems Interconnect model for communications (OSI) whereby software modules communicate by calling layers of "stacked" functions. Modules communicate by passing messages. The formats and sequences of messages that may be exchanged by a set of communicating modules are called *communication protocols* (or just *protocols*). So, on the computer initiating a communication, a communications API provides the software that initiates the communication with an interface to a communications stack, and the communications stack emits a protocol. Figure 3.1 shows an example of application modules communicating via a communications stack. For the communications to make sense, the protocol must be acceptable to the receiving end. The stack on the receiving end accepts the protocol messages and presents them to the application software module through a communications API on that system. Usually, the software on both sides uses the same communications API. They must use the same protocol; otherwise, one side doesn't know what the other is talking about. There are two protocols mentioned in Figure 3.1. The ap-

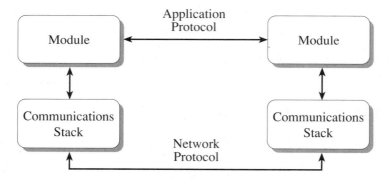

Figure 3.1   **Application Modules Communicate via Stack**

plication protocol contains the messages that the applications wish to exchange. The network protocol is the representation of the application's data on the network. The network protocol will contain all of the application's information, but may contain additional information, for example, check sums to ensure that the data is correctly transmitted.

Communications between software modules on dissimilar computers have another problem: data items on the computers may not have the same digital representation. For the communications to be effective, the data must be transformed from its representation on the source computer to an equivalent representation on the destination computer. This function is often called the *presentation service*, and should not be confused with software that renders images on terminals.

A *paradigm* is a style, or form, of doing something. Communication paradigms are styles of communication. To understand communication paradigms for software, think of how humans communicate. After all, the software modules that are communicating are often agents carrying out human communication. Humans communicate by declarative ("X has happened"), imperative ("Do Y!"), and requests ("Can you tell me Z?"). The communication is sometimes directly with and to the other party, for example, during a telephone call; sometimes it is indirect and initiated without the other party being available, for example, to an answering machine. Sometimes it is between two individuals (one-to-one), sometimes it is among group members (many-to-many), and sometimes it is broadcast from one person to many, for example, when an announcement is made over a public address system. Sometimes the communication is short and discrete, for example, when the electric company sends a bill and the customer replies with a payment. It may be continuous or dialogue-oriented, for example, when someone calls you on the telephone to conduct a survey. Sometimes the communication uses basic communication stacks, for example, using the human voice carried through the air, and sometimes it is carried across technologically sophisticated communications media, for example, satellite links.

Distributed business systems are conducting the affairs of humans, so it is natural for their implementation to mimic the paradigms of human communication. Thus, having a number of communications paradigms is natural for the builder of distributed applications.

3.1.2 Making Communications APIs Easy for the Programmer

Before investigating various communications paradigms, let's discuss a few concepts used to design a good communications API. It is important to do this, because the communications API will be the fundamental tool set used by application programmers in expressing the interaction of the modules of your application. A good communications API should have the following characteristics:

- It should be appropriate to the communications tasks it is meant to accomplish. This means the API should handle the types of communications functions most often needed in distributed systems. The interface should grow in complexity as the communication tasks grow in complexity. Simple things should be simple to do, and more complex tasks may require a more complicated interface.

▌ It should be consistent in the way it accepts arguments, returns data, and handles errors. The error handling facilities, in particular, need careful design, because error handling is among the most difficult problems the programmer will encounter.

▌ It should be intuitive to use. This means the programmer shouldn't be surprised by the results of successful or unsuccessful communications calls, and the use of the API shouldn't be error-prone.

We have already touched on one area where a communications API can help a distributed application programmer: built-in presentation services can off-load the problem of transforming data representations among heterogeneous computers. Another area where a communications API can simplify programming is by providing *location transparency*. Basically, applications want to communicate with other parts of the application, regardless of where the other parts are and without the tedium and difficulty of locating them. Imagine if you had to give the sequence of telephone circuits to use in connecting you to a person you are calling! It's bad enough having to remember a phone number—you'd really prefer to dial the *name* of the person you are calling! The provision of presentation services and location transparency are indicative of a high-level communications API. In fact, the higher the level of the communications API, the less distributed the application "feels." Also, the application designers and programmers can concentrate more on the business of the application and less about low-level communications details. Now, on to some communication paradigms!

3.2   Request/Response—"Ask and Ye Shall Receive"

One of the simplest interactions between computer programs is the *request/response* paradigm. In this style of programming, one program, called the *requestor*, asks another program, the *requestee*, to do something. The request can be to provide some information or take some action and report on its success or failure. The requestee performs the action and usually returns a result. In the communication jargon, a requestor is often called a *client*, and the requestee is called a *server*. The server carries out the wishes of its clients by performing a *service* for them. In a well-designed system, a client that makes a request for a service should know

1. what data the service requires

2. what data the service will return

The client should *not* know

3. where the service is located

4. how the service processes the request

5. how the service was created

The first two principles form a contract between the client and the server. The third principle, called *location transparency*, allows the service to be moved to a new location without the client's knowledge. One might want to do this, for example, if the computer on which the service is executing is to be brought down for maintenance. The fourth principle is called *implementation transparency* and exhibits *information hiding*. It allows the reimplementation of the service without any change to the client should a new, better, or cheaper algorithm for implementing the service be found. Figure 3.2 diagrams the request/response paradigm.

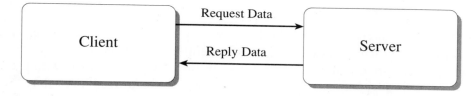

Figure 3.2 **Request/Response Interaction**

The implementation of a service may be such that the service calls other services to do its work. When this happens, the server becomes a client, that is, the notion of client and server are roles that software modules assume in their interaction with each other. The TRANSFER service shown in Figure 3.3 uses two other services (CREDIT and DEBIT) to do its work. In effect, TRANSFER is like a prime contractor that uses other services as subcontractors.

3.2.1 Procedure Calls—Near and Far

A number of methods can be used to create request/response behavior. In a simple *procedure call*, an invoking procedure provides arguments to an invoked procedure. Control is passed to the invoked procedure, and the invoker suspends operation until the invoked procedure completes. The invoked procedure performs its function and returns a result. Execution resumes in the invoking procedure at the statement after the procedure call invocation. Here, both calling and called procedures are executing in the same address space, the invocation is synchronous, and communication between the procedures is arranged for by the compilation sys-

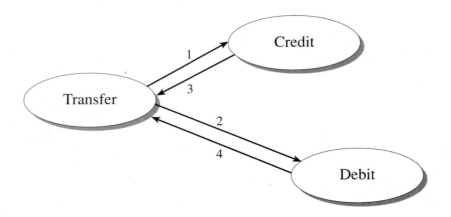

Figure 3.3   Service Using Subservices via Fan-Out Parallelism

tem. By synchronous, we mean that the invoking procedure is not executing while the invoked procedure is executing. The system locates the called procedure at linkage or run-time and creates argument passing and return areas within the common address space for the inputs and outputs of the invoked procedure. So, procedure calls are a form of request/response built into the programming language.

A programmer can also create request/response interactions by passing messages between modules executing in different address spaces, possibly in different computers. This may be done explicitly by the application using a communications API designed for such communications, or it may be done by a compilation system that converts procedure calls in one address space to procedure calls in another. The latter case is called a *Remote Procedure Call* (or *RPC*).

3.2.2 Elements of Request/Response Communication

The important elements of request/response communication include the following:

■ A *Request/Response API* which provides interfaces to request that a service be executed, allows data to be passed to the service, and provides for reply data that results from the service's execution.

■ The invoking module (also called the requestor, caller or client) sends a request to a server.

■ The invoked module (also called the server) processes a request sent by a client.

■ The communication protocol is a simple "one-over(request)/one-back(reply)" protocol.

▪ Request data (if any) is passed from client to server.

▪ Reply data (if any) is returned from the server to client.

▪ The communication (in its basic form) is *synchronous to the client—* when a client makes a request, it will not continue execution until the response from the server is received, that is, the processing of the client is synchronized with the processing of the server.

▪ The method by which error conditions are signaled to the communicating modules is either as error returns on the call or as *exceptions* raised by the run-time system.

The last point is particularly important, because even such a simple interaction as request/response is fraught with error possibilities, such as these:

▪ What happens if the server doesn't exist when a request is made?

▪ What happens if the client doesn't exist when the server is ready to send the reply?

▪ What happens if the request contains data the server doesn't understand?

▪ What happens if the reply contains data the client doesn't understand?

▪ What happens if the server abnormally terminates while processing the request? Will the client find out? Will it wait endlessly for the result, which won't be forthcoming, to be returned?

▪ What happens if the communication line is cut during transmission of the request or the reply?

▪ What happens if this interaction is the fourth in a set of six interactions that need to be accomplished to perform the entire business function, and it fails? Parts of the business function have been performed and parts have not.

In these cases, you want the application programmer to be notified of the error condition in a timely manner. You also want the system to clean up any mess that has been created as a result of the erroneous condition. As you will see later in this chapter, this cleanup can be accomplished simply via a technique called a *transaction*.

3.2.3 Asynchronous Request/Response—Fan-Out Parallelism

Sometimes a client can do processing while the server is executing its request. For example, Figure 3.3 shows a banking application that enables the transfer of funds from an account in a savings database to an account in a checking database. Transfer is essentially two actions: debiting one account and crediting the other. There is no reason why these operations cannot proceed in parallel, so long as the results of both are checked and there is a way to ensure that either both operations happen or neither of them happens. In Figure 3.3, the TRANSFER service initiates parallel requests via flows 1 and 2 to the CREDIT and DEBIT services. The replies return in flows 3 and 4.

We call this type of parallelism *fan-out parallelism* because it allows one module to distribute—that is, fan-out—requests in an overlapped fashion to a set of server modules. Fan-out parallelism reduces response time at the client. Presumably the multiple actions it initiates can be executed in an overlapped fashion, for example, having the debit and credits execute at the same time. A communications API that allows fan-out parallelism will also require functions to determine when the reply to a request is available. Typically, procedure call syntaxes for request/response do not allow fan-out parallelism. This is because the language semantics of a procedure call is usually synchronous. That is, the caller of a procedure doesn't gain control until the called procedure has completed execution. One way to achieve fan-out parallelism via procedure calls is to create a fan-out of executable contexts, called *threads*, in the requesting module. This separately executing thread can then issue a synchronous procedure call while its creator thread issues its own synchronous procedure call.

Fan-out parallelism is essentially *asynchronous request/response* at the client. This means that, while a request is being processed in the server, the client can be performing other work (including initiating other requests). Later, the client becomes synchronized with the response to the request by checking or waiting for a reply. Note that the asynchronicity of fan-out parallelism is not evident to the server. The server receives a request, performs it, and returns a result. It doesn't know whether the client is blocked awaiting its results or has fanned-out other requests.

3.2.4 Pipeline Parallelism—When Passing the Buck Is a Good Thing

By hiding the operation of a server from its client, another form of parallelism may be introduced into the communications system. A service that is invoked by a client may perform part of the work and then delegate the remainder of the work to another service. The delegate completes the work and responds to the client. While the delegate is working on the remainder of the service, the original server can be working on the first part of a different client's request. This type of delegation allows *software pipelines* to be constructed. Each stage in the pipeline performs some fraction of the total operation and passes its results off to the next stage. The terminal stage responds to the client. Figure 3.4 shows the flow of a two-stage software pipeline. The client makes a request (flow 1) and receives a response (flow 3 or 4), just as in the request/response paradigm previously discussed. However, the processing is performed by two servers, each doing part of the work. The initial server, identified in Figure 3.4 as STAGE-1, performs some of the processing. If it is unsuccessful, it returns a failure status (flow 3) to the client. If it is successful, it passes on the work (flow 2) to the server identified as

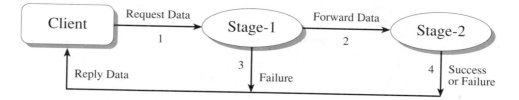

Figure 3.4 Pipeline Parallelism—Two-Stage Service Pipeline

STAGE-2, which completes the work, returning either success or failure (flow 4), depending on its part of the work. Note that the client is unaware of the facts that there are two stages. We term this type of parallelism *pipeline parallelism*.

How might pipeline parallelism be used in an application? Suppose a credit card authorization system wishes to validate the use of a credit card. Furthermore, suppose the customer is required to provide a password with each use of the credit card. Authorization might consist of two steps:

1. ensure the customer has provided a correct password

2. ensure the customer is a customer in "good standing"

These authorization rules may be done via a two-stage pipeline, as depicted in Figure 3.5. The client software module accepts input from a device where the credit card is being presented for use. The client calls the "AUTH" service (flow 1) to get the authorization and is expecting a NO or YES answer. The "AUTH" service performs the following functions:

▪ It looks up the customer's entry in the password database. If the customer is not found or if the password is incorrect, it returns NO (flow 3)

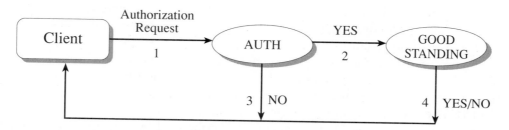

Figure 3.5 Pipeline Parallelism in Authorization System

to the client. If the customer successfully passes the password check, the AUTH service "passes the buck" (flow 2) to the GOOD_STANDING service.

▪ GOOD_STANDING checks the customer's credit. While GOOD_STANDING is checking a client's credit limit, the AUTH service may have begun work on another authorization request, from a different client.

▪ GOOD_STANDING replies to the client (flow 4). If the purchase would exceed the amount allowed, it returns NO. Otherwise, it returns YES.

Note that the work of AUTH and GOOD_STANDING may, thus, be overlapped. That is, AUTH may be checking the password for customer 2, while GOOD_STANDING is checking the account of customer 1. This behavior, which allows a better throughput, is hidden from the client. The client doesn't know which module replies to it—it only "knows" it is supposed to get a YES or NO.

3.3 Conversations—When Once (Over and Back) Isn't Enough

When ordering a meal in a restaurant, the customer and the waiter engage in a dialogue. Multiple interactions may range over various items, and depending on particular selections, other questions and answers may be developed. Finally, both parties come to an understanding of what is to be delivered as the meal. Likewise, it is sometimes the case that a number of messages need to be exchanged between software modules to complete a business operation. We give an example in the next section. In such a situation, we say that the modules are conducting a *conversation*. Implicit in the notion of a conversation is the notion of state. Whenever one side communicates with the other, both sides of the conversation "remember" the point (that is, the state) to which the conversation has progressed, and subsequent interactions are relative to that point. In the restaurant situation just mentioned, the waiter and the customer are both aware of the progression of the questions and answers through the presentation of the menu. In software, state is represented by the values associated with data items (for example, variables) and the locations of the instruction counters in the conversing modules.

Figure 3.6 depicts the flow of data between modules conducting a conversation. The client initiates the communication with a connection message sent to the server (flow 1). In response, the server sends two messages to the client (flows 2 and 3). The client sends another message to the server (flow 4), which sends a single reply message (flow 5). The sequence is terminated by the server sending a disconnect message to the client (flow 6).

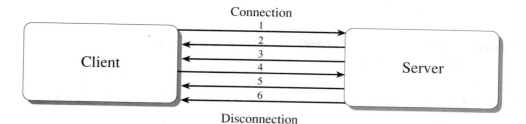

Figure 3.6   **Conversational Programming Paradigm**

3.3.1 An Example of the Use of Conversations

One common use for conversations is to buffer portions of a lengthy reply from a server to a client. In this situation, a client requests information from a server. The server has a lot of reply data, so much, in fact, that the client cannot accept it all at once. In this case, the server might only send part of the data and indicate to the client that it has "more" reply data. The client accepts the initial amount of reply data, processes it, and when it is ready, requests that the server send some "more." Here, the server keeps several items in its state including the fact that there is more data to be sent and the starting point of the reply data that has not yet been sent. When the client asks for "more," the server starts sending from this point.

If the protocol between the client and server allows the client to ask for previously sent reply data, then the server will also have to keep the data it previously sent and also state variables to indicate what and where that data is so it can "back up" the state.

3.3.2 Application Protocols for Conversations— Who Says What/When

The protocol for request/response is very explicit: The client asks, the server replies. In a dialogue, however, multiple messages may be flowing in both directions between the communicating modules. For correct behavior, some rules need to be observed. In the buffering example cited previously, it serves no purpose for the server just to keep sending information to the client. The whole purpose for the buffering is for the server to hold the information until the client is ready to accept it. The set of rules by which a conversational application exchanges messages is called an *application protocol*. In addition to specifying the formats of messages, application protocols indicate the allowable points when either side may send data.

For example, it is generally a *protocol violation* for both sides of a conversation to be awaiting a message from the other party.

3.3.3 Conversational Termination—When There Is No More to Be Said

In a request/response interaction, the interaction terminates normally for the client when it receives an answer from its server. For the server, it terminates when the answer has been sent to the client. Abnormal termination may occur when, for example, the server fails while processing the request without returning a response. In such a case, the client

- waits forever for the result, or
- learns of the server's failure through some means, or
- gives up waiting, or
- is told by some other software to stop waiting

For a conversation, the termination will normally happen by agreement between the modules. One side or the other will terminate the conversation, which is presumably accepted by the other. If either side should "disappear," the other side needs to be notified so that it can stop sending or awaiting messages. A special case of this arises when the communication channel between the conversing modules becomes inoperative. Here, each side is seen by the other as disappearing, and both need to be notified that the conversation can no longer continue.

3.3.4 Context—Remembering What Has Been Discussed

When two software modules are conversing, it is necessary for them to keep state. Otherwise, they have amnesia, in which case each message needs to contain an entire history of the conversation up to that point. Such a situation is quite difficult (and unnatural) to program. State is represented by the setting of data items in the modules. Thus, in the previous example, the server buffering data for its client "remembers" how much has been sent. A more subtle form of state is the location of the instruction counter in a conversing module. The instruction counter indicates what instruction is to be executed next, and thus implies what the module "expects" to happen next.

The elements of conversational communication include the following:

- A *Conversational API*, that is used by applications to initiate, exchange messages over, and terminate a conversation.

- The module initiating the conversation sends a setup request to a module that is to be the partner of the conversation. This request may contain application specific data.

- The communication protocol is determined by the application. In *two-way alternate conversations* (the type available in the TUXEDO System) either party is *capable* of sending a message, but at any given moment, only one party is *permitted* to send a message. A party may yield the right to send to its partner.

- The communication is *asynchronous to the sender*. This means that when the party controlling the conversation sends a message, it may continue execution before its partner receives the message. In fact, it may send multiple messages to its partner before granting its partner the right to send messages. The sending party does not know when a message is received or acted upon. Synchronization may be achieved by an application protocol. For example, the sender could grant send-control to its partner and wait for the partner to send an acknowledgment message that it (the partner) has received and processed the previous message.

- The conversation is normally terminated by agreement. Either side may abnormally terminate by disconnecting. As will be described in more detail in Chapter 11, "Conversational Communication," in the TUXEDO System, clients initiate conversations with partners called *conversational services*. Normal conversation termination occurs when the conversational service returns from execution with a success indication. Abnormal conversation termination is achieved in the client by calling a disconnect function. The conversational service abnormally terminates a conversation by returning a failure.

- The method by which error conditions are signaled to the communicating modules is either as error returns on the call or as *exceptions* raised by the run-time system.

3.4   Events—Things Happen

Request/response interactions are a form of polling. The requestor is asking for some information from, or for an action to be taken by, a server. The server replies when asked, but otherwise is idle. Sometimes software would rather not ask—polling can be tedious and resource-consumption intensive. Rather, it would like to be notified when the information it wants is available or, more generally, that "something has happened." In this case, the module that is the target of the communication does not know when the communication is to take place and may, in fact, be doing something else when the event occurs. For example, the software handling a terminal might like to be advised when the system is going to be taken off-line for maintenance, so that it can advise the person using the terminal. Otherwise, the system will be "taken down," and its users will have no clue as to what is happening. However, the terminal handler is not just waiting for the system to go down. Its normal job is to "listen" for input from the terminal.

We call an unsolicited communication of this form an *event*. An event has an *event generator* and *event targets*. The event generator is the software module that notices that some condition has arisen and wishes to tell another. Presumably the target software module "knows" what to do when it receives notification of any particular event. If not, it might ignore the event or assume that the event is something catastrophic and cease operations.

3.4.1 Simple Events

With simple events, an event generator notifies one or more targets that it knows are interested in the event. Figure 3.7 depicts such a situation. Here, a client module is the target and is being informed by an administrative server module of the "System Going Down" event. An event generator may know which targets to notify either because of a priori agreements, such as a statically configured set of targets, or because one or more such targets have previously informed the generator that they are interested in notification when the event is generated. In this latter scenario, the target "registers" directly with the event generator. This implies

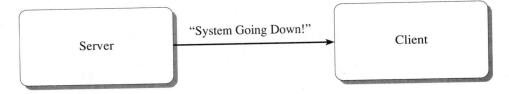

Figure 3.7 Client Being Informed of an Event

that the targets know which modules are, in fact, the generators of each event. To deliver the events to the known targets, the event generator explicitly provides the system with addressing information for the target modules.

By their nature, events are generated and delivered to targets, whether or not the target is idle or occupied doing something else. The target is interrupted from the work it is doing to process the event. Presumably the target takes note of the event, possibly performing some actions as a result of it, and may return to its previous work. Just as it is not easy to perform a task while being constantly interrupted, programming to handle events, which are in effect interrupts, is also difficult. One way to handle this is to deliver the event in a slightly less intrusive manner to the target, so that if the target is busy when the event is delivered, it is not interrupted. Rather, the event is kept pending, and when the target becomes idle, it is notified. The situation is akin to waiting for someone to stop talking before speaking to the person.

The elements of simple event communications include the following:

■ An *Unsolicited Notification API* which is used to send event notifications to targets.

■ *Event generators* are executables which send an event notification to targets it knows about.

■ *Event targets* are executables that are notified when events are generated.

■ Event targets are directly known by event generators.

■ *Event data* may be associated with an event at the time the notification is sent. This data is made available to event targets.

3.4.2 Brokered Events—Man in the Middle

One limitation of simple events is that somehow event generators must find out who the potential targets of the events are. Because new targets and, for that matter, new generators may come and go, the problem starts to get out of hand. For example, an application may be extended so that an "old" event is generated from a "new" subsystem. How are the "old targets" supposed to know about the new "generators" or vice versa? One way to handle this situation is to have a software module, called an *event broker*, whose job it is to accept target registrations and to deliver events. Targets "register" their interest in events with the broker. Event generators send their events to the broker, which in turn passes them on to registered targets. Event generators and targets need only to inform the broker, which takes care of the rest. Of course, "taking care of the rest" may be a complex job. For example, a registered target may cease operation without ever telling the broker, which will not be able to deliver the event to the defunct target. Figure 3.8

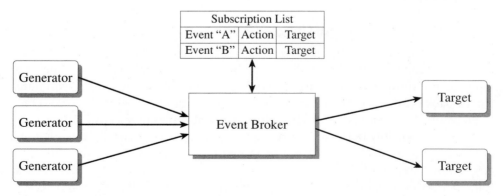

Figure 3.8 **Delivery of Events via a Broker**

depicts the flow of information through an event broker. Here, event targets register with the broker, which keeps a subscription list of such registrations. Event generators inform the broker when they wish to indicate an event has occurred. The broker fulfills the subscriptions by taking actions to notify the targets.

The elements of brokered event communications include the following:

- *Event identifiers* are used to name events.

- An *Event API* which is used to generate, subscribe to, and receive events.

- *Event generators* are executables which indicate that an event has occurred.

- *Event targets* are executables that register to be notified when events are generated.

- Event generators and event targets are mutually anonymous.

- *Event data* may be associated with an event at the time the event is generated. This data is made available to event targets.

3.5 Queues—Deferred Communication

Sometimes it is not possible, required, or desirable, for application programs to communicate *on-line*. Rather, the communications between the modules are deferred over time. An analogy from everyday experience occurs when you leave a message on a telephone answering machine.

To effect *deferred communication* between modules, it is necessary for them to "leave messages" for each other. If the communication is to take place across a reboot of the computer, it will be necessary to leave the messages on persistent storage. The persistent storage on an answering machine is the magnetic tape or disk inside of the device.

3.5.1 Examples of Queue Usage

One use of a queue is to buffer data for an unavailable software module. Perhaps the computer on which the module is to be run is currently "down." Then the input to the module can be saved on a queue and released when the computer comes back on-line. Another case in which queues can be used is to buffer communications between systems that are operating at different speeds. Suppose one computer is generating input to a second computer faster than the second computer can process it. The input can be stored in a queue on either the source or target computer until the target computer is ready to process it. Of course, at some point the consumption of the messages must be faster than their generation. Otherwise, the storage queues will fill up.

3.5.2 Essentials of Queued Access

The important elements of queued communications include

- a *queue*, which is the storage mechanism to hold messages until they are processed

- a *Queuing API*, which provides interfaces to allow modules to store (enqueue) and retrieve (dequeue) messages from queues

- enqueuing modules, that put messages on queues

- dequeuing modules, that take messages off queues

The purpose of a queue is to perform time-independent communication. The queue itself is a message repository. Thus, when applications communicate via queues, they do so by data shipping messages to and from queues.

Note that, in a distributed system, a queue and its enqueuing and dequeuing modules may all exist on different computers. However, to simplify matters for the application programmer, the queue should also be location-transparent to its enqueuing and dequeuing modules. Figure 3.9 depicts a queuing system composed of a single application module enqueuing messages, a single application module dequeuing messages, and an application queue, each on its own computer. When the application modules use the queuing API to access the queue, they are performing data shipping. As discussed in Chapter 2, data shipping is accomplished through some type of software, for example, distributed file system software, which does function shipping to accomplish the task. For simplicity, in Figure 3.9, we do not show the system software that ships messages to and from the remote queue.

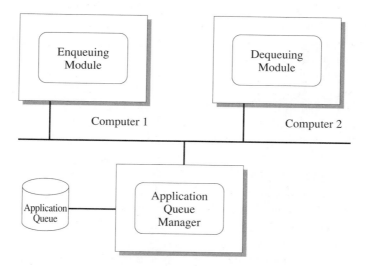

Figure 3.9   **Queuing Interaction**

3.5.3 Queue Ordering—When Arriving Early Does Not Always Count!

Although queues are data structures that are characterized by a first-in, first-out (*FIFO*) principle, there are a number of times when FIFO needs to be violated. Driven by a need to model the application's business rules, such overrides to FIFO ordering might include the following:

- *Prioritized messages*, which should be dequeued before lower priority messages. Messages of the same priority could be accessed in a FIFO manner.

- *Prenatal messages*. These are messages that are put in a queue but are not allowed to be dequeued until a specified *birth time*.

- *Specially ordered messages*, which are placed before or after other enqueued messages.

- *LIFO (last-in, first-out) ordering*. Here, the messages most recently put in the queue have the highest priority.

3.5.4 Replies and Queues

In effect, a queued message is a request for some future processing. The queue serves as a place to hold the input to these requests. However, the enqueuer cannot be assured when the processing will take place. In fact, when the processing of the message does take place, the enqueuer may no longer exist! If the processing is to return some results, it can do so through another queue. The originator of the request, if it still exists, can access the response through this *response (or reply) queue*. If the originator is no longer in existence, an "heir" will be responsible for processing the reply when it becomes available.

Typically, an enqueuing module will write one or more items to a queue. At a later time, it may look at the reply queue to see what replies are available. The association of replies to requests may be difficult unless the queuing system, or the application, arranges for some method of correlating replies with their associated requests.

Note that the terminology of queuing is very similar to the request/response paradigm mentioned previously. The main difference is that request/response happens on-line, whereas queuing uses permanent storage to allow deferred communication between modules. Additionally, there is an anonymity present between the enqueuer and the dequeuer of messages on a queue. Similar to the event broker, the queue is monitored and controlled by a broker called the *queue manager*, as shown in Figure 3.9. The queue manager is responsible for enqueuing messages from message producers and providing them to message consumers that request them via dequeue operations.

Because the semantics of request/response and queuing are so similar, it is possible to construct software that translates between them. For example, a *forwarding*

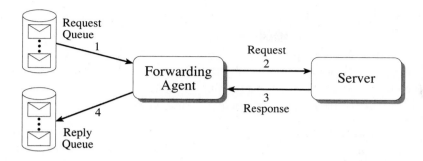

Figure 3.10   **Forwarding Agent Converts Queue Operations to Request/Response**

agent, as shown in Figure 3.10, may read a queue (flow 1), perform a request/response on-line (flows 2 and 3), and store the reply in a reply queue (flow 4). The server thinks it is talking on-line to its client. But it is really talking to a surrogate client, that is, the forwarding agent. The real client, or its successor, will get the server's response later in a response queue.

3.6   Data Representation for Communications—It's All in the Presentation

An important part of the communication paradigms previously presented is the representation of messages sent among the communicating modules. The possible number of types of data structures that might be communicated is limited only by the imagination of the architects of the application protocol. Several generic types include the following:

- Arbitrary, unformatted data.

- String data, typically from the printable character set.

- Structured data composed of aggregates of elemental types from the programming languages involved. This type includes, for example, COBOL records and C structures. Structured data representation is largely positional in nature, and requires a priori knowledge of the structure of the item by the communicating modules. That is, each side must have known or have access to the layout of the data.

- Tagged data items. Here, the value of each data item is accompanied by a description of the item. That is, the collection of items is *self-describing*. Note that because such data contains its own description, it might occupy more space. However, because it contains its own description, the structure of the data can be "learned" and "modified" at runtime. This provides an enormous amount of flexibility in architecting communicating applications, because "new" data elements can be added without affecting old programs.

▌ Arguments passed to procedures. Typically these are either elemental or aggregate data types defined by the language in which the invoked procedure is written. Such arguments are usually positional in nature (i.e., the "first" argument, the "second" argument, etc.).

All of the formats above may be used in any of the communications paradigms described previously in this chapter. Because communication may take place between software modules that are executing on computers with differing data representations, for example, between a client running on a SPARC processor and a server running on a Pentium processor, the data structures must be transformed to be understandable to the receiving module. Such a transformation process is often called the *presentation service* and was briefly described in the terminology section of this chapter. If the data formats are understood by the communications stack, it is possible for the stack to perform the presentation service. If the format of a message is not understood by the communications stack, then the communicating application modules themselves have to perform the presentation service.

3.7   Error Conditions—"Are You Still There?"

The most difficult part of programming and administering a distributed system arises from the very fact that the system is distributed. In a distributed system involving independent computers, although the failure of some computers may cause parts of the application to halt execution, other parts of the application may continue to execute. When operating parts attempt to interoperate with failed parts, failure scenarios will arise which might be difficult for the programmer and the administrator to anticipate. We've all experienced such a situation when we've been "cut off" during a phone conversation. Neither party knows what happened nor what to do next. Each may try to call the other, only to get a busy signal! Because the application is distributed, its parts, and therefore the state, that is the operational status of those parts, is distributed.

In a distributed application, there is no one place to go to find out "what is happening" when failures occur. The types of errors that can occur include the following:

▌ Computer hardware failure. Here, one of the nodes running part of the application fails.

▌ Network failure. Here, the communication links between some, or all, of the nodes fail.

▌ Software failure. Here, either the system software, for example, a communications stack or the application software, fails.

▌ Combinations of hardware, network, and software failure.

It may be possible to recover from some of these failures. For example, if an application server module stops, it may be possible to start a replacement. If a computer fails, it may be possible to shift its processing to a backup computer. If the network fails, it may be possible to reroute traffic around the failed link, or it may be possible to do limited processing without full connectivity. The difficulty of turning these "possibilities" into "realities" is being able to recognize what is happening and to take corrective action. This is easier said than done. Chapter 16, "Failure Handling," describes how many of these conditions are handled by the TUXEDO run-time system.

3.7.1 Designing for Error Conditions

Because there are so many points where error conditions may arise in distributed systems, system software and application software should be acutely aware of them. Suppose a banking application wants to debit a customer's account. There are two broad categories of failure that the application may encounter:

- Application semantic failure. For example, suppose a customer has a zero balance, wants to make a withdrawal from her account, and the bank does not permit overdrafts. Here, the business rules have been violated, and the procedure should not continue. The application actually performs correctly by not completing the withdrawal function.

- Communication failure. Something went wrong in executing the communications API. For example, perhaps the server is no longer running. Here, the system cannot perform a function that is allowed by the business rules.

Usually, these two failure modes are independent of each other. The business rules of the application are communications-independent, and the communications system is a general purpose one, knowing nothing of the actual application (while it is possible to build applications specific communications APIs, we do not consider such in this book). The key is to allow both types of failures to be indicated by the system. For example, the request/response paradigm should allow both an application-level success/fail indicator, as well as a communications API success/fail indicator.

3.7.2 Time-Outs—"How Long Do I Have to Wait, Forever?"

Many failures will result in a communicating software module "hanging," that is, waiting for a message that either is not going to be sent or cannot be delivered. This can be difficult for the application programmer to handle. One way that a communications API can help is by providing the notion of a *time-out*. Here, requests to wait for a message are satisfied either by the message being received or by the system indicating that a time limit for waiting has been exceeded. In the latter case, there is "good news" and "bad news." The good news is that the application is not waiting forever; the bad news is that it cannot be sure what happened. Note that a time-out is indicated as a system error rather than an application semantic error. Of course, it is always possible for the message to arrive just after the time-out has been signaled. Here, the application "thinks" no message is forthcoming, but, in fact, one has arrived. To provide a consistent view to the application, the best thing for the communications API to do is to discard such *stale messages.*

3.8   Transactions—Undoing the Past

When an application encounters an error, it sometimes wishes it could "just start over" or "forget the whole thing." *Transactions* enable precisely this by providing an application with a tool to undo the effects of some operation that it previously performed. Note that the execution of the past operation cannot be undone, because it is an historical fact. Rather, the side effects of the operation can be undone. For example, the database updates that occurred during the operation may be rolled back, so that the updated values return to their original values. We will not go into the technical fine points of transactions in this book. We suggest [Gray-Reuter] for those interested. Instead, we provide an informal discussion.

3.8.1 The Transaction Notion

The most important property of a transaction for a programmer is its *atomicity.* The idea is as follows. An application brackets some code by using transaction boundary calls, such as "begin_tran" and "end_tran." Whatever happens, all of the effects of the execution of code between the brackets, that is, between the "begin_tran" and the "end_tran" statements, or none of the effects, must be permanent. This allows a number of operations to be executed as if they were one operation. This is what is meant by atomicity. In a previous example, where an application wanted to transfer money from one account to another, the desired effect is for both the credit and debit operations to take place. What definitely is not wanted is for only one of them to take place. By bracketing the operations with transactional notation, the system recognizes that both, or neither, must be done.

The selection of what actions must be atomically done is part of the application. In effect, they represent some of the rules of the business being programmed. For example, for the transfer operation, the rule would be "every successful transfer operation must include both a successful debit operation and a successful credit operation." Thus, it is the application that knows where transaction brackets must be applied, and so it is the application designer and programmer who must provide them.

3.8.2 How Transactions Help a Programmer—"Back to Square One"

The main value of transactions to a programmer is that they ensure the atomicity of a set of operations that together form a business rule. Without transactional support, an application programmer must provide logic to ensure that the rules are enforced. For example, in the case of the funds transfer previously cited, if the computer hardware fails when only one of the operations has been completed, the databases are left in an inconsistent state. When operations are restored, remedial action must be taken to correct things. Such actions are called *compensating transactions*. Compensating transactions can be very difficult to program because there must be available somewhere, the state of progression of the business function and enough information to complete it or to undo it. Moreover, the execution of a compensating transaction can itself be disrupted, requiring another compensating transaction. Thus, the application must at ALL points be sure that enough information is available for future processing to ensure that the transaction can be completed or rolled back. For complex transactions that involve multiple operations, perhaps across multiple computer systems, this can be extremely difficult and error-prone. In effect, a programmer has to build an application-specific transaction system!

3.8.3 Transactions in a Distributed Environment— When Infection Is a Good Thing!

What do transactions mean in a distributed environment? When an application begins a transaction, it is indicating that, until it indicates the completion of the transaction, the work it is about to do must be done atomically. When an application module that has begun a transaction communicates with a remote module that is also part of the application, the work done by the remote part should also be included in the transaction. That is, ALL of the work, whether done locally or remotely, is bound by the same atomic properties. Thus, when an application that is in a transaction communicates to a remote part, we say that the remote part becomes *infected* with the transaction. Moreover, if the remote part communicates with yet another remote part, the other remote part also becomes infected. Note that, in general, transactional infection is a good thing because, as previously explained, if any of the local or remote parts fail, the entire set of work is restored to its original conditions.

Of course, transactions are not always needed to envelope communications. For example, some communications may only be informational in nature, and their successful completion may not be important. In other cases, certain application protocols and semantics may not require transactions.

3.8.4 Resource Managers—A Generalization of Databases

Previously, we mentioned that it is not the execution of operations that are undone when a transaction rolls back, it is the effects of those operations that are undone. What do we mean by this?

The execution of application software changes the "state" of an application. The state is represented by the contents of the computer's memory, both temporary and permanent. In general, the execution of a transaction changes the permanent memory of the application. For example, debiting a bank account changes the state of the account permanently, until another state change of the account occurs.

The permanent state of an application is realized in the storage memory it occupies. This permanent memory is usually organized into file systems and database systems. These storage mechanisms are referred to as *application resources* and are accessed via software called *Resource Managers*, or *RMs*. Access to application state stored by an RM is via the Resource Manager's API. Resource Manager APIs include file system interfaces, record manager interfaces, and relational database management system (RDBMS) interfaces (the standard RDBMS interface being SQL).

Note that an application may access multiple RMs in performing a business operation. For example, a checking account system may be implemented in terms of one RDBMS, and a savings system using another RDBMS. The business operation of transferring funds from the checking system to the savings system involves two distinct RMs. To support complex business operations, RMs are usually *transactionally aware*. Because a business operation may involve several operations on an RM, with each operation changing different state parts, and because the desired effect is to execute a transaction, business oriented RMs, such as RDBMSs, usually provide the transaction notion. Such transactions are "intra-RM" transactions, and may be delimited by transaction demarcation functions that are provided as part of the Resource Manager's API. In general, RMs are able to provide the atomicity principle within an instance of that RM, for example, within a database or, perhaps between multiple instances of the same vendor's RM.

Distributed applications, however, are increasingly using multiple RMs to complete a business operation. In fact, a well-designed distributed application does not know how remote operations are implemented. In particular, the RM used by a server to do its task should not be known by a client. This allows the implementation of the server to change, and possibly to use a "new and improved" RM to retain the state of the operation's effect. When an application uses multiple RMs, there is a need to provide for inter-RM transactions. Such transactions are referred to as *global transactions*.

3.8.5 Global Transaction Managers—Orchestra Conductors of Transaction Systems

The infection of the remote parts of an application does not suffice to support the transaction notion. Someone must remember what application parts were infected, and tell them when the application has ended the transaction either to complete or rollback their work. The "someone" is called a *Transaction Manager*, or *TM*. TMs are software systems that propagate transactions when communications take place and that coordinate the termination of a transaction, whether it is successful or not. Because RMs actually hold the state of the data, however, they also have a role to play in global transactions.

A TM is responsible for:

■ accepting an application's requests to start and end transactions. In this regard it provides an API for delimiting transactional boundaries

■ propagating the transaction when communications take place

■ interfacing to RMs to inform them that global transactions are operative and instructing them during the termination and recovery phases of transactions

Whereas TMs take a *coordinator role* for transaction completion, RMs take a *subordinate role*. An RM is responsible for:

■ accepting transaction delineation commands from the TM

■ performing work under the auspices of the transaction. Typically the RM provides the *consistency*, *isolation*, and *durability* properties of the transaction

■ accepting commands to perform the phases of the commitment algorithm from the TM, in particular

■ awaiting a transaction outcome of the second phase, as directed by the TM

To use an analogy from music, TMs are like orchestra conductors. They have the big picture, including the total score, and the parts each of the RMs, like the individual musicians, is to play. TMs direct the RMs during the course of the transaction, most importantly during the "commitment finale."

3.8.6 Transactions and Queues

Previously, we spoke of the queuing paradigm for deferred communication. Queues are storage systems through which application components may communicate in a deferred manner. Note that queues are passive in nature, they accept requests to store or remove items, but they never initiate such actions. A queue is, in effect, a specialized RM, and the storage mechanism for queue elements is called a *queue base*. Requests for future processing, that is, future application state changes, may be stored in queues and may be later extracted. Queues themselves are part of the state of an application. Because queues are RMs, they may be transactional in nature. This means that an enqueuing operation may be contained within a transaction. If the containing transaction does not complete, the enqueuing operation is rolled back. That is, upon rollback, the item is removed from the queue. Another way to say this is that enqueued messages appear in a queue, and thus are available for subsequent dequeuing, only after their containing transaction commits. Likewise, a dequeuing operation that is contained within a rolled back transaction leaves the item in the queue, and thus available for (re)processing at a later time.

The concept of transactional queues is very powerful because it enables the construction of a set of transactions linked over time. Figure 3.11 depicts a module which reads a queue (flow 1), performs some database interactions (flow 2), and enqueues a result (flow 3). In this regard, the module is a type of business filter.

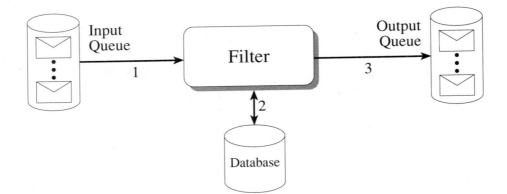

Figure 3.11 **Module Filtering Input into Output**

The result may be input to another filter operation. The set of such filters may comprise the steps of some business operation, also known as *work flow processing*. Because queues are subject to transactions, the execution of each filter step within a transaction is resilient to failure. If a transactional filter fails during execution, its inputs will be restored, its outputs eliminated, and any side effects it performed, for example, database updates, erased. In effect, the filter is enabled to reexecute.

3.8.7 Transactions and Events—"If Anyone Has an Objection to This Union . . ."

We have discussed the concept of transactional infection across communications. For request/response, servers become infected with a client's transaction. Likewise for conversational communication, the "callee" may become infected with a transaction the caller has initiated, so that any RM work it does is also part of the same transaction as the caller. In the previous section, we have discussed the significance of transactions and queues. What does the transactional notion mean for events?

At first thought, it may seem that events and transactions are disjointed. An event may be regarded as a statement that "something has happened," and thus not be subject to rollback. Targets or subscribers of the event are passive.

However, another interpretation of event communication may be possible. The publisher of a brokered event may wish to perform an action, providing there are no "objections" to it. In this regard, the posting of the event may be within a transactional bracket. When this occurs, if the infection is carried by the broker, event targets may also be infected with the transaction of the poster. If any of the subscribers to the event "object" to it, they may abort the transaction. In such a case, any transactionally aware RMs modified by the event's poster or other subscribers will be rolled back. Because subscribers are anonymous to the poster and other subscribers for brokered events, the poster only finds out that the effect of its posting wasn't a "good idea," although it doesn't know "who" objected to it.

For example, suppose in a computerized car auction system, the ANNOUNCER module wishes to put a car up for auction. It could begin a transaction, put a description of the car into the CARS_ FOR_SALE table of the AUCTION database, and post a "CAR_AVAILABLE" event. The entry in the CARS_FOR_SALE table is only pending and will not be permanent until the transaction commits. The data accompanying the posting of the CAR_AVAILABLE event might be details about the car, including its registration number. After posting the proposed availability of the car, the ANNOUNCER would like to commit the transaction, making the car details permanent in the CARS_FOR_SALE table. The registered target modules for the CAR_AVAILABLE event might be software components representing car wholesalers who bid on such cars. Another such subscriber might be the POLICE module, which reviews all such offerings to make sure the registration number of the car isn't on a stolen car list. If it is, the POLICE Module could abort the transaction, thereby removing the pending record from the CARS_FOR_SALE table.

3.9   Application Administration

So far in this chapter, we have concentrated on the means to construct distributed applications. In that regard, we have described techniques and communication methods to enable you to build distributed applications. Such applications are meant to mechanize the operation of an enterprise. After constructing and testing applications, companies deploy them. At this point a person other than the application's creator(s) may put the software into operation and ensures that it operates satisfactorily.

Many organizations focus on the costs of creating an application, but forget about the costs of running it. Administration is required to ensure that the business functions the application automates are carried out in a correct and timely fashion and that the users of the application, including your company's employees, electronic customers, and business partners, continue to receive the services, at the required service levels, that the application is meant to deliver.

Ultimately, the goal is self-administering and self-healing distributed applications. To achieve this, applications and the software upon which they are constructed need to be instrumented to provide a knowledge base and access to the knowledge base, upon which automated administrative software can be constructed. Then, generic and application-specific software needs to be written to provide for the automated administration. In the following sections, we will cover a number of techniques to enable such a system.

3.9.1 Administrative Tasks

Typically, administration of an application includes the following:

- installing the application software on its host computers
- setting configuration parameters to adapt the application to its operating environments
- tuning the environment, such as the computers' operating systems, to accommodate the application
- tuning the application so as to best take advantage of its execution environment, including usage patterns imposed by the user community
- starting and stopping parts, or all, of the application, as appropriate
- monitoring the application's execution to ensure it delivers adequate service to its users
- responding to alarms, including attempted security violations, that the application generates as it executes
- upgrading the application as new versions or components become available
- installing "software patches" as faults in the application's implementation are corrected

As previously noted, administering a distributed application will be more complex than the administration of a single computer application. Because it is partitioned, some parts may fail whereas others continue to operate, and some, or all, of the parts may be remote from the operator.

Although an application may be distributed, its administration may be distributed or centralized. The choice will depend on the geographic scope of the application, its size, and many other factors. Certainly, it is highly desirable if a distributed application can be administered from a single location. Administration of a distributed application requires that the administrative software itself must be distributed on the same computers as the application. However, the human interface to such distributed administrative software could be from a single administrative console. Such a console allows the operator to interrogate the application's components, to receive alarms from them, and to reconfigure or operate the application via various administrative commands.

In addition to allowing administration from a central console, a number of other facilities are required to ease the administration of distributed applications, including

- standardized programming interfaces to administrative data of the distribution framework

- presentation and modification of administrative data through administrator-friendly techniques, such as Graphical User Interfaces (GUIs)

- facilities to allow applications to provide administrative hooks for application components

3.9.2 Application Definition—"Just What Is an Application, Anyway?"

Our definition of an application is informal. An application is the software and permanent resources (databases, files, RMs, etc.) used to automate a business function. A distributed application is one that runs on multiple computers. Applications are extended by adding new functionality. This is done by adding new software and possibly new resources. In order that the boundaries of an application be understood, it is often useful to define the application through some configuration system. Typically, this identifies the code, data objects, and computer resources that comprise the application. Note that an application may "talk" to another application. In such cases, one might view the union of the two applications as one big application. However, implicit in the notion of an application is that it can be addressed and administered as an entity. So, we differentiate between two applications that happen to interact and the parts of a single distributed application that *must* interact. The former are two federated applications, each with independent administration. The latter represents one administrable entity.

For example, suppose a company has sales people who are paid partly on commission and partly on an hourly basis. The company has two systems, one for the payroll department and one for the sales department. The main purpose of the payroll system is to automate the payment of compensation to the company's employees. The purpose of the sales system is to track potential and executed sales. Each system is administered by its separate division. To compensate sales people based on the hours they work, data is entered by the payroll department from the time cards they receive from the sales department. To compensate the sales people based on their actual sales, the sales system needs to communicate to the payroll system the amount of sales made by each sales person. Here, within the same company, we have two independent systems that need to communicate.

3.9.3 An Introduction to MIBs—"What's to Administer?"

Applications contain lots of information, both static and dynamic. Static information changes infrequently and may include definitions of the software modules that comprise the application, database definitions, and computer configurations. Dynamic information changes frequently and will typically include the state of an application's permanent resources and information about the operation of the application (e.g., response time of the last executed transaction). To administer the operation of an application, it is necessary to understand the concepts the application embodies. In turn, this requires an explanation and classification of the items within the application. Such a classification may include very general information that is application-independent, such as the types of computers on which the application executes, and information that is very application-specific, such as a banking application that may indicate the total amount of deposits received during the day. We use the term *Management Information Base* (*MIB*) to indicate the classification of items in an application. Note that the term MIB is often associated with network management protocols, in particular, the Simple Network Management Protocol (SNMP)[SNMP]. Here, we use the term more generally, to mean any classification of a system's data.

In this book, we are concerned with distributed business applications, and thus turn our attention to the classification of those items particular to such. Moreover, because we are not discussing any particular distributed application, but rather a class of distributed applications, in this chapter we will confine our discussion to the general MIB properties for distributed applications. In Chapter 17, "A Tour of the TUXEDO Management Information Base," we will present details of the *TMIB*, the MIB provided by the TUXEDO System.

A MIB is composed of a set of *administrative class definitions*, called *classes*, for short. The classes represent concepts found in the application. Each class has a set of attributes (or properties) that characterize individual items in the class. Each item in a class has particular values for the attributes. Such values distinguish one item from other items in the class. So as not to sound too abstract, let's see what this means, in practice, for a distributed business system.

Suppose we have a system that has a lot of modules communicating via the request/response paradigm introduced earlier in this chapter. In the MIB for this system, we might have a class for "MODULE." One attribute associated with the "MODULE" class might be "NAME." Another might be "TYPE." Values for the name might be the actual executable program names. For TYPE, values might include "CLIENT" and "SERVER." MODULES of type "CLIENT" might have transitory attributes such as "NUMREQUESTS" that indicates the number of requests a particular CLIENT has initiated. Values associated for NUMREQUESTS would be an actual number, like 5122.

The value of using a MIB is that it provides the base on which to query and update the configuration and operation of a system. A query is used to report how things are going. Updating a MIB has the effect of changing the configuration or operation of the application. For example, one attribute of the MODULE class might be the "STATE" attribute, whose values could be "ACTIVE" or "INAC-TIVE." In a banking application where software modules inside Automated Teller Machines (ATMs) communicate to software inside server machines, changing the STATE attribute from ACTIVE to INACTIVE of the member of the MODULE class, whose NAME is ATMCONTROLLER and whose TYPE is "CLIENT," might mean that the software controlling a particular ATM should be turned off, thus rendering the ATM inoperable.

3.9.4 MIBs for Distributed Business Applications— Spreading the Classes Around

We will briefly describe the administrative class definitions one might find in the MIB for a distributed business system. Certainly, the configuration on which the system runs would be in the MIB. This would include the computers and associated network's attributes on which the application executes. Next, the software modules should be available in the MIB. Attributes of this class might include the role(s) the module plays in the system, for example, servers and clients. Next, the MIB might include classes describing the operation of the application, including counters and meters for various communication activities, for example, number of request/response activities, time for such, etc. Note that, to accommodate this, the MIB itself needs to be distributed. Permanent resources, for example, databases or queues accessed by the application, might also be represented in the MIB.

3.9.5 Accessing a MIB

A MIB is a set of administrative class definitions that describe an application and thus is a kind of database for the application information. As such, it needs a well-defined API.

3.9.5.1 Programmatic Access

To access the MIB, its contents should be published; an API to access the MIB is required. A MIB's API should allow the retrieval and modification of MIB data. Given an API to the MIB and a description of the MIB's classes and their attributes, it is possible to write programs to query or modify the MIB. This is a very powerful concept, for it allows application specific administration programs to be written. Figure 3.12 depicts a customized administration application that starts another server when the response time that the application is delivering becomes unacceptable. To do this, it asks the MIB of the system what the average response time is (flows 1 and 2). Finding that it exceeds the operational requirement of 2.5 seconds, the administration application then directs the MIB to start another server (flows 3 and 4). The interaction with the MIB is via a programming interface.

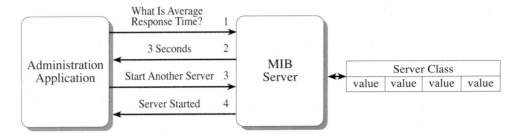

Figure 3.12   **Custom Administrative Application**

3.9.5.2 Human Access

By having administrative data presented intuitively, operators can more quickly understand operational abnormalities of an application and can take proper corrective action in a timely manner. As an enhancement to this capability, it is also helpful for documentation, training, or expert systems to be tied into the administrative facilities of the distributed application. When something goes wrong, the goal is to enable the operator to realize quickly what has happened and to be able to ask the system for recommendations on corrective action.

To allow humans to administer a system without writing code, a human interface is needed. Such might be a Graphical User Interface (GUI). This is a program that renders classes and attributes from the MIB on a screen and allows queries or updates by manipulations of the screen representation of the classes.

Figure 3.13 shows the relationship of the MIB, its API, custom applications, and a GUI that allows human access. The MIB is accessed via its API. The GUI and custom applications are built using this API.

3.9.6 When You Want to Tell the System to Do Something— Tell it to the MIB

A MIB's API provides two generic kinds of access. *GET operations* read the MIB, thus providing the caller with information about the configuration and/or operation of the system. A *SET operation* modifies attribute values in the MIB, thus changing the configuration or operation of the application. Both GET and SET operations are initiated by software external to the MIB. That is, in this role, the MIB is a passive entity, waiting to be polled for information (GET) or to be told to change its operation (SET). In Figure 3.13, arrows marked with the GET/SET symbol indicate flows of requests and responses to and from the MIB for GET and SET operations.

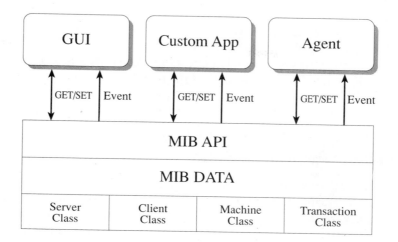

Figure 3.13   Modules Access MIB via its API

3.9.7 When the System Wants to Tell You Something— The MIB Speaks

However, the MIB is not totally passive. Things happen in a system. Disks fill up, clients join or leave the system, software fails, communications get interrupted— all without being told to do so! The MIB itself is changing in response to application actions and to real world events, such as communication devices failing. These are system level events, whose occurrence may be reflected in the values of MIB data, and which are "yearning" to report their occurrence! To be complete, the MIB's API needs not only to respond to GET and SET operations initiated from outside the MIB, but also to be able to report spontaneous internal developments, via an API, to interested external parities. We have already seen a way to do this. By using the event communication paradigm presented previously in this chapter, it is possible for the run-time system to report spontaneous changes to the MIB. To notify a human administrator, all that is needed is to write a program that subscribes to such events, and performs an appropriate notification action, for example, displaying an alarm indication on a console. We now see the purpose for the arrows marked by the word Event in Figure 3.13—they indicate events being generated inside the MIB and being sent to target modules.

3.10   Managers and Managed Entities— Answering to a Higher Authority

As previously mentioned, one of the substantial challenges of distributed business applications is their operational management. This includes oversight of the hardware on which they run, and their software components. A number of standards and products, for example, HP's Openview [HP-Openview], have emerged for managing such systems. Generally, these systems provide a *management framework* in which distributed systems and applications, referred to as *managed entities*, may be administered. In general, the role of the managed entities is to

- accept commands from the manager to report on their operation
- accept instructions from the manager to modify their operation
- inform the manager of anomalous behavior

We can see how this can be done, with the concepts previously discussed. Using its MIB, a distributed application may accept GET commands to report to a manager. Likewise, it can accept SET commands from the manager. Finally, using an event system, it can report to the manager. What is required is a set of software modules, called an *agent*, which sits between the application and the manager, accepts GET and SET commands from the manager, translates them into MIB operations (using the MIB's API), and also subscribes to MIB events and translates them into notifications to the manager. Figure 3.13 shows that an agent is, in effect, another application that uses the MIB's API.

3.11 Security—You Are Authorized to Read this Section

Centralized applications are easier to protect from security violations than distributed ones. Distributed applications offer more access points for malicious people to intercept valid data, disrupt operations, or generate fraudulent input. As business applications become more distributed, they must be protected from such invalid access. Some aspects of security can and should be provided by the infrastructure upon which distributed applications are built. For example, messages between application modules may be *encrypted* to ensure privacy. On the other hand, some aspects of security are, in fact, application-specific. For example, a bank may have a rule that large loan requests must be approved by a certain level of authority, and the "loan application" system may be required to enforce this rule.

No security system is "airtight," if for no other reason than the employees of an enterprise can inadvertently, or purposely, compromise its security systems. Nevertheless, it is reasonable for businesses to expect the distributed computing software upon which they base their distributed applications to provide generic security facilities to protect the operation of their systems.

The topic of computer security is quite large and complicated. We will introduce the main ideas here, and in Chapters 6, 9, and 15, we will relate them to the TUXEDO System. The main areas of security include *authentication*, *authorization*, *privacy*, and *auditing*.

Authentication is the act of ensuring that the user of a system is who he, she or it claims to be. We say "it" because a user need not be a person, it could be another system. In addition to a system authenticating its users, the users want to authenticate the system. That is, they want to be sure that, when they log onto a system, it is the real system and not some fake system. When each party is satisfied that the "other" one is who it declares to be, we say that the parties are *mutually authenticated*. Authenticated users are called *principals*. Typically, a user proves his identity by revealing some secret, such as a password, shared with the system.

Authorization means allowing or disallowing principals access to resources or facilities within a system. For example, only the principal whose name is "administrator" might be able to read and write a password file. An *Access Control List (ACL)* is a list of principals who can access a given resource.

Privacy means the assurance that messages transmitted between computer programs cannot be understood by unauthorized people. Privacy of messages is usually achieved by *encrypting* them before they are sent and *decrypting* them upon receipt.

Auditing is the recording of accesses made to a system. Such a recording may be later used to determine which principals performed, or attempted to perform, actions that read or modified data within the system.

3.12 Summary

The main challenges in creating and deploying distributed business applications include appropriate and easy-to-use communications systems for designers and programmers and coherent and useful management tools to configure and operate such systems. We have described a number of techniques that application architects can use to design communications among the modules of a distributed application. The goal should be comprehensible, modular systems that operate in a robust fashion. When the inevitable failures occur, the programmer should be given useful tools to diagnose and repair them. Likewise, the administrator of such systems should be given powerful, intuitive, and easy-to-use tools to cope with failures and enforce security.

II   Overview of the TUXEDO System

So far, we have examined the spectrum of distributed computing software. Chapter 3, "Communication and Administration Paradigms for Distributed Business Applications," described in general terms the features needed for building and administering a distributed business application. In the next three chapters, we present an overview of how these concepts are realized in the TUXEDO System by introducing the system's main features and architecture. Chapter 4, "Application Development—Overview," presents the building blocks you will use to write a TUXEDO application. Chapter 5, "Application Administration—Overview," introduces the tools you will use to configure, start, stop, and monitor a TUXEDO application. Chapter 6, "The Anatomy of a TUXEDO Application," shows you how all of the components of the TUXEDO System fit together.

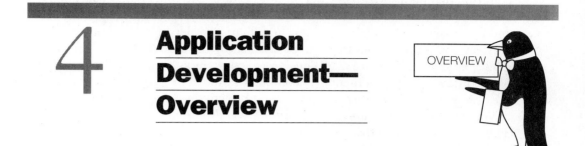

4 Application Development— Overview

In this chapter, we introduce the various concepts and tools available to designers and programmers of TUXEDO applications. We start by defining TUXEDO clients, servers, and services, because these are the building blocks of every TUXEDO application. We finish by introducing other features of the system, such as transactions, events, and application queues, that TUXEDO programs use when they communicate with each other.

4.1 TUXEDO Clients

A TUXEDO *client* is a software module that gathers and presents data to a TUXEDO application for processing. Client software can reside on a personal computer (PC) or a workstation (WS) as part of the front end of an application responsible for gathering input from users. For example, in a securities trading application, TUXEDO client software resides on the PC that a trader uses to enter customer orders to buy and sell securities. The trader, who is a user of the application, enters data using the keyboard and mouse. This data then becomes the input to a TUXEDO function-shipping request sent to a TUXEDO server which will process the trader's order.

Alternatively, a TUXEDO client can be embedded in software that reads a communication device where data is collected and formatted before being processed by TUXEDO servers. For example, in a cellular telephone application, a client program monitors telephone switching systems looking for call detail records originating from cellular phones. When one is found, the client formats it and sends it to a TUXEDO server. The server then determines the probability that the call being made is a fraudulent use of someone's cellular phone number.

4.1.1 Identifying Clients in Your Application

An important part of building a distributed application that meets the needs of your enterprise is identifying the various ways input from the outside world is gathered and presented to your business logic for processing. For example, a company that publishes mail-order catalogs can receive orders to buy its goods in a number of distinct forms: orders taken over the phone, orders received by mail, and orders received via fax machines. In each case, orders must be converted into an electronic form so that they can be fulfilled by the application's ordering programs, as shown in Figure 4.1. Thus order-entry clerks might convert voice and paper orders by entering them on a computer terminal or PC. On the other hand, fax orders might be readied for processing directly by computers capable of receiving fax orders; no human intervention would be required to input an order. The software modules that gather and render orders ready for processing are this application's TUXEDO clients.

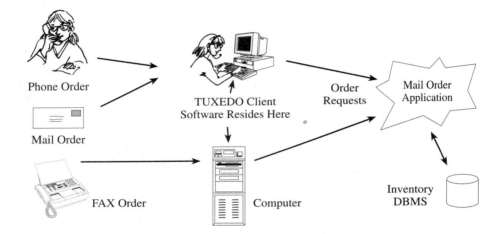

Figure 4.1   **Orders Being Converted into TUXEDO Client Requests**

An important point of this example is that in a distributed business application, the TUXEDO client software normally resides very close to where data is gathered from sources outside of the application. The TUXEDO clients bring the orders into the application. They do this by shipping them to functions for processing. These functions are called TUXEDO service routines and are introduced below. The function shipping itself is performed when a TUXEDO client issues a call to a TUXEDO communication routine that is responsible for transmitting the order to a TUXEDO service routine.

Regardless of the type of TUXEDO application you are building, it is important to identify how and where data enters your application. This enables you to write TUXEDO client programs that effectively gather, format, and ship data to your application processing functions.

4.1.2 The Structure of TUXEDO Clients

Almost any kind of software module can be a TUXEDO client program. The only real requirement of such a program is that it be able to call routines in the TUXEDO communications library. These routines are collectively known as *ATMI*, for Application-to-Transaction Monitor Interface. Simply by calling the ATMI client initialization routine, your program becomes a TUXEDO client. That is, it becomes recognized by the TUXEDO System as an entity that can initiate work within a TUXEDO application.

Once your program has become a client, it is said to have "joined" a TUXEDO application. It is then able to define transaction boundaries and call other ATMI routines that allow it to communicate with other programs in your application. Your program can also "leave" a TUXEDO application by issuing the ATMI termination routine. Leaving a TUXEDO application tells the TUXEDO System that your program no longer requires resources of the system and it should no longer be tracked as a TUXEDO client—that is, the TUXEDO System should stop accounting for the program's activities.

As the designer or developer of a TUXEDO client program, you have complete control over your program's structure. Where and when you call ATMI library routines depends on your business rules and your application. Of course, there are some simple sequencing rules your program must obey when calling ATMI routines. For example, your program must join an application before calling any communication routines. But it is up to you at what point your program joins a TUXEDO application or which TUXEDO application it joins. In fact, your program can join one TUXEDO application, do some work, leave, and then join a different TUXEDO application to do different work.

The basic structure of a TUXEDO client program is shown in Figure 4.2, and it contains:

- the program's starting point, the C language's **main** in this case

- your program's code (that is, data structures, conditionals, loops, etc.)

- calls to the TUXEDO libraries, which is where the ATMI routines reside

- calls to whatever other libraries your program needs (for example, graphics or math libraries)

4.1.3 How Client Programs Use TUXEDO

Client programs access the TUXEDO System by calling the TUXEDO ATMI library of C routines or COBOL procedures. The majority of routines in the ATMI library fall into one of three categories: buffer management, transaction control, or communications.

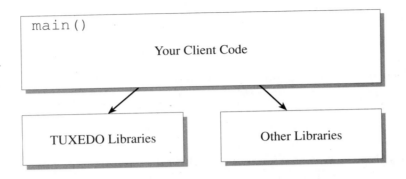

Figure 4.2 **Structure of a TUXEDO Client Program**

Before a client program can send its data to another TUXEDO program, it first must allocate a memory area, called a *typed buffer*, from the TUXEDO runtime system. A typed buffer is a memory buffer that has an identified format associated with it. Examples of typed buffers are C structures or COBOL records. All ATMI routines that send or receive application data do so in the form of typed buffers. These buffers offer many advantages to programs communicating data with each other. We cover them later in this chapter and, in much more detail, in Chapter 8, "Typed Buffers."

The ATMI library offers several calls to define and control TUXEDO *global transactions*. Using global transactions in your application gives you control over defining discrete units of work that can span multiple programs and resource managers in your distributed application. All the work performed within a single TUXEDO transaction, regardless of where those programs reside, is treated as a logical unit. Thus, if any one program cannot complete its task successfully, then all of the work done by programs in the transaction will be undone, as if the unit of work were never started. We cover TUXEDO global transactions more thoroughly later in this chapter, and Chapter 14, "Transactions in the TUXEDO System," is dedicated to the topic.

Most of the calls in the ATMI library support the different communication styles available to programmers. These calls are the ones that tie distributed programs together by allowing them to send and receive data to one another. Several of the next sections in this chapter, as well the chapters in Part III, "Application Development of a TUXEDO," describe the calls used to affect the different styles of ATMI communication. These include all of the communication paradigms described in Chapter 3, "Communication and Administration Paradigms for Distributed Business Applications."

4.1.4 What's Required to Run a TUXEDO Client

Once you've written your TUXEDO client program, it must be compiled and linked with the TUXEDO ATMI and run-time libraries and with any other libraries your program uses. You can do this on the computer on which the program will run (for example, a PC or WS). Or you can compile it on another machine and bring it over to the run-time machine as a ready-to-run executable —for example, a real-time device like a cash register.

The bare minimum required to run a TUXEDO client is a diskless computer that has a modest amount of memory, network connectivity, and the ability to load a program into memory. Automated teller machines (ATMs), cash registers, and hand-held devices such as personal digital assistants (PDAs) all meet the requirements. TUXEDO client programs can also run on the wide variety of general-purpose computers and operating systems available on the market, such as PCs running DOS/Windows, Mac/OS, and Unix-based systems.

4.2 TUXEDO Servers and Services

When we introduced TUXEDO clients, we mentioned that they gather and send your application's input data to procedures in other programs that process the data according to your application's business logic. These other programs are called TUXEDO *servers*. The business logic they contain is encapsulated in processing procedures called TUXEDO *services*. A TUXEDO server is a collection of one or more TUXEDO services. The TUXEDO service routines are the targets of clients' requests for processing. When a client wants to perform an operation, say "BuyStock," the procedure to which its data is shipped is a TUXEDO service. This routine could be a C function or COBOL procedure of the same name. Figure 4.3 shows a TUXEDO server containing two service routines, "BuyStock" and "SellStock." From the client's perspective, it requests specific services, and actually knows nothing about servers themselves or how services are packaged within servers.

The next few subsections talk about the important aspects of TUXEDO Servers and Services. These include their structure, the resources they access, the naming convention used to identify them, and how they can best be deployed in your distributed business application.

4.2.1 Services Embody an Enterprise's Business Rules

In Chapter 2, "Distributing Data and Logic," we introduced the notion of application function shipping and discussed how applications adhering to this model were partitioned into two distinct parts: the client and the service. In the

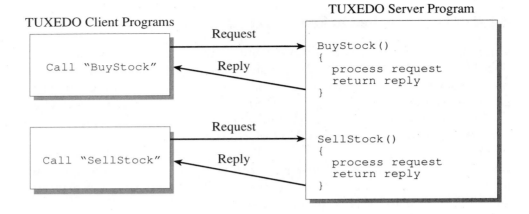

Figure 4.3   TUXEDO Server with Two Services

TUXEDO System, services are the set of routines that embody an enterprise's business rules. That is, the application designers decide on the set of logical services that define their business, and then write the set of corresponding routines that implement them. Once defined, these routines make up the allowable set of services offered to clients for the purpose of processing the data that clients bring into the application.

In our mail-order example, you could imagine that "Add_Cust," "Retrieve_Cust," "Place_Order," and "Cancel_Order" would be among the services offered to TUXEDO client writers. A well-defined set of services greatly simplifies the job of writing TUXEDO client programs. This is because the options for processing external data are limited to the published set of TUXEDO services written for the application. More importantly, a TUXEDO client program that invokes "Place_Order" has no knowledge about how an order is actually placed, which databases are involved, or the location of the data. If the implementation of these services changes or if the databases are moved to new machines, the client programs are not affected. This is because they use TUXEDO's ATMI routines for invoking services by name—for example, "Place_Order"— rather than by address. Previously, we called such names *location transparent* because a service name, like "Place_Order," implies no particular network address or physical location.

4.2.2 What Defines a TUXEDO Service

TUXEDO service routines have the following three properties:

▪ A service is a C routine or COBOL procedure that implements a business task. For example, the "Place_Order" service updates the Order database with the customer's order. It then updates the Credit Card database so that the customer can be billed. Finally, it prints the appropriate shipping ticket so that the fulfillment center can ship the ordered items to the customer.

■ A service routine has a logical name, such as "Place_Order", that is used by clients for addressing it. This name can be the same as the routine name, or it can be an alias for it. Thus, an application might map the service name "Place_Order" to the C routine **place_order**.

■ A service routine has well-defined inputs and outputs so that clients can use them correctly. For example, the "Place_Order" service might require a C structure that contains, at the very least, the customer's account number and an array of items ordered. If all goes well, the service returns a different C structure that contains a confirmation number and an indication of whether any of the items were not in stock.

From the client's point of view, these three properties define a *contract* for a TUXEDO service routine. The contract consists of the following:

■ the name of the service

■ the service's required input parameters

■ the specific processing on those inputs

■ the output values or list of errors that will be returned to the client as a result of the processing

The beauty of these contracts is that once they are defined, the client writer and the service writer can implement their respective programs completely independently from one another. This is because each knows exactly what is expected of the other. Also, each has a wide degree of freedom in terms of fulfilling their tasks, so long as they obey the stated contract.

For example, the service writer can implement "Place_Order" either as one large service procedure or as one of a collection of smaller services. Because the TUXEDO System allows services to act as clients by allowing them to invoke other services themselves, the writer of "Place_Order" might actually use three other services to complete its contract. That is, "Place_Order" first calls "Access_Orders" to update the Order database. It then calls "Update_Billing" to update the customer's billing record. Finally, it calls "Print_Ticket" to issue the shipping ticket. The "Place_Order" service might call each of these services serially or it might call them in an overlapped fashion, using the fan-out parallelism technique described in Chapter 3, "Communication and Administration Paradigms for Distributed Business Applications."

Figure 4.4 illustrates the steps taken by "Place_Order" to complete its contract. Because the client sees flows 1 (the request) and 8 (the reply) only, it can't tell whether "Place_Order" is a monolithic service or just a starting point for calling many smaller, more specialized services. Flows 2 through 7 are seen only by the **place_order** service routine.

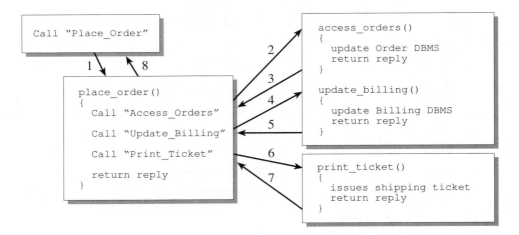

Figure 4.4   One Service Making Use of Three Other Services

This example illustrates an important point. When choosing the list of services that make up your application, it is worth the effort to define the basic tasks performed in your business, such as accessing a central database or printing shipping tickets. From these fine-grained services, you can write coarse-grained ones, as shown above in the example of "Place_Order". In fact, you could decide that client programs may choose from only a small number of coarse-grained services. The most basic, fine-grained services would not be available to them.

4.2.3 Request/Response Services

A TUXEDO *request/response service routine* is similar to a procedure call insofar as it accepts input parameters, processes these, and then possibly returns output parameters and a return value. Once a service routine completes, there is no state information or context maintained by the TUXEDO System with respect to any particular pair of client and service. That is, once a reply is returned, the client and service are dissociated from one another. The client will most likely invoke another service to perform some other function, while the service routine will most likely service another client's request. If state information needs to be retained between a client and a service, then programs would use a variant of the TUXEDO service routine called a conversational service.

4.2.4 Conversational Services

A TUXEDO *conversational service routine* allows a client to have an application-defined interaction with a service that can be more complex than the simple request/response interaction. With a conversational service, a client first makes a logical connection with a named service, and then receives a *descriptor* for subsequent interactions. The client and service then partake in an application-defined set of send-receive exchanges. This set of exchanges forms an application protocol. Normally, the service routine terminates the conversation by returning. This signifies to the client that the conversation has ended. This exchange is analogous to a telephone conversation where the caller and callee exchange one or more "messages" until the call ends and they both hang up.

In our mail-order example, one service that lends itself naturally to being conversational is "Browse_Catalog" which can be used to find a particular item given a general description. Let's say that a caller wants to know all the different styles of hats that the mail-order company sells. The operator answering the customer's request can select "Browse_Catalog" from the menu. This initiates a conversational interaction with a service routine whose function is to return a set of records, five at a time, each of which describes the style, color, size, and price of a specified piece of clothing available for purchase. After the first five hats have been seen, the operator can ask for the next five records, and so on, until all hat records have been seen.

This interaction is conversational because, while the operator is looking at a set of records, the service routine is maintaining state information about which are the next set of records to return. When the client needs to see the next set of records, it sends a message over to the service asking for the next set and the service replies with the next batch. This exchange occurs until the service routine has no more records to return at which time it ends the conversational service. At this point, the client and service are dissociated from each other, and any resources they were maintaining are freed (for example, the database cursor that was used to keep track of the inventory browse).

4.2.5 The Structure of TUXEDO Servers

As mentioned earlier, a TUXEDO server program encapsulates one or more service routines into an executable program that can be started, stopped, and monitored by the TUXEDO administrative system. The TUXEDO System imposes a particular structure on servers. As shown in Figure 4.5, a server contains three kinds of software:

▌ The TUXEDO run-time system. The starting point of a server program (known as **main** in C) is supplied by the TUXEDO run-time system. This allows the TUXEDO administrative system to have better control over starting and stopping servers. Once started, the TUX-EDO run-time system controls the dispatching of clients' requests to application service routines within the server. The TUXEDO run-time system also manages the TUXEDO-related resources that a server requires for communicating with clients and other servers.

■ Application Service Routines. As the application developer, you are responsible for writing these. They embody your application's business logic.

■ Application Server Initialization and Termination Routines. In addition to supplying service routines, you can also write server initialization and termination routines. Typically, these routines are used for opening and closing resources, such as databases, that your services will access. The initialization routine is called by the TUXEDO run-time system after the program has become a TUXEDO server but before it accepts and dispatches any service requests. Likewise, the termination routine is called once a server has processed its last application request after receiving an administrative message telling it to shut down.

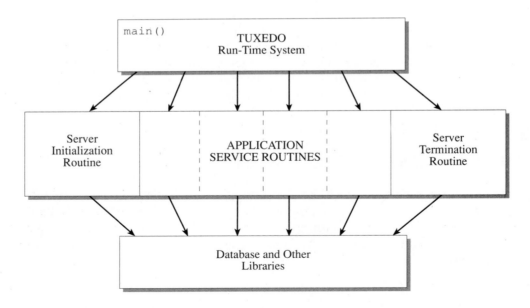

Figure 4.5   Structure of a TUXEDO Server Program

▪ Other libraries. Your service routines will typically access resources on behalf of clients' requests. Often, a service accesses a relational database via embedded SQL. However, your services can access any libraries that they need to complete their job. This might include non-SQL databases, file managers, or other application-supplied libraries, such as validation routines.

4.2.6 Tips on Constructing Your Application's Services

Here are a few principles to follow when designing your application's services.

Information Hiding   Define service contracts, as well as the data that flows between client and server, to be as independent as possible from their implementation. That is, don't have a client ship information to a server about the client's input gathering techniques, such as the positions or names of fields on electronic forms. These should be hidden from the server so that the client can freely change them without causing code to change in the server. The converse should also be followed: a client shouldn't know about a server's implementation details, such as its database schema and record layouts. These will most certainly change over time, so you should restrict the knowledge of your database organization on a "need to know" basis.

Service Layering   As much as possible, a service should perform one task instead of many. Don't be tempted to put too much—or too little—functionality in any individual service routine. You should strive to have a well-defined set of simple services that perform your business' elemental tasks. From these, you can construct more complex services simply by reusing the simpler ones in combination, as we saw in Figure 4.4.

Business Objects   Design your services around the objects of your business and the ways in which they are manipulated. In our mail-order example, the business objects are orders and inventory items. The services reflect the kinds of manipulation required of these objects: "Add_Cust," "Retrieve_Cust," and "Place_Order". You should organize services into servers around the set of related or common objects that they manipulate. For example, the services "Add_Cust" and "Retrieve_Cust" both access the customer DBMS and should probably reside in the same server, whereas "Place_Order" accesses the orders DBMS and should be in a separate server. Initially, the two DBMSs might be located on the same machine, but as the business grows, they might each need their own machine. Having the services grouped around common objects allows servers to move easily if the objects they manipulate move.

4.3 Application Queues

As introduced in Chapter 3, "Communication and Administration Paradigms for Distributed Business Applications," *application queues*[1] are an important tool for building distributed applications that communicate in a deferred or *time-independent* fashion. The TUXEDO System provides programming and administrative tools for using application queues in your programs. This section introduces the main features of the TUXEDO application queuing subsystem from the programmer's point of view. Chapter 12, "Application Queues," provides more detail, and Chapter 17, "A Tour of the TUXEDO Management Information Base," covers the administrative aspects of application queues.

4.3.1 Queue Spaces and Queues

Unlike the TUXEDO System's request/response and conversational paradigms, where a client names a service with which it wishes to communicate on-line, when you use its application queue functions, your program names a *queue space* and a *queue name* that it wishes to access. A queue space is a collection of disk-based application queues. Your application can have one or more queue spaces each of which can contain one or more application queues. Because application queues reside on disk, the messages stored in them are guaranteed to be available across failures that cause the machines in your application to be rebooted.

Application queue communication is characterized by a program accessing a queue, as opposed to communicating on-line with another program. Both TUXEDO client and server programs can enqueue messages into or dequeue messages from application queues. Moreover, any number of clients and servers can access the same queue. Like service names, queue space and queue names are location-transparent strings, as in "Payroll_Queue" or "MyBatchQueue." The benefit to the programmer of dealing with location-transparent names is that the programmer has no knowledge of where its application queues are located. Also, queues can be moved around by the administrator, so that no client or server programs accessing the queues have to change.

4.3.2 Communicating Through Application Queues

Application queues are ideal to use when programs need to communicate in a time-independent fashion. Time-independence means that programs operate independently from one another and do not need to synchronize their communications on-line. Rather, they synchronize by leaving messages for each other in

---

[1]Application queues are also referred to as the /Q sub-system in the TUXEDO System Documentation [TUXEDO].

application queues. As we mentioned previously, this is analogous to people leaving messages for each other on answering machines rather than having phone conversations.

In determining where application queues fit in your application, you need to consider where time-independent synchronization naturally occurs in your business. Let's look again at our mail-order example. Imagine that the "Place_Order" service not only updates the Order database, but it also enqueues an order message for the shipping department, which is responsible for fulfilling orders.

Orders are enqueued to disk because the shipping department has its own set of rules for determining when it ships merchandise, and these rules may have little relationship to the time orders are placed. For example, all orders destined for a certain part of the country might be handled at only one time of the day to ensure that they arrive at that part of the country on time. Thus, the shipping department's application might have different queue spaces for different time zones. Within each time zone queue space, there might be separate queues for each state within that time zone.

Figure 4.6 shows the Eastern Time Zone queue space along with queues for four states in that time zone. The "Place_Order" service enqueues each order to the queue space and queue appropriate for the order's destination. Orders are safely stored on disk until the shipping department dequeues them for fulfillment.

4.3.3 Application Queues: More Than Just Waiting in Line

In their simplest form, application queues allow programs to put messages into disk-based queues so that they can be dequeued in a first-in, first-out (FIFO) order. Although FIFO ordering will serve many applications well, some businesses require more sophisticated facilities from their queues, like priorities and time-based dequeuing.

The TUXEDO System's application queue feature allows a program to have fine control over the relative and absolute ordering of its enqueued messages. Likewise, a program dequeuing a message can specify attributes that influence which message it wishes to dequeue. The next two subsections will introduce these.

4.3.3.1 Enqueuing Options

The three main ordering attributes a program can specify when enqueuing messages are priority, birth time, and ordering overrides. Messages also have tags associated with them for the purpose of identity.

Each message can be enqueued with a priority between 1 and 100—the larger the number, the higher the priority. Priorities imply to the enqueuer that a message with a higher priority will be dequeued before a message with a lower one.

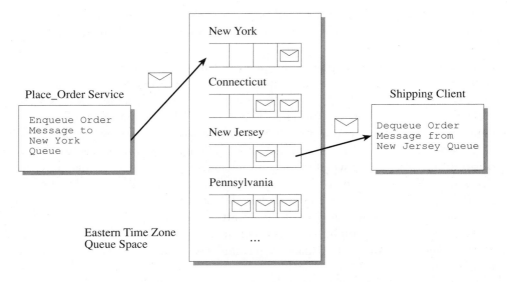

Figure 4.6   Mail-Order Application's Time Zone Queue Space and Queues

Some applications have a natural need for priority queue ordering. Drawing on our mail-order example again, if a customer is willing to pay extra for overnight delivery, then that customer's order will be enqueued with the highest priority to guarantee that the shipping application will dequeue it before all other orders that do not require overnight delivery.

A message can be assigned a *birth time* when it is enqueued. A birth time is a time, specified in either absolute (for example, January 16, 2000 at 7:00 a.m.) or relative (for example, 2 days from now) terms, before which a message cannot be dequeued. Birth times are useful when information is known in advance of the time it can be used or processed. For example, in advance of a one-day sale, a store manager could set the sale prices for all items affected. This information can be enqueued with the absolute birth time of the morning of the sale. Then all programs that dequeue price information would not see the sale prices until that morning. Before the sale date, the pricing information was stored safely on disk in a price queue, but no program could see it.

Sometimes your application might require that messages be placed out of order on a queue. There are two attributes that you can put on a message to affect this behavior. You can state either that a message should be enqueued ahead of a specific message (the equivalent of someone allowing a friend to "cut" in line just ahead), or that a message should be enqueued at the head of the queue (the equivalent of the neighborhood bully cutting in front of everyone to be first in line!).

Because out-of-order enqueuing allows for expedited handling of messages (not to mention the antisocial tendencies that follow), an administrator must configure a queue so that it is allowed at the programming level. For example, a brokerage application might require strict FIFO ordering on all orders enqueued and destined for the stock market. Any out-of-order orders could be in violation of market trading rules requiring fairness.

Whenever a message is enqueued, the TUXEDO application queue manager returns a receipt called a *message identifier*. Each message identifier is unique across all messages in the same application queue space. If an application program moves a message from one queue to another, it receives a new message identifier each time it is enqueued. A message identifier is used when your program wishes to enqueue another message immediately ahead of the one identified.

Another type of message tag exists called a *correlation identifier*. Correlation identifiers are assigned optionally by the application and may or may not be unique. These identifiers are supplied along with the message when it is enqueued. Unlike the message identifiers handed out by the TUXEDO System every time a message is enqueued, correlation identifiers do not change if a message moves from one queue to another. Thus, the original enqueuer can use a correlation identifier to track its message. Correlation identifiers are also used to match request and reply messages. That is, a program that dequeues a message can extract that message's correlation identifier and reuse it when it enqueues the reply. In this manner, the original enqueuer can correlate its requests with replies.

4.3.3.2 Dequeuing Options

When dequeuing messages, a program has three choices. It can dequeue the message at the head of the queue, it can specify a message by its unique message identifier, or it can specify a message by its (possibly not unique) correlation identifier. If there are multiple messages on the same queue with the same correlation identifier then the one closest to the head of the queue is taken. Of course, the queue's ordering requirements are obeyed so that, for example, the one with highest priority is taken first.

The nonuniqueness of correlation identifiers can be used to split up a single physical queue into multiple, logical queues. Recall Figure 4.6, where messages were enqueued to the shipping department by time zone and state, and each state had its own queue. Another approach that would have the same effect but would not require as many physical queues would be to have one queue and use each state's name as its correlation identifier, as shown in Figure 4.7. By doing so, the dequeuing program can dequeue by correlation identifier and get only those messages that matched the state identified, "NJ" in this case. Figure 4.7 shows that the client program dequeues the message at the head of the queue first (labeled 1) followed by the fourth message (labeled 2). It skips over other messages whose correlation identifiers do not match "NJ." At that point, the queue appears to be empty because there are no more messages that match the client's dequeuing criteria.

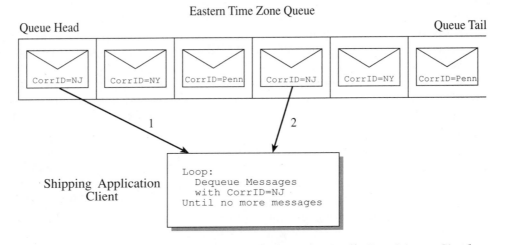

Figure 4.7 **Use of Correlation Identifiers to Logically Partition a Single Queue**

4.3.4 The Forwarding Agent

Along with its application queue mechanism, the TUXEDO System provides a special server whose job is to forward service requests residing on application queues to application servers. Let's say your client program tries to send an on-line request to a service routine only to find that the service is not available. This could happen because the service has not yet been started or perhaps the machine on which it was running crashed, thus making the service unavailable. Whatever the case, your client has just finished collecting and formatting important data that needs to be processed by a service routine that is no longer available.

One common use of application queues is for storing such requests and having TUXEDO's *forwarding agent* dequeue and forward them to service routines. From the TUXEDO programmer's view, the on-line service request that failed could be enqueued in an application queue for later processing. Thus, the program can recover from the on-line error by enqueuing the request to an application queue and still be given the guarantee that its request will be processed at a later time. Here, the program shifts from an on-line request/response, where the client waits synchronously for the response, to a time-independent request/response, where the client is guaranteed that its request will eventually arrive at a service but it most likely will not wait synchronously for a reply to be returned via an application queue.

4.4   Event-Based Communication

Both of the on-line communication paradigms discussed earlier in this chapter — that is, request/response and conversational—have in common the notion that some entity is waiting to service another's request. Having servers "at the ready" is practical due to the predictable nature of an application's business. For example, a bank expects to receive a certain number of debit and credit service requests at any given time. Thus, it is quite reasonable for a bank application to have servers ready to process debit and credit service requests.

In many applications, however, it may be impractical to have servers waiting to handle unexpected real-world events that affect a business. For example, an ATM running out of money might be viewed as an unexpected event that requires notification to be sent to a branch manager. As opposed to the branch manager's application offering services waiting for requests from ATMs for more money (which are supposedly few and far between), it is programmed to receive such events asynchronously. At the heart of event-based communication is the notion that application entities need to synchronize when unplanned or unscheduled events occur that need to be communicated to one or more application entities.

In Chapter 3, "Communication and Administration Paradigms for Distributed Business Applications," the concepts of both simple and brokered event communication were introduced. Here, we will introduce how these manifest themselves in the TUXEDO System.

4.4.1 TUXEDO Unsolicited Event Communication

ATMI has two mechanisms to handle simple events: single-program notifications and multiple-program broadcasting. These mechanisms allow your programs to communicate *unsolicited notifications* to client programs. The reason that the target programs must be clients (and not servers) is because servers are designed to receive "solicited" communication in the form of service requests. Clients, on the other hand, are designed to receive expected replies to requests that they initiate. That is, service requests are never destined to client programs; if they were, clients would then be servers!

Recognizing that sometimes your application might have to notify clients to tell them things that they need to know (for example, a new service has just come on-line), clients can be configured to accept and process unsolicited notifications. This is accomplished by configuring into the client an event-handling routine that is dispatched when an event arrives. Event handlers are procedures linked to client programs. They can be configured to be invoked immediately upon an event's arrival (that is, the client's current processing is interrupted to handle the event), or they can be configured to be invoked when the client finishes its current task (for example, after the client finishes gathering data from the screen and pauses waiting for more input).

The single-program notification mechanism allows a client or server to send an unsolicited notification, along with any data, to a single client program. This is most often used when a server processing a client's request finds that something has occurred that requires the server to notify the client with a message other than its reply—that is, an out-of-band message. As shown in Figure 4.8, let's say that the client program in an ATM requests money to be withdrawn from a customer's account. If the server program accessing the customer's account finds that the request will take longer than a minute (because its first attempt to access the database failed), it might send an unsolicited notification to the ATM client program telling it to put a message on the screen informing the customer that her request will take a little longer. After the client program handles the unsolicited notification, it returns to waiting for the promised reply so that it can dispense money to the patient customer.

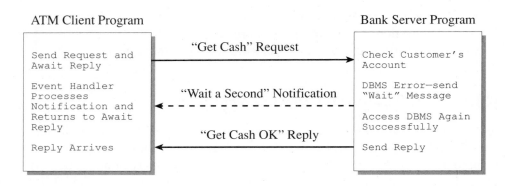

Figure 4.8   **Unsolicited Notification Example**

The multiple-program broadcasting mechanism is a generalization of the single-program notification mechanism insofar as it allows one or more clients to receive a single unsolicited notification. If, for example, the main bank server notices that the customer database has just been taken off-line, it could broadcast to all ATMs that it directly serves to put an "out of service" message on the ATM screen and to disable accepting new requests. Once the database is back on-line, the server (or some other program in the application) could broadcast another message to all the ATMs informing them that they can now accept new requests.

4.4.2 TUXEDO Event Brokering

The idea behind brokered events is to relieve an application from keeping track of which programs need to find out about an event's occurrence. Toward this end, ATMI contains a function that allows TUXEDO programs to *subscribe* to the events about which they are interested in hearing. The TUXEDO System's *EventBroker*™ keeps track of these subscriptions. ATMI also contains a function that allows clients and servers to *post* events that have occurred.

As shown in Figure 4.9, the TUXEDO System EventBroker receives all event postings and performs the actions associated with the subscriptions that match the posted events. Notice that a subscriber has no knowledge of which programs monitor and post events to which it subscribes. Likewise, a poster has no knowledge about which programs, if any, have subscribed to its events. The benefit of this anonymity is that subscribers can come and go without having to synchronize with posters, and vice versa.

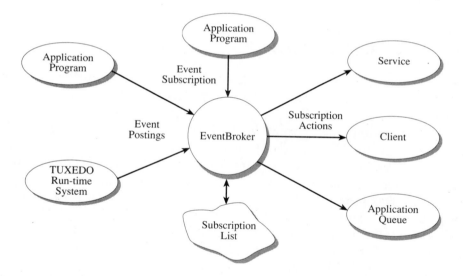

Figure 4.9 **Flow of Brokered Events from Poster to Subscriber's Action**

When a client or server subscribes to an event, it might be a TUXEDO System administrative event (for example, a server program just died) or an application event (for example, the ATM just ran out of money). In either case, the event is named by a string, just like service and application queue names.

As part of a subscription, a program specifies what action should take place when the event occurs. If the subscriber is a TUXEDO client, then it can receive an unsolicited notification, name a service routine that should be invoked, or name an application queue where the event's data should be safely stored for later processing. If the subscriber is a TUXEDO server then it can specify that the action be either of the latter two (that is, a service request or an enqueue to an application queue). As you can see in Figure 4.9, a program may or may not receive any notification of the event to which it subscribes. This is because the subscribing program does not have to be the target of the action associated with an event posting.

The TUXEDO System has been instrumented to post its own system events when they occur (Chapter 17, "A Tour of the TUXEDO Management Information Base," discusses this further). Application events are posted by clients or servers using an ATMI function. When an event is posted, the TUXEDO System EventBroker matches the posted event's name to subscriptions for the same event and takes the appropriate action called for by each subscription. The poster can wait for the EventBroker to complete the set of actions before continuing, or the poster can specify that it wishes to continue as soon as the broker is in receipt of its posting and thus not have to wait for the broker to complete all of the subscribed actions. Chapter 13, "Event-Based Communication," covers brokered events in more detail.

4.5   TUXEDO Data Types

Throughout this chapter, we have alluded to data being sent from client to server, from either of these to a queue, or from poster to subscriber via a broker. The TUXEDO System provides simple yet powerful tools for handling application data. Because an important goal of the TUXEDO System is to make it easier to write distributed applications, considerable attention was put into designing tools for creating, sending, and receiving application data. First, all ATMI functions that send or receive data do so in a common way: they use typed buffers. Second, your TUXEDO programs do not have to worry about translating data that crosses platforms with differing data representations. The TUXEDO System handles such translations, so that your programs can concentrate on their tasks. If your client needs to send an integer and a string to your server, for example, it does so without worrying whether the server has a different representation for integers, a different character set for strings, or different alignment requirements. Platform differences are another form of location transparency shielded from your programs by the TUXEDO System.

The next two subsections introduce the different ways data transparency is handled by the TUXEDO System.

4.5.1 Typed Buffers

A typed buffer is a memory area that has a *type* and a *subtype* associated with it. Type and subtype are string names that identify a set of characteristics belonging to a buffer. To illustrate, let's look at one of the simplest typed buffers provided by the TUXEDO System: the null-terminated string. The string typed buffer— whose actual type name is "STRING"— is an array of zero or more characters terminated by a null character. This buffer type is meant to be used in programs written in C. If your client program wishes to send a string to a service routine, it would allocate a typed buffer using the ATMI function to do so. This function requires the type name ("STRING"), the subtype name (null in this case), and the number of bytes you would like allocated. Returned to your program is a pointer to the number of bytes you requested. The TUXEDO System keeps track that the pointer returned to you references a null-terminated string (thus the name "typed buffer"). Your program then copies a null-terminated string into your typed buffer. The buffer is now ready to be sent to a server, placed in an application queue, or posted along with an event.

When you use ATMI's communication functions, the TUXEDO run-time system recognizes the type of the buffer you wish to send and processes it so that your data can be transmitted over any type of network fabric and protocol and to any type of CPU architecture and operating system supported by the TUXEDO System (more than twenty!). Returning to our STRING buffer example, the TUXEDO run-time system within a server receiving a string typed buffer detects that it has received such and performs the necessary processing to ready it for the service routine. When the service routine is dispatched, it is invoked with the string typed buffer ready to be used. The beauty of typed buffers in a distributed environment is that they relieve your clients and servers from the messy details of preparing data to be transferred between heterogeneous computers linked by various communications networks.

The TUXEDO System provides several built-in buffer types and allows you to customize these or provide your own (see Chapter 8, "Typed Buffers").

4.5.2 IDL Files and Stub Marshalling

The TUXEDO System provides an alternate form of data handling in the form of *TxRPC* [X/Open-TxRPC]. The TUXEDO System offers the language-based TxRPC as an alternate form of client/server communication that is based on *remote procedure calls* (RPCs). TxRPC is based on OSF DCE's RPC [OSF DCE RPC] but is enhanced to support global transactions.

The essence of an RPC is that it looks like a regular, local procedure call. However, when a C language function is called, the arguments passed to the function are packaged so that they can be sent to a server that performs the work of the called function. This argument packaging is called *marshalling*. Similar to the discussion on typed buffers, the function's arguments are marshalled in a way that allows them to cross network and platform boundaries and then unmarshalled at their destination before being passed to the invoked remote procedure ready for use. That is, neither the calling program (the client) nor the remote procedure (the server) needs to worry about the details of marshalling. Therein lies the transparency and the benefits of RPCs.

The marshalling and unmarshalling routines are automatically generated by the TUXEDO System's *Interface Definition Language* (IDL) compiler. An IDL compiler takes as input a description of a set of RPCs and outputs routines, called *stubs*, for the client and server programs. These stubs contain the marshalling and unmarshalling logic as well as the communication logic that allows a client and server to exchange marshalled data.

Chapter 10, "Request/Response Communication," discusses TxRPC in more detail. Also, Chapter 18, "Getting Applications to Work Together," talks about TxRPC in the context of TUXEDO applications interoperating with DCE applications.

4.6   Error Handling

As mentioned in earlier chapters, error handling in a distributed application is inherently hard because the logic of the application is distributed across a number of computers and networks, some of which fail while others continue to operate. Because the TUXEDO System was designed with program distribution in mind, special attention has been given to program error handling. This section introduces some of the tools that you can use when writing your distributed TUXEDO application.

One of the benefits of ATMI is that the programmer has control over some of the meta-aspects of the communications. That is, not only can one program easily pass data to another, but each can also influence other aspects of the communications, such as error data. In ATMI, a clear distinction is made between application and system errors. When a service routine encounters an application error, such as an invalid account number, the service needs to fail in such a way that the client knows that the service performed its duty but that it could not fulfill its request due to an application error. Contrast this with a system failure, such as the server crashing while performing the client's request. In this case, the client needs to know that the service routine did not perform its duty due to a problem with the underlying system itself. ATMI not only allows you to specify when application errors occur, but the TUXEDO System, as it monitors the application's and its own behavior, will also notify programs of system errors that occur when a remote partner encounters an unrecoverable error.

4.6.1 Time-Outs

One of the most difficult problems to cope with in a distributed application is when the application appears stuck and yet no explicit errors are being reported. Take the case where a service ends up in an infinite loop while processing a client's request. The client waits and waits and waits, and yet no reply is forth-coming. To prevent a client from waiting forever, the TUXEDO System has con-figurable time-out mechanisms. One type of time-out is called a *blocking time-out*, because it ensures that a program blocked waiting for something to occur will not wait much longer than the time-out value. Once the TUXEDO System detects a time-out, the waiting program is awakened with a system error informing it that a blocking time-out occurred. Note that blocking time-outs occur not only when clients wait for replies: if the internal buffers through which messages are trans-ferred are full then a client might time-out sending a request message to a server.

Another type of time-out that can occur in TUXEDO programs is called a *transaction time-out*. Because transactions tend to be resource-intensive while they are active (for example, database locks are held while a transaction progresses), an application might want to limit the amount of time its transaction resources are tied up. Transaction time-outs are discussed more in Chapter 14, "Transactions in the TUXEDO System," and Chapter 16, "Failure Handling."

4.6.2 Status Codes and Exception Handling

A different form of error handling is used when you write your application with TxRPC. Because RPCs take the form of a language's local procedure call, there is no transparent way to pass communications meta-information, such as communi-cation or system errors. Although application errors can be made part of the in-terface definition for an RPC in the form of a function's return value, system errors must be made an explicit part of your programs. TxRPC has two different ways of handling errors: *status codes* and *exceptions*. [OSF DCE RPC]

A status code is a new argument or return code added to your procedure defi-nitions. This argument or return code has a special data type for status codes and is reserved for use by the communications infrastructure to convey error informa-tion. The advantage of status codes is that they give your programs a high degree of control over error recovery at the point where errors are detected. The disad-vantage is that they add new parameters or return values to your functions that the local counterparts did not have.

When using exceptions, your procedure definitions are not altered to accom-modate system errors. Rather, your client programs contain special statements that bracket RPC invocations. These allow clients to *catch* errors *raised* by proce-dures running remotely in servers. Specifically, if a remote procedure encounters an error, it can raise an exception using a special TxRPC support library routine. The exception is transmitted back to the client and program control returns to the bottom of the client's exception bracket where the error is caught and pro-cessed. The reason that the exception is not processed at the point of the RPC s return is that the procedure definition has not been changed to accommodate re-ceiving such error returns.

4.7   Using Transactions in Your Application

Now that we have introduced all of the TUXEDO System communication paradigms, their methods of passing data, and the ways that they handle errors, the last tool to introduce is the *global transaction*. As discussed in the last chapter, transactions greatly simplify writing distributed applications. They also allow your application to cope more easily with a large set of problems that occur naturally in distributed environments—for example, machine, program, and network failures. One of the greatest strengths of the TUXEDO System is that the transaction semantic was built into the software and ATMI from the outset. That is, global transactions were not added to the TUXEDO System as an afterthought. They were woven into the fabric of the system and its communication APIs and protocols.

Although a global transaction itself is not a communication tool, the ability to define a global transaction around one or more communication calls makes it an indispensable tool for writing distributed applications. Not only does a global transaction allow the effects of your communications to be committed as an atomic unit, but, if an error occurs, it also gives you a simple, programmatic way to undo all the work that has been done so far.

Let's look one more time at our mail-order example to see the power of global transactions. Earlier in this chapter, we saw that the "Place_Order" service performs two operations: it updates the Order database and it enqueues the order to the shipping department. Not surprisingly, it is the intent of the business that either both of these actions happen together as a unit or neither of them is to occur should one fail. To accomplish this, the client program invoking the "Place_Order" service would bracket the call with a global transaction. This is done by using the ATMI begin-transaction function before issuing the service request and issuing the commit-transaction function after it. Because the service is invoked as part of a global transaction, all of its work will also be done on its behalf. We refer to the propagation of global transaction context from one program to another as *transaction infection*.

As shown in Figure 4.10, a server is infected with the client s transaction when the "Place_Order" service is invoked (flow 1). Thus, both the database access as well as the enqueue operation to the shipping application queue (flows 2 and 3) become part of the client's transaction. Should either operation fail, because of an application or system error, the work done in the transaction is rolled back to its state at the outset of this transaction. However, if both succeed (flow 4), the client's call to commit the transaction will cause the effects of the database update and the enqueued message to become permanent records of this transaction.

In Chapter 14, "Transactions in the TUXEDO System," we will cover transactions in much more depth and you will see how you can use transactions with each of ATMI's communication paradigms.

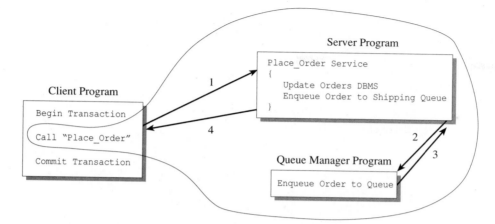

Figure 4.10 **Sphere of Infection within a Global Transaction**

4.8 Summary

Through ATMI and TxRPC, the TUXEDO System provides you with a wealth of programming tools that simplify the job of writing complex distributed applications. This is accomplished through a small number of powerful and integrated communication paradigms that are transactionally aware. The goal of these tools is to keep you focused on your application's business logic rather than on the details of your network and your application's physical configuration. When writing TUXEDO programs, you never have to worry about network addresses or the physical location of application objects. In fact, you do not even have to worry about using a directory to resolve a name to a physical address because this mapping is handled transparently by the TUXEDO System. Because the TUXEDO System's programming tools encourage modularity and encapsulation through function shipping, it is easy to modify isolated parts of your application without having to rewrite others.

In Part III, "Development of a TUXEDO Application," we will cover all of the programming aspects of ATMI and TxRPC in much more detail so that you will get a better idea of the options and features available to you.

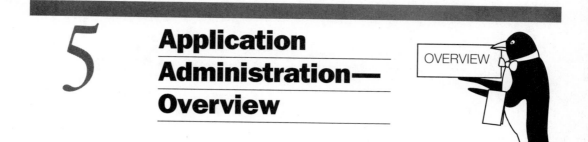

5 Application Administration— Overview

OVERVIEW

In Chapter 4, "Application Development—Overview," we introduced the TUXEDO application development environment—the concepts and tools available to designers and programmers to build TUXEDO applications. We discussed the structure of TUXEDO clients and servers and the different communication models provided by ATMI, the TUXEDO communications and transaction interface. In this chapter, we discuss what a TUXEDO application looks like from the perspective of the administrator. We also discuss what tools are available to simplify the complex task of administering a distributed application.

5.1 Application Administration—What Is it?

One of the most important characteristics of the TUXEDO System is the separation between the functions of the application designer and the application administrator. The TUXEDO ATMI programming model permits application designers to concentrate on the logic of the client and service modules instead of how these modules are built, deployed, configured, or monitored. Location independence and programming language transparency are the key elements in the ATMI model that permit this separation of functions. Thus, application designers can write code without having to worry about the location of the modules or the programming language they use. Application administrators can concentrate on the right deployment of the application modules without having to worry about the location's effect on the application code.

Figure 5.1 depicts a scene in which an application programmer is working with the logical modules of the application, and the application administrator is planning the deployment of these modules. Programmers and administrators cooperate to produce a well-running distributed system. But application administration is not only module deployment. Much more than that, application administration has to do with the ability to build, configure, manage, and monitor the different parts of a distributed application.

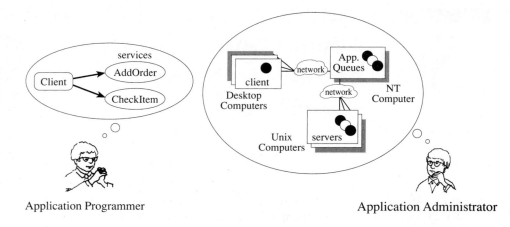

Figure 5.1 **Application Programmers and Application Administrators**

Application administrators build the distributed application with the cooperation of the application designers, operating system administrators, network administrators, and database administrators. Application administrators play a central coordination role that ensures the proper operation of the distributed application. Application designers help administrators to identify how services can be bundled into servers, if clients will be running on workstations, and what resources are used by the application code (for example, databases and buffer types). Operating system and application administrators collaborate to tune the operating system parameters to the application's needs. For example, they collaborate to set up the space required for shared memory and message queues. Network administrators and application administrators cooperate to define a computer network that satisfies the communications requirements. Database administrators help define the parameters needed to work with the databases used by the application.

The administration of a distributed application can be a complex task. Administrators need a set of comprehensive tools that simplify the administration process and address the following areas:

■ *Central Management:* The ability to supervise and manage the distributed application from a central console.

■ *Configuration Management:* The definition of the boundaries of the application and the arrangement of the different components of the application; the ability to rearrange the application modules or change their attributes while the application is active.

■ *Fault Management:* Ways to track the occurrence of faults and recovery actions performed by the system; in particular, there should be a way to be informed immediately of the occurrence of certain types of failures that require prompt response by the administrator.

■ *Security Management:* Ways to define who can access an application, to control unauthorized access to the resources provided by the application, and to alert when unauthorized accesses are attempted.

■ *Monitoring:* The capability to observe the operation of the application administrators should be able to obtain the status of the different application components.

■ *Performance Management:* The collection of statistics related to the operation of the application—administrators can use these statistics to tune the throughput of the application.

The TUXEDO administrative subsystem provides tools designed to meet these requirements. For example, the TUXEDO graphical interface—**xtuxadm**—is the control center for the administrator. With this tool, administrators can visualize the different parts of the application, obtain the status of the different modules, and detect and respond to failure conditions. They also can visualize the performance of the application and ensure that the application is properly secured. Further, application administrators can write their own custom administrative programs with the TMIB Interface, the TUXEDO administrative programming interface. The TMIB Interface uses an extension of ATMI that provides access to all entities defined within a distributed application. For example, administrators can obtain and change the attributes associated with a particular service, server, or machine. We explore these tools later in this chapter.

The following are examples of the different tasks involved in the administration of an application:

Application configuration management

■ Construct servers by grouping related services
■ Assign a location to each server
■ Replicate servers for high availability
■ Define what queuing model should be used for servers
■ Prepare the resources used by the application
■ Assign priorities and relative workload to services
■ Define what TUXEDO subsystems are required (for example, workstation handling)
■ Define what type of security is required by the application
■ Reconfigure the application by adding new machines or moving servers to other locations

Application monitoring, fault management, and security management

■ Activation and deactivation of the application

■ Observe the behavior of the application (for example, by obtaining statistics)

■ Detect and respond to failure conditions (for example, by migrating servers to other machines)

■ Detect and respond to heavy load conditions (for example, by starting new instances of a server, suspending certain services, or changing attributes like the time out values)

■ Detect security problems (for example, unauthorized access to a service)

As you can see, application administration involves very fine control over the construction and operation of the different parts of the distributed application. It has to deal not only with the hardware and the operating system but also with the different application components (clients and services) to ensure the proper operation of the automated business function.

5.2 What Is a TUXEDO Application?

We use the term "application" to refer to the set of programs and resources that computerize business functions. A TUXEDO application also includes the resources used by the TUXEDO system to support these programs.

A distributed TUXEDO application has these parts, as shown in Figure 5.2:

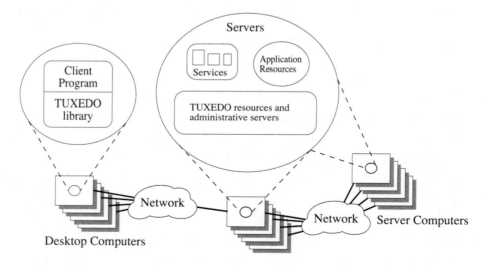

Figure 5.2 Parts of a Distributed TUXEDO Application

- client programs

- service procedures

- server programs

- resources used by the business logic such as databases, application queues, and events

- TUXEDO System resources and administrative servers

- operating system resources

- hardware resources

Client programs and service procedures contain the business logic of the application. Services typically access data resources controlled by a Resource Manager, such as a database system. Server programs group several related service procedures to optimize the processing of the business data. The TUXEDO System provides administrative functions via a set of utilities, server programs, and resources that store information needed or produced by the system (for example, configuration or events generated by the system to report faults and warnings). Also, the TUXEDO System uses operating system resources, such as shared memory and disk space data needed for the operation of the system. Finally, the different parts of the application can be distributed over a set of different computers. That is, client and server programs can be executing under different computing environments, for example, clients on desktop Windows machines and servers on one or more server machines (Unix, NT, or NetWare platforms).

Clients, servers and services are entities that require administrative control. A primary concern of TUXEDO System administrators is how to organize and maximize the use of their computing resources by distributing the processing required by clients and servers among the computers available to the application. TUXEDO administrators have fine-grained control over the following:

- the definition of servers

- the location of servers in the computer network

- the number of server instances

- the queuing discipline used by servers

- the service load and priority

- the routing criteria used by the system

- the grouping of servers

- the security methods used by the application

We introduced the concept of a MIB in Chapter 3, "Communication and Administration Paradigms for Distributed Business Applications". The administrative information needed to control a TUXEDO application is contained in the *TUXEDO MIB (or TMIB)*. The TUXEDO administrative subsystem uses the information in the TMIB to set up and control the run-time environment needed by the different parts of the application.

It is the TMIB that formally defines a TUXEDO application. With the TMIB, administrators can easily define and control the structure of their distributed business applications. The definition of this structure includes the distributed computer environment used by the application, client and server environments, and TUXEDO System components needed to control these environments.

5.3 The TUXEDO Management Information Base (TMIB)

The TMIB defines a classification of the manageable objects within an application. The TMIB is composed of a set of administrative class definitions that represent all parts of a TUXEDO application. Each class in the TMIB has a set of attributes that characterize the common properties of all objects that belong to that class. The attributes carry a set of permissions that define who can retrieve or update those attributes. Objects are distinguished one from each other by the unique values that they have for certain attributes. For instance, computers in the machine class are identified by unique machine names.

The classes and attributes that make up the TMIB are published in the TUXEDO Reference Manual [TUXEDO] and are accessible through a programming interface. Application designers, administrators, and independent software vendors (ISVs) can use this specification in a program to customize the administration of their applications.

Figure 5.3 shows a conceptual view of the TUXEDO MIB. There, the client class contains all active client programs ("OrdEntry" is one). The "AddOrder" service is an instance in the service class, and the "order-reg" server is an instance in the server class. Some of these instances are related. For example, the "order-reg" server executes in the machine "NewJersey" and offers the "AddOrder" service.

The TUXEDO MIB is a "virtual" database that hides the distribution and implementation of the classes. The TMIB defines the concepts and objects that the TUXEDO System knows about. When the TMIB is populated with values, a part of a TUXEDO application is defined. The TMIB has a persistent part and a dynamic part. The persistent part defines permanent resources used by the application, that is, the configuration of the application. The dynamic part reflects run-time attributes of the application.

Examples of permanent objects and relationships defined in the configuration are

- the machines used by the application
- the associations between servers and machines

■ the networking attribute values

■ other information that defines the boundaries of the application

Administrators can change the configuration attributes or add new objects at any time by changing the TMIB.

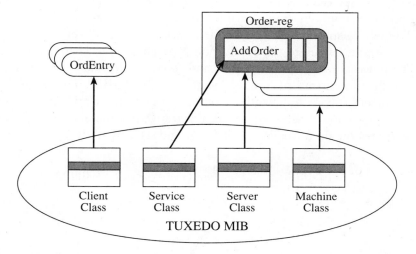

Figure 5.3 The TUXEDO Management Information Base

The dynamic part of the TMIB includes the state of the permanent resources and information related to the operation of the application, for example, statistics and other information that are needed only when the application is active. The dynamic part of the TMIB is also called the "Bulletin Board" because it is the place where global or local state changes to the TMIB are "posted." The Bulletin Board is a run-time representation of the TMIB that is replicated on every computer declared in the application configuration.

Figure 5.4 shows the basic classes that make up the TUXEDO Core MIB. An arrow between two classes denotes an "are-associated-with" relationship between these classes. For example, a machine is associated with a domain. The domain concept is used to represent an application that is independently administered and is the basis of the TUXEDO interoperability strategy. It can be used to build highly scalable applications consisting of multiple domains. In Chapter 18, "Getting Applications to Work Together," we discuss the facilities provided by the TUXEDO System to allow interoperation between different domains.

A domain is composed of one or more machines. Within a machine, related servers are grouped to provide optimal access to the application resources (for example, a database). Servers are also associated with a particular queuing model (as described in Chapter 6, "The Anatomy of a TUXEDO Application"). Services are associated with procedures and are bundled with a particular server. They may also be associated with a data-dependent routing criterion—we explain this concept later in Chapter 6. Clients are attached to or execute within a particular machine.

Recall that a server's physical location is completely hidden from clients that request services simply by using a name (for example, "GetOrder"). This allows TUXEDO administrators to change certain characteristics of servers or resource managers without having to tell application programmers to change their client's code. The physical properties of servers and service routines are under complete control of the administrator (they are specified in the TMIB). The assignment of servers to queues, any data-dependent routing criteria, the relative priority of services, and access control lists—all are administrative parameters that help administrators control the performance, availability, and security of the application.

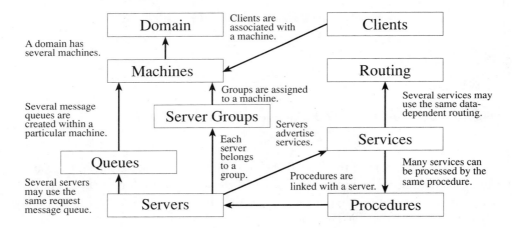

Figure 5.4   A Subset of the TUXEDO Core MIB

5.4   The TUXEDO System Administrative Environment

The TUXEDO administrative subsystem was designed to provide administrators with centralized control of the application configuration, monitoring, fault management, security management, and performance management of a domain. The administrative subsystem was also designed to automate critical aspects of the management of a distributed application. For example, the TUXEDO System performs automatic restart and recovery of servers, manages load balancing and context sensitive routing, controls the duration time of a request or a transaction, and can automatically begin a transaction before a particular service is invoked.

From the central console, administrators can make decisions based on a global view of the entire application (see Figure 5.5). They can observe the status of each part of the application, dynamically change the configuration, review the diagnostics issued by a particular component, visualize the statistics collected by the system, and monitor the clients using the application.

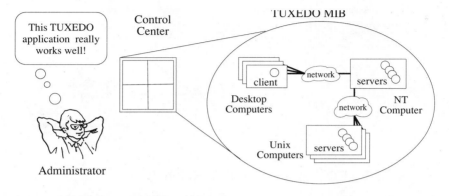

Figure 5.5   TUXEDO Control Window to Your Distributed Application

In the TUXEDO administrative model, a *domain* defines the scope of the administrative tasks. Each TUXEDO application, as defined by the TMIB, is a domain and is administered independently of other domains. Moreover, multiple domains can be administered from the same console.

As Figure 5.6 suggests, the TMIB is the "heart" of the TUXEDO administrative subsystem. It contains all the information necessary for the operation of the application. TUXEDO administrative tools are constructed around the TMIB and provide different types of interfaces to administrators. For example, administrators can use the graphical interface and the command interpreter supplied with the TUXEDO System to administer their applications.

The TUXEDO System provides the following administrative tools:

■ A central console from which administrators can observe the behavior of the entire application. They can also define the boundaries of the application from this central console.

■ A set of utilities to activate, deactivate, configure, and manage the application.

■ A published specification of the Management Information Base with a programming interface that allows custom application management.

■ An event mechanism that informs administrators of faults or exceptional events detected by the TUXEDO System or the application logic.

■ A set of administrative servers that automate most of the management aspects of the distributed application.

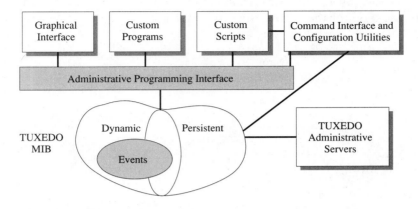

Figure 5.6 **TUXEDO System Administration Tools**

Some of the TUXEDO features should be explicitly configured by the administrator via the definition of administrative servers in the TMIB. Examples of these configurable features are workstation handling, application queuing, interdomain communications, event handling, and access control. These advanced services are described in more detail in the next chapter.

5.5 Using the TUXEDO Administrative Tools

In this section, we discuss the operational aspects of the TUXEDO System administration. We introduce the most important tools used by administrators: the graphical interface, the administrative programming interface, and the utilities for application activation and configuration.

To prevent "unexpected" changes to the TMIB, roles and associated permissions are defined to access the TMIB. The TUXEDO System distinguishes three types of users of the information in the TMIB: the application administrator, operators, and end users. Administrators have complete control of the TMIB, and they typically configure the static (or persistent) part of the application. They also change this configuration as required by the growth of the application. Operators monitor the operation of the application. They activate or deactivate the application and change parameters to adjust to heavy load or failure conditions. However, they usually cannot add new parts to the application. End users have read-only access to certain parts of the TMIB. They typically access the TMIB via a program that uses the administrative programming interface. Administrators and operators can be the same person, and administrators can always adjust the access permissions for operators and end users.

5.5.1 Administering Your TUXEDO Application with xtuxadm

The best tool to manage the TUXEDO System is the graphical interface (**xtuxadm**). Administrators can use **xtuxadm** to configure and monitor the operation of their TUXEDO applications. **xtuxadm** uses the X Window System [X-Window].

The basic goal behind the design of the graphical interface was to provide a visual metaphor of the TMIB and the TUXEDO administrative tasks from a central screen. This screen presents, in graphical terms, the information stored in the TMIB. The design of the screen minimizes the number of operations (mouse clicks) required for administering your application and maximizes the display of the administrative information needed to monitor your application. For example, the screen gives you a direct view of the events generated by the TUXEDO System. For these reasons, we also call this screen the "Application Mission Critical Control Center." An example of this screen is shown in Figure 5.7.

Figure 5.7　**xtuxadm Main Window**

Starting **xtuxadm** is very simple. It starts in the background after the administrator types:

```
$ xtuxadm
```

When **xtuxadm** starts up, the TUXEDO Application Administration Main Window pops up. This window is divided into five basic sections: pull-down menus in the menu bar, the power bar, the icon area, an event log area, and the status bar. The pull-down menus give you lists of choices. For example, the Exit command is located at the bottom of the File menu. The Help menu on the right side of the screen gives you access to the TUXEDO on-line documentation subsystem. The penguin icon in the upper right corner flaps its wings when the administrative subsystem is busy performing a particular administrative function.

Below the pull-down menus, you will see the "power bar." This bar is composed of a set of buttons that represent the most common administrative operations. For example, you can activate (boot) or deactivate (shut down) the entire application, a set of selected machines, a particular server group, or a particular server. You can migrate a group of servers defined on a particular machine to another machine. If you click on the "config" button on the power bar, you will switch to the "Configuration Tool Window." From this window, you can add entities to the TMIB or change the attributes of existing entities. If you click on the "stats" button, the "Statistics Tool Window" will appear. This window displays statistics as a bar chart, and you can choose from different categories, for example, domainwide, machine-specific, or server group statistics. The other buttons in the power bar allow you to administer the different entities defined in the TUXEDO Core MIB: the domain global parameters, machines, server groups, servers, services, clients, and data-dependent routing.

The icon area contains icons representing instances from the class selected in the power bar. In our example, the administrator has selected the "machines" button, and the icon area shows a set of icons representing the machines currently defined for this TUXEDO domain. The representation of each machine uses icons that carry visual status information. For example, the icon shows the machine type, if a machine is active or inactive, and if servers are active or inactive on the machine.

You can perform administrative functions in several ways: by using the pull-down menus, by clicking on the buttons of the power bar, by using "drag and drop," or by clicking on an icon in the icon area. For example, you can select a machine that is inactive and drag the icon to the "activate" button to start up all the servers defined for this machine, or you can activate several machines by using the "activate" button directly. If you double click on an icon in the icon area, the next level of instances in the TMIB for that icon will appear on the screen. For example, double-clicking on a particular machine icon will display the server groups defined in that machine.

Events generated by the TUXEDO System are reported in the event log area. By single-clicking on a particular machine icon, you will be able to visualize the event log for that machine. Exceptional conditions reported by the TUXEDO System such as a "machine failure" are reported via a pop-up screen. This event may require that you verify the network connectivity, and you may have to "migrate" the services offered by this machine to another machine. Server migration allows administrators to deactivate all servers in a particular server group and reactivate instances of these servers in another machine.

Finally, the status bar at the bottom of the main window is updated to display errors or the number of entities in the icon area.

5.5.2 Administering Your Application with the TMIB Interface

Although the TUXEDO System provides a complete set of administrative tools, your application may require more specialized administration. In Chapter 3, "Communication and Administration Paradigms for Distributed Business Applications," we introduced the concept of a programmable MIB. The TUXEDO System enables such programming with the TMIB Interface, the TUXEDO administrative programming interface.

The TMIB Interface is an extension of ATMI that defines the structure of messages sent to the administrative services supporting the TUXEDO MIB (also called, the TMIB). These messages are sent via the ATMI verbs. The structure of the messages is defined in FML typed buffers (we will explain the Field Manipulation Language in Chapter 9, "Joining and Leaving the Application"). You can access all of the classes in the TMIB with the TMIB Interface. Later in Chapter 17, "A Tour of the TUXEDO Management Information Base," we discuss in more detail how administrators and programmers can use this interface.

The TMIB Interface provides two types of access to the MIB: a "GET" operation that reads information from a particular class and a "SET" operation that modifies the attribute values of a particular object in the TMIB. Actions are typically performed by changing the state of the selected object. For example, by changing the state of a machine to "active," you activate the machine and all servers defined in that machine. From the programming perspective, the TMIB is a passive "agent:" it awaits to be polled with a "GET" operation or to be told to change its state with a "SET" operation. This is illustrated in Figure 5.8 with pseudocode that retrieves all machines active in the TMIB (upper box) and that "shuts down" the machine "manufac2" (the lower box).

The combination of the TUXEDO EventBroker™ facility (see Chapter 6, "The Anatomy of a TUXEDO Application") with the TMIB Interface gives you a more dynamic administrative tool. You can write a program that detects changes in the TMIB and automatically generates an event. Another program can subscribe to this event and produce an action in response to the event. Events are the standard way used by the system to notify of changes in the TMIB. If the EventBroker facility is not enabled, all system events are redirected to the Event log class in the TMIB.

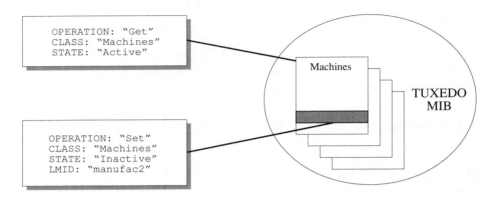

Figure 5.8   GET and SET Operations on the TUXEDO MIB

The TMIB Interface also allows you to write self-adapting applications. That is, application programmers can use the information in the TMIB within their application programs to modify dynamically the behavior of the application. For example, in a banking application, access to an automatic teller machine (ATM) can be self-configured to shut off access to the device when the ATM is running out of currency. This is shown in Figure 5.9.

5.5.3 Other Administrative Utilities

In addition to the graphical and the administrative programming interfaces, the TUXEDO System provides several scriptable utilities useful for automating ad-

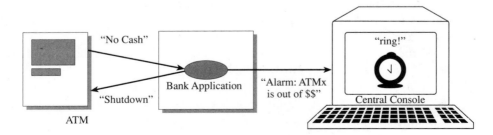

Figure 5.9   Self-Administered Application

ministrative tasks. With these utilities, administrators can configure, monitor, and start up or shut down the applications (or parts of it). In Chapter 15, "Application Administration and Monitoring," we will discuss these utilities in more detail.

5.6 Summary

The TUXEDO System provides administrators with a comprehensive administration facility that allows complete configuration, monitoring, and control of a distributed business application. Administrators can easily control the growth of their application by deploying more servers or by partitioning the application into a federated set of domains.

This chapter presented an overview of the different resources that a TUXEDO administrator can use to control the structure and behavior of an application. We introduced the concept of the TUXEDO Management Information Base (or TMIB), and we discussed the different elements that make up this repository of information. We also discussed how to control a TUXEDO application via the **xtuxadm** graphical interface and the administrative programming interface.

In Part IV of the book, "Administration of a TUXEDO Application," we present more details about how you can use the administrative programming interface, and we give you a few tips that will help you control the structure and behavior of your distributed business applications.

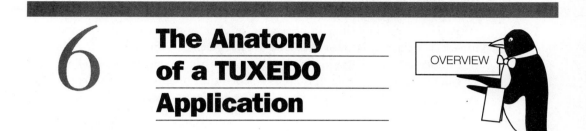

6 The Anatomy of a TUXEDO Application

OVERVIEW

Earlier, we described the development paradigms used by programmers to construct clients and servers. We also discussed the tools used by administrators to manage distributed applications. In this chapter, we explain the architecture of a TUXEDO-based application. We also discuss the different resources used by the TUXEDO System to control the definition and operation of a distributed application.

6.1 Hiding Complexity to Make Building Distributed Applications Simpler

The TUXEDO System client/server model simplifies the programming of distributed applications by introducing several types of transparency:

■ *Location transparency:* Users, clients, databases, and application services are never tied to fixed locations; hiding the location of the different application modules and resources simplifies the development of the distributed application and improves the administration capabilities—for example, a resource such as a server can be moved to a new computer without impacting clients or other servers.

■ *Network transparency:* The TUXEDO System hides the complexity of the network and the multiple networking protocols used in the communication among the machines involved in a distributed application; application programmers do not have to worry about how to access the network or how to deal with machines that have different byte ordering—they just invoke service modules, post events, or enqueue/dequeue messages.

■ *Implementation transparency:* Clients do not know the internal structure of a service, and the implementation of a service can be changed without having to alter the client program; application programmers can also use different programming languages to create the client and the server.

■ *Administration transparency:* Client and service programmers do not need to know how load balancing or routing is applied to a service request, how security is enforced by the administrator, or even how services are grouped into servers; administrators are free to change the configuration (for example, relocate servers or add new machines) without having to alter client or service modules; in general, there is a separation of administrative concerns and application logic.

The architecture of the TUXEDO System is centered around these transparency types. For example, the ATMI interface provides automatic name resolution—there is no explicit binding to a server—and application programmers always use constructs that emphasize location transparency. The following sections discuss the basic and advanced functionality that implement these transparency types in the TUXEDO System.

6.2 Portability—A Key Characteristic of the TUXEDO System

The TUXEDO software runs on numerous platforms and provides interoperability between all of them. That lets the application development team concentrate on their application, instead of the networking and the heterogeneity of the data formats across the various platforms.

6.2.1 Server Platforms

The TUXEDO System allows for applications that run on a wide variety of platforms ranging from POSIX-compliant systems like SCO's UnixWare, IBM's RS6000 AIX, Hewlett-Packard's HP-UX, and Digital Unix to POSIX-like systems like SCO's Open Desktop, to much different environments like Microsoft's Windows NT, and Novell's NetWare. Important with regard to application programming is that the same TUXEDO interfaces are available and identical on all of these platforms. This means that the application can be written without worrying about platform-specific changes to the distributed business application.

Of course, an important part of a distributed system is the networking between the various nodes. The TUXEDO System supports a single networking abstraction at the transport level to several types of networking interfaces. One is the sockets interface, which is used primarily for TCP/IP communications. Another networking interface that is supported is the TLI (or the corresponding X/Open XTI) interface. This interface commonly provides access not only to TCP/IP but also to IPX/SPX, X.25, and other networking protocols where the provider has a TLI interface. A NETBIOS interface can also be used on platforms where it is supported. The important thing is that the TUXEDO software will run over a variety of networks and, best of all, it is transparent to the application programmer. Details such as network addresses and devices are configured by the administrator and completely hidden from the application. The application programmer need not know the underlying networking paradigm (connection or connectionless), the media, the protocols, or the data representation. The application programmer is free to concentrate on application-level protocols.

With the advent of businesses that regularly span national boundaries, distributed business applications need to worry about providing information in multiple languages. The TUXEDO software has been internationalized such that all messages from the software, both in response to using the development tools and event log messages, can appear in different languages. By simply setting one or two operating system environment variables, the user can control the language for TUXEDO System messages and the date and time formats. The default language is "C" which provides for U.S. English messages and date/time format.

Summing up, one of the strengths of the TUXEDO System is that it runs on a wide variety of platforms and networks, but the application programming interfaces are the same across each of the platforms, and the networking is completely transparent to the application programmer. This eases the development complexity, preserves the large investment in developing the application, and provides for flexibility in deploying the application across multiple platforms in a distributed environment.

6.2.2 Client Platforms

In the previous section, we discussed the platforms where all of the TUXEDO software runs, including application servers. Client programs can also be run on these platforms with the benefit that they are directly connected to the computers where the servers run and inherit the security of the local operating system. Clients running on a server platform are called *local clients*.

In contrast, there are potentially many computers used by single persons that also participate in the application. These computers have irregular availability (that is, the owners may turn them off when not in use), and therefore, are not the best place to put application servers accessing shared databases that need to be available all the time to many users! These computers are called *workstations*, and they typically execute *workstation clients*. A workstation client does not need all of the TUXEDO run-time software, just the front end of all of the TUXEDO primitives and the networking software needed to connect the workstation client to a server platform.

The use of workstations helps in off-loading work from machines that contain not only TUXEDO application servers, but often serve as the database engines. Handling the overhead of character echo for ASCII terminals or handling processing for X Windows displays can present a large load on the server machine which can be migrated to workstations closer to the user.

All of the server platforms can also support workstation clients. The distinction between workstations, PCS, and servers is blurring and what may be server platforms in one application may be workstation platforms in another. In addition to the server platforms, desktop environments such as MS DOS, Windows 3.1, Windows 95, Windows NT, MacOS, OS/2, and NextStep can all be used to build workstation clients, and the TUXEDO System is becoming universally available. So whatever your desktop choice, chances are that you can write and run TUXEDO client software there.

6.3 The TUXEDO System—A Service Request Broker

The TUXEDO System is a *Service Request Broker (SRB)*. As such, the TUXEDO System provides an infrastructure for efficient routing, dispatching, and management of application service requests, event postings and notifications, and application queue enqueuing and dequeuing. This infrastructure consists of the TUXEDO run-time system, a set of administrative servers, and the TUXEDO MIB.

Figure 6.1 shows a conceptual representation of the architecture of a distributed TUXEDO application. Client programs request services via the ATMI or the TxRPC interfaces (see Chapter 4, "Application Development—Overview"). Server programs group several services, and these services are invoked according to the rules defined by ATMI and TxRPC. Application designers construct client and server programs by linking the TUXEDO run-time system with their application code. The TUXEDO run-time system provides the implementation of ATMI.

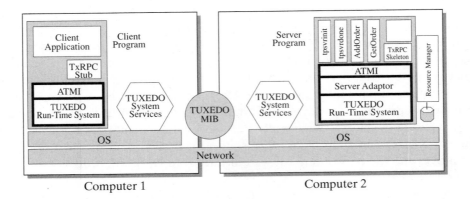

Figure 6.1   Conceptual Architecture of a Distributed TUXEDO Application

As shown in Figure 6.1, client and server programs have different structures, but they both use the basic infrastructure provided by the TUXEDO run-time system. The TUXEDO run-time system provides the basic SRB functionality for both clients and servers. This functionality includes

- resolving service requests (assign a server to process each request)
- preparing messages for transmission (encode/decode, compress/uncompress)
- propagating the transaction and the security contexts
- sending and receiving messages between clients and servers

Recall from Chapter 4, "Application Development—Overview", that the starting point (**main()** in C) of a client is controlled by the application program, whereas on the server side, the starting point is controlled by the TUXEDO libraries. We call this special component the *server adaptor* (or *standard main* in the TUXEDO manuals). The server adaptor provides several functions:

- invokes the routines provided by application programmers for server initialization and termination routines
- provides automatic advertisement of the services bundled with a server (services are registered in the TMIB)
- invokes services within the transaction and security contexts of the calling client
- dispatches service invocations (maps a service invocation to the routine implementing that service)

A set of system servers provides the administrative services needed by the TUXEDO System. These administrative services can be basic and advanced. Basic services are always available when an application is active. Advanced services need to be explicitly configured into the application by the administrator.

The following are the basic system services:

- naming
- application activation and deactivation
- dynamic application reconfiguration
- fault management
- intramachine and intermachine application communications management
- transaction management

And the following are the advanced system services:

■ workstation handling

■ security management

■ application queue management

■ event management

■ interapplication communication

Note that, from the programmer's perspective, there is no distinction between basic and advanced services. All of ATMI and TxRPC can be used. The distinction is purely administrative, and to exploit all of ATMI and interdomain communication, the advanced services must be configured in the TMIB.

In the following sections, we explain these features in more detail, and we discuss what their effect is on your distributed application.

6.4 The TUXEDO Run-Time System—The Basic SRB

Before we can describe the TUXEDO System services in more detail, we are going to make a short detour to describe the functionality provided by the TUXEDO run-time system libraries. These libraries are the heart of the SRB.

6.4.1 Anatomy of Client and Servers

Figure 6.1 gives you a global perspective of the different elements of the TUXEDO SRB. In Figure 6.2, we have expanded the TUXEDO run-time system to show you how the SRB processes a service request. A client invokes the "GetOrder" service with data stored in a typed buffer. The TUXEDO run-time system processes this service request. First, the naming facility is used to find if the "GetOrder" service is currently available in the TMIB. Then, the software verifies in the TMIB if the service is associated with a *data-dependent routing* criterion (discussed later in this chapter). If so, the system uses the data in the buffer for the routing algorithm. The routing algorithm selects a group of servers that can process the service request. To refine this selection, the system also maintains a set of metrics in the TMIB. These metrics help the TUXEDO SRB balance the workload between servers advertising the same service in the TMIB. Then, a message is prepared for the selected server and a predefined (or application defined) priority is assigned to this message. If the server is on a machine that uses a different byte ordering, then the message is automatically marshalled and finally, sent to the server.

Note that other basic TUXEDO administrative servers may be used in the transmission of the service request to the final destination. We will cover this aspect later in this chapter.

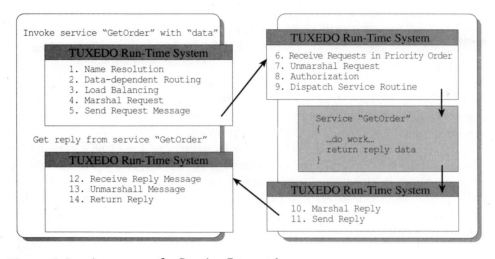

Figure 6.2 **Anatomy of a Service Invocation**

On the server, the TUXEDO run-time system retrieves request messages in priority order. Each message is unmarshaled and passed to the Server Adaptor. The Server Adaptor performs an authorization check on the requested service by verifying that the service can be invoked by the end user using the client program. Then, the Server Adaptor finds the address of the routine that implements the service and dispatches that routine with the typed buffer that came with the message. The service routine executes and returns a reply (also a typed buffer). The TUXEDO run-time system prepares the reply message for the client. Then, it marshals the message (if the client machine has a different byte ordering) and sends the message to the client. Finally, the TUXEDO run-time system on the client retrieves the reply message, unmarshals it (if necessary), and delivers the typed buffer to the application.

The TUXEDO basic and advanced system services exploit the basic functionality provided by the TUXEDO run-time system. For example, enqueuing messages to an application queue is translated into a service request to the queueing service provided by the **TMQUEUE** server (see Section 6.5.2.2). The same applies to the posting of and event—the posting of an event translates into a service request to the EventBroker (see Section 6.5.2.3).

In the following sections, we give you more details on each one of the services provided by the TUXEDO run-time system. We can also call this library the Basic SRB.

6.4.2 Name Resolution

When a TUXEDO server is activated, it *advertises* the names of its services in the

Bulletin Board (the dynamic part of the TMIB—see Chapter 5). These service names are associated with the server's *physical address* so that the TUXEDO SRB can route requests to it. One of the TUXEDO System's most powerful features is its ability to hide completely a server's physical location and address from the application programmer. That is, the names programmers use in their applications are completely location-transparent. A client could issue a request to a service that debits a bank account simply by using the string, "Debit." However, this service may execute in another machine or even in another application.

When a client program asks for a service by name, the TUXEDO System consults its name registry in the Bulletin Board. The name registry provides the information necessary to convert the string name to a machine and a physical address of a server that advertised the service. Using this address, the TUXEDO SRB sends the request to the appropriate server wherever it may reside in your distributed application.

6.4.3 Intramachine Communication

The TUXEDO SRB uses memory-based *message queues* for the communication between processes executing within a particular machine. By default, clients and servers have their own message queues on which to receive requests and replies. However, administrators can change this default for servers. Note that these message queues are different from the application queues described in Chapter 4—they are administratively configured transient memory areas used for communication and are not seen by the application programmer.

6.4.3.1 Allocating Servers to Message Queues

When a server starts, a request message queue is automatically created for it by the TUXEDO run-time system. Then, its services are automatically advertised by the Server Adaptor. After this, the Server Adaptor waits for service request messages to arrive on the message queue. When a service request arrives, the TUXEDO run-time system dequeues the request and dispatches it to the appropriate service routine.

By default, each server has its own message queue. We refer to this as *Single Server, Single Queue*, or *SSSQ*. This default can be overridden, and the administrator can assign multiple servers to read from the same queue. We refer to this as *Multiple Servers, Single Queue*, or *MSSQ set*. Both SSSQ and MSSQ sets can be used in your configuration; however, any given server is assigned either to an SSSQ or an MSSQ set, but not both. Note that SSSQ/MSSQ are administrative concepts that are not seen by the application programmer—application programmers just request services.

6.4.3.2 *Single Server, Single Queue*

Think of SSSQ as the model found in most supermarkets (see Figure 6.3). That is, there are several checkout lines, each a separate queue feeding a clerk at a single cash register. The time you wait in line is determined solely by how fast the checkout clerk services the people in front of you. If the clerk is delayed because someone needs a price check or is paying in pennies, everyone else in the queue will suffer although there is usually no effect on people in other queues (unless their clerks are called over to help count pennies!).

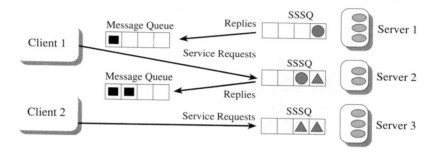

Figure 6.3 **Single Server, Single Queue (SSSQ)**

Having spent much time in checkout lines yourself, you might think there are no advantages to this scheme. On the contrary, this scheme can be used to load-balance and throttle work across several servers offering different kinds of services. Another example from the supermarket model is the "ten items or less" queue. For those clients (customers) with small requests (few items in their baskets) to be processed (checked out) by the server (clerk), having a separate queue can help raise throughput (quickly get you out of line) by guaranteeing cycles (cash registers) will be available for these small, but important requests.

6.4.3.3 *Multiple Servers, Single Queue*

On the other end of the queuing spectrum is the model found in banks: one line being serviced by several tellers all of whom can perform identical services (see Figure 6.4). There is a built-in load-balancing mechanism in this scheme because the next available teller will always take the next person in line. One important requirement must be satisfied for this scheme to work effectively: all tellers can perform any request put to him or her by a customer. Imagine waiting for a half-hour in line only to reach the next available teller and find that he or she cannot perform your task! You are then instructed to wait for someone else who can perform that duty. At this point you are thinking, "Why didn't I just wait for that person to begin with?" To make sure that such doesn't occur in the TUXEDO System, all servers that are set up to share a single queue must offer the exact same set of services at all times.

The main advantage of MSSQ sets is that they provide a second form of load-balancing at the individual queue level. That is, the TUXEDO System first performs load-balancing when choosing the server's queue to which a client's request should be sent. If that queue is part of an MSSQ set, then the dequeuing mechanism will perform its own load-balancing by giving the message to the first server that is idle. An important property of MSSQ sets is that they produce wait times with the smallest variance.

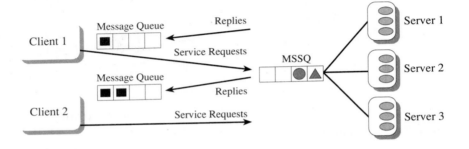

Figure 6.4   Multiple Servers, Single Queue (MSSQ)

6.4.3.4 Reply Queues

When a server belongs to an MSSQ set, it must be configured with its own (non-shared) reply queue. A server needs its own reply queue so that when it makes requests to other servers, the replies are returned to the requesting server and are not dequeued by other servers in the MSSQ set.

Figure 6.5 illustrates the flow of a client's request to a server on an MSSQ set (flow 1), server 2 dequeuing the request (flow 2), server 2 issuing a request (flow 3) that is handled by server 4 (flow 4), server 4 returning the reply to server 2's reply queue (flow 5), and, finally, server 2 returning the reply to the originating client (flow 6).

From the programmer's point of view, none of these queues are visible, nor whether servers belong to SSSQ or MSSQ sets. Request queues are strictly administrative entities. Using ATMI functions, your programs are concerned only with the names of your application's services, not where they reside nor from which queues they read.

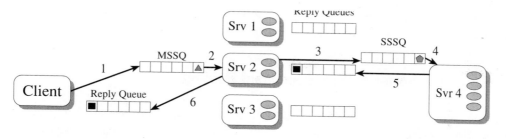

Figure 6.5   Reply Queues

6.4.4 Load-Balancing

In a TUXEDO application, separate queues for servers can be exploited to guarantee that resources will be available to process certain kinds of requests. If your application offers several services, some of which take little time to process, say, less than 75 milliseconds, and others which can take several minutes, then you probably would like the expensive services to have their own queues. Then, in the worst case, if many clients request the expensive services, their requests will queue and be processed one at a time, leaving plenty of resources available for the short, "bread-and-butter" services that make up the bulk of your application.

This type of load-balancing is inherent to queue-based function shipping and is one of the TUXEDO System's advantages over SQL-based data shipping approaches. With the latter, there is no way to guarantee resources to clients performing "bread-and-butter" requests because all data-shipping requests are treated equally by backend database engines. For example, if several clients simultaneously query a database with an expensive join operation, then all other "well-behaved" clients will feel the impact in terms of slower response times. However, with the TUXEDO System's administrative tools for allocating services to servers and servers to queues, it is straightforward to ensure that expensive operations use only a limited percentage of available resources.

6.4.5 Priorities

Just as assigning servers to queues supports modeling your business' throughput requirements, assigning priorities to services supports modeling any inherent priority requirements. The TUXEDO System allows you to assign priorities from 1 (lowest) to 100 (highest) to each service offered by your application. When a request is sent, it is marked with the priority of the service to which it is sent. When two requests arrive on a server's queue, the TUXEDO run-time system in the server will dequeue the message with the highest priority. In a brokerage application, for instance, you may want to give higher priority to buying and selling securities over providing quotes.

6.4.6 The Power of Data-Dependent Routing

One important feature of the TUXEDO System is its ability to perform *data-dependent routing*. This feature allows a client to send the same named service request to different service routines depending on the contents of the request's data. That is, the client issues a request for a service and, depending on the contents of specific data fields in the request buffer, the request might be sent either to the version of the service on machine 1 or to the version on machine 2. In the parlance of object-oriented programming, this is a type of *polymorphism* because the same operator (in this case, a service) may have multiple implementations depending on the context in which it is invoked (in this case, dependent on the data issued with the request).

One of the most common uses of data-dependent routing is for horizontally partitioning a database. In terms of relational databases, horizontal partitioning occurs when one logical table's rows are split across several physical tables according to its key values. As shown in Figure 6.6, a single logical database, whose key field is telephone number, is horizontally partitioned across two machines by area code. Thus, the database on computer 1 contains records only from the 908 area code, whereas the database on computer 2 contains records only from the 201 area code.

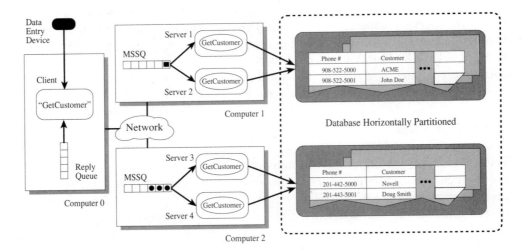

Figure 6.6 **Data-Dependent Routing**

In this case, the service routines processing the request are most likely identical because the only difference is in the data itself. In fact, just a few years ago, the 908 area code didn't exist, so all of the 201 numbers might have been housed in a single database. Once the 908 area code was created, the administrator could split the data according to the area code and transparently begin routing requests against the new area code to a new set of servers accessing a new database. Data-dependent routing is not seen at the programmer's level—it is strictly an administrative function performed while an application is running.

Another application might exploit the polymorphic quality of data-dependent routing by choosing to have a single named service with several different implementations. Imagine performing threshold-based data-dependent routing where, if an amount being transferred, for example, is greater than $10,000, then the request must be routed to a special version of the service that not only transfers the money but also performs several audits and security checks that the "less than $10,000" version of the "same" service does not perform.

Again, the important aspect of data-dependent routing is that the requester has no idea that it is occurring. It is precisely this level of transparency that allows administrators to split databases or introduce special versions of services, on-line, without changing one line of deployed client code!

6.4.7 Distributing Clients and Servers Throughout Your Network

The placement of TUXEDO client and server programs in your computer network is an important administrative issue. Several criteria need to be evaluated, such as where your databases are located, the power of the CPUs where your servers will run, and the number of client programs that will simultaneously access your servers.

With the TUXEDO System's function-shipping approach, you should place your clients and servers as physically close as possible to the resources that they will access. By doing so, you are likely to decrease the amount of time it takes for a service routine to access its resources, which should increase the number of service requests that servers can handle.

Another criterion to evaluate is whether your machines will handle clients, servers, or both. You could dedicate your smaller machines to handling traffic generated by clients, while dedicating larger machines for running servers accessing databases.

6.5　Basic and Advanced Administrative Services

In support of the transparency types discussed in Section 6.1, the TUXEDO System performs many of its distributed administrative functions via a set of specialized servers. Some of these servers are automatically defined when a distributed application is configured. These servers provide basic administrative services (see Section 6.2). Other servers need to be explicitly configured to enable specific advanced administrative services. For example, administrators need to specify in the TMIB the system parameters for workstation management or interapplication communication.

Figure 6.7 summarizes the TUXEDO System's basic and advanced administrative services. Advanced services are shown in shaded boxes. This figure is a blowup of the TUXEDO System Services hexagon in Figure 6.1. These services are explained in the following sections.

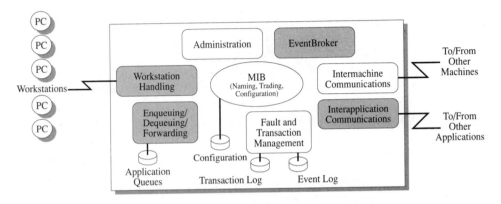

Figure 6.7 **Basic and Advanced Administrative Services**

6.5.1 Basic Administrative Services

In Chapter 5, we introduced the administrative environment provided by the TUXEDO System. In particular, we discussed the TMIB and the tools used by the administrator to control the operation of a distributed application. In this section, we discuss additional administrative functionality that is automatically provided when the distributed application is active. We also discuss the different resources used by the TUXEDO System to control the application configuration, fault management, and reliability.

6.5.1.1 Naming and Configuration

The TUXEDO System exposes to application designers three name spaces: service names, application queue names, and event names. The TUXEDO System is not aware of the application semantics of the names defined in these spaces—these names are just strings of characters. However, there is an important restriction that applies to these names: they cannot begin with a dot ("."). Because the TUXEDO administrative servers also use the TUXEDO System infrastructure, this restriction was necessary to distinguish system resources from application resources. Thus, service names such as ".TMIB", the administrative service for the TMIB, are reserved and carry specific system semantics and permissions. So, when you design your application do not use names that start with a dot.

In Sections 5.3 and 6.4.1, we introduced part of the functionality provided by the Bulletin Board. The Bulletin Board is a run-time representation of the TMIB that exists on every active machine defined in the TMIB. Because one of the TUXEDO System's goals is to provide very fast and efficient communications for large distributed applications, the Bulletin Board is implemented with high-performance memory caches that are available to all servers. The use of the TUXEDO System in numerous industry benchmarks (for example, TPC-A and TPC-C) is evidence that TUXEDO's techniques are among the best found in client/server middleware products.

Servers advertise their services in the Bulletin Board (flow 1 in Figure 6.8). However, this information must be reflected for the entire application in the TMIB. Thus, this information is propagated in a coordinated manner to all active machines involved in the application (flow 2 in Figure 6.8). The TUXEDO System uses two administrative servers to coordinate this mechanism:

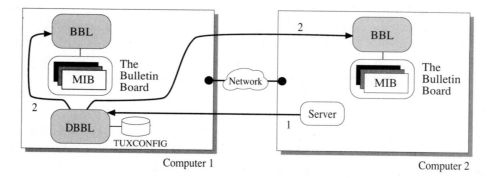

Figure 6.8   **The Bulletin Board, the DBBL, and the BBL**

- *The DBBL.* The *Distinguished Bulletin Board Liaison* server (or **DBBL**) is responsible for propagating the global changes to the TMIB and is the keeper of the static part of the TMIB; the **DBBL** also coordinates the state of the different machines involved in the application; there is only one **DBBL** for the entire application and it can migrate to other machines for fault resiliency.

- *The BBL.* The *Bulletin Board Liaison* server (or **BBL**) is the keeper of the Bulletin Board—there is a **BBL** on every active machine of the application;

the **BBL** coordinates changes to the local copy of the TMIB and verifies the sanity of the application programs that are active on the same machine as the **BBL**.

The **DBBL** and the **BBL** are started automatically when an application is activated by the administrator. Because the **DBBL** controls the global changes to the TMIB, it is the first server activated in the application. Then, a **BBL** is started when the administrator activates a configured machine. Both the **DBBL** and the **BBL** use information maintained in the static part of the TMIB—the application configuration.

The TUXEDO System allows administrators to preconfigure or dynamically configure a distributed application. Application administrators using this facility can specify how servers are grouped, where these groups are located, which machines are used by the application, and other information that help the system control the behavior of the application. This configuration is the static part of the TMIB, and it can be created entirely with **xtuxadm** (the TUXEDO graphical administrative interface).

Administrators can also use an ASCII file to specify the configuration. This file, called the UBBCONFIG file, can be used as input to the configuration loading utility (**tmloadcf**). This utility generates a binary version of the configuration, called TUXCONFIG. The TUXCONFIG file is used by the system to construct the Bulletin Board. It contains the persistent part of the TMIB in a "binary" representation that speeds the construction of the Bulletin Board. The **DBBL** maintains the master copy of this file (see Figure 6.8). A copy of the TUXCONFIG file is automatically propagated to the other machines involved in the application. This copy speeds the setup of the Bulletin Board on these machines.

6.5.1.2 Fault Management

The **DBBL** and the **BBL** also play an important role in the fault management mechanisms provided by the TUXEDO System. For example, the **DBBL** coordinates the state of the other machines active in the application. The **BBL**s are in charge of communicating state changes in the TMIB, and occasionally they send a message to **DBBL** indicating that "everything is all right" on that machine. Thus, the machine where the **DBBL** executes, is called the *Master* machine. The administrator can also configure another machine, the *Backup* machine, that can act as the Master machine. If the Master machine goes down, the administrator can perform a "master migration" that activates a new **DBBL** on the Backup machine. Administrators can also dynamically change the Backup machine. We will discuss these and other fault management mechanisms in Chapter 16, "Failure Handling."

Administrators need to understand why a failure occurred, and, for this reason, the TUXEDO run-time system records important events in a file, the Central Event Log. This file, called the *userlog* or *ULOG* file, keeps a journal of system error, warning, and tracing events. Application programmers can also use the ULOG file as a journal of records for debugging their distributed applications or to inform the system administrator of special conditions or states found during the execution of the application (for example, a failure in a security validation). There is usually a ULOG file on each active machine defined in the TMIB but, administrators can have a single file with the use of a networked file system. We discuss in more detail the structure of the ULOG file later in Chapter 15, "Application Administration and Monitoring."

6.5.1.3   *Intermachine Communications*

In Section 6.4.2, we discussed how memory-based message queues are used for interprocess communication within a machine. However, messages have to go across the network to other machines and delays may occur because of connection setups. The TUXEDO System architecture optimizes network communications by establishing a multiplexed "channel" between the machines involved in the application. TUXEDO messages flow in both directions over this channel, and the message traffic is managed by a specialized TUXEDO server called the **BRIDGE**.

The **BRIDGE** is a TUXEDO administrative server that is automatically activated on each one of the machines defined in the TMIB. The **BRIDGE** assumes a virtual one-hop network (see Figure 6.9). That is, the **BRIDGE** establishes a direct channel (network connection) with other active machines in the TMIB. When the **BRIDGE** is activated, it initially establishes channels only with the Master and the Backup machines. The channels to other machines are established only as needed—when the first service request flows between machines. Once the channel is established, it stays up until the application is deactivated. This lazy connect saves initialization time and network resources. Administrators, however, can explicitly force the creation of a channel between two machines.

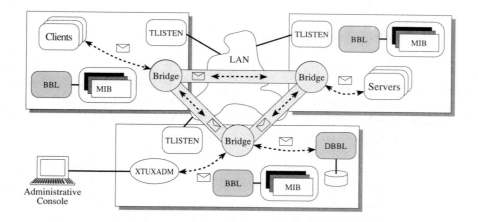

Figure 6.9   **The TUXEDO Network Manager—the BRIDGE and tlisten**

Activation of machines remote from the Master requires additional mechanisms. Of course, before a machine can receive any service requests, it must become part of a TUXEDO application. This is done by several bootstrapping utilities. In particular, a special program is needed to control incoming network connections and administrative requests generated by the TUXEDO System. This program is the TUXEDO listener, also called **tlisten**. Administrators must start a **tlisten** program on every machine defined in the TMIB.

tlisten receives remote commands from the **xtuxadm** graphical interface, the TMIB Interface, or the **tmboot** command to activate the **BBL**, the **BRIDGE**, and other servers defined in the TMIB for that machine. Administrators should configure the machine so that the **tlisten** is always running before the application is activated. Most operating systems automatically start a configured set of programs during the initialization cycle (for example, the Unix system starts all programs defined in /etc/rc). **tlisten** records events in a log file, and administrators can analyze the content of the log with a text editor (if necessary).

6.5.1.4 Transaction Management

The TUXEDO System uses optimized mechanisms for distributed transaction management. These mechanisms exploit asynchronous processing by handling the completion of a transaction in administrative servers rather than in application servers. This asynchrony allows application servers to be free to process service requests on behalf of different transactions, without having to wait for the completion of any transactions. This translates to better throughput for the application.

Transaction completion is controlled by the *Transaction Management Server* (or **TMS**). The **TMS** is defined by the administrator when a *server group* is specified in the TMIB (see Figure 6.10). A server group is associated with a particular transactional resource manager. When the server group is activated by the administrator, two or more **TMS** instances are automatically started. The **TMS**s wait for transaction termination messages to arrive at their message queues. A single **TMS** can coordinate the termination of a transaction with other **TMS**s. These transaction coordination mechanisms use optimized protocols to reduce the disk logging and the number of messages required to complete the transaction.

Finally, the **TMS** uses a log file, called the *transaction log* or *TLOG*, to record information needed for the recovery of a transaction if a failure occurs. There is one TLOG file on each active machine defined in the TMIB. The TLOG is created by the administrator using the TUXEDO administrative tools. When a server group migrates from one machine to another machine, the TLOG must be unloaded and reloaded on the new machine. We will discuss the TUXEDO transaction management mechanisms in more detail in Chapter 14, "Transactions in the TUXEDO System."

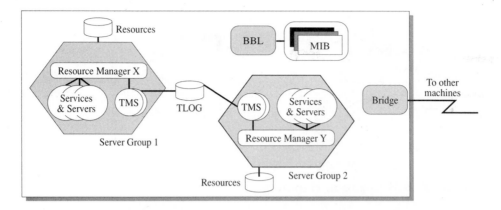

Figure 6.10   Server Groups, the TMS, and the TLOG

6.5.2 Advanced Administrative Services

The administrative services discussed in the previous section are implicitly defined in the TMIB, and the corresponding administrative servers are automatically started when a machine is activated. Advanced TUXEDO services, such as workstation handling, application queuing, event management, security, and interapplication communication, must be explicitly defined in the TMIB as one or more servers. In the following sections, we explain the functionality provided by these advanced administrative services.

6.5.2.1 Workstation Management

In Section 6.2.2, we discussed the differences between local clients and workstation clients. Local clients execute on a server platform, whereas workstation clients execute on a workstation—usually, a personal computer. Workstation clients don't need all of the TUXEDO run-time software, just enough to package up the information associated with the operation and get it to a system that does have all of the TUXEDO software. This includes the front end of all of the TUXEDO ATMI functions, plus the networking software. The only other information needed is a network address for the target machine, normally provided by the administrator.

The administrator configures in the TMIB one or more *Workstation Listeners* (*WSLs*) to listen for connection requests from workstation clients. Each **WSL** uses one or more associated *Workstation Handlers* (*WSHs*) to handle the client's workload. Each **WSH** can manage multiple workstations and multiplexes all requests and replies with a particular workstation over a single connection. We illustrated this architecture in Figure 6.11.

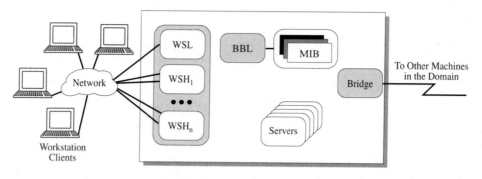

Figure 6.11   Workstation Handling

Using this architecture, a machine can handle thousands of workstation clients, far more than the number of local clients that could be handled by the same machine. Also, note that administrators can define several **WSL**s in the domain to distribute and balance the workstation communication load across the different machines in the domain.

From the client application programmer's point of view, this architecture is transparent. All of the client ATMI programming interfaces are provided for workstation client development. In fact, a few additional primitives are available on several of the workstation platforms to make better use of the features specific to those environments. For instance, under Microsoft Windows, there is an interface to set up receiving asynchronous messages from servers so that an application-specified event is generated on a Windows message queue.

6.5.2.2 Application Queue Management

In Chapter 4, "Application Development—Overview," we introduced the main characteristics of the TUXEDO /Q application queuing subsystem. This subsystem allows application programmers to write applications that communicate by accessing one or more application queues. However, programmers have no knowledge of where these application queues are located. This transparency permits application administrators to move application queues from one machine to another without having to tell programmers to change their application code.

Application administrators are in charge of configuring the /Q environment in the TMIB. This environment consists of the queue base, queue spaces, and queues needed by the application, and the TUXEDO System servers for enqueuing and dequeuing messages from a queue space. TUXEDO administrators can use the graphical interface or command line administrative tools to define queue spaces, queues, and the TUXEDO administrative servers in the TMIB.

Figure 6.12 illustrates the /Q administrative environment and provides an example of application queuing and forwarding. Imagine that the workstation client enqueues an order for a catalog item into the "OrderEntry" queue (flow 1) and a couple of days later, the workstation client accesses the "OrderStatus" queue (flow 4) to find the status of the order. Access to the queues in the "Order" queue space is controlled by a TUXEDO administrative server, called **TMQUEUE**, configured by the administrator to manage that queue space. The **TMQUEUE** server enqueues and dequeues messages for queues stored on a predefined queue space. By convention, the queue space name is associated with the administrative enqueuing service provided by the **TMQUEUE** server.

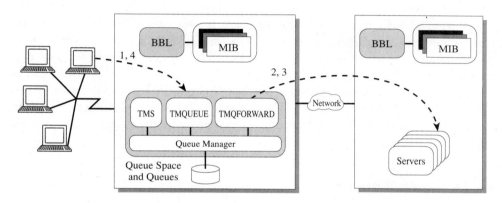

Figure 6.12   **Application Queue Management**

Orders stored in the "OrderEntry" queue may be processed by an application service. The TUXEDO System provides an administrative server, called **TMQFORWARD**, that dequeues messages from a queue and forwards (flow 2 in Figure 6.12) these messages to an application service. The use of the **TMQFORWARD** server requires the convention that a queue name is equivalent to a service name. This convention allows the server to dequeue automatically and to forward messages to a server advertising the application service.

Features discussed earlier, such as load-balancing, priorities, data dependent routing, and time-out, apply to these forwarded messages. If the requested service succeeds, then the reply message is enqueued to a predefined reply queue (flow 3 in Figure 6.12). If the service fails, then the initial service request is put back into the queue and **TMQFORWARD** will try later to forward this service request. When the retry limit is reached, the request will be stored in the error queue associated with the queue space. However, this behavior can be changed by specifying that replies from failed services be enqueued to a failure queue and that the corresponding service request message be removed from the queue. We will discuss this and other related characteristics of application queuing in more detail in Chapter 12, "Application Queues."

6.5.2.3 Event Management

In Chapter 4, "Application Development—Overview," we introduced the TUXEDO event-based communications paradigm. Application programs subscribe to events posted by another application program or to administrative events posted by the TUXEDO System. The TUXEDO System EventBroker keeps track of these subscriptions. The EventBroker receives all event postings and performs actions associated with the subscriptions that match the event. These actions are called *event notifications.*

The EventBroker consists of two administrative servers: the system event broker (**TMSYSEVT**) and the application event broker (**TMUSREVT**). Administrators need to configure these servers in the TMIB to enable event-based communication. Events posted by the TUXEDO System are filtered and distributed by the **TMSYSEVT** administrative server. Events posted by the application code are filtered and distributed by the **TMUSREVT** administrative server. This architecture allows the TUXEDO System to deliver events generated by the system without having "interference" (delays) from the events generated by the application.

6.5.2.4 Security Management

Application administrators should configure their applications with an appropriate level of security. They can use one of several incremental levels of security provided by the TUXEDO System. These security levels vary from no authentication for secure environments to an access control facility that filters who can execute a services, post an event, or enqueue (or dequeue) a message on an application queue.

The TUXEDO System uses the operating system security facilities to create a *trusted-base* for the servers and system resources. For example, an application can be configured so that all servers have restricted access to shared resources, such as shared memory and message queues. This restricted access uses operating system permissions so that only the application administrator can have access to these resources. As a result of this, servers must execute with the administrator's identity and permissions to be allowed to update the TUXEDO System resources. Another consequence is that the code of an application service must be trusted by the administrator. This implies that the code does not perform any malicious attack against the rest of the application.

On the other hand, clients are outside the trusted-base, and therefore, they are not trusted. With the TUXEDO System, administrators can use incremental levels of authentication and authorization to protect access to the application against unauthorized end users. For example, you can specify that clients must provide an application and an end-user password when they join the application. Also, you can control access to a service with an access control list (ACLs) that specifies who can execute the service.

Authentication is enforced by the TUXEDO run-time system when the client program joins the application. A TUXEDO administrative server, the **AUTHSRV** server, provides the authentication service that verifies whether the end-user joining the application exists in the TMIB and has the correct password. Administrators can also provide their own administrative service. Note, however, that the security service and the **AUTHSRV** are transparent to the application programmer.

To enable authentication and authorization services, administrators need to configure in the TMIB

▌ the **AUTHSRV** administrative server

▌ the identity and passwords of any authorized end users

▌ the access control lists enforced on services, application queues, and events

We will explain these security services in more detail later in Part IV, "Administration of a TUXEDO Application."

6.5.2.5 Cooperation Between Different Applications

By definition, a TUXEDO application is *autonomous*—administered independently from other applications. For this reason, a TUXEDO application is also called a *domain*. The scope of the administrative tasks is a primary factor in the architecture of a distributed application. Other factors could be the size of the application, the organizational policies within the enterprise, the trusted boundaries, and the groups of users that need access to shared resources and services.

A TUXEDO application can cooperate with other applications to form large federated applications. This cooperation consists of specifying what application services are accessible across applications. One application *exports* information about how to access a set of application services, and other applications *import* this information. An example of application cooperation is the catalog order company example that we used in previous chapters. The catalog company can organize its application around two separate applications: the Order Entry application and Warehouse application. The Order Entry application controls order placement (for example, by telemarketing representatives, phone operators, electronic mail, and fax), order status, customer billing and credit verification. The Warehouse application controls the stock of items in the catalog, updates to the catalog, and the delivery of ordered items to the customers. The Order Entry and the Warehouse application are not completely disjoint. For instance, the Order Entry application needs to know the availability of items stored at the Warehouse, and the Warehouse application may need to update the status of an order.

Thus, the Warehouse application exports information about how the Order Entry application can use some of its services to obtain the required information from the Warehouse databases. This information is reflected to Order Entry programmers as new services that they can use in their application. For example, application programmers could modify the "Place_Order" service to call the "Check_Item" service to find the availability of a particular stock item but they don't need to know that the "Check_Item" service is executed in another application. Hence, the TUXEDO approach for interapplication cooperation makes the mechanisms involved in this cooperation totally transparent to application programmers and emphasizes the role of the administrator as the person who controls this cooperation.

Our example can be extended as shown on Figure 6.13. A Warehouse can cooperate with other Warehouses or with other companies (Suppliers) to obtain items that are in short supply. These companies can also cooperate with other applications, and so on. The Order Entry application can be split across regional centers that may use the services exported by any of Warehouse applications. The Order Entry application may also use the services provided by other companies for credit card verification.

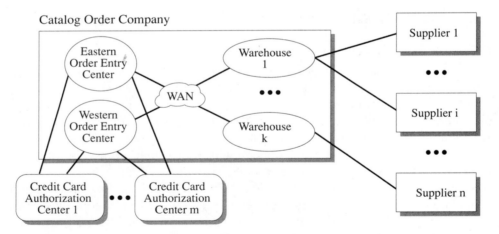

Figure 6.13   A Catalog Order System—An Example of Interapplication Cooperation

The TUXEDO System provides interapplication cooperation with the TUXEDO Domains facility. This facility consists of a set of administrative tools that allows administrators to specify which services are accessible across applications. We will discuss this administrative environment in more detail in Chapter 18, "Getting Applications to Work Together."

6.6 Summary

In this chapter, we provided an overview of the different architectural elements that make up a TUXEDO application. We discussed the basic and advanced services provided by the TUXEDO System. In most cases, the definition of the architecture of a distributed application is a task for application designers and application administrators. Application administrators enable the advanced TUXEDO services by defining the corresponding administrative servers in the TUXEDO TMIB. Administrators also decide how these administrative servers are deployed within the different computers used by the distributed application.

This chapter also ends our overview of the main features provided by the TUXEDO System. In the following part of the book, we will discuss how to develop applications with the TUXEDO ATMI interface.

III

Development of a TUXEDO Application

Part II, "Overview of the TUXEDO System," described the programming and administration interfaces and facilities provided in the TUXEDO System at a high level. This part of the book will describe the programming interface, ATMI, in more detail. It assumes some knowledge of the C and COBOL programming languages.

We start off with an introduction to the API as a whole, considering the philosophy behind the API design and characteristics common to many of the ATMI primitives. Typed buffers are used throughout the interface to allow for flexible representation of the data and are discussed next. Then, a chapter is devoted to each of the four communications paradigms: request/response, conversations, application queuing, and events. This part ends with a detailed discussion of how transactions can be used to bracket these communications calls to ensure that all or none of the work gets done.

7 Introduction to the Application Programming Interface

ATMI, the TUXEDO API, provides a unified interface for communications, transactions, and management of data buffers. This chapter will provide a road map to the TUXEDO application interface and will also describe the environments in which you develop and run your application.

The design goals of the interface were to provide an easy-to-use interface that is powerful, yet intuitive. A guiding principle was the "principle of least astonishment." That is, the primitives behave in a manner that would be expected by an application developer and, in cases where there might be multiple interpretations, the one that is least surprising is chosen.

The TUXEDO System runs in a large number of different environments. The important thing to remember is that the same TUXEDO application programming interface is used in all of these environments. This protects the investment in your application development, because the same software can be moved between the different environments, recompiled, and run. Further, the administration subsystem ties it all together, giving the administrator a single view of your entire application.

We will finish this chapter describing how to combine your application code with the TUXEDO run-time to create client and server programs. Using tools provided with the TUXEDO System, it's easy! We also indicate the differences in building clients and servers using the ATMI interface versus the RPC paradigm which is based on an interface definition.

7.1 The API and Language Environments

The two primary languages that are used for writing application clients and servers are C and COBOL. C++ can also be used for development. The style of the C and COBOL bindings are different, each using natural constructs for the associated programmers, so we will discuss them individually starting with C. Then we will consider mixed language environments and interoperability with other programming environments.

7.1.1 C Binding for ATMI Primitives

The C language interface for ATMI makes use of the full range of C language features. This includes the use of pointers for passing messages, pointers to pointers that allow for dynamically reallocating buffers to be large enough to hold incoming messages, function pointers for application handler or call-back functions, and C structures to provide input and output information for the various primitives. The application code can be written in either Classic C (the original dialect of the C language as proposed by Kernighan and Ritchie [Kernighan]), or ANSI Standard C [ANSIX3159]. The choice is based on what compilers are available on the development platforms and the style chosen by the development organization. Most platforms provide at least an option to compile using ANSI C. To get some of the benefits of ANSI C, such as stronger type checking of parameters, many applications are converting to or being written from scratch in ANSI C.

For the most part, the C++ language is a superset of the C language. As such, it can be used transparently for development with the TUXEDO software. The TUXEDO interfaces use the C calling convention which allows for the use of mixed C and C++ application software within the same program. The TUXEDO interfaces do not take advantage of any of the C++ features, such as C++ classes, but an application programmer can use whichever features are appropriate for the application. In fact, the function shipping model tends to push the application design toward being more modular, and this fits in well with the object orientation of C++. Applications can design objects and methods that abstract the TUXEDO interface. For instance, instead of sending a message to a service request to retrieve or update some data, the application can be designed or viewed as an operation or method on an object.

In the C binding, parameters to the communication primitives generally include a name, application data and its length, and control information. For example, the **tpacall** routine has the following prototype.

```
int tpacall(char *service, char *appdata, long datalen,
            long flags)
```

This is prototypical of many of the routines in the interface (some are simpler). Once you understand this, you're halfway there!

The name may be a service name or the name of a queue manager and an application queue or event name. Names are always string values assigned by the application. There are no arcane data types to be populated, and binding is automatically done by the TUXEDO System based simply on the string. Built into this automatic binding are factors such as network loads, load balancing between servers offering the same service, and routing based on application data. The application programmer doesn't need to worry about any of these details.

The application data is passed in a single data buffer that is allocated from the system. This will be discussed in much greater detail in the next chapter. The buffer contains all of the application information to be passed to the service, and the TUXEDO System transparently handles data conversion when moving the message between heterogeneous machines. This approach to presentation services allows for a single interface that handles any type of data in its local representation without application-level conversion.

All functions use copy semantics when dealing with input buffers. That is, the data is copied during the function call so that, upon return, the buffer can immediately be reused. This allows for greater and transparent parallelism in the application.

When messages are received, the system automatically grows the buffer dynamically to hold the message, if necessary, so that the application programmer doesn't need to worry about truncation of the message. Output buffer parameters require a pointer to a pointer to allow for reallocation of the buffer. In the case of **tpcall** which has both input and output data, two buffers are used instead of a single buffer. By using separate parameters for input and output, you have the choice of using two different buffer parameters, so that the data that is sent is preserved, or you can use the same buffer for both input and output. This is shown in Listing 7.1. Note that the third parameter for the **tpcall**, which is the request length, can be set to 0 because the system can compute how much data is to be sent. The second **tpcall** can be done without repopulating the request buffer because the reply for the first **tpcall** is received into a second buffer. The second **tpcall** uses the same buffer for the input and output, avoiding allocation of a third buffer.

```
char *buffer, *reply;
long len;
int ret1, ret2;

buffer = (char *)tpalloc("STRING", "", 100);  /* 100 byte request buffer */
reply = (char *)tpalloc("STRING", "", 100);   /* 100 byte reply buffer */
strcpy(buffer, "My data");
tpbegin(30,TPNOFLAGS);
                                              /* start 30-second transaction */
ret1 = tpcall("firstservice",    buffer, 0, &reply, &len, TPNOFLAGS);
if (ret1 != -1)
     ret2 = tpcall("secondservice", buffer, 0, &buffer, &len, TPNOFLAGS);
if (ret1 == -1 || ret2 == -1) {
     printf("%\n", tpstrerror(tperrno));    /* print error* /
     tpabort(TPNOFLAGS);                     /* rollback transaction */
}
else {
     printf("Application returned %ld\n", tpurcode);
     tpcommit(TPNOFLAGS);                    /* complete transaction */
```

Listing 7.1 *API Usage*

In most cases the control information consists of flags contained in a single, long integer. The flags allow for fine control of the operation without calling additional primitives. The flag values are common to most of the ATMI functions and include options that affect the nature of the current transaction, operation blocking, and interrupts. The default behavior of the API without setting flags is chosen to be what most applications would want in the default case. In Listing 7.1, the last parameter to **tpcall**, which is the flags value, is set to **TPNOFLAGS**. The call will automatically get a time-out if it takes too long, and will be included in the existing transaction.

Handling of time-outs and signals is built into the interface. You don't have to set alarms to make sure that a remote call comes back in a reasonable amount of time, and a single flag can be used to automatically restart functions after a signal is processed.

Call-back functions are defined or registered with the system for further control when the application needs to do more specific processing. In some cases, the application call-back function simply replaces the default function provided at link time. In other cases, the application can change the function on-the-fly by passing a function pointer. Call-back functions are used in the following cases:

■ handling notification messages (also called unsolicited messages) in clients

■ initialization and termination functions for servers

■ dynamically advertised services

On error, all of the C primitives return NULL (for pointers) or −1 (for non-pointers). Further information is available via an error variable, **tperrno**. This error variable is thread-specific in environments where multiple tasks share data. Some primitives also return an application return value from the server to the caller via another thread-specific variable, **tpurcode**. In Listing 7.1, error processing is done after the second **tpcall**. On an error return −1, a message associated with the error type **tperrno** is printed by calling **tpstrerror**. Otherwise, the returned application code is printed using **tpurcode**.

Transaction demarcation primitives, **tpbegin** and **tpcommit**, can bracket the communications calls. The TUXEDO System is responsible for keeping track of all of the work that is done between these calls, freeing the application programmer from this burden. Most important, the transaction semantics guarantee an all-or-nothing unit of work, as described in Chapter 3, "Communication and Administration Paradigms for Distributed Business Applications." The two **tpcall**s shown in Listing 7.1 will both be done or the effects will be rolled back as if they had never been called.

You will not see anything in the interface to directly indicate parallelism. If two asynchronous calls end up on the same queue or in two services that go against the same database transaction, they will be transparently serialized. Work on different queues or different database transactions will generally proceed in parallel. Partitioning application data to allow for more parallelism usually requires little more than administrative changes to route the data to the correct services. No changes to the application software are needed to specify parallel access.

You also will not see functions to access any resource managers that are used by the application. All RM actions are done by calling the RM's Data Manipulation Language directly, for example, executing an SQL statement for an RDBMS. There are a pair of functions to open and close all RMs associated with a client or server. This allows for portably setting up the connection between the TM and the RMs without specifying any information at the application level. The TM knows what to do based on the configuration and the way that the programs were built (more is said about this later in this chapter).

Finally, there are not any server primitives to do network and connection management, listening for requests, or dispatching services. All of this is handled automatically, as described in Chapter 9, "Joining and Leaving the Application." You do not need to know the server in which a service is running. You just concentrate on doing the work that your application needs to accomplish for each service.

The following is a table summarizing all of the ATMI primitives for both the C and COBOL bindings. Note that N/A indicates that the primitive does Not Apply for one of the bindings. These interfaces are described in chapters in Part III of this book as listed in the table.

API Group	C API Name	COBOL Name	Description	Chapter
Client Membership	tpchkauth	TPCHKAUTH	check if authentication is needed	9.2.1.2
	tpinit	TPINITIALIZE	used by a client to join the application	9.2.1
	tpterm	TPTERM	used by a client to leave the application	9.2.1
Buffer Management	tpalloc	N/A	create a message	8.1
	tprealloc	N/A	resize a message	8.1
	tpfree	N/A	free a message	8.1
	tptypes	N/A	get a message type and subtype	8.1
Message Priority	tpgprio	TPGPRIO	get priority of last request	10.3.2
	tpsprio	TPSPRIO	set priority of next request	10.3.1
Request/Response Communications	tpcall	TPCALL	synchronous request/response to a service	10.1.1
	tpacall	TPACALL	asynchronous request (fanout)	10.2.1
	tpgetreply	TPGETRPLY	receive asynchronous response	10.2.1
	tpcancel	TPCANCEL	cancel asynchronous request	10.2.1
Conversational Communications	tpconnect	TPCONNECT	begin a conversation with a service	11.1
	tpdiscon	TPDISCON	abnormally terminate a conversation	11.4
	tpsend	TPSEND	send a message in a conversation	11.2
	tprecv	TPRECV	receive a message in a conversation	11.2
Reliable Queuing	tpenqueue	TPENQUEUE	enqueue message to application queue	12.1.1
	tpdequeue	TPDEQUEUE	dequeue message from application queue	12.1.2

Table 7.1　The ATMI Interface (*cont.*)

API Group	C API Name	COBOL Name	Description	Chapter
Event-Based Communications	tpnotify	TPNOTIFY	send unsolicited message to a client	13.1.2
	tpbroadcast	TPBROADCAST	send messages to several clients	13.1.3
	tpsetunsol	TPSETUNSOL	set unsolicited message call-back	13.1.1
	tpchkunsol	TPCHKUNSOL	check arrival of unsolicited message	13.1
	N/A	TPGETUNSOL	get unsolicited message	13.1
	tppost	TPPOST	post an event message	13.2.2
	tpsubscribe	TPSUBSCRIBE	subscribe to event messages	13.2.1
	tpunsubscribe	TPUNSUBSCRIBE	unsubscribe to event messages	13.2.3
Transaction Management	tpbegin	TPBEGIN	begin a transaction	14.2.1
	tpcommit	TPCOMMIT	commit the current transaction	14.4.1
	tpabort	TPABORT	rollback the current transaction	14.4.2
	tpgetlev	TPGETLEV	check if in transaction mode	14.2.2
	tpsuspend	TPSUSPEND	suspend the current transaction	14.4.3
	tpresume	TPRESUME	resume a transaction	14.4.3
	tmscmt	TPSCMT	control commit return	14.4.1
Service Entry and Return	tpsvrinit	TPSVRINIT	server initialization	9.3.2
	tpsvrdone	TPSVRDONE	server termination	9.3.4
	service	N/A	prototype for service entry point	10.1.1
	N/A	TPSVCSTART	get service information	10.1.2
	tpreturn	TPRETURN	end service function	10.1.2
	tpforward	TPFORWAR	forward request (pipeline parallelism)	10.1.3
Dynamic Advertisement	tpadvertise	TPADVERTISE	advertise a service name	9.3.5
	tpunadvertise	TPUNADVERTISE	unadvertise a service name	9.3.5
Resource Management	tpopen	TPOPEN	open a resource manager	9.2.2
	tpclose	TPCLOSE	close a resource manager	9.2.4

Table 7.1 Continued

Note that there are actually two bindings from the C language. The first binding, the ATMI binding, listed in Table 7.1, is library based (system-defined library routines). The second binding, TxRPC, is language-based. It has what looks like calls to application routines, but the processing is done in remote servers. It is discussed further in Chapter 10, "Request/Response Communication."

7.1.2 COBOL Binding for ATMI Primitives

Many programmers are trained to write and maintain programs in the COBOL language. That is no problem in the TUXEDO environment because the TUXEDO System provides a COBOL binding for ATMI. The COBOL interface provides the same client/server model and similar semantics to the C interface but is quite different in appearance. Using C bit-twiddling and null-terminated strings is quite foreign to COBOL programmers. The COBOL interface provides the same functionality as the C interface but in a manner which a COBOL programmer would find comfortable.

Instead of using C header files, COBOL copy files are used to define records to pass information to and from the TUXEDO COBOL interface and among parts of the application.

In the COBOL binding, the communication **CALL**s generally need four parameters: a record that defines the name string and other control information for the call, a record that defines the data type, subtype, and length for the application data, an application record for the input/output data, and a status record to get the returned status information from the call. For example, Listing 7.2 shows a call to **TPACALL**.

```
01 TPSVCDEF-REC.
       COPY TPSVCDEF.
01 TPTYPE-REC.
       COPY TPTYPE.
01 DATA-REC.
       COPY User data.
01 TPSTATUS-REC.
       COPY TPSTATUS.
CALL "TPACALL" USING TPSVCDEF-REC TPTYPE-REC DATA-REC
       TPSTATUS-REC.
```

Listing 7.2 *Sample COBOL CALL*

The name string is stored in a predefined record structure, declared in a system-supplied COBOL copy file, **TPSVCDEF**. This record contains everything needed to define the communication operation, combining the service or queue manager name string and control information (that was multiple parameters in C). In Listing 7.2, it is named **TPSVCDEF-REC**. The C bit values in a single flag are replaced with flag words that indicate whether or not the option is in effect for the operation (for example, whether or not the operation should block). As in C, the default behavior is what we anticipate that most applications will use. In COBOL, the default is selected by setting the flag word to **LOW VALUES**.

Dynamically allocating space in COBOL is also not the norm. The COBOL application programmer uses application-defined records declared in the COBOL DATA section for describing the format of messages. In Listing 7.2, it is named DATA-REC. A second predefined record type is used to provide information about the record for communication operations and has an associated truncation indicator. In Listing 7.2, it is named **TPTYPE-REC**. This information includes the buffer type and subtype, and the record length. This record can be reused from call to call, assuming that the application is frequently using the same buffer type. When receiving a message, the data area cannot be dynamically reallocated to hold larger records, and it is possible that the buffer will be truncated. This is an additional detail that the programmer may need to handle. However, because COBOL applications generally work with fixed records, getting a record that is unexpectedly too big should not be a common occurrence.

Pointers to call-back functions are not needed. Functions to handle unsolicited notification are built into the program at fixed locations, and the programmer simply indicates which function to use for each purpose (see Chapter 13, "Event-Based Communication"). Dynamic service advertisement is done by program name instead of using function pointers (see Chapter 9, "Joining and Leaving the Application").

The return information for the TUXEDO COBOL interface is collected into a single predefined record structure that contains the operation return status, the application return code, if available, and possibly an event for conversational communications.

7.1.3 Other Language Environments

While some applications may use a single language, other applications will use a mix of languages based on either existing application software or the use of different languages in different environments. Applications can mix the languages, so, for example, a client could be written in COBOL, and the server could be written in C or vice versa. This allows for modules to be written in the most appropriate language, mixing old and new modules where necessary. Modules within a single program can also be mixed, although this is much less common.

Beyond C and COBOL, the TUXEDO interfaces can be called from any language that can call C-language procedures, either statically or dynamically. Many environments support dynamic linking, so that software objects can be dynamically loaded and executed. In the POSIX and X Windows arena, several command interpreters, such as the Desktop Korn Shell [Pendergrast] and TCL [Ousterhout], allow programs to be written in a high-level language that can call functions in dynamically loaded, shared objects. In the Microsoft Windows environment, Microsoft's Visual Basic can be used to write BASIC programs, or Borland's Delphi can be used to write Pascal programs, that call functions in a Dynamic Link Library.

Many third party vendors have extended their 4th Generation Language (4GL) products to specifically support the TUXEDO programming interface for client/server development, including the use of transactions. Using these languages greatly increases the programmer's productivity and provides for applications with state-of-the-art screen handling. The programmer may or may not actually see ATMI when using these tools.

Thus, the core interfaces for the TUXEDO System may be defined in C and COBOL, but there is a rich variety of languages available for developing distributed TUXEDO applications. Some of the factors that may influence your decision include the following:

- platforms where you want your client and server programs to run
- the ease-of-development of the various languages and development environments
- proficiency in a specific language
- availability of debugging tools
- the performance of the various environments (compiled or interpreted)
- cost

Chances are very high that, if you want to use a particular language or development tool, it will work with the TUXEDO System.

We are about to discuss the interfaces, paradigms, and features that you can use for creating your application. Before doing that, we will describe how to package the TUXEDO software with your own application software to create clients and servers.

7.2 Building Clients

As an application programmer, you write the application software that implements the external interfaces and business rules and actions, calling the TUXEDO software for the transaction management and communications between clients and servers. Once the client code is written, it is time to combine it with the TUXEDO software to produce an executable program. This step is simplified by a TUXEDO program to pull it all together.

The program **buildclient** takes a list of application files and libraries, compiles any C or COBOL source files using available compilers, and links them together with the necessary TUXEDO object and library files. The application programmer need not know the names of the TUXEDO libraries, or the operating system and networking libraries. To include an RM for use in a client program, the programmer simply specifies the name of the desired RM. The administrator preconfigures a table that has all of the information needed to include and use the RM: its name, the name of the data structure that provides access to its transaction primitives, and the object files and libraries needed. Listing 7.3 compiles a C client program, **empclient**, with an emp.c source file, an applib.a application library, and the MYSQL (pick your favorite) database.

It's that simple! You may not appreciate this simplicity unless you have ported an application between various platforms and realize how different compiler options and library names are between environments.

```
buildclient -o empclient -f emp.c -l applib.a -r MYSQL
```

Listing 7.3 *Creating a C Client*

To build a COBOL client, it is simply a matter of using the -C option, and specifying COBOL source code as in Listing 7.4.

```
buildclient -C -o empclient -f emp.cbl -l applib.a -r MYSQL
```

Listing 7.4 *Creating a COBOL Client*

When building a workstation client on a POSIX platform, it is simply a matter of including a -w argument on the command line to build the client. On other platforms, the compilation for a workstation client may need a bit more information, including the target platform. For instance, for DOS, the target compilation system and a memory model must be specified. For 16-bit MS Windows, the target must be specified along with a compilation system, a memory model, and a Windows definition file. Remember that, in spite of the fact that there are some platform dependent compilation options, the ATMI interface is completely portable and your software need not change as you move it to different environments.

We talked earlier about environments that interpret the application code and use execution of dynamically loaded libraries. In these environments, you do not even need to build the TUXEDO client. Generally, you need only indicate to the program where to get the TUXEDO software. For instance, in Microsoft's Visual Basic, a call to the primitive **tpbegin** for a client to start a transaction would require the definition in Listing 7.5.

```
Declare Function TPBEGIN Lib "WTUXWS.DLL" (ByVal opl As Long) As Integer
```

Listing 7.5 *Visual Basic Definition for ATMI Primitive*

This statement indicates that the Dynamic Link Library where the code lives is called WSTUXWS.DLL, the function takes a single parameter and it returns an integer. After including this line, the application programmer can simply call this primitive as if it were a built-in function. No compilation or linking is required. Once considered by some to be toys, more and more application programmers are turning to these front end graphical development environments to increase programming productivity in building client/server applications.

7.3 Building Servers

The process of putting together a server is similar to that for a client. It's a matter of combining the application service procedures that implement the business logic with the TUXEDO server adaptor that accepts messages, dispatches the work, and manages transactions (if they are being used by the application). As with building a client, there is a program to create servers. The program **buildserver** takes a list of application files and libraries, compiles any C or COBOL source files using the system compilers, and links them together with the necessary TUXEDO object and library files, and RM files if one is included.

Unlike a client, a server needs to advertise the services that it is making available to clients and other servers. In Chapter 9, "Joining and Leaving the Application," we will describe the four methods for indicating which services should be advertised for each server: at build time, at boot time, administratively while the server is running, and from within the server itself. Before a service can be advertised using one of these approaches, its associated service entry point must be defined when the server is built. The names of the service entry points, functions in C and programs in COBOL, are resolved to an address by the compilation system when the server is link-edited. Services names are then associated with the service entry points so that when a request is received for a service, the associated function or program can be called.

The easiest way to associate service names with entry points is to statically define the mapping when the server is built, using the -s command line option of **buildserver**. The simplest mapping is for each service name to match the name of the function or program implementing that service. That is, there is a one-to-one mapping of service name to function name. This is done by listing the service names when building the server. It is also possible to give an explicit mapping of service name to function name, or even map more than one service to the same function. This can be useful in designing an application in which many service requests come into a single service where the application does the dispatching based on the service name, possibly after doing some work that is common to all of the services.

To compile a C server program, **empserver**, with an empserver.c source file, an applib.a application library, and the MYSQL database with three services, A, B, and C, all mapping to a single function, MYFUNCTION, you could run the command in Listing 7.6.

A COBOL server would be built in the same manner by adding the -C command line option.

```
buildserver -o empserver -f empserver.c -l applib.a -r MYSQL
    -s A,B,C:MYFUNCTION
```

Listing 7.6 *Creating a Server*

Figure 7.1 shows the various pieces that are pulled together to build a client or server.

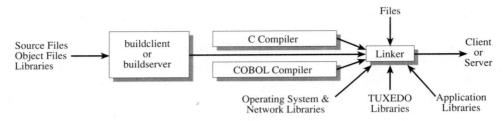

Figure 7.1   **Building Application Clients and Servers**

7.4   Building TxRPC Clients and Servers

The clients and servers in the last two sections were those that used the ATMI library interface. Building clients and servers that use the language-based approach of TxRPC will need a few additional steps. Figure 7.2 shows the steps needed to build an RPC server.

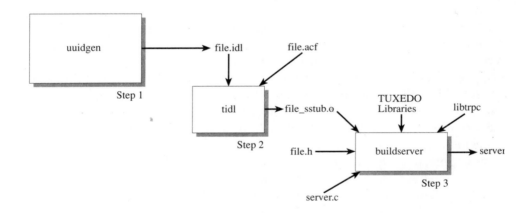

Figure 7.2   **Building an RPC Server**

Step 1. Run **uuidgen** to generate a template .idl file. The template includes a *Universal Unique Identifier (UUID)* that distinguishes this interface from all others. Edit the template to define the data types and functions in your interface using the Interface Definition Language. Some attributes of the interface can only be included using an attribute control file (.acf). These attributes include information relating to status variables and bindings.

Step 2. Run **tidl**, the IDL compiler, using file.idl and optionally file.acf, to generate the interface header file, file.h, and the server stub object file, file_sstub.o.

Step 3. After writing the server application code, server.c, run **buildserver** to compile it and link it with the server stub, and TUXEDO libraries, and the TxRPC library to generate a server.

To finish the client/server pair, the client program must be built. **uuidgen** is run only once for each client/server pair so that the UUID matches for the two halves. Figure 7.3 shows the remaining two steps.

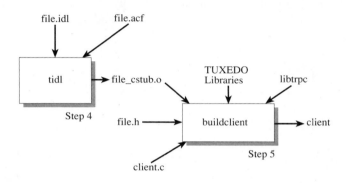

Figure 7.3   **Building an RPC Client**

Step 4. Run **tidl**, the IDL compiler, using file.idl and optionally file.acf, to generate the interface header file, file.h, and the client stub object file, file_cstub.o. It is possible to generate both the client and server in step 2 and avoid this step.

Step 5. After writing the client application code, client.c, run **buildclient** to compile it and link it with the client stub, the TUXEDO libraries, and the TxRPC library to generate a client.

So the additional steps in building an RPC client and server are the generation of the IDL template using **uuidgen** and defining the interface, generating the stubs using **tidl**, and linking in the stub files and the TxRPC library.

7.5   Summary

The TUXEDO System provides a wide range of communication paradigms and control over distributed transactions in a small, well-designed interface. The primitives are designed with the application programmer in mind. Whichever binding you plan to use, you can expect to find a consistent and easy-to-use (unastonishing) interface. Although the TUXEDO application programming interfaces are defined for the C and COBOL languages, the application software can be written in any language or development environment that can either statically or dynamically call the C or COBOL interfaces. The TUXEDO software runs on a large variety of computers and operating system platforms. However, the operating system and networking between computers is transparent to the application programmer—the same programming interfaces are available on each platform.

The chapter finished by describing how to build TUXEDO clients and servers. Building clients and servers requires listing which source, object, and library files to include in the executable programs, optionally including an RM. When using TxRPC, additional steps are needed to generate and incorporate the interface stub modules.

8 Typed Buffers

PROGRAMMING

The TUXEDO System allows programs to communicate with each other using different communications paradigms. In this chapter, we will discuss the format of these messages.

Message handling is one of the distinguishing features in the TUXEDO System. In the early versions of the TUXEDO System (before it was commercially sold as TUXEDO), one generic layer of routines was used to send and receive some message formats, but a second layer was provided to handle the special needs of the FML message format (described later in this chapter). Rather than continue to add a new set of routines for each new message format, the concept of typed buffers was born. Using this approach, operations, such as buffer initialization, data conversion for transmission between dissimilar machines and data-dependent routing, happen transparently to your applications. New routines need not be invented.

8.1 Using Typed Buffers: tpalloc, tprealloc, tpfree, tptypes

Typed buffers were introduced in Chapter 4, "Application Development—Overview." Remember that a typed buffer is a piece of memory allocated from the TUXEDO System that has a type and a subtype associated with it. The type and subtype are string names that identify a set of characteristics that belong to the buffer. The TUXEDO System keeps track of the buffer type so that it can perform subsequent operations on the buffer correctly.

To send a message using any of the ATMI communication routines, your application must first get a buffer from the system using the **tpalloc** routine, specifying its size (or 0 to get the default size), its type, and, optionally, its subtype. For example, the buffer type used for fixed collections of data elements (that is, structures or records) has a type of VIEW; the subtype is used to specify the record format name. This is shown in Listing 8.1.

Initially, the application does not have any typed buffers. The **tpalloc** routine is used to get or allocate a typed buffer, **tprealloc** is used to resize a typed buffer, and **tpfree** is used to free a typed buffer. These routines are similar to the ANSI C **malloc**, **realloc**, and **free** functions, but they know about types and subtypes. Specifically, when **tpalloc** is called, in addition to allocating space, an initialization function associated with the specified buffer type is called to set up the new buffer. **tprealloc** takes a pointer to a typed buffer and the new size. Note that be-

```
struct myview *view;
/* size will default to sizeof(struct myview) */
  view = (struct myview *)tpalloc("VIEW", "myview", 0);
/* view = (struct myview *)tprealloc((char *)view, 20);    */
. . . . .
  tpfree((char *)view);
```

Listing 8.1 *Typed Buffer Allocation Example*

cause it does not take a type and subtype, **tprealloc** cannot be used to change the type or subtype of a buffer. Instead, the original buffer should be freed and a new buffer type allocated to change types. **tprealloc** calls the reinitialization function associated with the buffer type. **tpfree** takes one argument which is a buffer pointer. It calls the uninitialization function associated with the buffer type. These associated functions are described later in the chapter.

Listing 8.1 shows the allocation of a VIEW typed buffer and subsequent freeing of the buffer. The size passed to **tpalloc** is set to 0 in this case because the size of the structure is fixed and can be determined by the TUXEDO run-time system. Calling **tprealloc** for fixed-size buffers is not commonly done—it is shown in a comment in the listing to give you an idea how to use the function.

When a message is passed to the TUXEDO run-time system for processing, such as sending a message to a service, the system knows what the type and subtype of the message are and can process the message appropriately. To restrict what buffer types are received by a service, the administrator can, as part of the configuration, specify input buffer types associated with each service. This technique can be used to eliminate the sending of message types that cannot be processed by a service and to simplify processing within the service. When the application service receives an incoming message, it receives both the message and its length. The **tptypes** routine can be used to query to get the buffer's type and subtype although many applications know the types with which they are dealing. The application can then process the message based on the buffer type.

At this point, COBOL programmers may be wondering how this works in an environment that (at least traditionally) lacks dynamic memory allocation. In COBOL programs, space must be statically declared in the DATA section instead of getting it from the system. In addition, another record must always be passed along with the typed buffer that indicates the buffer's length, type, and subtype. Thus, the advantages of typed buffers are preserved, but the method used for manipulating them differs between C and COBOL. Most of the rest of the examples in the book are in C, so here is an example in COBOL.

Listing 8.2 shows the use of a typed buffer in a COBOL program. The length, type, and subtype are set in **TPTYPE-REC**. The length, LEN, could be set to 0

```
01 TPSVCDEF-REC VALUE LOW-VALUES.
   COPY TPSVCDEF.
01 TPTYPE-REC.
   COPY TPTYPE.
01 DATA-REC.
   COPY APP-DATA.
01 TPSTATUS-REC.
   COPY TPSTATUS.

   MOVE LENGTH OF DATA-REC TO LEN IN TPTYPE-REC.
   MOVE "VIEW" TO REC-TYPE IN TPTYPE-REC.
   MOVE "myview" TO SUB-TYPE IN TPTYPE-REC.
   MOVE "MYSERVICE" TO SERVICE-NAME IN TPSVCDEF-REC.
*  Need to set up DATA-REC here
   CALL "TPACALL" USING TPSVCDEF-REC TPTYPE-REC DATA-REC
        TPSTATUS-REC.
```

Listing 8.2   *COBOL Use of Typed Buffer*

because the correct length can be determined from the specified type and subtype; in the listing, it is set explicitly to the length. This example takes a shortcut in setting all of the flags values in the **TPSVCDEF** record by initializing the record to LOW-VALUES.

8.2   The CARRAY and STRING Built-In Types

There are several buffer types that come with the TUXEDO System; they are built-in. The simplest built-in buffer type is just a collection of characters, called a *CARRAY (character array)*. This buffer type is used to handle data opaquely. That is, the TUXEDO run-time system does not interpret the characters of a CARRAY typed buffer in any way. You do not specify any subtype values for this buffer type. Unlike all of the other built-in buffer types, the CARRAY is not self-describing. *Self-describing*, as used in reference to typed buffers, means that the buffer's data type(s) and length can be determined simply by knowing the type and subtype, and by looking at the data. For CARRAY buffers, the data type is known, but because the system does not interpret the data, there is no way of knowing how much data to transmit during an operation. The application is always required to specify a length when passing this buffer type to ATMI communication routines. No data conversion is done when the CARRAY typed buffer moves between machines, and the system cannot automatically do operations, such as data-dependent routing (application hooks can be provided for this and other operations, as we discuss later in this chapter).

Another built-in buffer type is STRING. Like CARRAY, STRING is a collection of characters. However, it follows the C language convention for strings in that it consists of nonnull (where null is a hexadecimal 0) characters and is terminated by a null. Again, you do not specify subtype values for this buffer type. Unlike CARRAYs, the STRING typed buffer is self-describing. The data type is character, and the transmission length can be determined by counting the number of characters in the buffer until reaching the null character. Thus, it is not necessary for the application to specify the length for operations. The TUXEDO run-time can do data conversion automatically by converting characters when going between machines that have different character sets (for example, converting from the ASCII character set to the EBCDIC character set). An example of using a STRING typed buffer was discussed in Chapter 4, "Application Development—Overview."

CARRAY and STRING are simple typed buffers and have no variants in terms of subtypes. Two more powerful buffer types, FML and VIEWS, are also built-in and are described in the next sections. And if these four built-in types do not suit the needs of your application, then you can provide any number of specialized buffer types of your own, as described in Section 8.5.

8.3   The FML Built-In Type

Relational database vendors and their supporters have been stressing the importance of data independence for years [Date]. That is, you want to be able to access and update the data values without having to know how the data is structured and stored. Yet, most programs are written in languages that allow the programmer no data independence; you have to deal directly with data structures. If the structure changes, then your program must change. FML provides this data independence and a lot more.

8.3.1 What Is FML

FML stands for Field Manipulation Language. It is a data structure that stores tagged values. The values are typed and may be multiply occurring, and variable in length. It is an ideal data structure for communications, especially if you want flexibility in enhancing the application protocol as time goes on. With FML, you treat the buffer as an abstract data type and use FML operations to create, modify, delete, and access fields. In your application program, you simply access or update a field in the fielded buffer by referencing its identifier, and the FML run-time then determines where the field is and its data type to perform the operation. Figure 8.1 shows a conceptual view of a client adding a SALARY field to an FML buffer and sending it to a server via **tpcall**. The server can get the field by name, independent of any other fields that might be in the FML message.

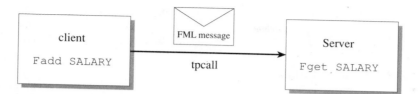

Figure 8.1 **FML Communications**

Each field consists of a field identifier, or tag, and the field value. For fields that can vary in length, a length is also stored with the field. A fielded buffer consists of a header with some housekeeping information and a collection of *identifier-value* pairs and *identifier-length-value* triples. The field identifier, called a FLDID, itself is composed of a unique number assigned by the application and the field type. In this way, the fielded buffer is self-describing. That is, each FML function understands the buffer format and can look at the buffer header to find the number of fields. Each function then searches the buffer, looking at each field. It uses the identifier to know the field's identity via the field number and interprets the contents using the field type, length, and value. Performance is improved by the internal use of indexes, but these are transparent to the application and are not transmitted, so as to save message bandwidth.

There are actually two interfaces to FML. One interface uses 16 bits for field identifiers and the lengths of fields. A second version uses 32 bits, hence the name FML32. The 16-bit version allows for up to approximately 8000 unique fields, character strings and arrays of up to 64,000 bytes, and similar lengths for the entire buffer. The 32-bit interface allows for millions of unique fields and buffer lengths of up to two billion bytes. The functionality between the interfaces is identical. Converting a program from one interface to the other can be as simple as including an extra line (a C header file) in your program. For these reasons, no further mention will be made of the distinction in interfaces. The term "FML" will be used for both.

Figure 8.2 shows a logical representation of a fielded buffer. It contains two types of fields: a NAME field that is a string value and a SALARY field that is a long integer. The NAME field is variable in length and has a length value. There are two occurrences of the SALARY field. Thus, there is a total of three field occurrences in the buffer.

The power of FML comes from its flexibility. Unlike C language structures or COBOL records, the size of the buffer is variable in length, depending on the

NAME/ STRING (32868)	9	John Doe	SALARY/ LONG (4197)	50000	SALARY/ LONG (4197)	60000
FLDID	LENGTH	VALUE	FLDID	VALUE	FLDID	VALUE

Figure 8.2 Fielded Buffer

needs of the application for each message. Character fields can also be variable in length; thus wasted space is avoided. Fielded buffers provide data independence to the application. When writing an application, you do not know how or where the data is stored within a fielded buffer. FML provides associative field access, so that you simply ask for the field by name and its value is then returned.

In many applications, you need to know the data type of a field and would retrieve the field value based on its native type. FML also contains conversion functions, so that you can store or retrieve a field in a particular data format, regardless of the underlying storage type. It also supports storage of more than one value for a field. The variable length format of fielded buffers allows for multiple field occurrences to be stored and retrieved.

The data independence provided by FML has another important advantage as your business application changes and grows. New fields can be added to a fielded buffer. They will be completely transparent to parts of the application that receive the buffer but do not know about these fields. You can implement new features that require additional data elements without having to rebuild all the software or changing message protocols, as is frequently the case with the use of fixed structures. This feature plus data-dependent routing allow for polymorphism, that is, different implementations or versions of a particular service with the same name.

This all sounds great, and you might be wondering what the disadvantages are in using this approach. The primary disadvantage is that your programs use function calls to access each field instead of referencing the structure or record member directly with language constructs. This function call has some overhead cost during development of your programs, and some cost at execution time. However, many applications find this small cost well worth the advantages of the data independence FML provides.

Let's look at a few more details of using FML in your applications.

8.3.2 Fields and Field Tables

Numeric field identifiers (FLDIDs) are the handles used to access and manipulate fields in a fielded buffer. The **mkfldid** primitive takes a unique number assigned to the field by the application programmer and combines it with the field type to generate a field identifier. Computers handle numbers easily. Programmers, however, would find it difficult to remember that the field identifier for NAME is 32868 along with every other field used in the application. So although FML can deal with numeric identifiers alone, applications normally use mnemonic identifiers, like NAME, that represent the fields.

Mappings between field numbers and field names are defined in a *field table*. A field table is stored in a file and is created and maintained with a text editor. For each application field, the file has a line that contains the name or mnemonic for the field, the unique number representing the field, and the field type. Most of the C language data types are supported: short, long, float, double, and char. In addition, the null-terminated string and character array carray data types are also supported.

In the small sample of a field table in Listing 8.3, the two fields shown in the fielded buffer in Figure 8.2 are defined. Lines beginning with # are comments. The NAME field is a string with field number 100; the SALARY field is a long integer field with field number 101. You are responsible for assigning names, numbers, and types to fields.

```
# Field Table
# name   number   type    flags   comment
NAME     100      string  -       Employee name
SALARY   101      long    -       Employee salary in dollars
```

Listing 8.3 *FML Field Table*

This table would be defined once for the entire application and replicated across as many machines as the application spanned including workstations (possibly using networked file systems).

There are two ways to make use of this table, depending on whether the field identifiers are defined statically at compilation time or dynamically at run-time.

The first approach is available at compilation time. When a C programmer is writing a program that calls FML routines requiring a field identifier, the simplest approach is to use a constant value for the field identifier. FML provides a program, **mkfldhdr**, that reads the FML field table and generates a C header file that you can include in your program for this purpose. For each field, a numeric constant is defined for the field name. These named constants or macros can be referenced directly within a program.

In the example in Listing 8.4, the field header file has definitions for the two fields defined in the field table in Listing 8.3. The actual numbers are generated by **mkfldhdr** and have meaning only to the FML run-time system. These defined symbols can be used directly as arguments to various FML functions. This approach is the most convenient way of writing application programs that use specific fields.

```
#define NAME      (FLDID) 32768
#define SALARY    (FLDID) 4197
```

Listing 8.4   *FML Field Header File*

The second approach is available only at run-time. Some application programs, particularly utility programs, may not know what fields they will encounter at run-time. For instance, a utility application might be given a list of field names to be processed in a fielded buffer. FML provides a run-time routine, **Fieldid**, that converts a field name to a field identifier. This could be used to convert the application field names to identifiers for access or update. Another application might print out field values along with the field names. In this case, the program knows the field identifier and needs the associated field name. For both of these mappings, name-to-identifier and identifier-to-name, the FML functions read the application field table at run-time so as to provide the desired information. Recall the discussion about the advantages provided by data independence. New fields can be added to the application simply by adding them to the field tables. These utility application programs could be written so that no changes would be needed to process the new fields.

In Listing 8.5, the SALARY field is used both statically (from the header file) and dynamically. Combining static and dynamic field naming, where appropriate, provides a powerful way to manipulate fielded buffers using the FML routines described in the next section.

```
#include "fml.h>"
#include "flds.h"                            /* generated by mkfldhdr */
FLDID fldid;
FBFR *fbfr;

fbfr = (FBFR *)tpalloc("FML", "", 0);              /* Allocate FML buffer */
salary = Fvall(fbfr, SALARY, 0);/* Get salary value using static field id */
fldid = Fieldid("SALARY");       /* Get fieldid dynamically using string name */
salary = Fvall(fbfr, fldid, 0); /* Get salary value using dynamic field id */
```

Listing 8.5   *Example Using Static and Dynamic Field Identifiers*

8.3.3 FML Functionality

FML is a rich language, with more than 80 routines in the interface. The typical working set has only about ten functions. One of the goals in designing FML was to provide an interface that was simple to use with a wide variety of operations (or methods) on the buffers. Because this book is not a reference guide, it is not our intention to review all the routines of FML. Instead, we give an overview here of the types of features supported.

As typed buffers, FML buffers are allocated, resized, and freed using TUXEDO primitives. **tpalloc, tprealloc,** and **tpfree** are used for these operations, as described in Section 8.1. If FML is used in a program independent of the TUXEDO System and typed buffers, native FML routines are provided for this purpose. To aid in allocating a buffer of the proper size, a routine exists to compute the needed buffer size based on the number of fields and data size estimates. Routines also exist to return the size of the buffer (this is useful in resizing the buffer), the amount of space currently used by a buffer, and the amount of space that is currently free.

The basic set of routines in the FML API provides access and modification of fields in the buffer. Routines exist to add, delete, and modify individual fields. Deletion can be done for a specific field occurrence, for all occurrences of a field, or for all occurrences of a list of fields. Fields can be accessed either by retrieving the value into an application area, by requesting that space be dynamically allocated and returned for the value, by getting a pointer to the value for either a specific field and occurrence or by sequentially scanning through the buffer, one field at a time.

In some cases, you do not need the value itself but merely need to check the existence of the field, or find out how many occurrences exist. Occurrences start numbering at zero and increase as new occurrences of a field are added. When an occurrence is deleted, the occurrence number for all occurrences greater than the deleted occurrence (if any) is decreased by one. That is, they shift lower. So in Figure 8.2 which had the salary values 50000 and 60000, deleting occurrence 0 of the SALARY field would leave the buffer with a single SALARY occurrence with a value of 60000.

FML also has routines that perform automatic type conversion. That is, a field can be specified for addition to the buffer in an application type and automatically converted to the proper type needed to be stored in the fielded buffer, as defined in the field table. Similarly, on retrieval, a field can be retrieved in a desired format independent of the type with which it is stored in the fielded buffer. A common example of this is converting numeric values to strings and vice versa.

The more powerful FML routines manipulate pairs of entire fielded buffers. Among the most straightforward are primitives to copy one fielded buffer to another fielded buffer and to move a fielded buffer into an uninitialized data area. There are also routines to compare fielded buffers, either all fields in both buffers or based on a specified list of fields in which the application is interested. There is also a routine to pull out or "project" fields from one buffer into another based on a specified list of fields.

The most powerful routines deal with merging two buffers. There are four ways to do this. In each, the routine takes a source and destination buffer and results are placed in the destination buffer.

1. Concatenation: The fields from the source buffer are added to the fields already in the destination buffer. If occurrences of a field exist in both the source and destination buffers, the occurrences in the destination buffer are preserved, and new occurrences are added based on the source buffer. For example, say the source buffer has one occurrence of B and one occurrence of C, and the destination buffer has one occurrence of A and one occurrence of B. The resultant destination buffer will have one occurrence of A, two occurrences of B (the first from the source and the second from the destination), and one occurrence of C. This is shown in Figure 8.3.

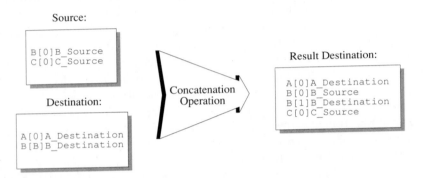

Figure 8.3 FML Concatenation

2. Join: This is similar to a relational database join operation. Fields that match on identifier and occurrence in the source and destination buffers are updated in the destination buffer with the value from the source buffer. If a field and occurrence do not appear in both the source and destination buffers, it will not appear in the resulting destination buffer. An example is shown in Figure 8.4 where only Field B occurrence 0 is in common in both buffers.

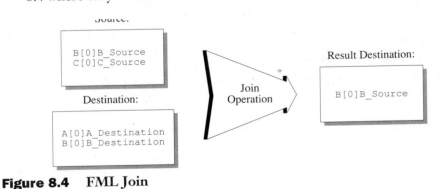

Figure 8.4 FML Join

3. Outer join: This is like a relational database outer join operation. The merge result is similar to the join operation but fields in the destination buffer that have no field identifier/occurrence match in the source buffer are not deleted. An example is shown in Figure 8.5. Notice that the occurrence of Field A appears in the resultant buffer.

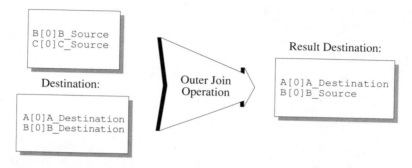

Figure 8.5 **FML Outer Join**

4. Update: Fields in the destination buffer are updated with fields from the source buffer. For fields that match on field identifier and occurrence, the value from the source buffer is copied to the destination buffer. Any field in the source buffer that does not have a matching identifier and occurrence in the destination buffer is added to the destination buffer (similar to concatenation). Fields in the destination buffer that do not have a match in the source buffer are left unchanged (similar to outer join). This is the most commonly used merge primitive. Examples of its use include updating fields in a database record and updating a buffer with new values from an input screen. Notice in Figure 8.6 that the value for Field C occurs in the resultant buffer.

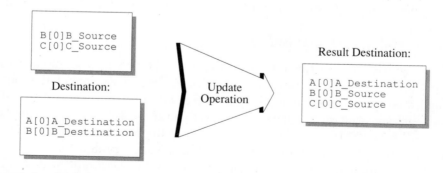

Figure 8.6 **FML Update**

Once you have updated your buffer, you might want to print it out. There are routines to print a buffer in a format that is human-readable. It consists of one line per field, with the field name, white space, and field value printed. A companion function can read the printed version of a buffer and construct a memory version. There are also routines to read and write a fielded buffer "internal" format. This format is the binary representation of the fielded buffer and is more compact than the external format. It is the format used for saving an FML buffer to disk when a person is not going to read it.

Finally, there is a set of routines for evaluating boolean expressions against a fielded buffer. For instance, you might want to check a fielded buffer to see if the NAME field has the value "Smith" and the SALARY field has a value greater than $55000. The expression would be

```
"NAME %% 'Smith' && SALARY[?] > 55000"
```

In this example, the "%%" operation indicates a pattern match instead of an exact equality. Remember that the SALARY field shown in Figure 8.2 had two occurrences. This sample boolean expression will check all occurrences of the SALARY field. If we wanted to check only the first salary field, then we would need to specify an occurrence number, as in SALARY[0]. The boolean expressions supported are quite rich and include most of the operations supported in the C language plus regular expression pattern matching, string comparisons, and matching against an array of field occurrences. Data conversions of the field types are also automatic. **Fboolco** is used to "compile" the expression and **Fboolev** is used to evaluate the compiled expression against any number of fielded buffers. An expression can also be an arithmetic expression, and routines are provided to evaluate an expression against a fielded buffer, returning an integer or a floating point result.

The FML routines provide more than just a replacement for access and update of individual fields in a record. Besides hiding the data representation and record format to give data independence, the FML interface equips the application programmer with a sophisticated set of operations for managing groups of fields.

8.3.4 FML as a Typed Buffer

Now that we have described the features provided by FML, it should be clear that there are many advantages to using fielded buffers in a distributed application. Fielded buffers are a convenient way to ship a collection of fields, perhaps different with each message, from a client to a server and back or to store in an application queue. Use of FML is highly recommended if the interface between clients and servers might change, because the impact of the change is minimal.

As an example of use, a data entry system could make use of FML buffers for all processing. All fields represented on the screen could be stored and updated using FML. Messages would be transmitted to application servers using an FML typed buffer. If messages come in from the screen with fields that are not needed or even known by the application program, they would be ignored. The reply message from the application would be used to update the screen fielded buffer using one of the merge operations. At this point, the screen would be repainted using the field values in the buffer. If there are fields in the FML typed buffer that aren't needed for the screen, again they would be ignored. This permits a very flexible communication mechanism between the data entry program and the application, allowing for fields to be changed in the screen definition and application software independently. In Figure 8.7, the FML buffer is shown with the EMPID and SALARY shared between the client and server, and attributes (fields) specific to the screen and the server.

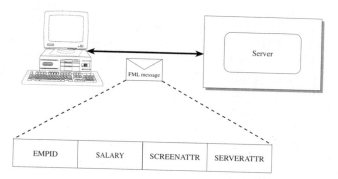

Figure 8.7   **Example Use of FML for Data Entry**

A program called **ud** that comes with the TUXEDO System is a driver program that uses FML buffers to execute service requests. It is good for bulk loading or batch processing. The program reads FML buffers in the printed format, takes the predefined SVCNM field as the name of the service to be executed, and sends the buffer to the service via **tpcall**. The reply FML buffer is printed out using the FML printed format.

Using FML, there are no fixed data structures of which you need to keep track. New fields can be added to the buffer without breaking or recompiling older programs, and it is easy to compare and merge information from the incoming message into an existing buffer. Of course, because these FML fielded buffers are being used as typed buffers, the TUXEDO run-time takes care of transformations like encoding and decoding when the message transfers between different machine types, and getting the buffer ready for transmission. This type of housekeeping work is transparent when you are writing programs, hence the power of typed buffers.

8.4 The VIEW Built-In Type

Not every application needs the power of FML. Nor will some programmers want to program in a way that requires a function call to access and update fields, either by style or for performance reasons. In this case, the normal use of C structures or COBOL records is provided by the VIEW typed buffer.

8.4.1 What are Views

A VIEW is simply a C structure or a COBOL record that has an associated definition of which fields and their types appear in the record in which order. VIEW records are "flat" data structures. That is, they do not support structures within other structures, nor do they allow for arrays of structures or pointers. They support integral data types like long integer, character, and decimal. Arrays of these integral types are also supported. By having these restrictions, you can convert VIEW records to FML records and back. This ability allows for an application to transmit messages as FML buffers for convenience, convert to VIEW records to manipulate the fields as structures, either for style or performance reasons, and then convert back to an FML buffer for transmission of the reply. In fact, this is required for COBOL programmers wishing to use FML messages because not all of the FML interface routines are supported in COBOL due to the lack of pointers in many COBOL implementations. So even if you choose not to use FML for the majority of your application programming, consider it as the transmission message format with VIEWS as the programming format. As described in the data entry program example earlier, new fields can be added to the application and the messages without updating existing programs, which will simply ignore these fields. In this way, the communicating programs need not predefine and/or share views.

Continuing with the earlier example, the C structure corresponding to the information stored in the FML buffer might look like the structure in Listing 8.6. Note that this data structure allows for up to two salary values. The C_salary member is used for a count of how many salary values are actually stored in the structure at run-time (this was transparent when using an FML buffer). That is, it indicates how many of the salary elements are populated.

```
struct employee {
        char name[16];
        short C_salary;        /* count of salary */
        long salary[2];
}
```

Listing 8.6 *C Structure Corresponding to view*

In COBOL, the record might look like Listing 8.7. This COBOL record holds the same information as the C structure. The FILLER is automatically generated by the view compiler (described next) and is used to align the COBOL elements with the equivalent C fields. COMP-5 is used instead of COMP to match the native C integer values.

```
05 NAME PIC X(16).
05 C-SALARY PIC S9(4)  USAGE IS COMP-5.
05 FILLER PIC X(2).
05 SALARY OCCURS 2 TIMES PIC S9(9) USAGE IS COMP -5.
```

Listing 8.7 *COBOL Record Corresponding to VIEW*

Views are described to the TUXEDO System using *view tables*. Once this is done, the generation of the C and COBOL definitions is automatic and ensures compatibility in a mixed language environment. The view definition process is described next.

8.4.2 View Definitions and the View Compiler

To use VIEW buffers, the C or COBOL record is first defined in a *view file*. The view file, like the FML field table, is created with any text editor. The description of the record is called a *view*. More than one view can be defined in a single view file. Each view is given a name. The name corresponds to the name of the structure in the C language and the name of the copy file that is included in a COBOL program. Within the description for each view, there is one line for each field. Lines beginning with # are used for comment lines and are ignored.

```
VIEW EMPSALARY
#TYPE    CNAME    FMLNAME  COUNT   FLAG    SIZE    NULL
string   name     NAME     1       -       16      "\0"
long     salary   SALARY   2       C       -       0
END
```

Listing 8.8 *View File*

Listing 8.8 is a sample view file for the C structure of Listing 8.6 and COBOL record of Listing 8.7. Each field description contains the following information.

■ Field type: This is the data type of the field. There are two additional field types besides those supported in FML. First, a native integer type can be specified because the use of integers within structures is so common. It corresponds to a short or long integer depending on the size of integers on the machine. Second, a decimal type can be specified. This corresponds to packed decimal in COBOL. For programming in C, a special data type is supported with a set of routines to do decimal arithmetic and conversions to other C data types. If the FML exchange feature is being used, then the data type can be defaulted to the data type of the corresponding FML field (remember that the field type is stored in the FML field table). In the example above, the first field is a string and the second is a long integer.

■ Field name: This is the name of the field as it appears in the C structure or COBOL record. Note that the CNAME field values in Listing 8.8 correspond to the names appearing in the C structure; in COBOL, they are converted to uppercase.

■ FML field name: If your application is going to be using the exchange feature to convert VIEWS into FML records and vice versa, then the name of the corresponding FML field must be given. This field name must appear in an FML field table.

■ Field count: This allows for fields with multiple occurrences.

■ Size: For strings and character arrays, this is the maximum length of the value. For decimal fields, it indicates the number of bytes allocated to hold the value and the number of decimal places to the right of the implied decimal point. It is ignored for other field types.

■ Null value: This is the application-defined null value for the field. That is, it specifies a value to be stored in the view when converting from FML to VIEWS for a field occurrence that does not exist in the fielded buffer, and similarly, indicates that a field occurrence should not be created when converting from VIEWS to FML. Default null values are defined for each data type, or the application can indicate that there are no null values for a particular field.

■ Flags: There are numerous field options. The flags can be used to control which fields are mapped from FML to VIEWS, and vice versa, and to affect handling of null values in the exchange. A flag is also supported to generate an additional count field associated with an application field to indicate the number of occurrences that are valid in the view. In the example above, the field C_salary or C-SALARY is such a field and is generated automatically because the flags field is set to C. Another flag is available to indicate that a length field should be associated with a string or CARRAY field. This is used to specify how many bytes are significant in a character array since, unlike FML, character array fields are of fixed length.

The view file is converted into some more useful information by the view compiler. The view compiler (a command called **viewc**) takes one or more view files as input and, for each one, generates a compiled view description, a C header file, and a COBOL copy file. The compiled view description is used by the the TUXEDO run-time system to interpret the record for operations ranging from converting VIEWS to FML, to encoding and decoding VIEWS sent between machines. More about this later. Let's first look a little closer at how the view-file and the view compiler are used.

Figure 8.8 summarizes the processing of the view description. The input view file, viewfile.v, has the input view description, such as that shown in Listing 8.8. The convention is that it ends with a ".v" suffix. The view compiler is run with the view file as input to generate a COBOL COPY file, such as shown in Listing 8.7, a C header file, such as shown in Listing 8.6, and a compiled description for use at run-time. The compiled view has a ".V" suffix; a .VV is used in environments without case-dependent file names. A view disassembler is also provided that can turn the compiled description back into a source view file.

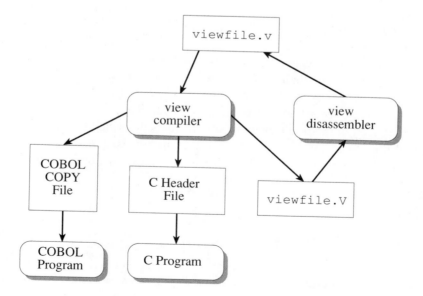

Figure 8.8　**View Compilation**

Once the view is compiled, the COPY and/or header files are used for development of the application. The compiled view description is used at run-time as described in the following section.

8.4.3 VIEW Functionality

Function calls are used to access and update all fields in FML buffers. When using views, the C language (for example, viewname.field or viewname->field) or COBOL language (for example, FIELD IN VIEWNAME) is used to directly access fields. The set of routines for manipulating views is much smaller, and typically none are used except as described below.

The most important view routines deal with conversion to and from FML buffers. Because all the information about field mappings (names, types, null value handling) is provided in view file description, it is simply a matter of passing the FML buffer, the view record, and the name of the view to the system for the conversion. Conversion from an FML buffer to a view is straightforward because the format of the view is fixed. This is shown in Figure 8.9. There is much more flexibility when going from a view to an FML buffer because the fielded buffer can have new occurrences added. Earlier we saw that there are four merge operations supported for fielded buffers. These same four operations can be specified to the primitive that converts from a view to a fielded buffer. The flags specified in the view description file that affect the conversion operation can also be changed at run-time. This allows an application dynamically to turn on and off which fields are transferred to and from the fielded buffer. Three other primitives deal with null values. One is a boolean that indicates whether or not a view field is null, and the other two can be used to set either a single field or all fields in a view to their defined null value.

There are two special conversion routines that convert views to and from another format. For example, one built-in conversion is to and from IBM-370 data formats. This would allow for an application to convert a view to an IBM-370 EBCDIC record and send the record directly to a COBOL CICS program, for example.

In addition, all of the boolean expression features described for FML buffers are supported for views. That is, a boolean or arithmetic expression can be compiled and evaluated against a view to return a boolean, integer, or floating point result.

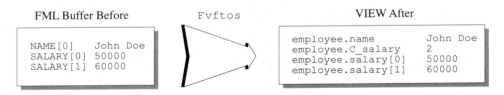

Figure 8.9   **Conversion from FML to View**

8.4.4 VIEWS as a Typed Buffer

VIEWS are a built-in TUXEDO typed buffer. They are provided as the way to use C structures and COBOL records with the TUXEDO System. In this way, the TUXEDO run-time system understands the format of these records based on the view description which is read at run-time. When allocating a VIEW, your application specifies a buffer type of "VIEW" and a subtype that matches the name of the view (the name that appears in the view description file). Since the TUXEDO run-time system can determine the space needed based on the structure size, your application need not provide a buffer length. The run-time system can also automatically take care of things, like computing how much data to send in a request or response, and handle encoding and decoding when the message transfers between different machine types. This simplifies the application programming job greatly in a distributed environment.

Listing 8.9 shows an example of allocating and populating a VIEW typed buffer. **tpalloc** is used to allocate the space. Thereafter, the buffer is simply treated as a normal C structure.

```
struct EMPLOYEE *ptr;

ptr = tpalloc("VIEW", "EMPLOYEE", 0);      /* sizeof(struct EMPLOYEE) */
strcpy(ptr->name, "John Doe");
ptr->salary[0] = 50000;
ptr->salary[1] = 60000;
```

Listing 8.9   *Example Using a VIEW Typed Buffer*

8.5   Custom Buffer Types

The STRING and CARRAY buffer types handle transmission of simple, non-fielded data. The VIEW typed buffer handles transmission of fixed, structured records. And the FML typed buffer handles transmission of varying length data with great flexibility in the fields contained in the buffer.

Still, you may find that none of these buffer types fills your application's special needs. For instance, your application may use a data structure that is not flat, that is, a data structure that has pointers to other data structures, such as a parse tree for a SQL database query. Or your application may require special encoding for a particular data structure that is not easily represented in a structure that can be defined with a VIEW buffer. In each of these cases, you can provide a custom buffer type and plug it into your application.

8.5.1 An Overview of the Typed Buffers Mechanism

A typed buffer is a data structure with application and system processing functionality. The typed buffer mechanism works by having access to information about each buffer type. The information is stored in a C structure for convenience, and an array of these structures defining the buffer types used by the application is built into each TUXEDO client and server. The default array has all of the types mentioned above. An application programmer or administrator can change the default array to take out unneeded buffer types and to add new ones. The information stored for each buffer type is as follows:

Buffer type: This is the name of the buffer type. It can be up to eight characters in length.

Buffer subtype: This is the name of the buffer subtype. It can be up to sixteen characters in length. The subtype is used to distinguish different processing needed for different formats of the generic type. In most cases, all buffers of a given type can be processed by a generic routine for the type, and the subtype value specified is the wildcard character "*". Any entries for a type that have a specific subtype must appear before the wildcard in the list, because a top-down search is done for a match.

Default size: This is the minimum size of the associated buffer type that can be allocated or reallocated. For buffer types for which this value is greater than zero and sized appropriately, the application programmer can simply specify a buffer size of zero when allocating or reallocating a buffer. Hence, it is both the minimum and default size.

The following are routines that need to be defined for each buffer type. If the routine is not needed for the particular buffer type, then it need not be provided (a null pointer is sufficient); the TUXEDO run-time system uses default processing.

Buffer initialization: This routine is used to initialize a newly allocated typed buffer. For instance, the application buffer type may need a buffer header or trailer added to the buffer.

Buffer reinitialization: This routine is called after a buffer has been reallocated to a new size. For instance, an application buffer type may need to fix up a header or trailer if the buffer size changes.

Buffer uninitialization: This routine is called just before a typed buffer is freed. An application may want to clear a buffer (for security or other reasons) before a buffer is released.

Buffer presend: This routine is called before a typed buffer is sent as a message to another client or server. There are two important operations to accomplish here.

First, the buffer may need to be prepared for transmission. This might involve removing information used locally, compacting any holes in the data, or flattening a record that contains pointers to other buffers. When the operation completes, the buffer must be ready to send. Second, this operation returns the length of the data to be transmitted.

Buffer postsend: This routine is called after the message is sent so that the application can return the buffer to its original state.

Buffer postreceive: This routine is called after a message is received. It allows the application a chance to fix-up the typed buffer before it is passed to the application. This might involve modifying or creating a header or trailer, generating an index, expanding a compacted buffer into an in-memory format, etc. This routine returns the length of the application data.

Encode/decode: This routine does all the encoding and decoding needed for the buffer type. The direction, encoding or decoding, is passed to the routine along with input and output buffers and lengths. The format used for encoding is left to the application, and, as with these other routines, can be dependent on the buffer type. Some buffer types might already be in a naturally canonical format that is understood on all platforms. Others might require byte reordering or character set conversions.

Routing: This routine is called with a typed buffer, its data length, a logical routing name that was configured by the administrator, and a target service. Based on this information, the application must decide the server group to which the message should be sent or indicate that it does not matter. This is where data-dependent routing is done.

Filter: This routine is called to evaluate an expression against a typed buffer, returning a match or nonmatch. For instance, if the typed buffer is a VIEW or FML, then the FML boolean expressions are used. It is used for evaluating matches for events by the Event Broker.

Format: This routine is used to make a printable string from a typed buffer.

Figure 8.10 shows how many of these typed buffer routines are called during the communication of a message from client to server.

8.5.2 Providing Your Own Custom Buffer Type

While this may seem like a lot of work, many typed buffers do not need all of these routines. Further, some of the operations, like initialization and providing a print format, may already exist. Most of the work is usually involved with producing a routine to do encoding and decoding. Most applications can be written using the built-in buffer types, and, if an application-specific buffer type is needed, at least these operations can be written once and hidden from the rest of the application.

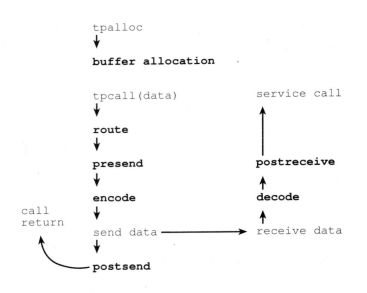

Figure 8.10 **Flow Through Typed Buffer Routines**

The steps involved in the installation of a new typed buffer is beyond the scope of this book. Suffice it to say, it is simply a matter of adding the information to an existing template file and compiling it to form a dynamically loadable object that is used by all TUXEDO and application run-time programs.

8.6 Summary

In this chapter, we have discussed the format of application messages sent and received by the TUXEDO communication primitives. This powerful mechanism used is called typed buffers which simply means that a type (and possibly subtype) are associated with the buffer when allocated from the TUXEDO system. From that point on, all manipulations on the buffer for formatting and transmission are transparent to the application.

We discussed the built-in buffer types. Besides simple character string types, the FML buffer type provides a flexible, variable length record, and the VIEW buffer type provides for fixed-format records.

Finally, if these built-in types do not meet your needs, then you can provide your own buffer type specifically suited to your application.

9 Joining and Leaving the Application

PROGRAMMING

Your application programs must register with the TUXEDO System and "join the application" before they can use any of the TUXEDO System's services. To provide effective administration, the TUXEDO administrative subsystem needs to keep track of all programs that access resources within your distributed business application, both clients and servers.

9.1 Clients

Recall from Chapter 4, "Application Development—Overview," that clients are the initiators of requests into your application. They can be attached to a terminal or a graphical interface, or they may be driven by input from a file, a device, a network, or another computer without any human interface whatsoever. From the view of the TUXEDO System, they are unstructured. That is, the application has complete control of its processing as well as its use of the TUXEDO System's services. The only requirement is that a client join an application before making any ATMI calls and leave the application before exiting. However, we will see that even these requirements can be relaxed under certain circumstances.

9.1.1 Joining the Application: tpchkauth and tpinit

A client normally joins the TUXEDO application by calling an initialization primitive, **tpinit** in C or **TPINITIALIZE** in COBOL (this is one of the few primitives where the name is not just converted to upper case). After calling this procedure, all of the other ATMI functions are available.

At initialization time, your client program must identify the TUXEDO application to which it should connect and it must identify itself to the application.

Identifying an application is provided through the operating system environment (on Unix, Windows, etc.), the system registry (on Windows NT), or the system directory (on Netware) on the computer where your client program is executed. This information is used to find or attach to the application. For the purpose of the example, Figure 9.1 shows the system environment being set from

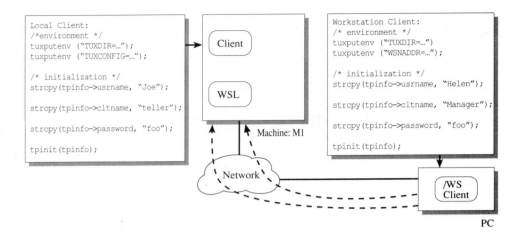

Figure 9.1 **Initialization Information**

within the client using the function called **tuxputenv**. More often, these values are set up on login or at least before executing the program, independent of the specific client program. Both local and workstation clients must have TUXDIR set to the directory where the TUXEDO System software is located. For a local client program on a server machine, the environment must have a pointer to the application configuration file, TUXCONFIG. For a workstation client that connects to the application via a Workstation Listener (**WSL**) and Workstation Handler (**WSH**), the environment must have information, such as a list of target network addresses for the **WSL**.

Although application identification is generally independent of the client program and the user, identification of the client program to the application is usually dependent on both the client program and the person executing it. Client program identification includes the identity of the user, security information, resource manager affinity, and flags to affect the behavior of subsequent calls to TUXEDO primitives. This information is passed directly to **tpinit**. In the example in Figure 9.1, each client sets a user and client name along with the application password. The following sections describe, in detail, the values passed during the initialization process.

9.1.1.1 Client Naming

Client programs have two names. One name, called a client identifier, is uniquely assigned by the TUXEDO System when the client joins the application. This name is passed to each service that is called on behalf of a client and can be used for unsolicited notification of clients. When joining the application, the client also can provide a symbolic user and client name that are used for security, administration, and communications.

When a client joins the application, a user name and client name can be passed to **tpinit**. There are no semantics implied for these values by the TUXEDO System; they are simply strings of up to thirty characters each. Normally, the user name field would be set to the name of the user running the application and the client name field might indicate the job function, role, or group associated with the user or client program. On operating systems that require a user name for logging in, this name could be retrieved and used. On the other hand, an application might choose to set the user name to a fixed value such as "teller1" at a particular position within a bank branch or based on the program name.

The user and client names are used to identify a client program in several important ways:

Security: When application security is configured for a per-user password, the client program must provide a password that matches the password associated with the user/client combination. Additionally, two client names are reserved for special semantics. **tpsysadm** is treated as the TUXEDO application administrator and **tpsysopr** is treated as the TUXEDO application operator.

Administration: Through the administrative interface, the administrator can see a list of all the clients that have joined the application. By giving meaningful names, the administrator can get a better idea of who is attached to the application, what workload is associated with the clients, and what types of services are being demanded by the associated clients.

Communications: **tpbroadcast** can be used to communicate with clients based on a name. The naming selection criteria includes machine name, user name, and client name, with wild-card values allowed for any or all of these values. The machine name is automatically assigned when the client joins the application. For workstation clients, the machine value is taken to be the computer where the workstation client is connected via the Workstation Listener and Handler. Thus, with an application-defined naming hierarchy, messages can be sent to specified groups of people or programs. For instance, a message could be broadcast to all users running a client program that joined the application with the "teller" client name, whether on a workstation or local to a server node. This is illustrated in Figure 9.2.

In Figure 9.2, sending a message to "teller" clients would go to Joe's client program which is directly on server machine M1 and to Tom's client program which is running on a workstation and connected to the application via machine M1. In this same example, a message to clients on machine M1 would go to the same two clients. Message broadcasting is also one of the mechanisms used for notification from the Event Broker. Although the user and client names are optional and can be left unset, they provide a powerful mechanism for administration and notification, and careful consideration should be given in assigning names to get the most benefit from them.

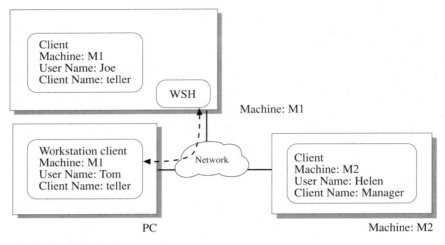

Figure 9.2 **Client Naming**

9.1.1.2 Application Password

We have already discussed security as it relates to joining the application. For general purpose client programs that are written to work with a variety of configurations, there is a primitive available to ask what level of security is enabled for this particular application. **tpchkauth** in C or **TPCHKAUTH** in COBOL returns whether the application requires no authentication, system authentication using an application password, or application authentication using an application password and per-user information (as described in Chapter 6, "The Anatomy of a TUXEDO Application").

Your client program normally calls **tpchkauth** before calling **tpinit** to determine what additional security information must be provided during initialization. When system or application authentication is configured, the application password must be specified when joining the application. The application administrator must inform users of the application password and the application programs must be written to accept the password from the users. Generally this is done by prompting for the password on the screen in a mode that either does not echo the typed characters or prints positional "x" characters (the latter is good visual feedback for the user but less secure because an observer could infer how may characters are in the password). The password is specified in the initialization information but the TUXEDO run-time system never ships it across the network (it is not vulnerable to attack in this fashion).

9.1.1.3 Group Association

Earlier, we talked about associating client and server programs with a resource manager. For most applications, the database access will occur from within the service functions. However, there are some applications that might want to access a database from within a client program and have the access within a global transaction, combined with other resource manager accesses taking place in servers. The administrator configures groups of servers that are associated with a resource manager including administrative processes to handle transaction coordination. By specifying one of these groups when joining the application, the client is associated with the group and the corresponding resource manager.

Figure 9.3 shows three clients with affinity to the ACCOUNT server group which has several servers and a DBMS, presumably holding the ACCOUNT database. By default, clients are not associated with any server group. Further, /WS clients cannot have affinity to a server group because they are not directly colocated with the server group.

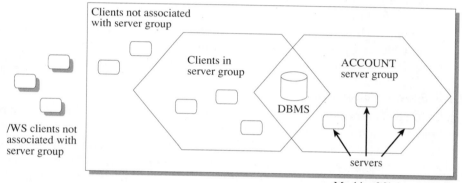

Figure 9.3 **Client Affinity with Server Groups**

9.1.1.4 Notification Mechanism

There are two other attributes that your client program can specify when joining a TUXEDO application: the notification method and the system access mode.

The notification method has to do with unsolicited notification messages sent via **tpbroadcast** and **tpnotify**. An example of an unsolicited notification might be when the administrator sends a message to all client programs that the system is going to be deactivated. An application could be designed to have high-priority messages sent to client programs; receipt would cause some window to pop up on the screen.

When a client joins the application, it can specify the mode by which it would like to receive these notification messages. If the application program doesn't want to be bothered with an unsolicited message, it is possible to ignore them completely. This is the simplest approach, but loses the advantages of using this feature. For the other two options, a call-back function that can be executed when an unsolicited message is received must be set up by the application. That is, the TUXEDO run-time system in the client will dispatch your call-back function when an unsolicited message arrives.

One method of notification is for the system to send an operating system signal to the client. This will interrupt what the client program is currently doing and process the message immediately. This option is not supported on all platforms due to limitations of the operating system; it also may restrict the client program to be running as the application administrator, which may not be the case. The default option is for the TUXEDO run-time system to check for any unsolicited messages whenever any of the ATMI primitives are called. This approach is called *dip-in*. The advantage is that it can be supported on all platforms and doesn't interrupt what the client is doing. The client has better control over when the message will be received. However, if the client doesn't dip-in for a while, then a message may go unnoticed for a long time. To avoid this problem, there is a primitive, **tpchkunsol**, that the application can call just to check for any waiting unsolicited messages.

If the client program doesn't choose a notification mechanism, one is assigned to the client either by the application administrator or it defaults to the dip-in mechanism.

9.1.1.5 System Access Mode

By default, all servers and local clients are directly attached to the Bulletin Board shared memory. Your application can be configured such that the BB is not accessible to an application outside of the TUXEDO ATMI calls. This mode of operation is called *protected mode*. When operating in this mode, the TUXEDO software must attach and detach to the BB for each call to ATMI, ensuring that the application does not accidentally scribble over the BB, causing failure on this node of the application. The price for this protection is additional overhead. The alternative is to have the shared memory always attached to the client or server. This mode of operation is called *fastpath* because access to the BB is as fast as accessing local program variables. This only makes sense for local clients and not /WS ones. Typically, applications would use protected mode during development to trap invalid memory references. Once the application is running satisfactorily, fastpath is used to get optimum performance.

The client can choose which mode is in effect when joining the application. If not specified, then the administratively configured option is used. In some configurations, the administrator may not want individual programs to pick their own choice. In this case, the administrator can pick a default mode, protected or fastpath, and also can specify that client programs cannot override the default.

9.1.1.6 Authentication Information

If your application requires authentication of individual users, it will be necessary in **tpinit** to furnish additional information for the application authentication service. This service is configured by the administrator to validate the per-user authentication information with the client and user names, indicating that the client program is or is not allowed to join the application. The TUXEDO System can't anticipate what the information will contain or its size. It is up to the client program to provide the data, in addition to the information described above. This data is passed to the authentication service without interpretation by the TUXEDO software. The only manipulation of this data is that, when it is transmitted over the network from a workstation client, it is encrypted for security. The authentication service was discussed in Chapter 6, "The Anatomy of a TUXEDO Application."

9.1.1.7 Default Initialization

You can see that the client initialization allows for specifying not only security information but also identification information and the operation mode. In applications where security is not used, the default values normally are sufficient. The user, client, and group names are not necessary, and the other options can be picked up from the configuration. In this case, the client need not explicitly join the application by calling **tpinit**. Instead, the client will implicitly join the application on the first call to most other TUXEDO API functions (excluding the buffer functions and **tpchkauth**). So, while all application clients will call the initialization function to join the application, some may do it implicitly.

9.1.2 Exiting the Application: tpterm

After a client program is finished processing requests for your TUXEDO application, the client should leave the application by calling the termination procedure, **tpterm**. This will unregister the client from the application, and free up resources that have been allocated while the client was part of the application. These resources include communications resources (conversational connections are closed), transaction resources (transactions are rolled back), IPC resources, and memory resources.

At a later time, if a client wants to join the application again, it is simply a matter of calling the **tpinit** primitive again. It is even possible to reset the environment so that the client will join another TUXEDO application. Although there is some overhead cost with joining and leaving an application, this approach can be used for toggling between multiple applications when necessary. The administrative GUI is an example of a client that does this.

What happens if you forget to call **tpterm** before your client program exits? In environments that support the use of **atexit** in C, the TUXEDO run-time system automatically sets up **tpterm** as a call-back function to be executed when the program terminates. That is, **tpterm** will be called automatically when the program exits, so that the client automatically leaves the application normally. There are some environments and some abnormal termination cases where these call-back functions do not work. In those cases, the client will continue to tie up resources. For workstation clients, the administrator can define inactivity time-outs after which the connection will be dropped and the client will be terminated from the application. For clients running on one of the server machines, the program termination will be detected after an administrator-defined period for sanity checking. The best approach is to ensure that every client program explicitly leaves the application before exiting by calling **tpterm**.

9.1.3 Example

All of the options your clients can set for **tpinit** are set in the structure called **TPINIT**. We have already discussed the various elements in a **TPINIT** structure. Listing 9.1 is the C-language definition.

```
struct  tpinfo_t {
        char    usrname[32];     /* client user name */
        char    cltname[32];     /* application client name */
        char    passwd[32];      /* application password */
        char    grpname[32];     /* client group name */
        long    flags;           /* initialization flags */
        long    datalen;         /* length of app specific data */
        long    data;            /* placeholder for application data */
};
typedef struct  tpinfo_t TPINIT;
```

Listing 9.1 *TPINIT Structure*

The **TPINIT** structure is used as a "TPINIT" typed buffer, a special buffer type that the TUXEDO System knows about. This buffer is allocated by the application, the values are set, and this typed buffer is passed to **tpinit**.

Listing 9.2 gives some sample C code for joining an application, with annotation in the C comments.

Note that a typed buffer is used in C for the **tpinit** call with additional space for user-specific data at the end of the buffer. The space is computed by calling **TPINITNEED**. This sample code uses hard-coded strings for the user name, and the application and per-user passwords. In practice, these values would be determined in an environment-dependent manner.

The interface for initialization is one place where the COBOL interface, although similar in functionality, has a different API. The COBOL interface does not use a **TPINIT** buffer. Instead, a **TPINFDEF** record is used to hold the information fields, and a separate data record is used to hold the per-user data. These two records plus a status record are passed to **TPINITIALIZE**. The **TPINFDEF** record format is shown in Listing 9.3.

Listing 9.4 shows an application code, written in COBOL, equivalent to the previous C sample code.

```
TPINIT *tpinitbuf ;                      /* initialization information buffer */
int     auth ;                           /* return value from tpchkauth */

/* Allocate TPINIT buffer with space for 16 bytes of application data */
tpinitbuf = (TPINIT *) tpalloc("TPINIT", NULL, TPINITNEED(16)) ;

if (tpinitbuf == (TPINIT *) NULL) {      /* check failure */
     (void) fprintf(stderr, "Failed for TPINIT buffer, %s\n",
          tpstrerror(tperrno));
     exit(1);
}
(void) strcpy(tpinitbuf->usrname, "usrname");
                                         /* hard-coded user name */
(void) strcpy (tpinitbuf->cltname, argv[0]) ;
                                         /* program name used as client name */
(void)strcpy (tpinitbuf->grpname, "") ;  /* not associated with an RM        */

/* set flags for dip-in notification and protected mode access */
tpinitbuf->flags = TPU_DIPIN|TPSA_PROTECTED;
switch (auth = tpchkauth()) {            /* check authentication level */
case TPNOAUTH :                          /* no additional authentication */
     (void)strcpy (tpinitbuf->passwd, "") ;
     break ;
case TPSYSAUTH:                          /* need application password */
     (void)strcpy (tpinitbuf->passwd, "app_password") ;
     break;
case TPAPPAUTH:
     /* Need both application password and per-user authentication data */
     (void) strcpy (tpinitbuf->passwd, "app_password") ;
     (void) strcpy ((char *)&tpinitbuf->data, "usr_password") ;

     /* Set length of per-user data */
     tpinitbuf->datalen = strlen ((char *) &tpinitbuf->data) + 1;
     break;
}
if  (tpinit(tpinitbuf) == -1) {          /* Join the application */
     (void) fprintf(stderr, "Failed to join application, %s\n",
          tpstrerror(tperrno));
     exit(1);
}
  /* APPLICATION CODE GOES HERE */
  tpterm();                              /* Leave the application */
```

Listing 9.2   *C Language Client Joining Application*

The application writer is in complete control of the client initialization and termination, as shown in these examples. In contrast, most of the processing is automatic for servers, as described in the next section.

9.2 Servers

The primary job of servers is to provide services to clients and other servers. They receive requests, process them, and return replies. The housekeeping involved in

```
05  USRNAME                    PIC X(30).
05  CLTNAME                    PIC X(30).
05  PASSWD                     PIC X(30).
05  GRPNAME                    PIC X(30).
05  NOTIFICATION-FLAG          PIC S9(9) COMP-5.
    88    TPU-SIG    VALUE     1.
    88    TPU-DIP    VALUE     2.
    88    TPU-IGN    VALUE     3.
05  ACCESS-FLAG                PIC S9(9) COMP-5.
    88    TPSA-FASTPATH        VALUE 1.
    88    TPSA-PROTECTED       VALUE 2.
05  DATALEN                    PIC S9(9) COMP
```

Listing 9.3   *TPINFDEF.CBL Record*

```
IDENTIFICATION DIVISION.
PROGRAM-ID. CLIENT.
AUTHOR. SDF.
ENVIRONMENT DIVISION.
CONFIGURATION SECTION.
WORKING-STORAGE SECTION.
01   TPSTATUS-REC.
COPY TPSTATUS.
01   TPINFDEF-REC.
COPY TPINFDEF.
01   TPAUTDEF-REC.
COPY TPAUTDEF.
01   USER-DATA-REC        PIC X(75).

PROCEDURE DIVISION.

CALL "TPCHKAUTH" USING TPAUTDEF-REC TPSTATUS-REC.
IF NOT TPOK
        DISPLAY "TPCHKAUTH FAILED"
        STOP RUN
END-IF.

MOVE "USRNAME" TO USRNAME.
MOVE "CLTNAME" TO CLTNAME.
MOVE SPACES TO GRPNAME.
SET TPU-DIP TO TRUE.
SET TPSA-PROTECTED TO TRUE.

IF TPNOAUTH
        MOVE SPACES TO PASSWD
        MOVE ZERO TO DATALEN
END-IF.
IF TPSYSAUTH
```

Listing 9.4   *COBOL Client Joining the Application*

```
              MOVE "MYPASSWD" TO PASSWD
              MOVE ZERO TO DATALEN
       END-IF.

       IF TPAPPAUTH
              MOVE "MYPASSWD" TO PASSWD
              MOVE "USRPASSWD" TO USER-DATA-REC
              MOVE 10 to DATALEN
       END-IF.
       CALL "TPINITIALIZE" USING TPINFDEF-REC
              USER-DATA-REC
              TPSTATUS-REC.
       IF NOT TPOK
              DISPLAY "TPINITIALIZE FAILED"
              STOP RUN
       END-IF.
*
* APPLICATION CODE GOES HERE
*
       CALL "TPTERM" USING TPSTATUS-REC.
       IF NOT TPOK
              DISPLAY "TPTERM FAILED"
              STOP RUN
       END-IF.
```

Listing 9.4   *COBOL Client Joining the Application, continued*

servers is more complex than that for clients. Services must be made known to all client and server programs joining the application, the server must respond to administrative requests to advertise new services and deactivate themselves, new servers must be able to take over for earlier failed servers, and transactions must be handled so that a server automatically joins a transaction started by the requestor. Because the processing is more complex, additional structure is needed in the server program. Unlike "unstructured" client programs, server programs are well-structured, and the TUXEDO System controls all of this high-level processing. When building a server program, a TUXEDO-supplied main function is included. In Chapter 6, "The Anatomy of a TUXEDO Application," this was called the server adaptor. This function includes all high-level control with the following application hooks:

- One-time call to an application initialization hook during server startup

- Calls to application service entry points for each request

- One-time call to an application termination hook during server shutdown

The following sections will discuss the main function and each of the application hooks.

9.2.1 The "Standard Main"

The "standard main" function or server adaptor serves as the C **main** function or the COBOL program entry point for a TUXEDO server. The logical processing flow is shown in pseudocode in Listing 9.5.

```
main
{
        Process command line options
        Join the application as server
        Advertise services
        Call Application Server Initialization Function, tpsvrinit
        Do {
                Dequeue request
                If Administrative Request {
                        Advertise Service or
                        Deactivated Server
                }
                Otherwise {
                        Join Transaction if Request in Transaction Mode
                        Dispatch Request to Application Service Entry
                }
        } Until Deactivated Request
        Unadvertise services
        Call Application Server Done Function, tpsvrdone
        Leave the application
        Exit
}
```

Listing 9.5   *Server Main Processing*

Parameters can be configured for a server in the TMIB which the server gets when activated. The parameters are divided into a set of standard administrative options and application parameters. The following administrative actions can be set from the command line.

▪ Services to be advertised can be specified on the command line. By default, all services indicated when the server was built will be advertised. It is possible to specify a subset of those services or even map new services to defined service entry point functions at server activation time.

▪ Because a server is activated by an administrative process, often over the network, the standard output and error output of a server would be lost unless redirected to a file. The default is to use the files "stdout" and "stderr" in the application directory. The file names can be modified at activation time.

▪ The administrator can specify that a log be kept of all service requests that are processed by the server. The service start and end times are also logged, along with the service name. A utility program, **txrpt**, is provided to analyze the output of this log based on service name.

▪ An argument consisting of two dashes (--) is used to indicate the end of the administrative options. Options following "--" are passed to the application server initialization function. If you look at the options passed to the server at activation time, you will see a few "hidden" administrative options that are added by the boot program.

After processing command line arguments, the server joins the application, similar to the way a client joins. One difference is that the server is running with the permission of the application administrator and need not be authenticated. As part of joining the system, the services indicated by the command line options are advertised as available. Before and after the main processing loop, while the process is joined as a server in the application, application hooks are called to allow one-time application processing. In addition to processing application requests, the processing loop handles administrative requests to advertise services and to deactivate. The main loop terminates after a deactivation request is received. All of its services are unadvertised. If it is the last server reading the queue, it will try to drain and process the message queue before deactivating. Before exiting, the server program terminates its participation in the application.

9.2.2 Server Initialization: tpsvrinit and tpopen

The TUXEDO run-time system calls your **tpsvrinit** call-back function after the server joins the application but before processing any application requests. It allows for one-time, application-specific initialization. The application command line arguments and an argument count are passed as parameters to the function and are normally processed using the **getopt** function. **tpsvrinit** is also commonly used to read any application configuration information from files, connect to a database, set up any memory data structures, and perhaps advertise server-specific services and subscribe to events.

For servers that will access an XA-compliant resource manager, for example, a database, as part of a global transaction, **tpopen** must be called to connect to the resource. It takes no arguments and the TUXEDO run-time system opens the RM that has been administratively associated with the server.

Because the server is part of the application when **tpsvrinit** is called, the processing may contain any of the ATMI primitives (except the two primitives that can be used to return from a service function, **tpreturn** and **tpforward**). They could be used to get information from another server via one of the communications mechanisms, to register with an application registration server, or any other application client/server processing that is needed. The only restrictions are that work that is started must be completed within the initialization function: transactions, conversations, and asynchronous requests cannot be outstanding when the routine returns control to the TUXEDO System. If, for some reason, the application is unable to complete its initialization, a return code of -1 from this function will cause the server to fail to activate.

Listing 9.6 shows an example **tpsvrinit** function that processes two command line options and opens any associated resource managers.

```
int
tpsvrinit(int argc, char **argv)
{
        int c, bopt = 0;
        char outfile[512];
        /* get -o outfile -b options */
        while ((c = getopt (argc, argv,"o:b"))  && c != EOF)
        switch ((char) c) {
        case  o':
                strcpy(outfile, optarg);
                break;
        case  b':
                bopt = 1;
                break;
        default:
                (void)userlog("WARN: Invalid command line option) ;
                return(-1);
        }
        if (tpopen() == -1) {              /* open any resource managers */
                switch (tperrno) {
                case TPEOS:
                    (void)userlog("tpopen failed, error %d\n", Uunixerr);
                  break;
                default:
                    (void)userlog("tpopen failed, %s", tpstrerror(tperrno));
                }
                return(-1);              /* don't let server activate */
        }
        return(0);
}
```

Listing 9.6 *C Server Initialization Example*

For COBOL programmers, the command line argument count and values are provided through the LINKAGE SECTION, as shown in Listing 9.7.

Default **tpsvrinit** and **TPSVRINIT** functions are provided in the TUXEDO run-time system. These functions simply open the resource manager associated with the server, if there is one and write a message in the event log. For applications that don't have application command line options and do not need additional initialization, the default can be used with no additional programming needed.

```
LINKAGE SECTION.
01 CMD-LINE.

   05 ARGC   PIC 9(4) COMP-5.
   05 ARGV.
      10  ARGS PIC X OCCURS 0 TO 9999 DEPENDING ON ARGC.
01 TPSTATUS-REC.
   COPY TPSTATUS.
PROCEDURE DIVISION USING CMD-LINE TPSTATUS-REC.
* User code goes here
EXIT PROGRAM
```

Listing 9.7   *COBOL Server Initialization Example*

9.2.3 Service Dispatch

The server main loop takes messages off the server's request queue and passes them to the correct application service entry function, based on the requested service name. Messages are taken off the queue in priority order. The administrator can set the priority for each service, and the application programmer can set the priority higher or lower on an individual message basis. Remember that the application message is a typed buffer. When it is passed to the service, the type and subtype can be determined using **tptypes**. Additional information passed to the service includes the service name, the client identifier of the original requestor, whether or not the work is in transaction mode, and whether or not the request is conversational. The service interface is described in more detail in Chapter 10, "Request/Response Communication."

When your application service completes its work, it must return control to the TUXEDO server adaptor. As part of returning control, it can choose to send a reply message back to the requestor or it can forward a request message on for further processing by another server. In either case, the server is finished processing the request and can go on to work on the next request without worrying about state for the current request. Even if the work is finished within a transaction, the transaction is completed by another server, freeing up the application server to work on the next request. In this way, the application can be partitioned into logical divisions of work, and the server is serially reused for job steps on behalf of clients and other servers.

The service termination functions, **tpreturn** and **tpforward**, are described in more detail in Chapter 10, "Request/Response Communication."

9.2.4 Server Termination: tpsvrdone and tpclose

After an administrative deactivation request is received by the server adaptor and the server stops processing requests, the server termination call-back function is called. A C **tpsvrdone** or COBOL **TPSVRDONE** call-back can be used for one-time application termination logic. Often, this function has operations that complete or undo the work done in the initialization function. This includes calling **tpclose** to close the open resource manager. It also might include writing out and closing application files, unsubscribing from events, and freeing allocated resources.

A default **tpsvrdone** function is provided in the TUXEDO libraries. This function simply closes the resource manager associated with the server, if there is one. For applications that don't need additional termination logic, the default function can be used with no additional programming needed. Listing 9.8 shows code for a sample **tpsvrdone** that is similar to processing that the default would do.

```
void
tpsvrdone(void)
{
        if (tpclose() == -1) {              /* close any open resource managers */
                switch (tperrno) {
                case TPEOS:
                        (void)userlog("tpclose failed, error %d\n", Uunixerr);
                    break;
                default:
                        (void)userlog("tpclose failed, %s", tpstrerror(tperrno));
                }
        }
        return;
}
```

Listing 9.8   *Server Termination Example*

9.2.5 Service Advertisements: tpadvertise and tpunadvertise

There are four ways that you can advertise service names.

Compile time: You must specify *service entry points* (C function names or COBOL program names) when you build your servers. The linker is used to map these entry point names to actual execution start addresses. This was described in detail Chapter 7, "Introduction to the Application Programming Interface." At compilation time, the administrator can also specify the default list of services to be advertised when the server is activated and the mapping to the entry point names. If you have many services, you can put the list of services in a file and reference the file name on the **buildserver** command line.

By default, a service name is assumed to map to a service entry point name with an identical name. But multiple services can be mapped to a single entry point and the service name need not match the entry point name.

This approach is static, determined at build time. The advantages of doing it early are that it serves as documentation of what services the server provides and makes it easy to get the right services advertised when the server is activated (the administrator can just say activate all of the configured services).

Configuration time: As mentioned earlier in this chapter, the command line options can be used to specify service names to be advertised and the associated entry point names. The default is to advertise all services defined when the server was built. However, the command line options can be used to override this list, activating a subset of the defined services or adding to the list. This approach is static, determined at configuration time. Note that the configuration can be dynamically updated but the change will take effect only the next time that the server is activated, so it is static in nature.

Administratively: A third mechanism is to administratively advertise or unadvertise a service for one or more servers. This can be done through the Administrative API, the GUI, or the command line interface (**tmadmin**). This approach and the following are dynamic.

Run-time using ATMI: The mechanism described in this section is to use the ATMI interface to dynamically advertise or unadvertise a service anytime during the life of a running server.

A service can be dynamically advertised by using **tpadvertise**. This is commonly performed in the server initialization function; it is less common for an application design to include advertising services from within a service although this is possible. One common use of dynamically advertising a service is for a general server to advertise a specific name based on the resources to which it provides access. For instance, a server that provides access to a database might advertise a name that implies the database name. Any client wishing to access the database sends a request to the generated name.

A second use might be for each server to generate a unique name and return that name to a client whose request is serviced. The client can use a generic name to get to any server offering the service and then use the unique name to go back to the same server for additional requests. This is pseudoconversational communication because the client communicates with the same server but does not tie up the server and the service is always entered from the top (the communication does not happen from within the service). Listing 9.8 shows generation of a service name including the process identifier (note that this will not be unique across multiple machines) and advertising it as part of **tpsvrinit**. Another approach would be to go to the TMIB and find the server's unique identifier and group number.

The **tpadvertise** function requires the name of a service to be advertised and a function pointer in C. The function pointer must match the pointer associated with one of the service entry points defined when the server was built. For COBOL, **TPADVERTISE** takes a service name and a program name. In this case, the program name must match one of the names defined when the server was built. Note that, in both cases, the function must exist within the server in which it is advertised.

Advertising a service has special implications when multiple servers are reading from the same queue (MSSQ). Because any of the servers can read a message off of the queue, then each of the servers reading the queue must be able to process any message put in the queue. This can be ensured only if all servers on the queue advertise the same services. The requirements for multiple servers reading a single queue are that they are the same program. Further, when one server advertises a service, the same service is automatically advertised for all servers on the queue. Similarly, when a new server is started on an MSSQ, it gets the same services that all of the other servers already have advertised. Note that the example in Listing 9.9 won't work as desired for servers on an MSSQ because all servers on the queue would advertise the special name (so it will not be unique to a single server).

Services can be dynamically unadvertised. The specified services can be services that were defined when the server was built, when the server was activated, or dynamically advertised. **tpunadvertise** simply takes a service name. When a service is unadvertised on a queue with multiple servers, the service is unadvertised for all of those servers. Requests already on the queue will be processed but no new requests can be submitted for an unadvertised service.

```
void SERVICE(TPSVCINFO *tpsvcinfo);            /* declare entry point */

int
tpsvrinit(int argc, char **argv)
{
        char service[15];
        argc = argc; argv = argv;              /* unused arguments */

        /* generate unique service name for single machine */
        sprintf(service, "SERVICE%ld", (long)getpid());
        if (tpadvertise(service, SERVICE) == -1) {
                userlog("Service advertisement for %s failed", service);
                return(-1);
        }
        return(0);
}
```

Listing 9.9 *Example of tpadvertise Call in tpsvrinit*

9.3 Summary

In this chapter, we described the way in which clients and servers become part of the application. Clients are completely under application control and join the application by calling **tpinit**, either explicitly or via the first ATMI call. They are started and terminated as needed by the application. Servers, on the other hand, are controlled by the TUXEDO System. They are activated and deactivated by the administrator. Servers have application hooks that are called during server initialization, to process application requests, and during server termination. Dequeuing requests and other control processing is done by the TUXEDO run-time system.

10 Request/ Response Communication

The request/response communication paradigm has been a fundamental part of the TUXEDO System since its inception. It is precisely this paradigm that implements the distributed function-shipping approach, which is one of the core values of the TUXEDO System. This chapter will present the programming tools that allow you to write distributed client/server applications using function shipping. First, we will present the two ways in which you can write simple, synchronous request/response programs. Next, we will describe the two ways in which you can add parallelism to your application by issuing and processing multiple requests simultaneously. Finally, we will show you how to manipulate the priorities of the requests sent and received by TUXEDO client and server programs.

10.1 Synchronous Request/Response

An essential element of many client/server communication frameworks is the synchronous request/response mechanism: a client program issues a request to a server program; it then waits for the server's response before performing any other operations. The client and server synchronize their communication on-line. The TUXEDO System offers two programmatically distinct ways of using the synchronous request/response mechanism in your programs: library-based ATMI and language-based TxRPC. As mentioned earlier, ATMI is a set of library functions that you call from within your programs, whereas TxRPC is a set of tools—a compiler and run-time libraries—that you use to make calling remote procedures as easy as calling local procedures.

10.1.1 Synchronous Call: tpcall

The ATMI function **tpcall** invokes an application-provided service routine and synchronously waits for a response. Recall from Chapter 4, "Application Development —Overview," that an application service routine offers a contract to the client who invokes it. The contract consists of the name of the service, its required input parameters, the specific processing on those inputs, any output values, and the set of errors that might be returned to a client as a result of the processing. You use **tpcall** to execute a service contract. Here's an example of how to call this ATMI function:

```
ret = tpcall(service_name, req_buf, req_buf_len,
             &reply_buf, &reply_buf_len, flags);
```

As you can see in Figure 10.1, the client supplies the service name and the request buffer to the service routine while the service returns the reply buffer and return code to the client. Let's now look at the parameters you can pass to **tpcall**. Since many of ATMI's functions use these same parameters in a consistent fashion, we will cover each parameter in detail here so that when we introduce other ATMI functions in later chapters you will already have a good idea of how those functions operate. We start with the C language version of **tpcall**. We will follow that by showing the COBOL version and pointing out its main differences from the C version.

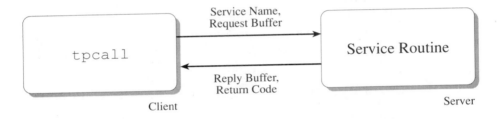

Figure 10.1   **Client/Server Interaction Using tpcall**

Service Name

This parameter is the string name for the service being requested. From previous examples, we have seen service names such as "Place_Order," "Access_Orders," and "Update_Billing." Service names are specific to your application, and they should name your business functions. They should encapsulate well-defined business functions—thus, the use of the term "function shipping" as a synonym for "request/response."

The fact that this parameter is a simple string rather than some sort of addressing structure makes ATMI simple to use and makes writing and understanding your distributed applications much easier. The meaning of the service name string is specific to your application rather than to your network or machine configuration. In designing ATMI, there were two requirements that led to the use of simple strings, like "Debit," for service names. The first was that programs should not have to manipulate network addresses. This tends to ruin any notion of location transparency. Imagine using names like "Place_Order@MachineA.CompanyX.com" in your application. Not only might the service move to another machine, but even if it stays put both the machine and company names might change.

The second design requirement was that programs should not have to consult a directory explicitly to resolve a name to something that can be used in a subsequent communication call. Why make two calls when one suffices? When using **tpcall**, the TUXEDO System does a few things transparently for you. Using its load balancing algorithms, the TUXEDO System first consults the Bulletin Board to pick a server having a relatively low load at the moment. It then resolves the service name to a fully qualified address for the chosen server. Finally, it sends the request on its way.

In the TUXEDO System, there is no value in returning fully qualified addresses to programs. This would only encourage programs to cache them thinking they would be saving on the cost of name resolution in subsequent calls. Unfortunately, your application could be dynamically changing which would make the addresses invalid. And even if your application wasn't changing very much, stashing away addresses completely thwarts the benefits of load balancing! For this reason, server addresses are not revealed to your programs.

Choosing service names and deciding what processing they will do is an important part of designing your TUXEDO application. If service routines are too "fine grained," then you run the risk of "showing through" to clients too much of the logic implementing your business functions. On the other hand, if your service routines are too "coarse grained," then you run the risk of burying the bulk of your business logic in too few services. Ideally, your application's portfolio of service routines should match the set of functions commonly performed by your business.

By the way, the service name is the only parameter **tpcall** requires to have a nonnull value. That's right; some service contracts can be fulfilled simply by calling them. No data is exchanged between client and server; rather, the mere mention of the service name by the client is enough for the server to know what to do. Such services are purely processing agents whose actions are implied by their service names. One example is a service that keeps track of a statistic: every time the service is invoked it increments a counter stored on disk. Another example is a registration service that keeps track of clients simply by the request's associated client identifier.

Request Buffer

More usual is the case where a service routine requires some parameters to fulfill its contract. These parameters are carried in a *request buffer*. A request buffer is always a typed buffer, and it contains the data a service needs to perform its service. The TUXEDO System imposes no limit on the maximum size of request buffers; you are limited only by the amount of memory that your programs can allocate.

One of the most powerful aspects of the ATMI communication verbs is that they can accept any type of input data. Because typed buffers can contain virtually any data type or structure that you can represent in the programming language you are using, a single set of communication verbs suffices for sending and receiving an unlimited number of data types. Thus, **tpcall**'s request buffer parameter can be either one of the typed buffers supplied with the TUXEDO System or it can be a custom buffer type defined specifically for your application.

A service routine can accept multiple request buffer types. For example, the "Place_Order" service might be written to accept both FML buffers and VIEW buffers. In fact, there are administrative options available to declare which buffer type or types a service routine is willing to accept. When specified, **tpcall** will return an error if the request buffer type is not on the service routine's list of accepted buffer types (that is, the client is not executing a service contract correctly). This provides for early error detection to avoid the potential overhead of sending network messages simply to get an error return.

Request Buffer Length

This parameter contains the size in bytes of the request typed buffer. As mentioned in Chapter 8, "Typed Buffers," most typed buffers are self-describing in terms of their length. This means that for such buffers you do not have to tell **tpcall** how many bytes are in your request buffer. Because the FML typed buffer switch routines use information stored in the FML buffer itself to determine the size of any given FML buffer, FML is a self-describing buffer type. However, the CARRAY buffer type, being an application-interpreted collection of bytes, does not carry its length information, so you must use this parameter to tell the TUXEDO run-time system how many bytes you wish to send. In most code listings in this book, you will see that this parameter is set to zero due to our use of self-describing buffer types, such as VIEWs.

Reply Buffer

This parameter is where the data returned from the service routine, in the form of a typed buffer, is placed. The client must pass to **tpcall** a typed buffer in which to place the reply data. This buffer can, in fact, be the request buffer, in which case the reply data will overwrite values present in the buffer before **tpcall** was invoked. If this is not the behavior you desire, then the reply buffer parameter should reference a different typed buffer.

In most cases, the types and subtypes of the request and reply buffers are the same, but this does not have to be the case. Just as service routines can accept multiple buffer types and subtypes, services can return one of several different buffer types as well. Typically, this feature is used when a single buffer type has several distinct sub-types, and the subtypes used for requests differ from those returned as replies. When the reply received differs in type or subtype from the reply buffer parameter passed to **tpcall**, the TUXEDO run-time system changes the reply buffer's type or subtype automatically. ATMI provides a function, **tptypes**, that your program can use to find out the type and subtype of the reply buffer returned.

Reply Buffer Length

Once **tpcall** returns, this parameter contains the length of the buffer received, even if the buffer type is self-describing in terms of its length. This is done so that your program can know how much total data is in the returned reply buffer. Also, you can compare the returned reply buffer length with the length of the reply buffer before you issued **tpcall** to see whether or not the buffer has grown. Recall from Chapter 8, "Typed Buffers," that ATMI transparently grows your buffers so that your programs do not have to worry about truncation and reallocation.

Flags

This parameter contains bit settings that influence the way **tpcall** works. In general, flags are used to override a function's default behavior. Here is a summary of the flags that you can pass to **tpcall**. The symbolic name of the flag is shown at left. Many of these flags are reused in other ATMI functions. We will cover them here and only mention them by name throughout the rest of the book.

TPNOTRAN. Call a service routine so that it is not part of your client's current transaction. You might use this option because you do not want any failures reported by the called service to affect your client's current transaction. When this option is not set, the called service will work on behalf of the client's transaction, if one exists.

TPNOCHANGE. Perform strong type checking on the returned output buffer. This option states to **tpcall** that your client is expecting the reply data to be of a particular buffer type. Specifically, it is requiring that the returned buffer match the type and subtype of the output buffer passed to **tpcall**. If a buffer type is returned that does not match the one provided, then **tpcall** returns an error. When this option is not set, **tpcall** returns in the output buffer whatever buffer type the service returned, and you can use **tptypes** to find out its type and subtype. You might use this flag to enforce a service contract's reply buffer type—especially if the service returns only a single type. In the event that a service routine is updated to return a different buffer type, a client using the older version would get an explicit "output buffer type error" when it called the newer version of the service.

TPNOBLOCK. Do not block waiting to send the request if a blocking condition exists. If the TUXEDO run-time system processing **tpcall** would have to wait for some condition to pass while trying to send a client's request, then this option instructs **tpcall** not to send the request and to return control to the client. Blocking conditions typically occur when internal operating system or networking buffers needed for sending a request are temporarily full. When this option is not set, **tpcall**, upon encountering a blocking condition, either waits until the blocking condition subsides or until a time-out occurs. Recall from Chapter 4, "Application Development—Overview," that there are two types of time-outs: blocking and transaction.

TPNOTIME Do not generate a blocking time-out. When you use this option, your program is telling the TUXEDO run-time system that it is willing to wait indefinitely if a blocking condition is encountered. This option can be used only to override blocking time-outs; transaction time-outs cannot be overridden.

TPSIGRSTRT Restart processing after receiving an operating system interrupt. Some operating systems—most notably Unix—allow running programs to be interrupted, which causes them to stop doing whatever they were doing in order to process the interrupts. Programs use a facility called "signals" to interrupt each other. The **TPSIGRSTRT** option allows your program to specify that it wants **tpcall** to restart its processing after being interrupted by a signal and behave as if the signal had not arrived. When this option is not used, **tpcall** returns an error if it is interrupted either while trying to send a request or while awaiting its reply.

Listing 10.1 shows an invocation of the "Place_Order" service using **tpcall**. To fulfill this service contract, the client must send it a request in the form of an order. The service places the order—in a manner which is completely transparent to the client—and returns a reply in the form of a receipt.

```
#include "views.h"

struct order *req_buf;
struct receipt *reply_buf;
long reply_len;
int ret_val;

req_buf = (struct order *) tpalloc("VIEW", "order", 0);
reply_buf = (struct receipt *) tpalloc("VIEW", "receipt", 0);
/* put code here that fills in req_buf */
ret_val = tpcall("Place_Order", req_buf, 0, &reply_buf, &reply_len, TPNOBLOCK);
/* put code here that checks ret_val and processes reply_buf */
```

Listing 10.1   *tpcall Example*

Before calling **tpcall**, the request and reply typed buffers are first allocated using **tpalloc**. Both are VIEW buffer types, which means they will be manipulated as C structures. In this example, the subtypes of the request and reply buffers differ. The request buffer is a structure called **order** while the reply buffer is a different structure called **receipt**. In both calls to **tpalloc**, the length parameters are 0 because VIEWs are self-describing in terms of their lengths (that is, **tpalloc** can determine the size of each structure solely from its type and subtype). As described in

Chapter 8, "Typed Buffers," these VIEWs are first defined and compiled using the TUXEDO VIEW compiler **viewc** which generates a C header file, called **views.h** in Listing 10.1, containing the definitions of these two structures.

Once the request buffer has been filled in, the client calls **tpcall** passing it a reference to the order structure (**req_buf**). The client also passes to **tpcall** the *address* of the address of the reply buffer (**&reply_buf**) where the reply will be placed. The reason that the address of **reply_buf**'s address is passed to **tpcall** is because the TUXEDO run-time system might return a pointer to a different data buffer than the one to which **reply_buf** points. By passing the buffer pointer's address, the run-time system is free to "swap" buffer pointers with the program calling **tpcall**. It might need to do this to allocate a larger buffer so as to prevent the caller from having to worry about truncation and reallocation in the event that a buffer of a larger size than expected is returned. Preventing truncation is more a concern for buffers that vary in size, such as FML, as opposed to fixed-sized buffers, such as VIEWs.

Let's now turn our attention to the COBOL procedure, **TPCALL**. Listing 10.2 shows the same invocation of the "Place_Order" service written in COBOL.

The semantics of **tpcall** and **TPCALL** are nearly identical. The main difference is how typed buffers are used. Because standard COBOL does not provide for pointers and dynamic memory allocation, the C mechanism for allocating buffers along with their type via **tpalloc** would not have worked. Instead, COBOL programs explicitly assign type and subtype information to COBOL records predefined in the **WORKING-STORAGE SECTION**. That assignment is done in a record (**TPTYPE**) that is separate from the data record itself. In Listing 10.2, we see that this is accomplished by assignments to the **REQ-TYPE-REC** and **REPLY-TYPE-REC** records. These records are declared in the **COPY** files, **ORDER.cbl** and **RECEIPT.cbl**, respectively, each of which was generated by the TUXEDO VIEW compiler **viewc**.

Because dynamic memory allocation is not available in COBOL, another difference in COBOL ATMI is that truncation of reply buffers is possible because COBOL records cannot be grown automatically by the TUXEDO run-time system. Note above that in preparing the reply record's type information, the length of the record where the reply data is placed must be passed to **TPCALL**. After **TPCALL** returns, the program can check **REPLY-TYPE-REC** to see if the reply data was truncated because it could not fit in the reply data record. Unless an application error exists, truncation cannot occur in this example because a specific record type, the **RECEIPT** record, is returned.

Another interesting difference is how options are passed to the COBOL version of ATMI routines. COBOL programs deal with options by setting individual values to **TRUE** or **FALSE**. In Listing 10.2, you can see a line of code where the **TPNOBLOCK** value is set to **TRUE**. Notice that the value is an element of a record called, **TPSVCDEF-REC**, the service definition record. This is the same record where the program places the name of the service to be invoked. One advantage of having the option values reside in the same record as the service name is

```
      WORKING-STORAGE SECTION.
*
      01 TPSCVDEF-REC.
         COPY TPSVCDEF.
      01 REQ-TYPE-REC.
         COPY TPTYPE.
      01 REPLY-TYPE-REC.
         COPY TPTYPE.
      01 TPSTATUS-REC.
         COPY TPSTATUS.
      01 REQ-DATA-REC COPY ORDER.
      01 REPLY-DATA-REC COPY RECEIPT.
*
      PROCEDURE DIVISION.
*
      MOVE LOW-VALUES TO TPSCVDEF-REC.
      MOVE "Place_Order" TO SERVICE-NAME IN TPSCVDEF-REC.
      SET TPNOBLOCK IN TPSCVDEF-REC TO TRUE.
      SET TPSIGRSTRT IN TPSCVDEF-REC TO TRUE.

      MOVE LOW-VALUES TO REQ-TYPE-REC.
      MOVE "VIEW" TO REC-TYPE IN REQ-TYPE-REC.
      MOVE "ORDER" TO SUB-TYPE IN REQ-TYPE-REC.

      MOVE LOW-VALUES TO REPLY-TYPE-REC.
      MOVE "VIEW" TO REC-TYPE IN REPLY-TYPE-REC.
      MOVE "RECEIPT" TO SUB-TYPE IN REPLY-TYPE-REC.
      MOVE LENGTH OF REPLY-DATA-REC TO LEN IN REPLY-TYPE-REC.
*
*  FILL IN REQ-DATA-REC RECORD WITH APPLICATION DATA
*
      CALL "TPCALL" USING TPSCVDEF-REC, REQ-TYPE-REC, REQ-DATA-REC,
            REPLY-TYPE-REC, REPLY-DATA-REC, TPSTATUS-REC.
```

Listing 10.2   *TPCALL Example*

that, once you set up this structure for a particular service name and its options, your program can reuse it each time it needs to invoke that service.

10.1.2 The Service Template

Now that we have seen what the client program must do to call a service, let's look at what the service writer must do to process a client's request. Essentially, a service routine is invoked with a request buffer, processes it, and returns a reply buffer. Writing a service routine is different from calling one because instead of your program calling a TUXEDO System ATMI verb, the opposite happens: the TUXEDO Server Adaptor calls your service routine. This can be seen in Figure 10.2.

When you write a service routine, it must conform to a template after which all service routines are modeled. A service routine is invoked with one argument, a *service information structure*, that contains the elements shown in Listing 10.3.

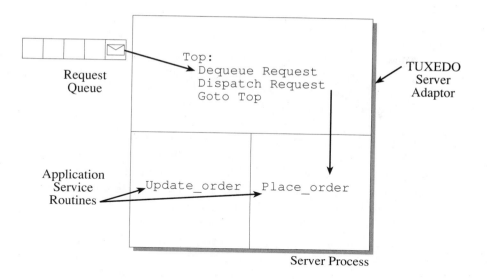

Figure 10.2 **The TUXEDO System Dispatching an Application Service Routine**

Let's look at each of these elements in detail.

Service Name

Your service routine can extract the service name from the name element with which it was invoked. Now, this might sound peculiar at first since you would think that a service would know its own name! In fact, most of the time a service does not need to consult the name element because it knows on behalf of which service name it is working. Here are some cases where it might need to find out its invoked name.

A TUXEDO System administrator is free to assign service name aliases to service routines. The actual C routine name for a service could be different from the

```
struct tpscvinfo {
        char        name[32];      /* service name */
        long        flags;         /* options about request */
        char        *data;         /* request data */
        long        len;           /* request data length */
        int         cd;            /* connection descriptor */
        long        appkey;        /* application key */
        CLIENTID    cltid;         /* client identifier */
};
typedef struct tpsvcinfo TPSVCINFO;
```

Listing 10.3 *Service Information Structure*

service name advertised to clients. For example, the routine whose C symbol is **empapp_add_v2** could have as its advertised name "Add_Employee." Aliasing is another form of location transparency because the service routine might change its C symbol with, say, every new version. The benefit to your client programs is that they are not disrupted by service routine name changes; they continue to invoke "Add_Employee" regardless of the routine's actual C name. From the perspective of the service routine, there might be situations where the routine needs to reference its invoked name, let's say because it calls a generic routine that writes a message in the application's error log. In this case, it is helpful if it referred to the name that clients used to invoke it, rather than its actual routine name.

Another use for service name aliasing occurs when a single service routine performs many different services. Such a service needs to know its invoked name to determine which service to perform. For example, the "Debit" and "Credit" services perform many of the same operations, such as account validation. Of course, the main difference ultimately comes down to the arithmetic operation performed against the account: "Debit" subtracts money from an account whereas "Credit" adds to an account. Thus, a banking application might choose to provide a single service routine, **Update_Acct**, for both of these operations, and have the routine use the invoked service name to decide which one to perform at run-time.

Request Data

The request data element is the typed buffer sent to a service. Recall from the previous subsection, that this was **tpcall**'s request buffer. A service can choose to accept as its input one or more kinds of typed buffers. In the most straightforward case, a service routine accepts only one particular buffer type and subtype. A slightly more general version of that same service might be written to accept its input in the form of multiple subtypes of the same buffer type, or even as multiple buffer types. In the case of a single routine that performs multiple services, it might be written to process several different buffer types or subtypes. For example, our **Update_Acct** routine requires a VIEW whose subtype is "debit_struct" when it is invoked as "Debit," whereas it requires the "credit_struct" subtype when it is invoked as "Credit."

Request Data Length

This element contains the length of the request buffer. This is an important piece of information for buffer types whose length cannot be determined by their type or subtype alone, for example, the CARRAY buffer type. It is ignored in other cases.

Flags

This element contains options and attributes that affect the behavior of a service routine. For example, one of the settings available to the service is whether or not it was dispatched in transaction mode. Another flag informs it whether or not the client expects a reply. When a service is used in a conversation, the flags also tell it whether the client or the service has sending rights.

Connection Descriptor

When a service is constructed to have a conversation with a client, then this structure element holds the *connection descriptor* for the conversation. This descriptor is used for referencing the conversation in subsequent calls that send or receive data on the conversation. A service is designed to be either a request/response service or a conversational service; it cannot be both. Thus, this element has no relevance for request/response interactions. Conversational services are covered in Chapter 11, "Conversational Communication."

Application Key

The *application key* is a value assigned to every client that has been authenticated as part of joining a TUXEDO application. This authentication is done either by the authentication mechanism supplied with the TUXEDO System, or it can be a replacement authentication mechanism provided by your application. When a client program joins an application by calling **tpinit**, it is assigned an application key value that accompanies every request the client sends to services and every message the client enqueues in application queues. The application key is each client's credentials and is used for access control purposes. We should point out that client programs never see the keys assigned to them at authentication time; rather, the authentication mechanism makes keys available only to the TUXEDO run-time system which appends them transparently to all clients' requests.

Many applications find the TUXEDO System's use of the application key for access control purposes sufficient (see Chapter 17, "A Tour of the TUXEDO Management Information Base," for more details). These applications' services, then, would have no further use for the application key. However, there are other applications that not only want system-level access control but they also want to use clients' credentials to perform their own application-level access control. As you can see in Listing 10.4, the **Update_Acct** service uses the application key as the parameter to a function that determines whether a particular client has the authority to debit amounts over $99,999.

Client Identifier

Each client program that joins a TUXEDO application is also assigned a unique *client identifier* for the purpose of event notification. If a server needs to contact a client with anything other than the reply the client is expecting, then it uses the client identifier to address the client that should receive the event notification.

For example, imagine that a client makes a request of a service to buy stock. Rather than have the service wait until the order completes before sending the reply, the server could forward the client's order to the market—that is, to the

```
#include <atmi.h>

void Update_Acct(TPSVCINFO *svcinfo)
{
        debit_struct deb;
        credit_struct cred;

        if (equal(svcinfo->name, "DEBIT")) {
                /* service was invoked to perform debit */
                deb = *(debit_struct *)(svcinfo->data);
                if ((deb.amount > 99999) && !verify(svcinfo->appkey)) {
                        /* client is not allowed to debit large amounts */
                        strcpy(&deb.status, "Permission Denied");
                        tpreturn(TPFAIL, -1, &deb, 0, TPNOFLAGS);
                }
                /* otherwise perform debit and return balance */
                deb.balance = new_balance;
                tpreturn(TPSUCCESS, 0, &deb, 0, TPNOFLAGS);
        } else {
                /* service was invoked to perform credit */
                cred = *(credit_struct *)(svcinfo->data);
                ...
        }
        ...
}
```

Listing 10.4   *C Language Service Routine Example*

computers that actually perform stock trades—and send a reply back to the client right away informing it that it will notify the client later when the order has completed. Just before doing so, the server will record the client's identifier, along with its order number, so that when the order is later completed, the server can send the client an asynchronous event notification that its order was filled or the reason why it failed to fill. ATMI's event notification methods are discussed in Chapter 13, "Event-Based Communication."

Listing 10.4 shows an example of how a service routine is written in C and how to use the service information structure passed into a service.

In COBOL, dispatching a service routine is done differently than in C because the server adaptor cannot start a COBOL program with the set of data elements described above. Instead, it dispatches the COBOL program whose first order of business is to call back the server adaptor to get these elements. Thus, all COBOL service routines start by calling the COBOL ATMI function, **TPSVCSTART**. Listing 10.5 shows an example of how this is done.

You might have noticed that **TPSVCSTART** takes the same parameter as **TPCALL**: the **TPSVCDEF-REC** record. This record contains all the elements that a service needs to begin its processing, including the service name used to invoke the calling program and all option settings (for example, the "no reply is wanted" setting).

```
   WORKING-STORAGE SECTION.
*
01 TPSVCDEF-REC.
   COPY TPSVCDEF.
01 TPTYPE-REC.
   COPY TPTYPE.
01 DATA-REC.
   COPY User Data.
01 TPSTATUS-REC.
   COPY TPSTATUS.
*
   PROCEDURE DIVISION.
*
CALL "TPSVCSTART" USING TPSVCDEF-REC TPTYPE-REC DATA-REC TPSTATUS-REC.
```

Listing 10.5   *COBOL Service Initialization Example*

10.1.3 Returning from a Service: tpreturn

In Listing 10.4, there are a couple of calls to the function **tpreturn**. This is the function used to end a service routine and return a reply to a client. **tpreturn** is similar to the C language **return** statement insofar as it returns control back to the higher-level routine that invoked it. In the case of a TUXEDO service, the higher level "routine" where control is returned is the server adaptor. Here is the function prototype for **tpreturn**:

```
void tpreturn(int return_value,long return_code,
              char *reply_data,long reply_len,long
              flags)
```

Let's now look at the parameters that **tpreturn** accepts and what they are used for.

Return Value

The return value informs the server adaptor whether or not the service completed successfully from the application's point of view. If the service routine performed its part of the contract successfully, then setting the return value to **TPSUCCESS** informs both the TUXEDO run-time system and the client of the service's success. On the other hand, if something went wrong in the service routine, for example, a customer's account number was not found in the database, then the service routine can set the return value to **TPFAIL** indicating that the service could not fulfill the contract. In Listing 10.4, the service fails if the amount being debited is larger than $99,999 and the client does not have permission to debit such large amounts (as determined by passing the client's application key to an application-supplied routine that verifies the client's credentials).

The return value is also sent back to the client along with any reply. The client can use the return value to determine how to handle the reply. For instance, a service might return one buffer type on success but a different one if the service fails. Perhaps the buffer returned in the failure case contains detailed information needed by the client program to inform the end user why the service failed. Such information is not needed when the service succeeds.

It is important for the TUXEDO run-time system to know about the success or failure of a service. Although the TUXEDO run-time system does not understand what success or failure means in terms of your application, when a service participates in a TUXEDO global transaction, a service's success is a vote of confidence in the transaction, whereas a failure indicates to both the client and the TUXEDO run-time system that the transaction must be rolled back. Upon seeing a service failure return value, the TUXEDO run-time system notes that the transaction must ultimately be rolled back—in fact, it marks the transaction internally as *abort-only*. So, even if the client ignores the failure return value and accidentally tries to commit the transaction, the TUXEDO run-time system will ensure that all the work done on behalf of the transaction is rolled back. In Chapter 14, "Transactions in the TUXEDO System," we will cover how a service participates in global transactions.

Return Code

The return code is an application-defined value that can be returned to the client along with the reply, regardless of whether or not the service completed successfully. Moreover, a return code can be sent even when no reply buffer is sent, in which case the return code is the reply. The return code is defined as a long integer and is used to carry a code that means something to the client (the TUXEDO run-time system does not interpret the code's value). Because a service is, in fact, a function, albeit one that is remote to the client, then the return code can be used like a function's return value. After **tpcall** completes, a client program can access the called service's return code via the variable, **tpurcode**.

Say that your application's convention is to return a value less than zero when services fail. Moreover, you have defined values for half a dozen distinct reasons why services can fail. Then, the return code can be set to one of these six negative values so that the client can understand immediately why its request failed. From Listing 10.4, we see that –1 is used in conjunction with **TPFAIL** to denote that the service failed because the client failed the verification test for debiting large amounts of money. The service could also fail because the account number is invalid. In that case, the service would call **tpreturn** with a return value of **TPFAIL** and a return code of –2.

There are advantages to decoupling a service's level of success (its return value) from its return codes. The return value provides a simple, unambiguous, binary method for declaring a service's success or failure to both your client and the TUXEDO run-time system, whereas the return code gives your service the flexibility to differentiate particular reasons for success or failure. Services can do this because they are not constrained to using particular values to denote application successes and failures. Your application can define positive numbers, negative numbers, prime numbers, or Fibonacci numbers as your services' return codes. And, you can define different ranges of numbers for success and failure conditions. You should think of the return code as an extra data item that you can use to pass information between a client and a server.

Reply Data

The reply data parameter is the data buffer sent back to the client that initiated the request. This buffer ends up in the reply buffer parameter of **tpcall**. Usually, the buffer passed into the service—the request buffer element of the service information structure—is the same buffer used for the reply. But, as we have mentioned before, this does not have to be the case. A new buffer of the same or different type or subtype could be used for the reply. It is worth noting that the buffer used for the reply is freed by the server adaptor. This is because **tpreturn** does not return control to its caller, the service routine. This makes things easy if your service uses for its reply the same buffer it was given at the start of the service. That is, the server adaptor allocates the memory for the buffer before dispatching your service, and it frees it after your service calls **tpreturn**. If your service allocates and uses a different buffer for the reply, then having the server adaptor free that buffer ensures that your server does not incur memory leaks by allocating buffers which are never freed.

Reply Length

As we have seen before, this parameter is necessary only for those buffers whose length cannot be determined by the buffer itself (for example, CARRAYs).

Flags

Most ATMI calls have a "flags" argument. As we saw previously, **tpcall** makes extensive use of this parameter for specifying options that affect its behavior. However, in the case of **tpreturn**, this parameter currently does not have any defined options.

As you can see, **tpreturn** does quite a lot! With one call your service routine can

- end the service and return control to the server adaptor
- indicate to both the client and the TUXEDO run-time system whether the service completed successfully or not
- return reply data to the client in the form of a typed buffer
- return an application return code to the client in the form of a long integer
- ensure that its work on behalf of the client's global transaction has quiesced so that ultimately it can be committed or rolled back.

10.1.4 TxRPC

The other set of tools available for writing synchronous request/response applications in the TUXEDO System is that of TxRPC. As we have already mentioned, TxRPC is based on OSF's DCE RPC facility enhanced to support transactional communication. Specifically, TxRPC is DCE RPC extended by X/Open's TX transaction demarcation API [X/Open-TX] and enhancements to the IDL so that RPCs can be bracketed within transaction boundaries.

RPCs are a form of communication in which what look like regular, local procedure calls are actually calls to procedures that are executed in other address spaces, possibly on other computers. The trick is that when a local procedure call is made, the invoked procedure issues communications calls to a server which, in turn, dispatches a procedure that actually does the intended work. As you can see, this is clearly a form of distributed function shipping. Also, by their very nature, RPCs are a form of synchronous communication because the caller waits for the called procedure to finish, just as it would if the procedure were directly linked to the calling program.

RPCs are defined using an *Interface Definition Language* (IDL). The IDL is used to describe the procedures—C functions, there is no COBOL support—that will be called by client programs but which will actually be executed in server programs. These procedures are called *operations* in RPC parlance, and an interface definition may contain one or more operations. An operation defined in IDL contains information about the syntax of the function called, its parameters, and their data types. It also contains information about which parameters must be present when the function is called, known as [in] parameters, which ones are returned when the function returns, known as [out] parameters, and which ones are both "in" and "out" parameters, known as [in,out] parameters. IDL definitions also contain unique interface definition numbers and version numbers. In a nutshell, IDL definitions are concrete representations of service contracts.

Listing 10.6 shows an IDL file for an interface that offers both debit and credit operations.

Other than the function prototypes and the data type information in Listing 10.6, you will see a very long string of numbers and letters on the first line of the IDL. This is this interface's *universal unique identifier* (uuid). This identifier

```
[uuid(E168C700-A9AE-1111-9A3F-9302C1160000),version(1.0)]
interface My_Bank_App
{
        int debit([in] int account, [in] int amount, [out] int *balance);
        int credit([in] int account, [in] int amount, [out] int *balance);
}
```

Listing 10.6 *IDL for the Interface My_Bank_App*

uniquely defines this interface definition across all applications and all networks. Every IDL interface must have a uuid. You get a uuid by running a program called **uuidgen**. Its output is an interface definition template complete with its own uuid. Once you have the template, you use your favorite text editor to fill in the specifics of your interface contracts. The interface in Listing 10.6 is called **My_Bank_App** and it contains two operations, **debit** and **credit**.

Unlike ATMI services, which have no inherent administrative relationship with one another, RPC operations are bound together by the interfaces in which they are defined. That is, as ATMI service names, **debit** and **credit** are independent services. Unless they are written to use shared data (for example, a common global variable), there is nothing about them that requires that they reside within the same server. However, as shown in Listing 10.6, **debit** and **credit** are two operations defined within the same RPC interface, **My_Bank_App**. As such, they must always reside within the same server—regardless of whether they share any data. In fact, the interface name is the unit of administration in the TUXEDO System (and in DCE, too). Recall from Chapter 7, "Introduction to the Application Programming Interface," that interface names, not individual operations, are advertised when RPC servers are built.

Once you have an IDL file, you need to compile it into *stubs* which are linked to your client and server programs. As shown in Figure 10.3, you pass your IDL file through the TUXEDO System's TxRPC IDL compiler whose job it is to generate three output files:

∎ A client stub file. This is a surrogate for the real function that your client wishes to invoke. It is linked to the client program instead of the

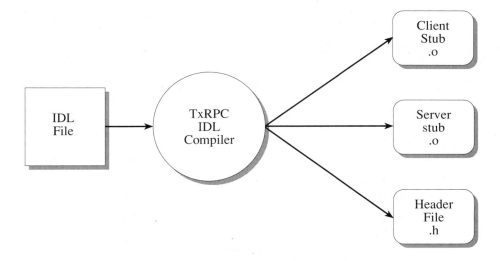

Figure 10.3 Compiling IDL File into Stubs and Header Files

real function (which is linked to the server). The client stub contains calls to the TUXEDO run-time system which package and send the input parameters in the form of a service request. The client stub also unpacks any output parameters and the function's return value received from the server. The packing and unpacking of arguments is referred to as marshalling and unmarshalling, respectively.

▮ A server stub file. This is a surrogate routine that the server calls when it receives a request to dispatch the function. The server stub unmarshalls the input parameters and calls the actual function that the client wants invoked. When that function returns, the server stub marshals the output parameters and the function's return value, and ships them back to the client in the form of a reply.

▮ A header file used by the stubs and, more importantly, by the programs that call the client stubs. This file contains data type information and the function prototypes for the operations defined in the IDL file.

Because IDL files are compiled into stubs containing executable marshalling code, the C data types that can be expressed in IDL are far richer than those expressed as VIEW typed buffers, which are interpreted at run-time. The power of typed buffers does not lie in the expressive power of any one particular data type. Rather, it is the fact that with typed buffers your application can choose from a variety of data types each offering unique advantages to your applications. On the other end of the data marshalling spectrum, IDL offers the most expressive power—indeed, a superset of the C language—due to its compilation into code tailored specifically to marshal each defined data type and no other. The downside is that its format is fixed, requiring recompilation of both client and server when it is changed.

IDL files are portable across platforms because they contain source statements. The same IDL file can be compiled into a client stub on one computer and compiled into a server stub on a different computer. For example, you may want to compile your IDL files into client stubs on your Windows 95 PC and link them to your client programs while compiling those same IDL files into server stubs on your HP/UX RISC machine where they will be linked to your servers that execute there.

The general flow for an RPC is illustrated in Figure 10.4 using the **debit** operation from our example in Listing 10.6. When the client program calls **debit**, the client stub is invoked. It marshals the operation's [in] parameters, **account** and **amount**, and uses the underlying TUXEDO System communication infrastructure to send the request to the server. The client stub then blocks waiting for the reply. The server receives the request, unmarshals the parameters, and dispatches the debit function. When **debit** returns, the server stub marshals the [out] parameter, **balance**, and the operation's return value, and sends them back to the client in the form of a reply. The client unmarshals these and returns them to the client program in the form of the function's return value and **balance**.

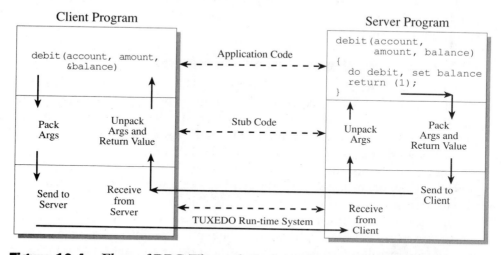

Figure 10.4 **Flow of RPC Through Stubs and TUXEDO Runtime**

In addition to the IDL compiler, the TUXEDO System supplies TxRPC run-time support libraries that help your programs manage memory and communication errors. You use the TUXEDO System's **buildserver** and **buildclient** programs to generate executable programs that link to the stubs and these libraries, as described in Chapter 7, "Introduction to the Application Programming Interface." The area of RPC programming is much larger than can be covered in this book. You can read more about it in [OSF DCE]. One area we will cover later, in Chapter 18, "Getting Applications to Work Together," is how you can use TxRPC so that your TUXEDO applications can interoperate with DCE applications.

Although both TxRPC and ATMI support synchronous request/response communication, each has a distinctive approach and inherent advantages. The obvious advantage of TxRPC is that it mimics local procedure calling conventions. To that end, any C data structure that you can pass to a local procedure can also be specified in IDL and passed to a remote one. On the other hand, ATMI is a collection of library routines. As such, each routine's behavior is controlled by arguments passed to it, some of which are processed by the application (for example, request data) and some of which are processed by the TUXEDO run-time system (for example, flags). Thus, one of ATMI's advantages is its expressive power and the control you have when programming with it. Another advantage is the breadth of supported communication paradigms. Let's now turn back to ATMI and look at its parallel request/response constructs.

10.2 Parallel Request/Response

ATMI provides important variations to the synchronous request/response construct that help increase the performance of your application by adding parallelism to the basic request/response mechanism. These variations are described in the next two subsections.

10.2.1 Fan-Out Parallelism: tpacall and tpgetrply

Both **tpcall** and TxRPC are designed so that a client synchronously waits for a server's reply. In many cases, a client can do no other processing until its reply is returned. However, there are times when a client can do other tasks—including making other service calls—while its request is being processed and would not like to wait synchronously for its reply. That is, the client would like to issue its request, regain control to do something else, and, at some later time, check for its reply.

The ATMI functions **tpacall** and **tpgetrply** give client programs a way to issue service requests asynchronously (in fact, the first "a" in **tpacall** is for "asynchronous"). Think of these two functions as the two halves of **tpcall: tpacall** sends a request to a service routine and **tpgetrply** receives the reply. The difference is that, after a request is sent, tpacall returns control to the client program rather than waiting for the reply. It also returns a receipt, known as a *call descriptor*, that can be used when calling **tpgetrply** to specify exactly which reply the client is interested in getting.

As introduced in Chapter 3, "Communication and Administration Paradigms for Distributed Business Applications," this form of asynchronous processing is called fan-out parallelism because a client is allowed to issue several requests via **tpacall** before retrieving any replies. That is, a client's requests can be fanned out simultaneously to several services for processing. If the services reside on different computers or on different processors of a multiprocessor computer, then the client's requests can proceed in parallel.

Let's look more closely at each of these two functions. We will start with **tpacall**. The parameters passed to **tpacall** are service name, request buffer, request buffer length, and flags. Because **tpacall** can be thought of as the "send half" of **tpcall**, these parameters have a meaning identical to those described earlier in this chapter for **tpcall**. Thus, the service name parameter contains the name of the service routine to which the request buffer is sent. The request buffer is a typed buffer whose length is specified by the request buffer length parameter (unless the length of the buffer can be inferred from its type in which case you can set the length to 0). Last, with one exception we will describe below, the flags are a subset of those passed to **tpcall**.

There really are only two new semantics introduced in **tpacall**. The first one is the call descriptor returned for later use in retrieving the request's reply. The second is a new flag (**TPNOREPLY**) that allows the client to specify that it does not want a reply. In fact, should the service send a reply when the client uses this flag, the

TUXEDO System will discard it. We should point out that not receiving a reply is different from receiving a reply that has no data (that is, a null reply). With the former, the client has no idea when (or even if!) the service routine completes its request, nor can it find out whether its request succeeded or failed. With the latter, the client will receive a reply with an empty data buffer. It will know whether its request succeeded or failed, and it will get an application return code in the **tpurcode** variable.

Here is an example of how you use **tpacall**:

```
cd = tpacall("debit", req_buf, 0, TPNOTIME);
```

Notice that the call descriptor is returned as the function's return value and placed in the variable, **cd**.

Let's now look at **tpgetrply**. As the "receive half" of **tpcall**, **tpgetrply** takes a pointer to a reply buffer, a pointer to the reply buffer's length, and flags as its parameters. These parameters are used in the same way as they are for **tpcall**. In addition, **tpgetrply** takes a new parameter: a pointer to a call descriptor. Each invocation of **tpacall** returns a unique call descriptor whose scope is limited to the program that issued the call. A client program uses a call descriptor to correlate a reply with a previously issued request. The call descriptor is both an input and an output parameter to **tpgetrply**. On input, the call descriptor is used to tell the TUXEDO run-time system which reply to return (or which one to wait for). Your client programs are responsible for keeping track of call descriptors and correlating them with returned replies. Once a reply has been retrieved, its call descriptor is no longer valid. Shortly, we will see how the call descriptor is used as an output parameter.

Let's look at an example of how you call **tpgetrply** using the call descriptor, **cd**, returned above.

```
ret_val = tpgetrply(&cd, &reply_buf, &reply_len,
                    TPSIGRSTRT);
```

In this example, the client will retrieve or possibly wait for the reply associated with call descriptor **cd**, and no other. If your client program has issued several requests with **tpacall** and has no preference about which of its pending replies to wait for, **tpgetrply** has a flag setting (**TPGETANY**) stipulating that the TUXEDO run-time system should return any available reply. So that the client knows which reply was returned, **tpgetrply** also returns the call descriptor associated with the reply as an output parameter. If no replies are available, then **tpgetrply** waits for one to arrive—unless the **TPNOBLOCK** flag is used, in which case **tpgetrply** returns immediately if no reply is available.

In Listing 10.7, you can see how **tpacall** and **tpgetrply** are used together. Because the program uses the **TPGETANY** flag on the first call to **tpgetrply**, it uses a generic variable, **cd**, in which to get the returned call descriptor. The program then compares the value of **cd** to those returned by **tpacall** to determine which reply was actually received. Depending on the outcome, the program uses the other call descriptor to get the second reply (and does not use the **TPGETANY** flag).

```
int deb_cd, cred_cd, cd;
...
debit_buf = (struct debit *) tpalloc("VIEW", "debit", 0);
credit_buf = (struct credit *) tpalloc("VIEW", "credit", 0);
/* put code here that fills in the two input buffers */

deb_cd = tpacall("Debit", debit_buf, 0, TPNOFLAGS);
cred_cd = tpacall("Credit", credit_buf, 0, TPNOFLAGS);
/* both services are processing in parallel */
/* wait for either reply to arrive first */
tpgetrply(&cd, &outbuf, &outbuf_len, TPGETANY);
if (cd == deb_cd) {
        /* received reply for debit request */
        /* do any post-debit processing, then get credit reply */
        tpgetrply(&cred_cd, &outbuf, &outbuf_len, TPNOFLAGS);
} else {
        /* received reply for credit request */
        /* do any post-credit processing, then get debit reply */
        tpgetrply(&deb_cd, &outbuf, &outbuf_len, TPNOFLAGS);
}
```

Listing 10.7 *Example of Fan-Out Parallelism Using tpacall and tpgetrply*

In addition to fan-out parallelism, there is another thing you can do with **tpacall** and **tpgetrply** that you cannot do with **tpcall**: you can retry waiting for a reply after a blocking time-out occurs. Let's say your program is waiting in **tpgetrply** and the function returns with an error indicating that a blocking time-out has occurred. Your program can decide if it wants to call **tpgetrply** again and continue to wait for the reply. It can do this because call descriptors are not invalidated when blocking time-outs occur. You cannot retry a timed-out **tpcall** because there is no call descriptor generated for the request sent.

If your program doesn't want to retry a timed-out **tpgetrply**, it can call **tpcancel** with a particular call descriptor. This tells the TUXEDO run-time system that your program no longer wants to wait for that particular reply. If and when a reply arrives for a cancelled call descriptor, the TUXEDO run-time system automatically disposes of it.

Note, however, that retries are not allowed when a transaction time-out occurs. In this case, all call descriptors associated with the transaction are cancelled, and the transaction is flagged so that it will be rolled back.

10.2.2 Pipelined Parallelism: tpforward

Recall the example in Chapter 3, "Communication and Administration Paradigms for Distributed Business Applications," where a client makes a credit card authorization request. The client called a single service routine, "AUTH." However, to fulfill the credit card authorization contract, the "AUTH" service authorized the customer's password and then it forwarded the rest of the work of the contract to another service, "Good_standing." This service ensured that the customer was still credit-worthy. The advantage of forwarding the request to another service is that the forwarding service ("AUTH") is free to do work for another client because it has passed the responsibility of completing the first client's request to another service ("Good_standing"). When the "Good_standing" service is finished, it returns the reply directly to the client.

This type of forwarding from one service to the next was referred to as pipelined parallelism because many clients' requests can be in the contract-completion pipeline at once. That is, while client A's request is being processed by "Good_standing," client B's request is being processed by "AUTH." Without this form of parallelism, client B would have to wait for both the "AUTH" and the "Good_standing" services to complete client A's request before they could begin processing B's request.

ATMI offers this form of parallelism through the verb **tpforward** which service routines use to forward work to another service. This verb is a mix of **tpreturn** and **tpacall** with the **TPNOREPLY** flag set. At the point where a service routine has finished its part of the contract, it uses **tpforward** to do two things:

1. It ends the service routine and returns control back to the Server Adaptor. In this regard, **tpforward** acts like **tpreturn**.

2. It names a service routine to be invoked to process that portion of the original request still requiring processing. In this regard, **tpforward** acts like **tpacall**.

In fact, the parameters that you pass to **tpforward** are identical to those passed to **tpacall**: service name, request buffer, request buffer length, and flags. The only difference is that there are no flag options defined for **tpforward**. This is partly because **tpforward** does not return to the program that called it (that is, your service routine), and partly because the behavior of **tpforward** is controlled by the TUXEDO run-time system.

Taking our credit card authorization example again, Figure 10.5 shows the ATMI calls used by each program as well as the flow of messages between them.

1. The client uses **tpcall** to issue a request to the "AUTH" service. This request flows to Server 1 which offers the "AUTH" service.

2. The "AUTH" service verifies that the customer's password is correct, and then, using **tpforward**, forwards the data buffer to another service, "Good_standing." At this point, Server 1 is free to process new requests for its "AUTH" service.

3. The "Good_standing" service verifies that the customer is credit-worthy, and then uses **tpreturn** to send a reply back to the original client. The TUXEDO

run-time system ensures that enough addressing information is available at
Server 2 so that it can respond directly back to the original client.

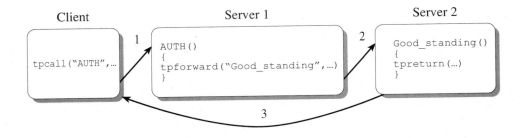

Figure 10.5   **Service Using tpforward to Forward Request**

Notice that the client is not aware that request forwarding is taking place. In
accordance with the principle of encapsulation, the client is aware only of the
contract offered, and has no knowledge of how the service goes about fulfilling its
obligation. This also extends to the "Good_standing" service which has no knowledge that it was invoked by a service calling **tpforward**. In fact, it cannot tell the
difference between being invoked directly by a client using **tpcall** or **tpacall** or by
a service using **tpforward**. In some cases, this application's clients might need to
use the "Good_standing" service directly.

The architectural feature that makes request forwarding possible in the
TUXEDO System is the use of *reliable messages* as the underlying mechanism
by which programs communicate. Recall from Chapter 6, "The Anatomy of a
TUXEDO Application," that the TUXEDO System uses message queues to pass
messages between programs on the same machine. **BRIDGE** programs deliver
messages between programs on different machines. The combination of the two
allows messages to be passed reliably—that is, with proper ordering and with no
duplication or loss of messages. Moreover, clients and server do not set up their
own private communication channels. Rather, they exchange messages over communication channels established and maintained by the TUXEDO System. Thus,
it is relatively straightforward for servers to forward the responsibility of responding to clients waiting for replies. In systems where clients and servers communicate via private channels (for example, pipes or sockets), true request forwarding is
nearly impossible because servers cannot easily delegate (that is, forward) their
end of a network connection to another server—let alone to a server on another
machine.

10.2.3 Using Parallelism: Think Globally, Act Locally

The beauty of ATMI's parallel request/response constructs is that they are local optimizations preserving the global nature of the request/response paradigm. Regardless of which techniques are used, the goal is the same: a client sends a request to a server, the server fulfills the service contract, and a reply is sent back to the client. So, when you design your application, you think first in terms of which services you need to model your business without worrying about which ATMI constructs to use. This keeps the task much simpler. Then, once you have defined your set of services and their interface contracts, you can decide locally (at each client and service) whether to exploit techniques for gaining processing parallelism.

Upon examining the services that your client programs need to call, you might find places where it makes sense to use **tpacall** for invoking several services at once. Of course, this affects only the client programs because converting a set of **tpcall**s to pairs of **tpacall**s and **tpgetrply**s has no affect on the interface contract or the service routines themselves.

Likewise, breaking up a single service routine into several smaller ones linked together with **tpforward** might not only keep each individual service in the forwarding chain simpler, but it could also lead to performance improvements due to pipelined parallelism. And as we mentioned earlier, doing so has no impact on client programs.

10.3 Request Priorities

ATMI allows you to control the priority at which a request is sent to a server. Priorities affect the order in which servers dequeue and dispatch requests. If two requests are on a server's queue, the server dequeues the one with the higher priority. It does not matter whether the requests are for the same service or for different services. The server will dequeue the request with the highest priority. To prevent the situation where low-priority requests sit on a queue for too long, every so often the TUXEDO run-time system will dequeue requests in order of arrival on the queue.

Request priorities range from 1 (lowest) to 100 (highest). All services are given a starting priority of 50. A service's starting priority can be changed by the administrator during application configuration. Once you have defined your set of service routines, you can assign priorities to them. For example, your business might require that the services "Debit" and "Credit" have higher priority (75) than "Balance_Inquiry" (50).

10.3.1 Setting Request Priorities: tpsprio

At run-time, if your program needs to further refine a service request's priority, it can do so with the ATMI function **tpsprio**. This function allows a program to set the priority of the next (and only the next) request sent by any of **tpcall**, **tpacall**, or **tpforward**. It takes two parameters: a priority value and flags. You can use **tpsprio** in one of two ways. You can increment or decrement a service's configured priority, or you can specify a priority in absolute terms regardless of its configured value. Let's look at two examples. Using the first method, your program might do what is done in Listing 10.8. The priority of "Debit" is incremented by 10. So, if "Debit" is currently configured at priority 75, then, for this **tpcall**, it will be sent at 85. This method is useful when your application's configured priorities are modified by the administrator while the system is running in which case your programs cannot know a service's given priority. Using **tpsprio** in this manner, your program alters a service's priority relative to its currently defined administrative value.

```
tpsprio(10, TPNOFLAGS); /* increments configured priority by 10 */
tpcall("Debit", req_buf, 0, &reply_buf, &reply_len, TPNOBLOCK);
```

Listing 10.8 *Example Using a Relative Priority*

Using the second method, a program can set a request's priority to an absolute value. Listing 10.9 is an example. The application's rules are that priorities are not changed by the application's administrator; rather, programs have control over altering services' priorities based on data values. Thus, this program might know that "Debit" is configured at priority 75, but, because this request involves a large amount of money, it needs to send this request at a higher priority than normal.

```
tpsprio(85, TPABSOLUTE); /* sets priority to 85 */
cd = tpacall("Debit", req_buf, 0, TPNOFLAGS);
```

Listing 10.9 *Example Using an Absolute Priority*

10.3.2 Getting Request Priorities: tpgprio

Programs can find out at which priority a request was sent. After a program calls **tpcall** or **tpacall**, it can call **tpgprio** to find out the priority of the request just sent. This is useful if the program does not know a service's configured priority but needs to find it out for future reference. A service routine can use **tpgprio** to find out the priority of the request it is currently processing. The function **tpgprio** takes no arguments, and it returns a priority value between 1 and 100.

10.4 Summary

In this chapter we presented all of the TUXEDO System's request/response constructs. These fall into one of two categories: library-based ATMI or language-based TxRPC. ATMI offers a "classic" synchronous request/response mechanism (**tpcall**) as well as unique constructs for both fan-out (**tpacall** and **tpgetrply**) and pipelined (**tpforward**) parallelism. Because these constructs are available through a programming library, they give you flexible run-time options and good control over error handling. The data passed between clients and services is encapsulated in typed buffers which let your application communicate any number of data types through one set of ATMI routines.

TxRPC also offers a synchronous request/response paradigm. Because its syntax is meant to mimic the C language's local procedure calling conventions, it cannot offer either fan-out or pipelined parallelism. The bulk of the work you have to do to program using TxRPC is writing the IDL files that contain your application's interface contracts and linking your clients and servers to the stubs produced by the IDL compiler. Because they are compiled into marshalling code, the data types that can be expressed in IDL are as powerful—and in some ways more powerful—than the C language itself. Where the transparency of remote procedures falls down is in the area of error handling: your programs have to handle a whole new set of errors that were never possible when calling local procedures (for example, network errors).

Even though you can mix and match TxRPC and ATMI in your programs, you will probably want to stick with one or the other for consistency. You should use ATMI's request/response tools when your application requires any of the following:

▌ the performance benefits of parallel constructs,

▌ control over run-time options, such as those offered by **TPNOTRAN** and **TPNOBLOCK**, or

▌ use of the other paradigms offered in ATMI, such as application queuing or events.

If your application is largely based on synchronous request/response, you might choose the TxRPC approach, especially if your application needs more complex C structures or if it needs to interoperate with a DCE application (see Chapter 18, "Getting Applications to Work Together," for details).

11 Conversational Communication

PROGRAMMING

In Chapter 10, "Request/Response Communication," we saw several ways that you can program request/response communication in the TUXEDO System. One aspect common to all of them is that a client sends one request and receives one reply—unless **tpacall** with **TPNOREPLY** is used in which case no reply is received. Although this paradigm suffices for the majority of client/server interactions, there are times when a client and a server need to exchange more than just one request and one reply. Recall the "Browse_Catalog" example from Chapter 4, "Application Development—Overview," where the client asked for a description of all the hats offered by the mail-order company. Rather than the service returning all of them at once, which might be too burdensome for the client, the service returns only five a time. In this case, a single request has multiple "replies."

This chapter covers the nature of conversational interactions and shows you the ATMI functions that you use to write them.

11.1 What is Conversational Communication?

From a programmer's perspective, the essential difference between request/response and conversational communication is how client and server programs maintain and use state information during an interaction. With the request/response model, the client's request contains all the data that the service requires. The service processes the client's request using only that data and, when it finishes the service, returns a reply.

We call this interaction *stateless* because the service neither maintains nor uses any extra information about the client to process its request; all the information necessary to complete the work is in the request buffer. Any information that the service needs to maintain beyond the interaction is usually kept in some kind of database system that the service accesses. When the service finishes and returns a reply, there is no trace of the client left in the server or service. The service processes the next client's request with a "clean slate."

On the other hand, conversational programs build up and use application state information during their interactions. As we will soon see, even though data is sent and received between the client and the service, each program also maintains additional context or state information while conversing using a combination of its code position and stack data (known as local variables in C). By code position, we are referring to where a program is in executing its instructions.

With conversational communication, a program executes some instructions and then issues an ATMI communication call to synchronize with the program on the other end of the conversation. When one program sends data, its partner will not continue its processing until it receives the data. This is similar to coroutine processing where two programs are working together, but only one is executing at a time. In our "Browse_Catalog" example, the service maintains information about how many hat records have been sent to the client as well as which records to retrieve the next time the client asks for more. This information is maintained in local variables, and synchronization is performed by having the service wait for a client's message asking it for the next set of records.

Because programs having *stateful* interactions are synchronizing by using communication calls, they do not have to pass all of their state information back and forth each time they interact. Rather, they can keep some of their state in local variables and let the program's execution sequence set and use the state information as needed. There are some advantages in not passing all the state information in the communicated data. First, it decreases the amount of data sent through your networks. Second, it maintains the principles of encapsulation and data hiding because data that should not be visible outside of a client program will not be seen by a service, and vice versa.

11.2 Overview of the TUXEDO System's Conversational Interface

ATMI provides a set of verbs that allows your clients to interact with conversational service routines. These are **tpconnect**, **tpsend**, **tprecv**, and **tpdiscon**. As you can see in Figure 11.1, a client uses **tpconnect** to establish a conversational interaction with the service routine "Browse_Catalog." Both client and service then use **tpsend** and **tprecv** to exchange application data. A service routine normally terminates a conversation using **tpreturn**; however, if the client needs to "hang up" abruptly, it uses **tpdiscon** to end the conversation.

When the server adaptor receives a connection request, it dispatches the appropriate service routine. In this manner, a conversational service routine looks and acts just like a request/response service routine.

As Figure 11.1 shows, the client and service exchange data so that one of them sends data and the other receives data. In fact, ATMI permits only one of the two programs to have *send-control* of the conversation at any point in time. This greatly simplifies writing conversational services because you do not have to worry about potential error situations that are difficult to recover from. For example, if both

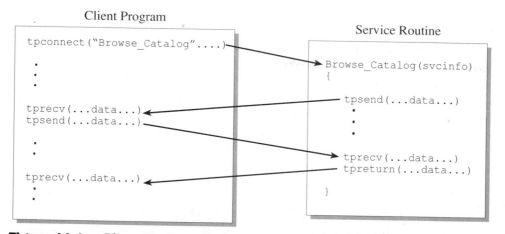

Figure 11.1 **Client Exchanging Data with a Conversational Service**

client and server call **tprecv** at the same time and neither had previously sent any data then both programs would hang!

Something that distinguishes ATMI's conversational communication model from those found in other conversational APIs (for example, X/Open's CPIC API [X/Open-CPIC]) is that the called program is a service routine as opposed to a stand-alone program that must itself handle polling for and accepting connection requests. The server adaptor contains all the necessary logic for listening, accepting, and ultimately tearing down connections with client programs so your services do not have to worry about connection management. This greatly simplifies programming conversational applications. Also, because the program being contacted is a service routine, just like in the request/response paradigm, learning how to use ATMI conversations is easy once you know how to write services.

Let's now look more closely at each of the ATMI functions used in conversational communication. Because the C and COBOL versions of these functions are used in the same way, only the C functions are shown throughout this chapter.

11.3   Initiating a Conversation: tpconnect

Client and server programs use the function **tpconnect** to set up a connection with a service routine to converse with it. Similar to other ATMI functions, **tpconnect**'s parameters are: service name, data buffer, data length, and flags. In this regard, the function looks just like **tpacall**, and in many aspects **tpconnect** has a lot in common with **tpacall**. Here is an example of calling **tpconnect**:

```
cd = tpconnect ("Browse_Catalog", init_buf, 0,
                TPSENDONLY|TPNOBLOCK);
```

The service name parameter names a conversational service. Even though there is a single name space for all of your service names, from an administrative viewpoint, service names are defined to be either request/response or conversational. Those denoted as request/response can be contacted only with **tpcall**, **tpacall**, or **tpforward**. Those denoted as conversational can be contacted only with **tpconnect**. This prevents potential programming errors by inadvertently trying to communicate with a service using the wrong client/server protocols.

Just like other ATMI functions, the data buffer parameter is a typed buffer, and the length parameter contains that buffer's length (that is, for those buffer types whose length cannot be inferred by their type and/or subtype). Sending data as part of **tpconnect** is optional. If it is present, then the conversational service will receive the buffer as part of its invocation.

The flags argument has familiar settings: **TPNOTRAN, TPNOBLOCK, TP-NOTIME**, and **TPSIGRSTRT** (see Chapter 10, "Request/Response Communication," for a detailed explanation of these settings). In addition, there are two new flags, **TPSENDONLY** and **TPRECVONLY**, that are used to state which program has initial control of the conversation—that is, which one is allowed to send data. Thus, if a client issues **tpconnect** with **TPSENDONLY** set, then it can, subsequently, use **tpsend** but not **tprecv**. Once the client has sent all of its data, then it can give its sending right to the service routine. Until that time, the service is in "receive mode" and cannot issue **tpsend**. Likewise, a client can issue **tpconnect** with **TPRECVONLY**, which means that it cannot issue **tpsend** until the service routine has explicitly yielded control of the conversation to the client.

```
            Client Program
buf = tpalloc("VIEW", "browse_struct", 0);
/* what to return */
strcpy(buf->desc, "hat");
/* how many records at a time to retrieve */
buf->cnt = 5;
cd = tpconnect("Browse_Catalog", buf, 0, TPRECVONLY);
. . .

            Service Routine
Browse_Catalog(TPSVCINFO *msg)
{
  get_items(msg->data->desc,
            msg->data->cnt, &recs);

  . . .
  tpreturn(TPSUCCESS,...);
}
```

Listing 11.1   *Setting Up a Connection with a Conversational Service*

Like **tpacall**, **tpconnect** returns a descriptor. The client program uses this descriptor to refer to the conversation in subsequent calls to **tpsend**, **tprecv**, and/or **tpdiscon**.

As shown in Listing 11.1, a conversational service is invoked just like a request/response service. The server adaptor calls the named application service routine with a service information structure, **tpsvcinfo** (see Chapter 10, "Request/Response Communication," for details). There are two items in this structure that are used only when the service communicates conversationally: the descriptor used to refer to the service's conversation with the client that invoked it and a flag setting (**TPCONN**) indicating whether or not the service routine has send-control.

If the client sent data along with its call to **tpconnect**, then the data is available to the service via the data pointer in the **tpsvcinfo** structure. This is a convenient way to pass to the service any initial data that it needs to take part in the conversational request. It is also more efficient for the client to piggyback its data as part of **tpconnect**, as opposed to issuing a separate **tpsend** call to get the conversation rolling. In Listing 11.1, the client sends data to the service as part of **tpconnect**.

11.4   Exchanging Data: tpsend and tprecv

Once the connection between the client and service routine is in place, the two programs can exchange data conversationally using the functions **tpsend** and **tprecv**. As their first parameter both of these functions take a descriptor that refers to the connection with the other program. Also, like all other ATMI functions that manipulate data, both have data, length, and flags parameters. Of course, **tpsend**'s data parameter points to a typed buffer to be sent (like **tpacall**), whereas **tprecv**'s is the address of a pointer to a typed buffer in which to place the data received (like **tpgetrply**). Listing 11.2 shows uses of both functions.

The flag settings are also familiar with both accepting **TPNOBLOCK**, **TPNOTIME**, and **TPSIGRSTRT**. Additionally, **tpsend** accepts a flag, **TPRECVONLY**, indicating that the sender yields send-control to the receiver, and **tprecv** accepts the **TPNOCHANGE** setting indicating that the received typed buffer must match the one passed to **tprecv** (**tpcall** and **tpgetrply** also accept this setting).

The conversational model in ATMI is asynchronous in the sense that **tpsend** does not wait for the program on the other end of the conversation to process its message. Instead, **tpsend** returns control to the calling program once its message has been sent. A program having send-control can issue several calls to **tpsend** without knowing exactly when the partner program actually receives its messages. However, so long as the conversation is not abruptly disconnected, the sender can rest assured that the receiver will receive its messages once (and only once) and in their proper order.

Both **tpsend** and **tprecv** take a parameter that we have not seen on other ATMI functions, the *return event* parameter. One characteristic of conversational

```
        Client Program
/* send data and yield control */
tpsend(cd, buf, 0, TPRECVONLY, &revent);

        Service Routine
if (tprecv(cd, &buf, &len, TPNOCHANGE, &revent) == -1) {
      switch(tperrno) {
          .
          .
          .
      /* an event (not necessarily an error) occurred on the connection */
      case TPEEVENT:
            switch (revent){
                .
                .
            case TPEV_SENDONLY:
                  have_send_control = TRUE;
                  /* return to processing received buffer */
                  break;
            }
      }
}
```

Listing 11.2   *Example of Client Granting Send-Control to Service*

communication is that while one program is talking another might encounter an error and have to "hang up," or the communication line between the two parties breaks causing both to encounter an abrupt disconnect. The return event parameter is where such events are returned. Other events are returned here as well, including an event indicating that the receiver now has send-control of the conversation and an event indicating that the conversation has terminated successfully.

Listing 11.2 shows an example of how a client turns over send-control of the conversation to a service and also how the service can detect that it has received the send-control event. Notice that the send-control event is detected as part of **tprecv**'s error processing. Even though this event is not an error, the TUXEDO run-time system uses a special error code to tell your program that a return event exists. Upon receiving this, your program should interrogate the value of the **revent** parameter to discover which event was actually returned. Unless the event signifies that the conversation has ended, normal processing can continue.

11.5   Ending a Conversation in the Service: tpreturn

Although either client or service can end a conversation, the way to do so to ensure successful results is for the service to call **tpreturn**. By doing so, the service routine completes, and control is returned to the server adaptor which takes care of sending the last data buffer (if any is provided) over the connection to the client and then tearing down the connection in an orderly fashion. Using **tpreturn** to end a conversation also simplifies your programs when the chain of conversations extends beyond one service routine. For example, let's say you have a client conversing with service X, and, as part of fulfilling its contract, service X needs to converse with service Y, as shown in Figure 11.2.

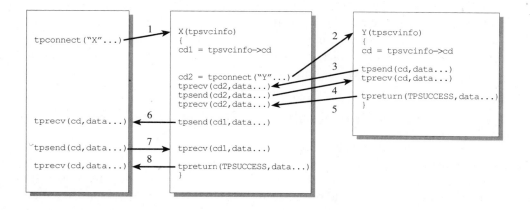

Figure 11.2   **Using tpreturn to End a Conversation**

As you can see, the client converses with service X with exchanges 1 and 6 through 8, whereas service X converses with service Y with exchanges 2 through 5. Notice that at exchange 5, service Y completes its work and uses **tpreturn** to end its conversation with service X. When service X's call to **tprecv** completes at exchange 5, service X also receives a return event indicating that the conversation has completed successfully. At this point, **cd2** is no longer a valid descriptor, and service X no longer has to worry about that conversation. Service X then converses with the client (using **cd1**), and when it has finished, it issues **tpreturn** (at exchange 8) to end the conversation.

Having conversational services complete in this order—that is, last connection made is the first one completed—makes programming conversational services much easier. This is because **tpreturn** does several things for you at once:

- It ends the service routine and returns control to the server adaptor.
- It sends the last data buffer over the connection.
- It tears down the connection in an orderly fashion once the data has been received by the program on the other end of the connection.
- It ensures that any transactionally protected resources are able to be committed or rolled back at a later time (that is, when the client calls **tpcommit** or **tpabort**).

Also, this model follows the one used in a chain of request/response services: a service that has itself called another service must wait for the latter service's reply before it returns.

The above illustrates what should be done when successful results are desired. When errors occur and your service needs to end abruptly because it can do no other useful work then it can call **tpreturn** with the **TPFAIL** setting at any time. When the Server Adaptor sees this, it automatically cleans up any open connections and any outstanding requests made with **tpacall**. It also rolls back any transactionally protected resources. The client finds out about this abrupt disconnection by receiving a return event indicating that the service encountered an error and its conversation with the service is now over.

11.6 Ending a Conversation in the Client: tpdiscon

Even though the proper way to terminate a conversation is for a service routine to use **tpreturn**, there are times when a client encounters an error and must "hang up" immediately. To do so, the client uses the function **tpdiscon**, which takes the connection's descriptor as its only parameter. This function sends a disconnect event to the service routine on the other end of the connection informing it that the client has terminated the conversation. A client can call **tpdiscon** even if it does not have send-control of the conversation in which case the service receives the return event in **tpsend**. Because the service can no longer communicate with its client and any attempt to do so will fail, the service should respond by issuing **tpreturn** with the **TPFAIL** setting. The TUXEDO run-time system then takes care of cleaning up all communication and transactionally protected resources on both ends of the connection.

11.7 Summary

In this chapter, we have seen how you can program conversational interactions between a client and a service routine. Because the conversational model is a generalization of the request/response model, writing programs that make use of conversations is quite similar to writing programs that use the request/response style of interaction. In deciding which of the two to use, remember that request/response communication is best suited for stateless interactions between programs whereas conversations should be used when your programs need to build and maintain state information.

You should keep in mind that applications using stateless interactions are, in general, less resource intensive and more scalable than stateful interactions. As we said at the beginning of this chapter, with a stateless request/response, a server is free to start new work once it has sent the response to its current service. This keeps servers busy processing services which helps keep throughput high. On the other hand, if a server is having a conversation with a client, then that server is dedicated to the client, possibly for several interactions as required to complete the conversation. During that time, no other client can use that server because it is keeping state information in its local variables and its flow of execution is dependent on interactions with the client.

The best way to ensure the efficient use of your conversational services is to minimize the number of synchronization points that ultimately rely on human intervention—in the time it takes a person to read a computer screen and make a decision, a stateless service might have processed several hundred service requests while a stateful one is idle waiting for someone to click the mouse!

12 Application Queues

PROGRAMMING

There are times when your programs cannot or need not communicate in an on-line manner using either of the request/response or conversational models. This is precisely why the TUXEDO System provides a means for your programs to store messages into, and retrieve them from, disk-based storage areas, called application queues. You should think of an application queue as a database of messages. Previously, we referred to this method as time-independent communication because programs that enqueue messages are not synchronized on-line with those that dequeue them; rather, they run independently from each other and rendezvous by exchanging messages.

Figure 12.1 shows the conceptual model for programs communicating via application queues. As shown in the figure, either a client or a service routine can access application queues. In fact, client programs can use application queues to

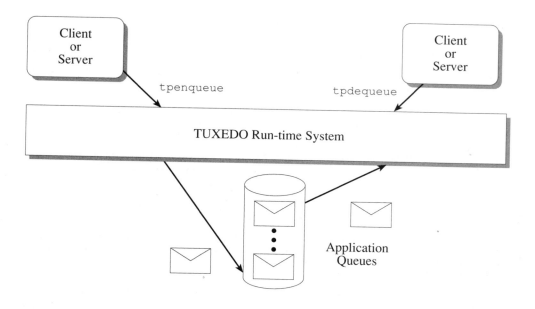

Figure 12.1   **Programming Model for Application Queues**

communicate among themselves—with no servers whatsoever present. This is because communication via queues is always initiated by application programs rather than by the TUXEDO run-time system which, in the case of the two on-line models, dispatch a service routine at a client's request. Figure 12.1 shows that application programs put and get messages from application queues using ATMI's **tpenqueue** and **tpdequeue** functions, respectively.

This chapter explains how to access application queues from within your programs using **tpenqueue** and **tpdequeue**. We'll show only the C functions because they are used in the same way as the COBOL versions of the same functions. Later in this chapter we describe the TUXEDO System's forwarding agent which allows you to combine request/response communication with application queuing.

12.1 Enqueuing Messages

You use the function **tpenqueue** to put a message into an application queue. You can put a message into a queue only if the queue already exists. Your application administrator uses TUXEDO administrative tools to create queue spaces and the queues that reside within them—if you need to brush up on the relationship between queues and queue spaces, see Chapter 4, "Application Development—Overview." Let's look at an example of how to call **tpenqueue**:

```
ret = tpenqueue("Payroll_Queues","Raise_Queue",&qctl,
           msg_buf,0,TPNOFLAGS);
```

Both queue spaces and queues have names that your programs use when they call **tpenqueue**. These two names are the first two parameters of the function. Like service names, these names are character strings and, as such, they provide for location transparency. For example, a payroll application might have a queue space named "Payroll_Queues" containing the two queues "Raise_Queue" and "Bonus_Queue."

The third parameter is called the *queue control structure*. It is used to control how a message is enqueued. It is also used to pass information to the dequeuer that is stored along with the message. We will look at the control parameter in detail after first introducing the rest of the function's parameters. The last three parameters are the usual ones: data, length, and flags. The data is the message to be enqueued, and it must be a typed buffer. As with other ATMI functions, the flags parameter allows your program to control how the TUXEDO run-time system handles a program's **tpenqueue** call. The settings for **tpenqueue** are the same as for other functions: **TPNOTRAN, TPNOBLOCK, TPNOTIME,** and **TPSIGRSTRT**.

Because the queue control parameter is where all the goodies are, let's now look more closely at it. As shown in Listing 12.1, this parameter points to a structure, **TPQCTL**. Some of the structure's elements are set by your program on input to

```
struct tpqctl_t {
        long flags;
        long deq_time;
        long priority;
        long diagnostic;
        char msgid[TMMSGIDLEN];
        char corrid[TMCORRIDLEN];
        char replyqueue[TMQNAMELEN+1];
        char failurqueue[TMQNAMELEN+1];
        CLIENTID cltid;
        long urcode;
        long appkey;
};
typedef struct tpqctl_t TPQCTL;
```

Listing 12.1   *Queue Control Structure*

tpenqueue, and some are set by the function on output. Because there are several options to choose from and you may be interested in only a subset of them on any particular invocation, you set only the ones in which you are interested and ignore the rest. One element in the structure is a flags word that you use to indicate which of other elements are to be used by **tpenqueue**. When you call **tpenqueue**, only those elements indicated as being set in the **flags** element are processed; all others are ignored by the function.

Let's look at an example of how you would use the queue control structure. Listing 12.2 shows you how to set a message's priority. Since **priority** is the only element set, only that value is used to influence the enqueuing operation; no other options are considered.

```
TPQCTL qctl;
qctl.priority = HIGH_PRIORITY;  /* Set the message's priority */
qctl.flags = TPQPRIORITY;       /* Indicate that priority is present */
ret = tpenqueue("My_Q_Space", "Queue_A", &qctl, msg_buf, 0, TPNOFLAGS);
```

Listing 12.2   *Enqueue Message with Specific Priority*

12.1.1 Input to tpenqueue

This section discusses all the items that you can set in the control structure on input to **tpenqueue**.

12.1.1.1 Priority

When a queue is created, it has ordering criteria associated with it. The three criteria to choose from are FIFO or LIFO (which are mutually exclusive), priority, and birth time. One of FIFO or LIFO must be specified, and either or both of priority and birth time can be also selected. If priority is an ordering criterion selected for a queue, then the control structure's priority element allows your program to set a message's enqueuing priority. The range of priority values is 1 through 100, inclusive, 100 being the highest priority.

Because messages are usually enqueued in the order specified for their queue and dequeued from the top of the queue, the priority selected for a particular message ensures that it will be dequeued before all others having lower priority values (unless ordering overrides are also enabled on the queue; see below). Listing 12.2 shows how to set a message's priority in the queue control structure.

12.1.1.2 Birth Time

If one of a queue's ordering criteria is birth time, then messages are ordered so that the ones whose times are earliest are dequeued before those with later birth times. Birth times come in two flavors: absolute and relative. The former is an unambiguous time (for example, December 15, 2005), whereas the latter is an amount of time to delay after a message is enqueued before allowing it to be visible to a dequeuer (for example, three hours from now). Because there is only one structure element for the birth time, your program has to specify via a flag setting which of the two is being used. Listing 12.3 shows how you would specify the relative time "an hour from now" where "now" is the time when the message is enqueued.

```
TPQCTL qctl;

qctl.deq_time = 3600;      /* Number of seconds in one hour */
qctl.flags = TPQTIME_REL; /* Indicates that a relative time is used */
ret = tpenqueue("My_Q_Space", "Queue_A", &qctl, msg_buf, 0,TPNOFLAGS);
```

Listing 12.3 *Enqueue Message with Relative Birth Time*

12.1.1.3 Reply Queues

When a program places a message in a queue, often it is a request for something to be done. Sometimes the enqueuing program expects a reply message. For the dequeuing program to know where to put a reply message, the enqueuer needs to specify the name of a reply queue. A reply queue can be the same queue into which the enqueuer placed the request message, or it can be a different queue—perhaps one that is dedicated to holding reply messages. Regardless, the reply queue must be the name of a queue that exists within the same queue space as the queue where the enqueuer placed the request message.

Listing 12.4 shows an example of a program enqueuing a message to the queue "Request_Q" and stating that its reply should be placed in the queue "Reply_Q." Both queues are in the queue space "My_Q_Space." Later, we will see how your program can get replies from a reply queue.

```
TPQCTL qctl;

(void) strcpy(qctl.replyqueue, "Reply_Q");
qctl.flags = TPQREPLYQ;
ret = tpenqueue("My_Q_Space","Request_Q",&qctl,msg_buf,0,TPNOFLAGS);
```

Listing 12.4   *Setting a Reply Queue Name Before Enqueing a Message*

12.1.1.4 Failure Queue

Another queue you can name as part of enqueuing a message is a failure queue. If a program dequeuing a message encounters a problem processing it, it can put a message in a failure queue indicating what happened. Like the reply queue, the failure queue must exist in the same queue space as the queue in which the initial message was enqueued. In fact, you can choose to use the same queue for both replies and failures, but we recommend using separate queues. One reason to have a separate failure queue is that its ordering criteria might be different from the reply queue's ordering criteria.

Naming a failure queue is similar to naming a reply queue: copy the name into the queue control structure and set a flag indicating that it is there.

12.1.1.5 Correlation Identifier

A correlation identifier is an application-defined tag that allows programs to correlate replies with their original requests. As part of enqueuing a message, you can specify a correlation identifier in the control structure. These identifiers can be unique but they do not have to be. In fact, the TUXEDO run-time system does not interpret them; they are simply a set of up to 32 characters defined by your application.

The usual way that correlation identifiers are used is shown in Figure 12.2. A program enqueuing a message specifies both a reply queue and a correlation identifier ("123.XYZ"). Another program dequeues and processes that message. As part of enqueuing a message to the reply queue, that program copies the original correlation identifier into the control structure for the reply message. When the program reading the reply queue dequeues this message, it uses the received correlation identifier to determine for which request this message is the reply.

Correlation identifiers can be used to partition a single queue logically into what appears as several smaller queues. For example, if every end user in your application

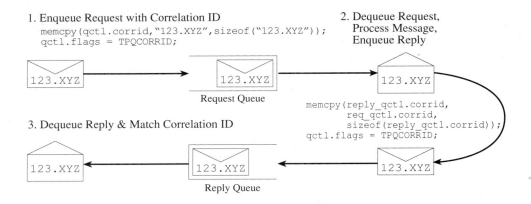

Figure 12.2 Using Correlation Identifiers

has a unique user name—specified when calling **tpinit**—then that name can also be used as the correlation identifier for all messages enqueued by each user. Thus, if all client programs specify the same reply queue and if each client dequeues only those reply messages tagged with its own correlation identifier, then it appears to each client program that it has its own personal reply queue because it sees no messages other than its own. An administrative benefit to this strategy is that administrators can use the application queue scanning tool to see which messages on the queue belong to which users. We'll cover dequeuing by correlation identifier shortly.

12.1.1.6 Ordering Overrides

As we discussed earlier, your application administrator may configure a queue to allow for out-of-order enqueuing. Because the purpose of queues is to provide some semblance of order, allowing programs to override the configured ordering should be done only after careful consideration. Once you decide that your application can benefit from isolated instances of out-of-order enqueuing, then your programs can specify one of two types of overrides in the control structure.

The first method allows your program to place a message at the top of a queue. As we said earlier, messages are dequeued from the top of the queue by default. So, by placing a message at the top of the queue, you are stating that your message should be dequeued and processed as soon as another program can get to it. This makes the most sense for queues configured with FIFO ordering because the message will actually be the first dequeued, rather than the last. On the other hand, using this override with queues configured with birth-time ordering does not make much sense because a message cannot be dequeued until its birth-time arrives, even if it is at the top of the queue.

The second method lets your program specify that a message should be placed immediately before another message. This override is useful when your program needs to enqueue separate messages but would like to keep them close together on the queue—again, this makes sense for FIFO ordered queues. To do so, your program needs to specify in the control structure the message identifier of the message that your new message should "cut in front of." As we will see in the next section, **tpenqueue** returns a message identifier for every message placed into a queue. For example, if your program has saved the message identifier for a previously enqueued message, then it is simply a matter of including it in the control structure as shown in Listing 12.5.

```
TPQCTL qctl;

(void) memcpy(qctl.msgid, prev_msgid, sizeof(qctl.msgid));
qctl.flags = TPQBEFOREMSGID;
ret = tpenqueue("My_Q_Space", "My_Q", &qctl, msg_buf, 0, TPNOFLAGS);
```

Listing 12.5 *Setting the Message Identifier for Out-of-Order Enqueuing*

12.1.1.7 *User Return Code*

Recall from the request/response and conversational models that when a TUXEDO service routine completes, it can specify a user return code in the form of a long integer. The service passes this code to **tpreturn** as a parameter, and the TUXEDO System makes this code available to the client in the variable, **tpurcode**. Similarly, when your program enqueues a message, it can specify a user code in the control structure so that a program dequeuing the message will receive it. One common use for this element is for setting a return code as part of enqueuing a reply message. Another place this element is used is in the queue forwarding service—we will be discussing queue forwarding later in this chapter. Unlike other elements in the control structure, your program does not have to declare in the **flags** element that the user return code is present. This is because it is considered an application data item and, as such, is not interpreted or processed by the TUXEDO run-time system.

12.1.2 Output of tpenqueue

When **tpenqueue** returns, it can set the values of a couple of items in the control structure. Before calling **tpenqueue**, your program uses the **flags** element to specify which values it is interested in getting upon the function's return. If a value exists, then it is returned in its corresponding element, and the flag bit for that value remains set. On the other hand, if the value is not available, then the flag setting is turned off indicating that no value is available for that element. There are two benefits to retrieving elements in this manner. First, new control elements can be added in an upward-compatible way. Second, network traffic is reduced because the only information passed back to your application is that in which it is interested in getting.

The following are the values that can be returned in the control structure.

12.1.2.1 Message Identifier

Every message enqueued has an identifier assigned to it by the TUXEDO System. This identifier is unique within the scope of a queue space. That is, no two messages within one queue space will ever have the same message identifier. You can think of a message identifier as a receipt returned by the TUXEDO System for each message that your program enqueues. Message identifiers have two uses. The first, discussed previously in this chapter, allows your program to enqueue a message just before another message already on a queue.

The second lets any program that has access to a message identifier dequeue the message associated with it. For example, let's say your application has a pool of programs that dequeue and process specific messages whose data meet some special criteria. That is, these programs are not supposed to dequeue arbitrary messages on the queue—just specific ones. When a program enqueues a message that meets the special criteria, it makes the enqueued message's message identifier available to the pool. When a program in the pool needs some work, it can pick up a message identifier, dequeue the associated message, and process it.

The code fragment in Listing 12.6 shows you how to retrieve a message identifier after enqueuing a message. First, you have to set the bit in the **flags** element indicating that you are interested in getting the message identifier. Then, after **tpenqueue** returns successfully, you check to see if the bit is still set. If it is, then the message identifier is in the appropriate element of the control structure.

```
TPQCTL qctl;

qctl.flags = TPQMSGID;                    /* want message id */
if (tpenqueue("My_Q_Space","My_Q",&qctl,msg_buf, 0, TPNOFLAGS) == -1){
        /* process error condition */
} else {
        /* tpenqueue succeeded */
        ...
        if (qctl.flags&TPQMSGID){          /* got message id*/
                (void) memcpy(msgid, qctl.msgid, sizeof(qctl.msgid));
        }
        ...
}
```

Listing 12.6 *Retrieving Message Identifier After Enqueuing Message*

12.1.2.2 Diagnostic

There are two ways for **tpenqueue** to fail. Either it fails because a problem occurs in the TUXEDO run-time system in the program calling **tpenqueue**, or it fails because a problem occurs at the queue manager trying to enqueue the message. When the former happens, **tpenqueue** returns an error value like any other ATMI function. That is, the function returns –1 and sets the **tperrno** variable to a value indicating the nature of the error. In this case, the nature of the error is such that a TUXEDO System queue manager could not be contacted for enqueuing the message.

In the latter error scenario, the queue manager itself encountered an error and could not enqueue the message. For example, the queue might be full. When this occurs, **tpenqueue** returns a special error value in **tperrno**, **TPEDIAGNOSTIC**, indicating that the real cause of the error can be found in the diagnostic element of the control structure. Listing 12.7 shows how you can do this. Unlike all other control elements, you do not ask for the diagnostic element in advance. This is so your program can see these errors regardless of whether it asked for them.

```
TPQCTL qctl;

if (tpenqueue("My_Q_Space","My_Q",&qctl,msg_buf, 0, TPNOFLAGS) == -1){
        /* process error condition */
        switch(tperrno) {
        ...
        case TPEDIAGNOSTIC:                 /* queue manager error */
                switch(qctl.diagnostic) {
                QMEINVAL:                   /* invalid qctl.flags specified */
                    ...
                QMENOTOPEN:                 /* queue manager not open */
                    ...
                QMEBADMSGID:                /* invalid message id specified */
                    ...
                }
        ...
        }
}
```

Listing 12.7   *Checking for Queue Manager Errors*

12.2   Dequeuing Messages

To take a message out of a queue, you use **tpdequeue**. Once a program dequeues a message, it is no longer there for any other program to see—unless, of course, the dequeuer's transaction rolls back in which case the message remains on its queue. Unlike a relational DBMS, where entries in the database are more frequently read and updated than they are deleted, entries in a queue exist solely to be consumed—that is, deleted. If a message actually needs to be updated, then it can be dequeued and reenqueued within the scope of a global transaction. However, this is not the usual way application designers have used the TUXEDO application queuing feature. Processing queued messages is a lot like processing electronic mail: you read a message out of your in-box, process it, and discard it. In this context, it sounds quite odd to think of "updating" your mail messages.

Naturally, the function **tpdequeue** looks quite similar to **tpenqueue**:

```
ret = tpdequeue("Queue_Space","Queue_Name",&qctl,&msg_buf,
                    &len,TPNOFLAGS);
```

Like all ATMI functions that return application data, **tpdequeue**'s data parameter is the address of a pointer to a typed buffer where the message is placed, and the length parameter is the address of a long integer where the length of the returned message is placed. Because queues are not restricted in the buffer types they can hold, a program dequeuing messages might need to use the function **tptypes** to find out the buffer types of its dequeued messages.

12.2.1 Input to tpdequeue

As input to **tpdequeue**, the control structure is used to specify which message to dequeue. There are three different ways you can dequeue messages. The default way is simply to dequeue the message at the top of the queue. Or, you can specify that you want a message with a particular correlation identifier. Last, you can ask for a message by its message identifier.

To get a message by correlation identifier or by message identifier, you need to copy the identifier into the control structure and set a bit in the **flags** element indicating which type of identifier you are using. Listing 12.8 shows an example using the correlation identifier.

```
TPQCTL qctl;

(void) memcpy(qctl.corrid, my_corrid, sizeof(qctl.corrid));
qctl.flags = TPQGETBYCORRID;
ret = tpdequeue("My_Q_Space", "My_Q", &qctl, &msg_buf,&len,TPNOFLAGS);
```

Listing 12.8 *Dequeue Message by Correlation Identifier*

If you are using the default method of dequeuing from the top of the queue, then you can also specify in the element that, if the queue is empty, you are willing to wait for a message to arrive. When this flag setting is not used and the queue is empty, then **tpdequeue** returns a diagnostic indicating that no message was available for dequeuing.

A queue that appears empty might actually have messages on it. However, those messages are not available because other programs might have dequeued them as part of their global transactions. If any of those programs roll back their transactions, then the messages associated with those transactions will become available for dequeuing. A queue might also appear empty when all of its messages have birth times that have not yet arrived.

12.2.2 Output of tpdequeue

Of course, the main output of **tpdequeue** is a message which is placed in a typed buffer and returned to your program via the data parameter. In addition, your program can receive information about the message, such as its priority and message identifier. As we described above, the way you ask for this information is by setting bits in the **flags** element of the control structure before calling **tpdequeue**. If a message is successfully dequeued, then the values for those items you specified will be in their corresponding elements in the control structure, and the flags bits stay set. If a value is not available, then the bit setting will be turned off indicating that no meaningful value is present in the corresponding element. The items that you can retrieve are the priority, the message identifier, the correlation identifier, the reply queue name, and the failure queue name. With the exception of the message identifier, which is set by the TUXEDO System, none of these elements will have values unless they are defined and set by your application when the message was enqueued.

The other elements returned in the control structure are the user return code, the application key, and the client identifier. As we saw previously, the user return code can be set to any long integer value by the program enqueuing the message. The other two values should look familiar. They are both associated with clients, and we saw them previously in the service information structure for request/response and conversational services. These values are set by the TUXEDO System. Because your dequeuing programs may want or need to know the identity of the programs that enqueued the messages, the TUXEDO run-time system keeps track of the originating client's authentication key and its client identifier along with each message. In the upcoming section on message forwarding, we will see that these values come in handy when messages are forwarded to request/response service routines.

If the queue manager encounters an error dequeuing a message, the diagnostic element in the control structure is set to reflect the error. You can check for a dequeuing error in the same way we saw previously for enqueuing errors in Listing 12.7.

12.3 Forwarding Queued Messages to Servers

Using the TUXEDO System's application queue forwarding agent, your programs can combine on-line request/response communication with time-independent, disk-based queuing. Here is the model you use to do this. You start with a set of request/response service routines. That's right, the same ones that your clients contact using **tpcall** or **tpacall**. Next, you look at your client programs and decide where it makes sense to enqueue requests for those service routines. One place, for example, might be where service requests fail. If **tpcall** fails, as part of your error checking code, your program could decide that, in some cases, it would be advantageous to enqueue the request data intended for the service routine. Perhaps **tpcall** failed because the service requested was not available due to a network failure that precluded your client from contacting the server. So, if you enqueue the request, the application queue forwarding agent could forward it to the service at a later time when the service is available. Listing 12.9 shows how the client's code might look.

```
if (tpcall("Place_Order",reqbuf,0,&rplybuf,&rlen,TPNOFLAGS) == -1) {
    /* tpcall failed; process errors */
    switch(tperrno) {
    case TPETIME:        /* timeout could be due to network failure */
    case TPENOENT:       /* service is not available */
        (void) strcpy(qctl.replyqueue, "Order_Reply_Q");
        qctl.flags = TPQREPLYQ;
        if (tpenqueue("Q_Space","Place_Order",&qctl,&reqbuf,0,TPNOFLAGS) == -1){
                /* tpenqueue failed */
                /* report to end-user that request cannot be sent or stored */
                ...
        }
        /*
         * report to end-user that service request has been safely
         * stored on application queue for later processing
         */
        break;
    ...
    }
}
```

Listing 12.9   *Enqueuing a Request after tpcall Fails*

In Listing 12.9, the client has decided that if either of two errors occur, it is appropriate to enqueue the request for subsequent forwarding. Notice that the queue name matches the service name. Thus, the queue named "Place_Order" is where all requests destined for the service of the same name reside until they can be forwarded. The forwarding agent, **TMQFORWARD**, dequeues messages and calls **tpcall** to send the message to a request/response service routine. You will also notice that the message is, in fact, the request buffer itself. Because the service might return a reply buffer as part of issuing **tpreturn**, the client needs to specify a reply queue where the forwarding agent should enqueue the reply buffer.

From the service's standpoint, it cannot tell whether the request came from an on-line client or from a queue read by the forwarding agent, which behaves like a client when it issues **tpcall**. This, in fact, is the power of the forwarding agent: the service routine writer does not have to know that clients are enqueuing requests for later transmission. Thus, your application can reuse service routines for time-independent communication as you find appropriate.

In case a service routine needs to perform additional security checks on the message forwarded to it, the forwarding agent makes sure that the originating client's application key and client identifier are passed along to the service routine. Recall from the previous section that this information is available in the queue control structure for every message dequeued. Also, because a service might return a user return code as part of **tpreturn**, this code is enqueued along with the reply. The forwarding agent does this as part of enqueuing the reply message.

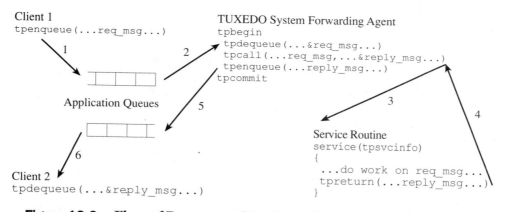

Figure 12.3   **Flow of Request and Reply via Forwarding Agent**

Figure 12.3 shows that the forwarding agent uses a global transaction to guarantee that the client's request is delivered to the service routine for successful processing. Actually, this guarantee is based on three transactions that, taken together, guarantee that both the client's request and the service's reply are delivered. In order, these are:

1. If the client's call to **tpenqueue** succeeds (flow 1), then the request is guaranteed to be in the request queue and available for dequeuing. The TUXEDO System application queue manager uses its own transaction to commit the request message to disk. Of course, the client can also define its own global transaction to bracket the call to **tpenqueue** to protect it against any communication errors that might occur between it and the queue manager.

2. The forwarding agent has its own global transaction (which encompasses flows 2 through 5). If the invoked service ends by issuing **tpreturn** with **TPSUCCESS**

set, then the forwarding agent commits its transaction which atomically removes the message from the request queue, commits any work that the service did, and ensures that the reply message is on the reply queue. If the service fails and calls **tpreturn** with **TPFAIL** set, then the forwarding agent will issue **tpabort**, which rolls back the global transaction. This means that the request will not be removed from the request queue so that it can be processed later when it has a better chance to succeed. Also, any transactional work that the service did will be rolled back.

3. If the client's call to **tpdequeue** succeeds (flow 6), then the TUXEDO System's queue manager uses a transaction to guarantee that the reply is removed from the reply queue. As with the initial client, this dequeuing client can also define its own global transaction to ensure that the reply does not get lost in the event of a communication failure between it and the queue manager.

12.4 Summary

This chapter has presented the way you can write programs using the TUXEDO System's application queue communication paradigm. This model manifests itself in two ATMI functions, **tpenqueue** and **tpdequeue**, that offer a feature-rich set of queuing semantics, yet are easy to use and understand because they "look and feel" like the rest of ATMI.

In addition, we covered the forwarding agent, which is a system-supplied server built upon these primitives, that allows you to combine both the request/response and the queuing models. This allows you to add much flexibility to your application because your application is no longer constrained to do all of its work on-line. Thus, if some part of your application is unavailable, work for that part of the system can be enqueued and processed later when it is available again.

When the application queuing subsystem was originally designed, consideration was given to adding the time-independent queuing semantics to the on-line verbs, **tpcall** or **tpacall**. For example, a new flags setting could have been added to **tpacall** indicating that the request should be enqueued rather than processed on-line.

Although this might have worked, it would have severely limited the functionality of the application queue feature as described in this chapter. Specifically, all the features available via manipulation of the queue control structure would not have been possible without completely redesigning **tpacall**. Rather than doing that, it was clear that a new set of functions was needed specifically for queuing. One of ATMI's distinctive characteristics is that it supplies the right set of tools for the set of jobs likely encountered, rather than trying to provide a one-size-fits-all tool that would not fully satisfy any one job.

13 Event-Based Communication

PROGRAMMING

Most of your business' work is initiated by real-world events that are quite predictable. For example, mail-order houses *expect* orders to come in. Often though, business events occur that are not predictable (for example, a stock's price reaching a certain level) or are even undesirable (for example, a machine crashing). Yet these events still have an important impact on your application, and they must be handled properly and without the overhead of polling.

The fourth major communication paradigm offered in ATMI is event-based communication. Unlike the client/server models where a server is waiting at-the-ready to process a client's request, the essence of event-based communication is that a program being contacted is not waiting for that communication to take place. Rather, it registers that it is willing to be contacted, but it does not actively wait or poll for communication to occur. This is because it is busy doing other things. The client is usually notified in a manner that takes it momentarily away from its current work to handle the result of some unforseen event. As we will see in this chapter, ATMI offers several variations on this model, from a simple, unsolicited client notification construct to a brokered event mechanism that combines event-based communication with the request/response and application queue communication models.

13.1 Unsolicited Event Notification

Unsolicited notifications are used to communicate with client programs. We use the term "unsolicited" because, by their very nature, clients do not wait for other programs to initiate communication with them. If they did, then they would be servers.

In Chapter 4, "Application Development—Overview," we introduced the notions of single-program notifications and multiple-program broadcasting as ways for either clients or services to communicate unsolicited data to client programs. The former is done using the ATMI function **tpnotify** whereas the latter is accomplished using **tpbroadcast**. Here is an overview of how you use this form of communication. First, a client program registers a function, known as a *call-back*, with the TUXEDO run-time system. A client uses the ATMI function **tpsetunsol** for this purpose. Then at some later time, either a client or a service generates an unsolicited notification using one of **tpnotify** or **tpbroadcast** which sends a typed buffer to one or more clients, respectively.

Depending on which notification method the client chose during its initialization—that is, when it called **tpinit**—the TUXEDO run-time system at the client performs one of three actions. If the client chose signal-based notification, then the TUXEDO run-time system immediately dispatches the client's registered call-back function along with the data. Because the client is most likely busy doing some other processing when the notification arrives, the TUXEDO run-time system puts that work on hold before dispatching the call-back function. After the client processes the data, the TUXEDO run-time system returns it to whatever it was doing prior to receiving the unsolicited notification.

If the client chose to defer notification until it "dips into" the ATMI library, then the unsolicited notification is held until the client calls an ATMI function. At that point, the TUXEDO run-time system dispatches the client's registered call-back function along with the data. As we mentioned in Chapter 9, "Joining and Leaving the Application," the advantage of this method is that it does not depend on operating system signals—which are not supported on all platforms—and it does not interrupt the client's work-in-progress. There is an ATMI function, **tpchkunsol**, whose sole purpose is to "dip into" the ATMI library and check for any pending unsolicited messages. If any exist, they are dispatched to the call-back function. This function is useful when your client has no other ATMI work to do other than to check for pending unsolicited messages.

Last, if the client chose to ignore such notifications altogether, then the TUXEDO run-time system drops the notification and its data. The client is never made aware that it was sent such a message. Moreover, the program that sent the notification is never made aware that the client did not receive its notification. The nature of unsolicited event notifications is that they are not acknowledged—more on this as the chapter proceeds.

13.1.1 Registering Call-Back Functions in C: tpsetunsol

Sometime soon after a client joins an application, it should call **tpsetunsol** to register its call-back function. The job of the call-back function is to handle unsolicited messages that are sent to the client from either **tpnotify** or **tpbroadcast**. The function **tpsetunsol** takes one argument: a pointer to a function that conforms to the function prototype of an unsolicited message handling routine. Let's say that your client wants to use the function **my_unsol_hndlr** for this purpose. To conform, that function must accept three parameters, data, length, and flags, where data points to the typed buffer that is the unsolicited message, length is the buffer's size, and flags are not currently used. Thus, a call to **tpsetunsol** registering **my_unsol_hndlr** would look as shown in the top half of Listing 13.1.

```
/* call tpsetunsol to register new handler function */
prev_hndlr = tpsetunsol(my_unsol_hndlr);

/*
 * Elsewhere in your program is the
 * definition of the registered handler.
 */
void
my_unsol_hndlr(char *data, long len, long flags)
{
        /* handle unsolicited message here */
        return;
}
```

Listing 13.1 *Registering an Unsolicited Notification Handler in C*

As the function's return value, **tpsetunsol** returns the pointer to the function previously installed to handle unsolicited notifications. If none existed, then a null function pointer is returned. The call-back function itself would look like the template for **my_unsol_hndlr** shown in the bottom half of Listing 13.1.

When your client receives an unsolicited notification, the TUXEDO run-time system dispatches **my_unsol_hndlr** with the message. Once inside the call-back function, minimal processing should be done on the message because your client was busy doing something else before being interrupted to handle this message. In fact, the TUXEDO run-time system won't let your client use any ATMI communication verbs while in the call-back function—the run-time system might have been in the middle of an ATMI call when it dispatched the call-back function! You are, however, allowed to use ATMI's typed buffer functions in case you want to copy all or parts of the message into another buffer for later processing.

If you have ever used the call-waiting feature with your phone, this processing should sound analogous. First, you have to sign up for call-waiting on your phone line (**tpsetunsol**). Then, when an unsolicited call (**tpnotify**) comes in while you are using the line, you are notified of it via a clicking sound. Then, you put on hold the first caller and handle the new one (dispatch the call-back). Using common courtesy, you acknowledge the new call and either quickly extract any information, or, if that is not possible, you tell the caller that you will call him/her back when you are finished with the first call (process the message and return from the call-back).

13.1.2 Registering Call-Back Functions in COBOL: TPSETUNSOL and TPGETUNSOL

If you are familiar with COBOL, you might have taken one look at **tpsetunsol** and thought, "How can I do that in COBOL?" Because you cannot pass function pointers as parameters in COBOL, ATMI's COBOL version of this function, **TPSETUNSOL**, works somewhat differently than the C version. However, the end results are the same: your program registers an unsolicited message handling routine and returns the name of the previously registered one. Here is how it works. The ATMI COBOL routine **TPSETUNSOL** predefines the names of sixteen functions that you can choose from for handling unsolicited messages. To register a call-back function, you pass **TPSETUNSOL** the number corresponding to the routine that you would like to register, and it returns the number for the previous one.

The first eight predefined functions, **_tm_dispatch1** through **_tm_dispatch8**, are the names of C functions that match the parameter definition for **tpsetunsol**. That is, through the COBOL routine **TPSETUNSOL**, you can register—by its number—a C call-back function that the TUXEDO run-time system dispatches to handle unsolicited messages. If your application has a mix of C and COBOL clients, then being able to register a C handler allows your programs to share one handler across both types of clients. Listing 13.2 shows an example of registering a C handler through the COBOL **TPSETUNSOL**.

```
WORKING-STORAGE SECTION.
*
01 CURR-ROUTINE PIC S9(9) COMP-5.
01 PREV-ROUTINE PIC S9(9) COMP-5.
01 TPSTATUS-REC.
   COPY TPSTATUS.
*
PROCEDURE DIVISION.
*
* Register the C unsolicited message handler called _tm_dispatch7
*
MOVE 7 to CURR-ROUTINE.
CALL "TPSETUNSOL" USING CURR-ROUTINE PREV-ROUTINE TPSTATUS-REC.
```

Listing 13.2   *Registering a C Unsolicited Handler in COBOL*

In Listing 13.2, the program passes to **TPSETUNSOL** the number 7 to register the predefined function, **_tm_dispatch7**. You are then responsible for writing a C function called **_tm_dispatch7** whose parameters are a pointer to a typed buffer, its length, and flags—just like the function **my_unsol_hndlr** in Listing 13.1. When you compile your client, you must make sure to link in your version of **_tm_dispatch7** so that it is used in place of the default, predefined version which does nothing.

The next eight predefined functions, **TMDISPATCH9** through **TMDISPATCH16**, are the names of COBOL programs. These are used when your application is one hundred percent COBOL. Because they are the names of COBOL programs, these "routines" take no parameters. You register these names in the same way as shown in Listing 13.2, except that you use numbers in the range 9 through 16.

When one of these COBOL programs is registered, the TUXEDO run-time system dispatches it when an unsolicited message arrives. One of the first things the dispatched program must do is call the ATMI COBOL routine, **TPGETUNSOL**, to fetch the unsolicited message from the TUXEDO run-time system—similar to the way **TPSVCSTART** fetches a service request. **TPGETUNSOL** returns a data record (the unsolicited message itself), the data record's type and subtype in a separate **TPTYPE** record, and any status information in a **TPSTATUS** record. Listing 13.3 shows an example of how to call **TPGETUNSOL** at the start of the COBOL unsolicited handler, **TMDISPATCH9**.

```
IDENTIFICATION DIVISION.
PROGRAM-ID. TMDISPATCH9.
*
DATA DIVISION.
WORKING-STORAGE SECTION.
*
 01 TPTYPE-REC.
    COPY TPTYPE.
 01 TPSTATUS-REC.
    COPY TPSTATUS.
 01 DATA-REC.
    COPY Msg Data.
*
PROCEDURE DIVISION.
*
CALL "TPGETUNSOL" USING TPTYPE-REC DATA-REC TPSTATUS-REC.
*
* Process unsolicited message here and return.
*
```

Listing 13.3 *Using TPGETUNSOL to Fetch an Unsolicited Message*

13.1.3 Client Notification: tpnotify

The function **tpnotify** was originally conceived to meet the requirement that sometimes services need to send data in an unsolicited fashion directly to clients. A function to do this could have been designed to allow a service to notify only the client that invoked it. This would not have required clients to have identifiers nor for servers to receive them on every invocation because their identities are always known implicitly by the TUXEDO System. However, having explicit client identifiers that your application can use and keep track of makes for a much more general-purpose function whereby any program, client or service, can specify a particular client to be notified simply by referencing its identifier.

Either a client or a service uses **tpnotify** to send an unsolicited message to another client. From our discussion of service routines in Chapter 10, "Request/Response Communication," recall that each time a service is dispatched, it contains the client's identifier (**CLIENTID**) as part of the service information structure. This tells the service routine exactly which client initiated the request.

A **CLIENTID** is the first parameter passed to **tpnotify**. The next three parameters are—surprise!—data, length, and flags. Data points to a typed buffer, and length specifies its size. The flags parameter can be set to any of **TPNOBLOCK**, **TPNOTIME**, or **TPSIGRSTRT**. Recall our example from Chapter 4, "Application Development—Overview," where a client requests money from an ATM. The service processing the request encounters a delay so it notifies the client "out-of-band" that its request will take a few extra seconds. Listing 13.4 shows how the service might do so using **tpnotify**.

```
#define WAITSTRING "Please wait; trying again."
get_cash(TPSVCINFO *svcinfo)
{
        char *string;

        /* update DBMS and place new balance in data buffer */
        while (access_dbms(svcinfo->data) == ERROR) {
                switch(db_errno){
                case TRY_AGAIN_LATER:
                    /* notify client to put delay message on screen */
                    string = tpalloc("STRING", NULL,sizeof(WAITSTRING)+ 1);
                    strcpy(string, WAITSTRING);
                    tpnotify(&svcinfo->cltid, string, 0, TPNOFLAGS);
                    tpfree(string);
                    sleep(wait_amount);
                    break;
                ...
                }
        }
        /* return updated buffer with new (lower) balance */
        tpreturn(TPSUCCESS, 0, svcinfo->data, 0, TPNOFLAGS);
}
```

Listing 13.4   *Using tpnotify to Send an Unsolicited Notification*

When a service is contacted by another service, the original client's identifier is passed down the chain of requests so that each service can know on whose behalf the work is being done. Figure 13.1 shows how a downstream service can use **tpnotify** to send an unsolicited message back to the originating client. During its processing, **svc_2** finds that it needs to send an unsolicited notification to the client (flow 3). To do so, the service references the client identifier element of its service information structure (**info->cltid**) which contains the originating client's identifier. The client identifier was forwarded to **svc_2** by the TUXEDO run-time system from the client (as part of flows 1 and 2) through **svc_1**. The TUXEDO run-time system in the client dispatches the client's call-back routine, **my_hndlr**, to process the notification sent to it by **svc_2**. After sending the notification, **svc_2** continues its processing and forwards the request on to **svc_3** (flow 4) which finishes the request and calls **tpreturn** to send a reply back to the waiting client (flow 5).

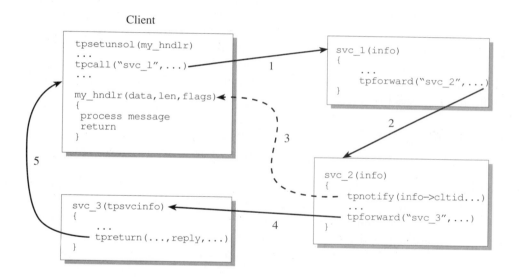

Figure 13.1 **Calling tpnotify from within a Service**

Even though a service receives a **CLIENTID** as part of a specific request, the service can share it with any of your application's other clients or services so that they can also contact the originating client via **tpnotify**. For example, your application might choose to have services send **CLIENTID**s to a special service which keeps track of them for later use. Or, your services might put them in a DBMS along with other data, like the application key, so that other programs can query them. Last, because information about clients is kept in the TUXEDO System MIBs, programs can get access to **CLIENTID**s by using the TUXEDO System's administrative programming interfaces—see Chapter 17, "A Tour of the

TUXEDO Management Information Base," for details. For instance, you could write a program to retrieve all clients associated with a particular TUXEDO Workstation Listener that you are about to shut down and notify each of them about the imminent shutdown.

A service sending a message to a client using **tpnotify** is the reverse of a client sending a message to a service using **tpacall** with the **TPNOREPLY** flag set. With **tpnotify**, a service routine's message is sent to a client and that is the end of it; there is no reply sent back to the service. The service has no assurance that the message is delivered to or processed by the client unless the client executes an agreed-upon action that the service can detect.

The reason for this lack of assurance has to do with the nature of the unsolicited notification paradigm. Clients are structured to initiate requests, not receive them. In fact, you should not think of unsolicited notifications as requests because they are not. Rather, they are messages delivered to the client on a "for your information" basis and are delivered on a "best effort" basis. As we mentioned previously, a client might not even completely finish handling an unsolicited notification while in its call-back function. We recommend that if you find that your application requires more assurance about messages sent from server to client or those sent between clients, then you should design your programs to use application queues instead.

13.1.4 Broadcasting to Client Groups: tpbroadcast

Let's say you would like to send the same message to a set of clients. This is when you would use **tpbroadcast**. The main difference between it and **tpnotify** is the way your program identifies the clients that should receive the message. When using **tpnotify**, a program targets a particular client by directly using its **CLIENTID**. With **tpbroadcast**, a program uses a combination of logical client names that are mapped to one or more **CLIENTID**s. We first covered client naming in Chapter 9, "Joining and Leaving the Application." As a refresher, here are the three names used to logically identify a set of targeted clients:

■ **Logical Machine Identifier** (LMID). As we saw in Chapter 5, "Application Administration—Overview," your TUXEDO application programs are configured to run on machines that have logical names. The logical name for a machine can be the same as its real (or physical) name. Having a level of logical naming insulates your configuration from hardware changes. From a client naming standpoint, specifying an LMID identifies all the clients associated with that machine. This includes both client programs running natively on that machine and clients who access your application via Workstation Handlers that run on that machine. The value for an LMID comes from the machine definitions that are part of your TUXEDO System MIB.

■ **User Name.** The user name component comes from the **usrname** element in the **TPINIT** structure that each client passes to **tpinit** when it joins the application. Usually, this is the name of the user running the client program. However, this name can really be anything you choose because the semantics of this name are completely defined by your application.

■ **Client Name.** Similar to the user name, the client name comes from the **cltname** element in the **TPINIT** structure that is passed to **tpinit**. Although there are no semantics defined for this string either, applications have been known to use it for identifying roles that users have within their applications.

These three names are the first three parameters of **tpbroadcast**. A null value for any of these denotes a wild card which means that all **CLIENTID**s are taken into account for that name. Specific values for one or more of these parameters reduces the scope of the target set of identifiers only to those that match the given names. The last three parameters are the usual suspects: data, length, and flags. Their meanings and values are identical to those for **tpnotify**.

Using the example in Figure 9.1 again, let's say that you wanted to send a message to all tellers (client name) on machine M1 (LMID) telling them that their machine is going down an hour earlier than usual. Your program would call **tpbroadcast** as shown in Listing 13.5.

```
#define EARLYSTRING "Your machine is coming down an hour earlier."
char *string;

string = tpalloc("STRING", NULL, sizeof(EARLYSTRING) + 1);
strcpy(string, EARLYSTRING);
tpbroadcast("M1", NULL, "teller", string, 0, TPNOFLAGS);
```

Listing 13.5 *Using tpbroadcast to Send a Message*

One reason to restrict the broadcast only to tellers is that there might be other client programs on that machine that do not have users looking at screens. Thus, sending the message to those programs would be a waste because they have no one to tell.

Messages sent via **tpbroadcast** are dispatched to a client's call-back function. In fact, unless your application puts something special in the data, a client cannot tell the difference between a message sent via **tpnotify** or **tpbroadcast**. Like **tpnotify**, messages sent with **tpbroadcast** are not guaranteed to arrive nor do they have replies. As we said earlier, unsolicited notifications should be used to convey informational messages to clients that, if lost in transit because of a network failure, would not adversely affect the running of your business. For sending event-based messages of greater importance to your business, the TUXEDO System EventBroker should be used.

13.2　Brokered Events

Brokered events allow programs to post events without having to worry which other programs are supposed to receive notification of an event's occurrence. Although **tpnotify** and **tpbroadcast** require your programs to specify some form of a client name to which an event notification is sent, posting events through the TUXEDO System EventBroker does not. In fact, a key value provided by the EventBroker is that subscribers and posters, who have no knowledge of each other, can still communicate with one another. As you can imagine, this is the ultimate in location transparency!

Any client or service can subscribe to an event using the ATMI function **tpsubscribe**. An event is simply a name represented by a string, such as "Inventory_Low." This is consistent with the other location-transparent names used in ATMI—that is, service names and application queue names. Essentially, an event subscription consists of the event's name and an associated action to perform when that event is posted. Any client or service can post an event using **tppost**. Event names are the rendezvous points for subscribers and posters. To post an event, a program specifies an event name and, optionally, a typed buffer that contains any data associated with the event. Last, programs can use **tpunsubscribe** to remove subscriptions from the EventBroker's list of active subscriptions.

The TUXEDO System EventBroker is a set of system-provided servers that keep track of all the event subscriptions in your application. When events are posted, the EventBroker invokes the required actions for subscriptions that match the posted events. As we mentioned previously in Chapter 4, "Application Development—Overview," the possible actions are to send an unsolicited notification to the subscriber, to send a service request to a named service routine, or to enqueue the posted data to a named application queue. Figure 13.2 shows the EventBroker performing a subscriber's requested action using the poster's data.

Let's now look at the details of the three ATMI verbs that you use to program brokered events. We will look at the C versions only because the way they are used is almost identical to their COBOL counterparts.

13.2.1　Subscribing to Events: tpsubscribe

Because there is a lot of flexibility in defining an event subscription, the best way to see what one looks like is to introduce the function prototype for **tpsubscribe**. Next, we will cover each of its parameters.

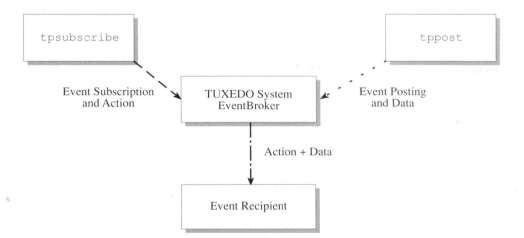

Figure 13.2   **Event Broker Combining Action and Posted Data**

```
long tpsubscribe(char *eventexpr, char *filter,
                 TPEVCTL *ctl, long flags)
```

The first parameter, **eventexpr**, is the event name itself. Actually, this string—an array of up to 255 characters—is a regular expression for one or more event names. That is, the event expression can contain metacharacters that represent one or more characters. The regular expressions themselves are patterned after those found in many Unix System commands, specifically, the line editor, **ed**. By allowing regular expression pattern matching, a single subscription can be used for several events that match a given event expression. For example, the event expression "^auth.*_error$" would match all event names starting with the substring "auth", followed by zero or more other characters (denoted by ".*"), and ending with the substring "_error". So, both "authentication_error" and "authorization_error" event names would qualify.

The name space for events is partitioned into two sets. The first set contains the names of your application's events. The second set contains the names of the predefined TUXEDO System administrative events. Event names in this latter set are prefaced with a "." so that they do not clash with your application event names, which are not allowed to begin with ".". For example, to subscribe to all TUXEDO System administrative events pertaining to clients, your program would specify the expression "\\.SysClient.*". Because the dot is also a metacharacter in the regular expression syntax, the first instance is prefaced (aka "escaped") with "\\" so that it will evaluate to the character ".", rather than to its metacharacter meaning. However, the second dot is the metacharacter for "any single character" and therefore is properly unescaped.

Because every subscription has an associated action, regular expressions allow programs to map a single action to possibly many events. Contrast this with having a unique subscription for each event. Of course, if your program needs to perform a different action for each and every event, then it cannot have a blanket subscription covering a set of events. In that case, it should subscribe to each event individually. By carefully choosing the names for your application's events and their associated actions, subscribers can exploit regular expression pattern matching to get the most out of each subscription.

The second parameter, **filter**, specifies an optional boolean filter rule that the EventBroker applies to the posted data. The posted data must "pass" the filter rule before the broker will invoke the subscription's action. A filter rule lets a program tailor a subscription to its needs by specifying that it is interested in a particular event only if the posted data matches the filter's criteria. Let's say, for example, that a brokerage application has an event called "High_Volume" which is posted when a particular stock's trading volume is abnormally high. Two of the fields in the posted typed buffer are "Symbol" and "Ask_Price." A program can specify a filter rule stating that it wants to know about the "High_Volume" event only when the symbol is "XYZ" and the asking price is greater than $100. If the filter rule doesn't pass, then action associated with the "High_Volume" subscription is not performed.

Filter rule formats and syntaxes are specific to the buffer types of the posted event data. For some of the buffer types supplied with the TUXEDO System—that is, FML, VIEWs, and strings—there are predefined filter rule syntaxes and functions to evaluate them. For FML and VIEW buffers, the TUXEDO System uses the boolean expression compiler, **Fboolco**, described in Chapter 8, "Typed Buffers." The filter rule for the string buffer type is a regular expression—using the same syntax as the event expression strings. If you have created your own buffer type, then you can define your own filter rule syntax as well as a customized filter rule evaluator that the EventBroker invokes whenever it receives an event accompanied by your custom buffer type—also covered in Chapter 8, "Typed Buffers."

To complete the subscription, the subscriber specifies an action to be performed when an event is posted that not only matches the event expression, but whose data also passes the filter rule (if one has been specified). The EventBroker dispatches the action using the poster's data as input to the action. Thus, the subscriber specifies the action but the poster supplies the data for its invocation.

Your programs use the third parameter of **tpsubscribe**, **ctl**, to specify one of three types of actions to be performed when the subscription is fulfilled. If your program is a client, then it can specify that the EventBroker notify it of the event via **tpnotify**. This is accomplished by setting the event control structure **ctl** to NULL. As with any unsolicited notification, your program must first register a call-back function using **tpsetunsol** before it can receive and process notifications from the EventBroker. If your client needs to know the name of the posted event, the poster should include it as part of the data buffer sent to subscribers.

There are two other actions that either a client or a service routine can specify via the event control structure: dispatch a service routine or enqueue a message to an application queue. Listing 13.6 shows the event control structure, **TPEVCTL**.

```
struct tpevctl_t {
        long flags;
        char name1[32];
        char name2[32];
        TPQCTL qctl;
};
typedef struct tpevctl_t TPEVCTL;
```

Listing 13.6 *Event Control Structure*

As we saw in the last chapter for the queue control structure, the **flags** element in the event control structure is used to specify how to interpret the remaining elements. To specify that your program wants the EventBroker to fulfill a subscription by calling a service routine, it sets **TPEVSERVICE** in the **flags** element and puts the name of the service to invoke in the element **name1**. Listing 13.7 shows an example of how a program subscribes to the event named "X" with the action of invoking the service named "Y."

```
TPEVCTL ctl;

ctl.flags = TPEVSERVICE;
strcpy(ctl.name1, "Y");
tpsubscribe("X", NULL, &ctl, TPSIGRSTRT);
```

Listing 13.7 *Using the Event Control Structure to Set an Action*

The subscriber has no idea which of the possibly many instances of service "Y" will be invoked because the TUXEDO System load balances between them. If a particular server subscribes to an event, and wants to make sure that it (and no other) receives the event notification via a service request, then it should advertise a unique service name that only it offers and use that service in its subscriptions.

Service routines dispatched by the EventBroker are no different from those invoked directly by clients using **tpcall**. However, they are executed for their side effects and not their return values that is, the data returned as part of **tpreturn**. By side effects we are referring to the effects of invoking a service, such as updating a database or printing a report. The reason that a service routine's reply is not of value during subscription fulfillment is that the poster is not able to receive it. If you think about it, the notion of a reply runs counter to the anonymous communication offered by brokered events. That is, an event-posting program cannot easily expect a reply if it has no idea with whom it is communicating. Thus, the TUXEDO run-time system drops any reply returned to the EventBroker by a service routine.

The other action that programs can specify is to enqueue the posted data to an application queue. This method is very useful when programs want to make sure that notifications are not lost. For example, when client programs are stopped at 5 P.M. because the people using them leave for the day, events might still occur that they want to find out about when they come back in the morning. Enqueuing the posted event to an application queue allows users to dequeue any events that they would have otherwise missed if they were sent on-line via unsolicited notifications.

To specify that your program wants the EventBroker to enqueue the posted data, it sets **TPEVQUEUE** in the **flags** element of the event control structure. It also needs to specify the queue space and queue name in the **name1** and **name2** elements, respectively, where the EventBroker should enqueue the message. Your program can also specify options in the queue control structure element **qctl** so that you can tell the EventBroker precisely how the message should be handled. For example, you can specify a correlation identifier that the EventBroker should use or the priority at which it should enqueue the message. In fact, any queue control option setting that can be given as input to **tpenqueue** can also be specified as part **tpsubscribe**. Listing 13.8 shows an example of a call to **tpsubscribe** that specifies in which queue space and queue to enqueue the posted data, as well as the priority to be used when doing so.

```
TPEVCTL evctl;

evctl.flags = TPEVQUEUE;    /* indicate action: enqueue posted data */
strcpy(evctl.name1, "My_Queue_Space"); /* name of queue space */
strcpy(evctl.name2, "My_Event_Queue"); /* name of queue */
evctl.qctl.priority = LOW_PRIORITY;   /* specify queuing priority */
evctl.qctl.flags = TPQPRIORITY;     /* indicate that priority is set */
handle = tpsubscribe("rare_event", NULL, &evctl, TPSIGRSTRT);
```

Listing 13.8 *Setting the Enqueue Action in the Event Control Structure*

There are two other flags that can be set in the **flags** element of the control structure. The first is **TPEVTRAN** which is used to tell the EventBroker that this subscription's action should be done on behalf of the poster's global transaction, if one exists at the time of the posting. We'll discuss this more in Chapter 14, "Transactions in the TUXEDO System."

The other flag setting is **TPEVPERSIST** which tells the broker that the subscription should persist in the active subscription list even if the resource being accessed by the action is not available. For example, the service that is supposed to be called might not be available at the time posting is made. If the subscription is not a persistent one, then it is deleted if the resource is unavailable.

As you might have noticed, these two flags, **TPEVTRAN** and **TPEVPERSIST**, have meaning only for the two actions that are set from within the event control structure. Because the third action, **tpnotify**, is specified by setting the control structure to NULL, these options do not apply. Of course, neither of these options makes much sense for unsolicited client notifications anyway.

When **tpsubscribe** successfully registers a subscription with the EventBroker, it returns a handle for the subscription that any program can use later for removing it via **tpunsubscribe**. We will look more closely at tpunsubscribe shortly.

13.2.2 Posting Events: tppost

Like all other ATMI functions that communicate application data, **tppost** takes as its parameters a name and the usual triple: data, length, and flags. Here's an example of calling **tppost**:

```
ret = tppost("Inventory_Low", data, 0, TPNOREPLY);
```

The first parameter is the event name. When received by the EventBroker, all subscriptions are evaluated against the event name for matching purposes. Those whose event expressions successfully match this name pass the first test.

The second test is against the data. The second parameter passed into **tppost** is a typed buffer containing the posted data, and the third is its length (that is, for buffers whose length can't be inferred). For those subscriptions having an optional filter rule, the data buffer is evaluated against the rule. If it passes, then the subscription's action is taken. Otherwise, the subscription is passed over.

The last argument is the flags parameter, and it has settings that we have covered before: **TPNOTRAN**, **TPNOREPLY**, **TPNOBLOCK**, **TPNOTIME**, and **TPSIGRSTRT**. Of these, **TPNOREPLY** is of interest as it informs **tppost** not to wait for the EventBroker to dispatch all of the actions associated with subscriptions that successfully matched the event name and filter rule. As soon as the EventBroker has been notified of the event, **tppost** returns, and the caller proceeds in parallel with any actions dispatched by the EventBroker.

When this flag is not used, **tppost** waits for the EventBroker to finish dispatching all the actions for matching subscriptions, and then returns to the caller the number of subscriptions fulfilled in the variable, **tpurcode**. Even though the poster does not know the nature of the actions or the identities of the subscribers, it can know how large or small an audience it had for its event!

13.2.3 Unsubscribing to Events: tpunsubscribe

Programmatically, there are two ways to remove event subscriptions from the EventBroker's active list. The first is to use **tpunsubscribe**, and the second is to use the TUXEDO TMIB API to directly update the event MIB. We will discuss the first method here. Writing programs that use the TMIB API is covered in Chapter 17, "A Tour of the TUXEDO Management Information Base."

The first parameter to **tpunsubscribe** is a subscription handle returned previously from tpsubscribe. The second parameter is the flags settings (**TPNOBLOCK**, **TPNOTIME**, and **TPSIGRSTRT**). A client should remove its "personal" subscriptions before exiting. These are the ones whose actions call for the EventBroker to send it an unsolicited notification directly. Obviously, these subscriptions are of little value once a client is no longer around to be notified. If the client fails to remove these subscriptions before exiting, the EventBroker will remove them when it finds out that the client is no longer active.

Subscriptions calling for services to be invoked or data to be enqueued in application queues are not automatically cleaned up after their subscribers exit. This is because the actions of these subscriptions are not associated with the subscribing programs. The EventBroker can still enqueue a message into an application queue even after the client program that made the subscription terminates. If one of these subscriptions is not tagged as being persistent, then it is removed either when a program issues **tpunsubscribe** against its subscription handle or when the EventBroker determines that the named resource (service or queue name) is unavailable. On the other hand, if it is marked as persistent, then the only way to remove it programmatically is by calling **tpunsubscribe**—unless, of course, you write a program that accesses the event MIB directly.

The function **tpunsubscribe** also allows a wild-card value, −1, for the subscription handle. The wild-card handle allows a program to tell **tpunsubscribe** to remove all of its nonpersistent subscriptions. This makes it convenient for a program to remove a set of subscriptions with a single call. The wild card works only against a program's nonpersistent subscriptions because the whole point of persistent subscriptions is that they are supposed to remain active until explicitly removed by a call to **tpunsubscribe** with the associated handle.

13.3 Summary

In this chapter, we have covered the various ways that your programs can communicate using event-based notifications, a communication paradigm that is quite distinct from the request/response, conversational, and queuing paradigms. ATMI provides two approaches for this purpose. The first is an unsolicited event notification mechanism whereby one program can send an unsolicited message to one or more named clients programs. The functions **tpnotify** and **tpbroadcast** are used for this purpose. We also described how clients can receive such messages by registering call-back functions that are dispatched when these notifications arrive.

The second class of event-based communication is ATMI's brokered event mechanism. Using the TUXEDO System EventBroker, programs do not have to know about each other to communicate. Rather, using **tppost** and **tpsubscribe**, programs communicate through an intermediary whose role is to keep track of active subscriptions and dispatch actions for subscriptions that match event postings. Event subscriptions are quite rich in their semantics. Not only are there several communication techniques to choose from for dispatching a posted event's data, but there are also powerful pattern matching and filtering techniques that your programs can use to tailor subscriptions to their needs.

14 Transactions in the TUXEDO System

In Chapter 3 we gave a brief overview of the transaction notion, and in Chapter 4 we gave an introduction to the use of transactions within a TUXEDO-based application. In this chapter, we delve deeper into the transactional features of the TUXEDO System. Before doing so, we provide some additional transaction-specific terminology.

14.1 Transaction Terminology

A *transaction initiator* is an application software module that establishes the beginning of a transaction. A *transaction terminator* is an application software module that signals that a transaction is to be completed. Transactions which complete successfully are said to *commit*, and those which complete unsuccessfully are said to *abort* or *roll back*. Usually, a transaction's initiator and terminator are required to be the same software module. The instructions which initiate and terminate a transaction are said to *bracket* the transaction. Figure 14.1 depicts the bracketing of application code by initiation and successful termination pseudoinstructions. A *transaction coordinator* (or just *coordinator*) is a software module that executes the logic to terminate a transaction. It may, or may not, be the transaction's initiator or terminator.

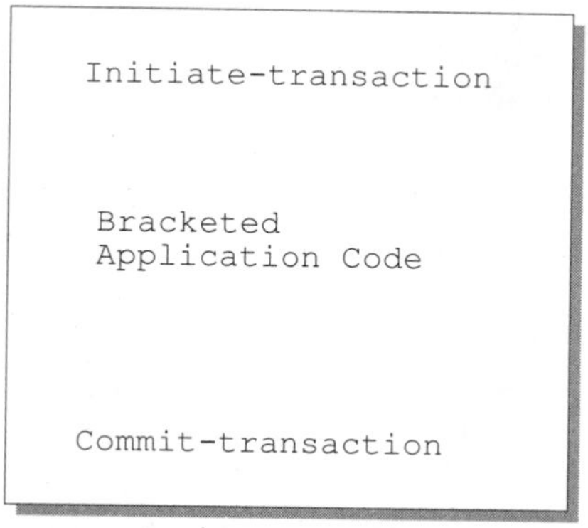

```
Initiate-transaction




Bracketed
Application Code




Commit-transaction
```

Figure 14.1   **Transaction Bracket**

Two-phase commit-presumed abort (2PC-PA) is an algorithm used to ensure the *atomicity* of a committing transaction. We draw an example from everyday experience to illustrate how 2PC-PA works. Suppose you need to meet with several parties. You instruct your administrative assistant to set up the meeting. It is mandatory that ALL the parties must be at the meeting for the meeting to take place. Your assistant picks a time suitable for you and calls the parties to see if they can attend the meeting. As each person agrees to attend the meeting, your assistant notes the person's consent and tells him to "pencil it in" in his appointment book. Your assistant also indicates that he will be "getting back" to the person with an indication of the status of the meeting. "Penciling it in" indicates that the time is to be reserved by the attendee (i.e., can't be used for something else), but might be freed up, if the other people can't make that time. If everyone can make the meeting, then your assistant, as the meeting coordinator, can PEN the time in your appointment book. He can then get back to everyone and tell them to change the pencil indication to a pen indication in their appointment books. If, in canvassing the potential meeting attendees, your assistant discovers that someone can't make the meeting, then he should get back to those he has contacted previously and tell them they don't have to reserve that time anymore (i.e., they can erase their pencil indication). The meeting is canceled, and the process might have to begin with a new time.

The process to set up the meeting has two phases. The first phase is getting in touch with everyone, making sure they can make the appointed time, and having them reserve the time. This phase culminates with the recording of the fact by the coordinator that everyone can make the meeting. Once this is recorded in the appointment book of the coordinator, the decision to hold the meeting at the appointed time has essentially been made. Even if the coordinator becomes unavailable, your appointment book can be consulted to see if the meeting is "on." If the meeting time is recorded in pen in your appointment book, the meeting must have been successfully established. If there is no appointment recorded, it is unclear if the meeting is to take place. In this case, one might presume that the meeting has not been successfully established. The second phase of the process to set up the meeting occurs when the coordinator informs everyone that the meeting is "on."

2PC-PA for transaction commitment works in much the same fashion as the meeting coordination. In *phase one*, the commit coordinator issues *prepare notices* to transactionally aware resources involved in the transaction (similar to the meeting coordinator calling the potential attendees). The resources promise to make the results of the transaction permanent (like the attendees promising to reserve the time for the meeting by "penciling in" the meeting time), but do not actually do so. Typically, the resources log information to disk to ensure they can complete phase two. If all the resources agree to commit, the commit coordinator logs the fact that all of the resources have agreed to commit (similar to the meeting coordinator penning the decision in your appointment book). This ends *phase one*, and the outcome of the transaction is effectively decided. In *phase two*, each of the resources is informed of the decision, and they permanently update their resources.

2PC-PA is the algorithm executed by the TUXEDO System transaction coordinator. In the 2PC-PA algorithm, the software plays two roles. The *transaction coordinator* executes the algorithm, and, in so doing, interacts with the *participants*, who act in a *subordinate role*. It is the coordinator which, based on information received from the participants, decides whether the preparation was successful. The participants play a subordinate role and wait to be instructed by the coordinator as to the outcome.

In a TUXEDO-based application, the TUXEDO System plays both the role of the transaction coordinator and transaction subordinate. In its role as transaction coordinator, the TUXEDO System is called the *Transaction Manager (TM)*. Database systems play subordinate roles and are called *Resource Managers (RMs)*. The TUXEDO System's Application Queuing Manager is a Resource Manager.

As a TM, the TUXEDO System performs the following actions for each transaction:

- It creates a *global transaction identifier* when the application initiates a transaction.

- It tracks the communications partners of the transaction initiator. This is required so that the TM "knows" which sites to contact during the execution of the 2PC-PA algorithm.

- It notifies the RMs of the global transaction identifier when they are accessed on behalf of the transaction. This allows the RMs to know which database records have been accessed on behalf of the transaction. Typically, the RMs would *lock* these records until the end of the transaction.

- It executes the 2PC-PA algorithm when the application indicates that the transaction is to be committed. This includes the notification of the partners during phase one, the logging of the successful outcome of phase one, and the notification of the partners in phase two.

- It executes the rollback procedure when the application indicates that the transaction is to be aborted.

- It executes a *recovery procedure* when failures occur.

To conduct the 2PC-PA algorithm, the TUXEDO System must keep track of the various transactions executing within the distributed system. There may be multiple transactions concurrently executing. To do this, the TUXEDO System creates a global transaction identifier for each transaction in the system. We will discuss transaction creation in the next section. When it comes time to commit a transaction, the coordinator must know which RMs throughout the distributed computation have participated in the transaction. The TUXEDO System tracks the flow of each transaction throughout the system. It can do this because it also manages the communications paradigms that the application programmer uses to create the flow.

When the application accesses a Resource Manager, the TUXEDO System communicates with the Resource Manager through an interface that is not seen by the application programmer. This interface, called the *XA Interface*, was originally conceived in the TUXEDO project and has been standardized by the X/Open Company [X/Open-XA]. The RMs must keep track of the various transactions and, typically, will create *local transaction identifiers* to do so. When RMs use local transaction identifiers, they must be able to provide a mapping of global identifiers to local identifiers.

14.2 Creating a Transaction

In the TUXEDO System, transactions may be initiated explicitly by the application or implicitly by an administrator. We describe both techniques in this section.

14.2.1 Explicit Transaction Initiation: tpbegin

You explicitly indicate the programmatic initiation of a transaction by a call to the **tpbegin** function. This function creates a global transaction, begins a transaction bracket in the invoking executable, and indicates to the transaction management system that the invoking executable is the transaction initiator. After starting a transaction, your program may update databases and communicate with other parts of the application. These partners may, in turn, update the same, or other, databases. No special syntax is needed for database interactions. In particular, the programmer does not need to tell the database systems on behalf of what global transaction it is updating the database—the system automatically does it via transparent calls to the XA interface. None of the updates made permanent or visible to application modules whose work is not part of the transaction until the application commits the transaction. An executable may be active in only one transaction at any given time, and **tpbegin** will thus fail if the application is already active in a transaction when it is called. This makes for a simple interface. The application need not "juggle" transactions and need not pass global transaction identifiers to database systems.

tpbegin takes two parameters. The first is a time-out value, and the second is a flags parameter. To ensure consistent behavior during update, transactions lock resources such as records. A transaction which never completes, or takes a very long time to do so, could prevent other transactions from accessing the records it has locked. The time-out parameter of **tpbegin** is intended to prevent this by putting a bound on the lifetime of a transaction. If a transaction has not entered its termination phase before its time-out parameter has been exceeded, the system will roll back the transaction. The rollback will unlock any resources locked during the transaction. This will allow other transactions to access them. The flags parameter to **tpbegin** is currently unused and reserved for future use. Listing 14.1 shows an example of a service routine that begins and commits a transaction.

```
DELETECUST (TPSVCINFO *tpscvinfo)
{
    if (tpbegin(60,TPNOFLAGS) == -1){/* tran should complete within 60 seconds */
                                    /* for some reason tran couldn't be started */
        userlog(...);               /* put an error in the log */
        tpreturn(TPFAIL, ...  );
    }

    EXEC SQL DELETE FROM T1 where ...

    if (tpcommit(TPNOFLAGS) == -1){              /* commit the transaction */
        userlog( ...  );     /* oops ..Commit failed !  put an error in the log */
        tpreturn(TPFAIL, ...  );
    }
    tpreturn(TPSUCCESS, ...  );
}
```

Listing 14.1   *Service Routine Initiates and Terminates a Transaction*

14.2.2 System-Initiated Transactions

Suppose that the service routine shown in Listing 14.1 is invoked by a client that is already in a transaction. Recall that transaction infection will infect the service with the client's transaction. Thus, the call to **tpbegin** within the service routine will fail, because it is already within a transaction. What is the programmer of the service routine to do to insure that his work is done within a transaction, yet that he doesn't try to start a transaction if he is already in one? There are two solutions to this problem. A service can find out if it is in a transaction by calling the function **tpgetlev**. It takes no arguments returning a 0 if the caller is not in a transaction and returns a positive integer if it is in a transaction. If the service finds out that it is in a transaction already, it need not call **tpbegin**. Otherwise, the service routine should begin its own transaction.

To relieve the programmer of the complexity of these decisions, the TUXEDO System provides a built-in solution via an administrative configuration option called *AUTOTRAN*. Services that are marked **AUTOTRAN** are encapsulated within the transaction of their caller, if one is in effect. If there is no transaction in effect, the TUXEDO run-time system automatically initiates one prior to invoking the service. If the service ends successfully, the system commits the transaction. Otherwise, it aborts it. A service which is configured as **AUTOTRAN** cannot tell if the transaction it is working on was started in its caller or by the TUXEDO run-time system. If the service of Listing 14.1 were configured as an **AUTOTRAN** service, the **tpbegin** and **tpcommit** function calls would not be present. Note that when the system initiates a transaction for an **AUTOTRAN** service, it will commit the transaction if the service calls **tpreturn** with a success indication. However, if **tpforward** is used by the application to end an **AUTOTRAN** service, then the TUXEDO run-time system also forwards to the destination service the responsibility for terminating the transaction. In effect, the destination service is treated as the transaction initiator.

One other place where the TUXEDO System initiates a transaction is in its Application Queuing System. When the **tpenqueue** or **tpdequeue** functions are called, they are done within the caller's transaction, if one exists. If the caller is not within a transaction, the **TMQUEUE** server starts a short-lived transaction to perform the queue operation. Additionally, a forwarding agent can be configured to dequeue requests and call the associated services. The response from each service is enqueued on a reply queue. The **tpdequeue**, **tpcall**, and **tpenqueue** are bracketed by a transaction in the forwarding agent.

14.3 Transaction Infection

In general, when an application module that is executing within a transaction bracket communicates with another module, the target of the communication is brought into the transaction. We say that the target becomes transactionally infected. The TUXEDO System keeps track of all infected sites, so that, at commit time, it will know which sites to involve in the 2PC-PA algorithm. Transactional infection happens transparently to the application programmer. Figure 14.2 shows a client C which begins a transaction and calls two services S1 and S2. The work that is done in both S1 and S2 is automatically performed as part of the transaction started by C. When C calls **tpcommit**, the work it has done, together with the work that S1 and S2 have done, are all atomically committed. If C rolls back the transaction, the work done by S1 and S2 are likewise undone. Infection is transitive: if an infected service itself calls a service, the infection will be passed on.

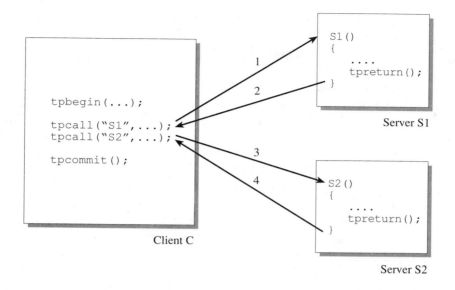

Figure 14.2   Client Infects Two Services with Transaction

14.3.1 A Second Pass at Commit

The earlier discussions of the 2PC-PA algorithm described its preparation and commit phases. There is actually another requirement for the algorithm to work successfully. Application manipulation of each resource that is to be considered part of the transaction must be completed prior to the preparatory phase for the resource. One way to ensure this is to arrange processing control so that no application work is proceeding on behalf of any resource at the time of the beginning of the first phase of commit. What is desired is that all work on behalf of the transaction has been stopped, thus allowing the orderly progression of the 2PC-PA algorithm. ATMI has been carefully designed so that processing quiescence can be guaranteed at commitment time. We discuss several examples of this design.

In Figure 14.2, client C creates a transaction. Let's call this transaction T. C also invokes services S1 and S2 via **tpcall** function calls. The use of **tpcall** by a client is synchronous in the client. That is, in Figure 14.2, C cannot proceed until the service it calls completes. When C calls S1 (flow 1), S1 becomes infected with T. When S1 calls **tpreturn** (flow 2), it has completed its work for T. Thus, when the **tpcall** to S1 returns in C, S1 is no longer doing any work on behalf of T. The situation is identical for the **tpcall** to S2 (flows 3 and 4). When C calls **tpcommit** to signal the termination of T, there is no work proceeding anywhere in the system on behalf of T. The system is quiescent with respect to T, and commitment can proceed. Note that, even if S1 and S2 had called other services to perform their work, and thereby had infected them with T, so long as S1 and S2 used **tpcall** by the time control was returned to C, no work would have been proceeding anywhere on behalf of T.

On the other hand, the use of **tpacall** is asynchronous in the caller. The service that is invoked can be executing at the same time as the client that invoked it. This means that it is possible for the client to call **tpcommit** while a service it invoked is still performing the service request. In fact, the service might be updating a resource that the client is trying to commit. For this reason, a call to **tpcommit** fails if there are any outstanding **tpacall** handles in the client. Likewise, a call to **tpcommit** will also fail if there are any open conversations started by **tpconnect**. In both cases, ATMI is protecting the application from inadvertently getting partial results from the commitment process.

We cite one more example of how the design of ATMI protects applications from premature calls to commit. When using ATMI, a service written in the C programing language terminates its work by calling **tpreturn**. The choice of this method was not arbitrary. A number of possibilities were considered. One of the foremost was having another function, say **tpsendreply**, to send back the answer, and just have the service terminate with the standard C **return** function. One problem with this approach was that, if **tpsendreply** actually sent the reply, the server might (inadvertently) continue to update the resource. We would then have the same problem as **tpacall**: the client could be trying to call commit while the server is still updating the resource. (Note that there is no function called **tpsendreply** in ATMI).

14.3.2 Preventing Infection

The TUXEDO System provides two ways to insulate a "callee" from the effects of a transaction active in the "caller". On the calling side, the use of the **TPNOTRAN** flag throughout ATMI prevents a module initiating a communication from propagating the transaction to modules it is trying to contact. On the called side, a module may use the **tpsuspend** function to extract itself from any transaction that has infected it.

14.3.3 Carrying Infection

If a module does not directly access a transactionally aware resource, it may still be desirable to infect it, because the module may call another module which does access such a resource. Figure 14.3 shows this happening in a TUXEDO-based application. In the figure, the client explicitly begins a transaction. Then it calls the TRANSFER service (flow 1). TRANSFER does not directly access any transactional resources. However, it calls the CREDIT (flows 2 and 3) and DEBIT (flows 4 and 5) services, both of which access (transactionally aware) RDBMS

(Relational Database Management Systems). During flow 1, TRANSFER becomes infected with the client's transaction and passes the infection on to CREDIT and DEBIT. The client terminates the transaction with a call to **tpcommit**.

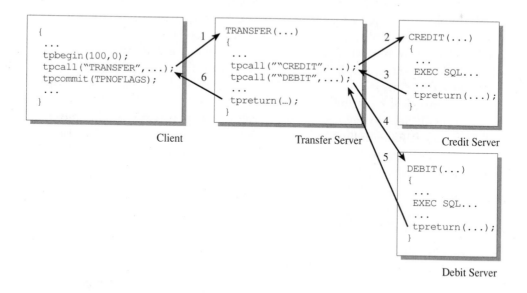

Figure 14.3   **Transaction Infection Passes Through Nontransactional Service**

14.4   Terminating a Transaction

Transaction termination is usually the responsibility of the software that started the transaction. For explicit initiation, the application module that called **tpbegin** should also call a termination procedure, either **tpcommit** or **tpabort**. Any time the TUXEDO run-time system initiates a transaction (as for example via **AUTOTRAN**), it will terminate it.

14.4.1 Committing Work: tpcommit

Successful termination of a transaction is indicated by a call to tpcommit. This signals that the application wants an execution of the 2PC-PA commit algorithm. As previously discussed, the 2PC-PA algorithm contains a decision point: the outcome of the algorithm is decided when the result is logged after phase one. In phase two, the TM informs the resource managers that they should make updates permanent and visible. Via the **tpscmt** function, ATMI allows the application to decide if it wants a return from its call to **tpcommit** after either phase. Returning after phase one may allow better response time from the invoking module to its caller, because it does not have to wait for the resource managers to be informed in phase two.

There are, however, two potential harmful effects of using **tpscmt** to return after completion of the first phase of commit. First, there is a small possibility that resource managers will renege on their promise to update their data, and thus the module calling **tpcommit** may be misled. The unilateral commitment or rollback of a transaction via an RM is called a *heuristic decision*. An RM might decide to take a heuristic decision because it no longer wishes to hold its locks. If one RM decides to heuristically commit its work, whereas another in the same transaction heuristically decides to roll back its work, the atomicity property of the transaction will be violated. A second problem with return to the application after phase one is that the application may try to access a resource updated during the transaction but be denied access. This could occur because locks acquired during the course of a transaction are released as part of the second phase of commit.

14.4.2 Rolling Back Work: tpabort

A transaction may be terminated with the restoration of all work to its initial state by an explicit call to **tpabort**. As described in Chapter 3, only the effects of a transaction are undone by a rollback. The fact that certain code was executed is a fact, and history cannot be rewritten. Moreover the "effects" that may be undone are those that are held by resource managers which themselves are transactionally aware (e.g., RDBMS systems or the TUXEDO System's Application Queue System). Usually, program variables and the like are not rolled back, although if access to them were via a transactionally aware resource manager, it is not inconceivable that they could be rolled back. Resources that are not transactionally aware or that are accessed outside of the transaction cannot be rolled back.

In addition to explicit rollback by the transaction initiator, it is possible for modules with which the initiator of a transaction communicates to require that a transaction be rolled back. For example, if a service routine calls **tpreturn** with **TPFAIL** as its return code, the enveloping transaction is marked by the TUXEDO run-time system as *abort-only*. This means that the only acceptable transaction termination is a call to **tpabort**. In effect, the called routine has veto power over the commitment of any transaction of which it is a part. An interesting case of this occurs in the event system, where subscribers, anonymous to the poster of an event, can abort a transaction that the poster has created.

14.4.3 Transaction Juggling: tpsuspend and tpresume

Sometimes, it may be desirable to temporarily remove an executing piece of code from the effects of a transaction it has started, but not yet completed. In particular, the code may receive inputs for a different transaction. For example, Figure 14.4 shows a client interfacing to three devices, D1, D2, and D3. The work from each device arrives in an interleaved fashion, and each device may have multiple inputs to be combined into a single transaction. One simple way to accommodate this is to have the client start a transaction associated with each device. When it receives input from the device, it activates the associated transaction and performs some work; then it deactivates the transaction. In between inputs, it is in no transaction, as all are in an inactive state. At some point, the client will receive input from a device indicating that the transaction that it initiated is to be completed. The client can activate and then commit or roll back the transaction for that device. To do this, the client will have to keep an association of each device with its transaction. In Figure 14.4, D1 is submitting inputs for transaction 33, D2 is submitting inputs for transaction 40, and D3 currently has no associated (NA) transaction. Note that the device/transaction association is state information kept in the client.

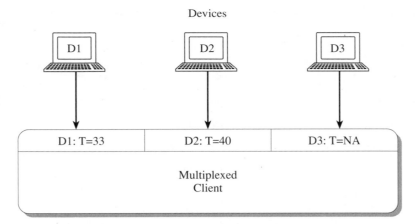

Figure 14.4 **Multiplexed Client Juggles Transactions via tpsuspend/ tpresume**

Another scenario where it might be desirable to temporarily deactivate a transaction is in a server. Suppose a server receives a request to perform some action and wishes to log the request to a database, regardless of the outcome of the transaction in which the request was received. If the service updates its log database as part of the originating transaction and that transaction aborts, the log information will also be rolled back. What the service would like to do would be to update its log in a transaction **different** from the one in which it received the request. One way to do this would be to call another service in **TPNOTRAN** mode, have that service initiate a separate transaction, log the information, commit the work, and then return to the original service. A more straightforward method would be to allow the server to suspend the transaction in which it was called, begin, do work for and commit another transaction, and then resume the original transaction.

To accommodate such needs, ATMI provides two simple, but powerful functions. **tpsuspend** is used to suspend a transaction, and **tpresume** is used to resume a suspended transaction. When an executable suspends a transaction, it is then permitted to activate a different transaction by calling **tpbegin** or **tpresume**. In this fashion, an application may "juggle" multiple outstanding transactions. To keep things simple, an execution context may have only one transaction active at any given time. Listing 14.2 illustrates the use of **tpsuspend** and **tpresume** within a service to log its input in a separate transaction. When a transaction is suspended, it is put into the *transaction orphanage*. The transaction orphanage is a collection of transactions which are not active in any executable. While it is in the orphanage, all the modifications previously made by a transaction are preserved in a pending state until the transaction is committed, aborted, or times out.

```
DEBIT(SVCINFO *s)
{
        TPTRANID t;
        tpsuspend(&t,TPNOFLAGS); /* suspend invoking transaction */

        tpbegin(30,TPNOFLAGS);   /* begin a separate transaction */
        loginputs(s);
        tpcommit(TPNOFLAGS);     /* commit it */

        tpresume(&t,TPNOFLAGS);  /* go back to original transaction */

        ......                   /* do work of service routine */

        tpreturn( .... );
}
```

Listing 14.2 *Server Logs Input in Separate Transaction*

It is also possible to resume a transaction in a process different from the one which suspended it. For example, a client may begin a transaction, perform work on it, suspend it, and communicate with a server. The server could resume the transaction, while the client goes on to begin another transaction.

tpsuspend takes two arguments. The first is a pointer to a location where the TUXEDO run-time system returns the *transaction identifier* of the transaction that has been suspended by the call to **tpsuspend**. The second parameter is currently unused and is reserved for future use. **tpresume** also takes two parameters. The first is a pointer to the transaction identifier of a transaction which is to be activated in the calling process. The second parameter is unused and is reserved for future use.

To ensure transaction integrity, the use of **tpsuspend** is subject to the types of restrictions previously described. For example, it is not permitted to suspend a transaction while asynchronous requests or conversations are outstanding.

14.4.4 More About Database Involvement

We have previously described the role that the TUXEDO System plays as coordinator of transaction commitment. During transaction commitment, database systems play a subordinate role. That is, they await directives from the TUXEDO System. It is important to realize that the details of 2PC-PA are hidden from application programmers. The goal in designing the TUXEDO System's transaction subsystem was to make transaction control simple and intuitive for the application programmer. Thus, the application sees functions like **tpbegin** and **tpcommit**, but not what goes on behind the scenes.

Behind the scenes, 2PC-PA is not a simple algorithm to implement. In fact, it requires close teamwork between the transaction coordinator and subordinates. This teamwork is enabled by an interface called XA. The model by which applications, transaction managers, and database systems "fit" together was created as part of the TUXEDO System. This model, as well as the XA and XATMI interfaces, have since been adopted by the X/Open Company [X/Open-DTP].

In Figure 14.5, we see two clients, C1 and C2 , a server called TELLER, and a service DEBIT contained within the TELLER executable. C1 begins a transaction by calling **tpbegin** and infects TELLER when it invokes DEBIT by using the **tpcall** function (flow 1). When C1 calls **tpbegin**, a global transaction identifier, let's call it T1, is allocated, and T1 becomes active in C1. When C1 calls **tpcall**, T1 is put into the transaction orphanage while the message is on its way to TELLER. When TELLER receives the message from C1, T1 becomes active in TELLER, thus removing T1 from the orphanage. The DEBIT service is thus executed in transaction T1. When DEBIT completes its work, it calls the **tpreturn** function to complete its work and to send a reply back to C1 (flow 4). While the result is on its way back to the C1, T1 is again placed in the orphanage. When the reply is received back in C1, T1 becomes active in C1. Meanwhile, DEBIT is free to work on a message associated with a different transaction, say T2, that was started by C2.

As explained in Chapter 6, servers receive messages in their main routine, called the Server Adaptor. The Server Adaptor, which is supplied with the TUXEDO System, dispatches the application written service routine. Before

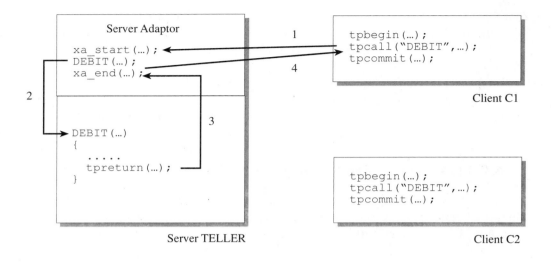

Figure 14.5 **Transaction Flows from Clients to Server**

doing this, however, the Server Adaptor inspects the message. If the message contains a transaction identifier, the server becomes infected with the transaction, thus removing it from the orphanage. The Server Adaptor uses the **xa_start** function of the XA interface to tell any RMs linked into the server about the infecting transaction. Thus, the RMs used by the server also become infected. After infecting the RM via the **xa_start** call, the Server Adaptor dispatches the actual service routine. When the service routine calls **tpreturn**, control returns to the Server Adaptor. The Server Adaptor uses the **xa_end** function of the XA interface to inform the RM that the executable is no longer infected with the transaction. The Server Adaptor then sends the reply to the client.

We show this scenario in Figure 14.5. The **tpcall** in C1 sends a message to the Server Adaptor in the TELLER server (flow 1). The Server Adaptor calls **xa_start** to infect the RMs used by TELLER, and then dispatches the DEBIT service (flow 2). The call to **tpreturn** in the DEBIT service returns control to the Server Adaptor (flow 3), which calls **xa_end** to inform the RMs that the transaction is leaving the TELLER executable. When the Server Adaptor sends the reply back to the client (flow 4), the transaction is disengaged from the server and put in the orphanage. The server has no further responsibility for the transaction, unless the application happens to call another service routine within the server as part of the transaction. In particular, the server is not needed to complete the outcome of the transaction. Note that the scheme of having the Server Adaptor infecting the RM may have an unnecessary overhead if the service routine doesn't do any RM operations. The calls to **xa_start** and **xa_end** would be wasted. A second scheme that some RM vendors use has the RM register with the TM when the RM has actually been called to do some work. At that time, the TM can indicate to the RM that the execution context is associated with a global transaction.

Again we stress that XA is a system level interface and is *never* seen by application programmers. It *is* seen by the implementers of transaction managers and resource managers. Likewise, the Server Adaptor is transparent to the application programmer. It is supplied as part of the TUXEDO System. An important design goal of the XA interface was the incorporation of arbitrary, transaction-aware RMs. That is, the goal was to allow users to "plug in" any software component that could partake in the 2PC-PA algorithm. Because arbitrary software was to be plugged in, it was assumed that the interfaces to such components would not be known to the TUXEDO System and could not be modified by it. This is fundamentally different from other transactional systems, such as MVS/CICS [IBM-CICS], where access to transactional resources must be via a TM provided API. TUXEDO itself does not supply such APIs. A programmer merely uses the RM's "native" API.

The execution of the 2PC-PA algorithm by the TUXEDO System is highly optimized—but none of the complexity of this optimization is known to the application programmer. Some administrative setup is required to define which RMs are active in the system, where their XA interface functions are located, etc. As discussed in Chapter 6, the actual execution of the 2PC-PA algorithm is conducted by special servers, called *Transaction Manager Servers* (*TMS*s). This fact is unknown to the application programmer but is configured by the administrator. Unlike other transaction managers, where the 2PC-PA algorithm is actually executed by application servers, the TUXEDO System gains more parallelism by disengaging an application server from a transaction when the server replies to its client and by performing commit processing for the transaction in a TMS.

14.5   Transactions and Communications Revisited

Let's briefly review the use of transactions and transactional infection among communicating modules.

Global transactions can be defined in either a client or a server. The closer the transaction definition is to the end user of the system, the more work can be included under the umbrella of a global transaction. The feature known as **AUTOTRAN** automatically performs the transaction bracketing on behalf of your services.

One simplifying aspect of global transactions is that the transaction terminator —the program that completes a transaction—is the only program that has to handle transaction outcomes. That is, transaction participants, which are always servers, do not have to worry about them.

14.5.1 Transactions in Request/Response Communications

There are two interface categories involved in the TUXEDO System request/response paradigm. For the first, use of the library-based calls (**tpcall** and **tpacall**), transactions are straightforward. The default is that services become infected with the caller's transaction. Infection can be prevented by using the **TPNOTRAN** flag in the caller. To ensure that all work on behalf of the transaction has ceased, all fan-out parallelism bracketed by the transaction must be completed prior to the call to **tpcommit**. That is, **tpgetrply** must have been called to resolve all outstanding transactional **tpacall** handles prior to calling **tpcommit**. Services which are invoked in a pipeline, that is, as a result of a call to **tpforward** in a previous service, are infected with any outstanding transaction.

The other category of request/response is language based TxRPC. Control of the propagation of a transaction to an invoked TxRPC procedure is specified in the Interface Definition Language (IDL) for the procedure, and thus is determined at compile time. Two mutually exclusive specifications are allowed. The **transaction_mandatory** clause indicates that the remote procedure must be invoked in a transaction. If none exists at the time of its invocation, an exception is generated. The **transaction_optional** clause indicates that the remote procedure may be invoked either in a transaction or not. If neither specification is used, the remote procedure is excluded from any outstanding transaction (the equivalent of **TPNOTRAN**).

14.5.2 Transactions in Conversational Communications

If a module begins a conversation after it has started a transaction, the conversational partner will be infected with the transaction. Commitment cannot take place until all transactional conversations have been terminated. This ensures that access to resources by the conversational partners has ceased. If a module begins a transaction subsequent to the initiation of a conversation, the conversational partner does not become part of the transaction. We show the distinction in Listing 14.3. The first code fragment begins the transaction before it begins the conversation, thus including the conversational partner within the transaction. The second code fragment begins the transaction after it has begun the conversation, thus excluding the conversational partner from the effects of the transaction.

In all cases, transactional infection may be prevented by using the **TPNOTRAN** flag on the call to **tpconnect** that begins a conversation.

14.5.3 Transactions and Application Queues

The interaction of application queuing and transactions was discussed in Chapter 3. Briefly, Application Queues are transactionally aware RMs used for deferred communication. Because they are transactionally aware, the effect of a **tpenqueue** or **tpdequeue** call within a transaction bracket is not made perma-

```
{
  ....
  tpbegin(300,TPNOFLAGS);              /* start a transaction */
  cd = tpconnect("GETPRICES", ... );   /* GETPRICES in transaction */
  ....
  tpcommit(TPNOFLAGS);
}


{
  ....
  cd = tpconnect("GETPRICES", ... );   /* GETPRICES NOT in transaction */
  tpbegin(300,TPNOFLAGS);              /* start a transaction */
  ....
  tpcommit(TPNOFLAGS);
}
```

Listing 14.3   *Conversational Partners and Transactions*

nent until the transaction commits. If the transaction rolls back, the enqueue or dequeue operation is undone. For enqueue operations, this means that upon rollback, the item that was to be enqueued will not appear in the queue. For a dequeue operation, this means that upon rollback, the item that was to be dequeued remains in the queue. Queuing operations can be excluded from outstanding transactions by using the **TPNOTRAN** flag during their invocation.

You may recall from Chapter 4 that the TUXEDO System provides a forwarding agent to convert a request stored on an application queue to an on-line service request. To do this, the forwarding agent starts a global transaction, dequeues a request, invokes the appropriate service routine, and, if the service succeeds, commits the transaction. By doing so, the forwarding agent atomically processes a queued request. If any failure had occurred, the transaction would have rolled back, keeping the request safe on the application queue for later processing. Transactions allow the forwarding agent to guarantee that it will process requests as if it processed them exactly once.

Queue operations that are not contained within a global transaction are effective immediately and cannot be undone.

14.5.4 Transactions and Simple Events

Transactions are not propagated from simple event generators to their targets. Thus, the client code that is invoked as a result of a **tpnotify** or a **tpbroadcast** call is not part of the caller's transaction, if one is active, because these events are one-way and unacknowledged. The system has no way of knowing when the target is quiescent with respect to the transaction. For safety, the client is thus excluded from the transaction.

14.5.5 Transactions and Brokered Events

If a module that is in a transaction calls **tppost**, the transaction will be propagated to subscriptions which involve transactionally aware resources. These may include calls to service routines and application queuing operations. In addition to the invocation of service routines and application queues, the EventBroker is capable of executing operating system commands, sending simple events, and writing to the user log in fulfillment of a subscription. Such actions are not transactionally aware and thus cannot be included in the poster's transaction. If the poster rolls back the transaction, the transactionally aware resources updated via subscription fulfillments will also be rolled back. Subscriptions involved in the transaction may render it abort-only. In order to ensure that the system is quiescent, so that commitment may proceed, **tppost** must be used in its synchronous mode. Infection of subscriptions can be prevented by using the **TPNOTRAN** flag on the call to **tppost**.

Figure 14.6 depicts the flow of a transaction from an event poster through the event broker to one subscription fulfilled by calling a service routine and another fulfilled by putting a message in an application queue. If both of the actions are performed successfully, then when the poster commits, the effects of the event's actions are also committed. If any of the actions fail, the effects of the event are undone. Similarly, if the event poster rolls back the transaction, the effects of the service routine are undone, and the message is removed from the application queue.

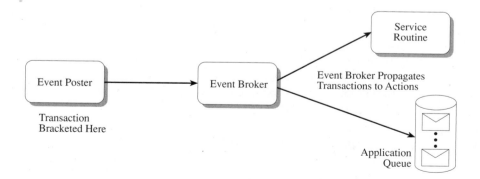

Figure 14.6   **Flow of Transaction through Event Broker**

14.6   Recovery—Picking Up the Pieces

During the 2PC-PA algorithm, enough information about the transaction is recorded, so that the transaction can be completed in the event of hardware and software failures. A goal in the design of the TUXEDO System was to make the programmer totally unaware of what happens during such a failure. *Recovery* is the term used to denote what happens when a computer that had been participating in transactions is restarted after a failure. In general, each computer may be the coordinator of some transactions and may be a subordinate to others. The TUXEDO System makes the completion of outstanding transactions completely automatic.

When a TUXEDO System computer is restarted, the TUXEDO transaction subsystem determines which transactions were active in the computer at the time of the crash. It does this by inspecting the transaction log to discover transactions for which that computer is the coordinator and by interrogating local RMs (via the **xa_recover** primitive of the XA interface) to discover transactions for which the computer is the subordinate. For those transactions it is coordinating, the transaction subsystem reinstructs all outstanding subordinates of the disposition of the transaction, that is, it completes the second phase of the 2PC-PA algorithm. For those transactions in which the restarted computer is a subordinate, it asks the transaction coordinator what the state of the transaction is. The coordinator informs it, thus completing the 2PC-PA algorithm. If the coordinator doesn't know about the transaction, the subordinate will roll back the transaction (that's where the "Presumed Abort" comes from in the 2PC-PA algorithm). Chapter 16, "Failure Handling," provides additional details on transaction recovery.

14.7   Summary

The TUXEDO System supplies transactional facilities that are intuitive to program and well integrated into its various communication paradigms. In particular, the transactional properties are designed to err on the side of safety when potentially "dangerous" or ambiguous constructs are used. Important aspects of the design of the TUXEDO System's transaction facility include the following:

- The application programmer sees a simple transactional programming interface.

- Time-outs are used to abort any transactions that are holding locks too long.

- Arbitrary transaction-aware Resource Managers (RMs) may be plugged into the system. Applications access an RM by using the RM's native API.

- Administration consists of allocating space for transaction logs and installing XA implementations from various resource manager vendors.

- Recovery is automatic.

IV Administration of a TUXEDO Application

Now that you have finished Part III, you should have a good grasp of what programming elements you can use to build your distributed applications. However, we have not yet discussed the details of what is involved in administering your applications. We introduced the basic elements in the administration of a TUXEDO application in Chapter 3, "Communication and Administration Paradigms for Distributed Business Applications," and in Part II, "Overview of the TUXEDO System." In the next four chapters, we will concentrate on the tools provided by the TUXEDO System for administering and customizing the administration of your distributed applications. Chapter 15, "Application Administration and Monitoring," presents the different tools you can use to administer your applications. Chapter 16, "Failure Handling," introduces the system capabilities for handling different kinds of failures and discusses how you can tune these capabilities. Chapter 17, "A Tour of the TUXEDO Management Information Base," covers the characteristics of the different objects that form a TUXEDO application. Finally, Chapter 18, "Getting Applications to Work Together," discusses the facilities provided by the TUXEDO System to allow interoperation with other applications.

15 Application Administration and Monitoring

In this chapter, we discuss in more detail the different steps involved in administering a TUXEDO application. First, we review the responsibilities of the TUXEDO administrator. Then we provide an overview of the different administrative tools that come with the TUXEDO System and how these tools are matched to the administrative tasks. And last, we discuss the administrative programming interface.

15.1 Responsibilities of TUXEDO Administrators

TUXEDO administrators configure, manage, and monitor the different parts of a distributed application. A primary concern of TUXEDO administrators is how to organize and maximize the use of their computing resources with the TUXEDO administrative tools. With these tools, administrators have centralized management and can make decisions based on a global view of the entire distributed application.

15.1.1 Tasks Performed by an Administrator

TUXEDO administrators have several tasks:

1. *Organize the application*. Administrators install the TUXEDO System and the application code on each machine required by the application.

2. *Ensure that all machines are properly tuned*. Administrators, in cooperation with operating system administrators, tune the system resources to the needs of the application.

3. *Preconfigure the application*. Administrators can preconfigure the components of the application (workstations, servers, resource managers, and system resources) to ensure a balanced data flow between the machines running these components.

4. *Activate and deactivate the application.* Administrators can activate (boot) or deactivate (shutdown) the entire application or parts of the application.

5. *Monitor the application.* Administrators should monitor the different application and system components to ensure the proper operation of the application. For example, under heavy load conditions, administrators can detect that more instances of a particular server may improve the throughput of the application.

6. *Diagnose and correct problems.* The TUXEDO System generates events in the TUXEDO event log file or via the system event broker. Administrators should monitor these events, diagnose problems occurring in the operation of the application, and then take corrective action. For example, servers running on a machine that goes down could be migrated to another machine.

7. *Enforce application security.* Administrators define the type of security required by the application. They define who can join the application or execute a particular service. Administrators also control application and domain passwords.

We will explain these tasks in more depth in the second part of this chapter.

15.1.2 The Central Coordination Role

TUXEDO administrators also play a central coordination role by working closely with application designers, operating system administrators, network administrators, and database administrators to ensure the proper management of the distributed business application. In this central coordination role, TUXEDO administrators need to know the status of a machine, network failures, database system failures, and other problems that have a global impact on the operation of the application. Of course, in some applications, all of these roles may be played by a single person.

Application administrators interact with application designers to identify which TUXEDO components should be included in the application configuration. For example, the administrator needs to know if clients will be running on a workstation, what database managers or resource managers will be used, if distributed transactions are used, what services require high priority, what buffer types will be used, or how data-dependent routing can be applied.

TUXEDO administrators interact with operating system administrators to tune the operating system parameters to the needs of the business application. An example is tuning the interprocess communication resources. Utilities are provided with the TUXEDO System to help the administrator size these resource requirements. Network administrators and TUXEDO administrators cooperate to define a computer network that maximizes the operation of the distributed application.

Network administrators provide network addresses or define workstation information in directories like the Novell Directory Service (NDS) or the NT registry. TUXEDO administrators cooperate with network administrators to define strategies to contain network failures and reduce their impact on a running application.

Database administrators provide the information necessary to "open" the database resources used by the application. TUXEDO administrators and database administrators also cooperate to solve failure situations that would prevent the normal operation of the application.

Although some of these interactions may appear complex, the TUXEDO System simplifies the administration process by allowing administrators to make decisions based on a global view of the entire application, rather than just the individual nodes. With this global view, the administrators can know the status of each node, server, service, or client. They can also identify network and database problems or performance bottlenecks in the application. Administrators can easily identify which nodes require attention and can use the administrative commands to respond to failures—for example, by moving servers to another node.

15.1.3 Administrative Tools

The TUXEDO administrative subsystem provides several tools designed to meet the different needs of application administrators. These tools include the following:

- The graphical interface (**xtuxadm**) provides centralized configuration management, start up, monitoring, and shutdown of the distributed application.

- The command interpreter interface (**tmadmin**) also provides centralized management and allows for scripted administration.

- A set of command line utilities allows easy activation (**tmboot**) and deactivation (**tmshutdown**) of the entire application or parts of the application (for example, certain machines, groups, or servers); command line configuration utilities (**tmloadcf** and **tmunloadcf**) are also provided to allow administrators to specify the application configuration in an ASCII file (called the UBBCONFIG file); scripting utilities (**ud** and **ud32**) can be used to send FML service requests to services in an active application.

- A programming interface, the TMIB Interface, allows administrators to customize or automate the administration of the application; the TMIB Interface provides access to the TUXEDO Management Information Base.

- An event management mechanism allows administrators to be informed of exceptional conditions reported by the TUXEDO System or the application; this event mechanism can be used with the TMIB Interface to construct programs that automatically respond to specific events.

In the following sections, we will explore how TUXEDO administrators can use this comprehensive set of administrative tools.

15.2 Structuring a Distributed Business Application

We have already discussed the TUXEDO programming model and how application designers structure the application into a set of modules that cooperate to achieve business' functions. Using the TUXEDO programming model, application designers can concentrate on the algorithms for the different modules (clients, services, queues, and events) and not on how these modules are built or deployed. Thus, the TUXEDO System provides application administrators with a lot of freedom to decide how to build, deploy, and manage the different application modules defined by application designers. In Chapter 7, "Introduction to the Application Programming Interface," we discussed how clients and servers are built with simple commands, and in this section, we will concentrate on the role of the application administrator in structuring the application.

15.2.1 Preliminary Steps

We will contrast the construction of a house with the construction of a distributed application. After understanding your requirements, your architects first specify the layout of the house, how the structures fit together, the type of materials used in the different parts of the house, and get a price estimate. Then, you get the basic materials and lay the foundation for the house. Finally, you start building your house. With a distributed application, there is design and planning work to be done up front to define the structure and the layout of the application. Then, administrators prepare the computing environment to receive the TUXEDO application, and finally, the application modules can be built and deployed.

Thus, the definition of the distribution of an application has three basic preliminary steps:

- First, administrators create a "configuration" (the TMIB) that defines the initial limits of the application. This TMIB defines the hardware and the software used by the application. The TUXEDO administrative subsystem uses the TMIB to control the run-time environment required by the application.

- Second, administrators lay the foundation for the run-time environment used by the application. That is, the TUXEDO System software and the application code must be installed on the machines used by the application. Also, the resources used by the application must be created on each machine. For example, the databases used by the application code must be created, and the corresponding DBMS code must be installed. TUXEDO System resources, such as the transaction log and the TUXEDO listener, must be created.

■ Third, administrators assemble the application. That is, service modules are packaged into servers, and the servers are built and deployed to maximize the processing of service requests generated by the clients.

As with a house, the application structure may be changed to adapt the application to the needs of the business. Dynamic configuration changes can be performed at any time with the TUXEDO administrative system.

15.2.2 Planning Leads to Better Results

Planning the architecture of a distributed application is not an easy task because of the number of elements that can have an impact on the performance, reliability, and security of the application. The TUXEDO System addresses this complexity by providing application designers with an architectural approach centered around two main principles: modularity and sharing. Modularity makes applications more manageable and easier to maintain and adapt to changes in the computing environment. Sharing common resources reduces cost and maximizes the use of the different computing resources. By using these two principles, you can simplify the application configuration. A TUXEDO configuration defines where the application modules will be running and how these modules will be grouped to share resources.

You do not need to predefine the application configuration all at once. You can start with the basic elements and then use the TUXEDO administrative tools to add or change the configuration as required. For example, the configuration could initially start with a single machine, and as the application grows, new machines and servers can be added dynamically.

There are many benefits in preconfiguring an application. From the architectural perspective, planning in advance results in applications with better security, reliability, and performance. From the operational perspective, administrators can be sure that modules will execute on suitable computing environments. Finally, operators and administrators should "practice" running the application (simulating failures) to understand how the TUXEDO System and the application behave together and to tune the system parameters to achieve the desired results.

15.2.3 Other Factors to Consider in Preparing to Administer Your Application

Availability, performance, and security are important factors that should be considered when you define an application. Because failures occur in distributed systems, you should consider architectures that avoid single points of failure. The

TUXEDO System provides several features that help you to structure your applications for high availability. For example, servers can be automatically restarted if they die, redundant servers can be defined on other machines, backup machines can be assigned to critical machines, and custom programs can be written using the TMIB Interface to respond to failure events generated by the system.

How you bundle application services into servers and how you place these servers on the different computing platforms will have a direct impact on the performance of the application. For example, conversational and request/response services must be bundled in different servers because conversational services tend to tie up servers for longer periods of time. Request/response services that use the same resources could be bundled in the same server to maximize the resource sharing. To decrease the access time to the data, servers should be placed as close as possible to these data resources, and servers that are frequently used could be placed on more powerful CPUs.

You can also use several tools to tune the performance of your applications. For example, you can give a different relative workload and priority to each service. The relative workload provides an idea how "expensive" is the execution of a service. The TUXEDO System uses this attribute to balance the load across servers that offer the same service. The priority attribute allows you to specify the "urgency" of requests to a given service: requests to services with higher priority are dispatched first. Also, you can use one of the different queuing models provided by the TUXEDO System to improve the performance of the application. For example, you can use the MSSQ model (see Chapter 6, "The Anatomy of a TUXEDO Application") to allow several instances of the same server share the same message queue.

Security is also an important element in the structure of an application. You may want to protect your applications from unauthorized access. The TUXEDO System provides authentication and authorization mechanisms that can be tuned to your needs. You can place nontrusted clients on workstations, protect access to secure services with access control lists, and protect access to the application with a password.

15.3   Activating a Distributed Application

Activating a distributed application means starting up the different components of the application—application servers and TUXEDO System components start running on each one of the machines defined in the TMIB. Once an application has been activated, service requests issued by clients can be performed with minimum delays. For example, there is no additional time for starting servers. Throughout the text, we have used the words *activate* and *boot* and the words *deactivate* and *shutdown* as synonyms.

15.3.1 Activation Management

The TUXEDO System provides four ways of managing the activation of an application:

- The **xtuxadm** graphical interface provides a menu and a simple drag-and-drop mechanism to activate or deactivate the application.

- The **tmboot** and **tmshutdown** commands can be invoked from the operating system command interface with in-line parameters that specify which parts of the application should be activated or deactivated.

- The **boot** and **shutdown** commands in the **tmadmin** command interpreter provide a way for activating or deactivating the application.

- The TMIB Interface provides a programmatic means for activating or deactivating the application (or parts of it) by directly changing the state of the TMIB.

One reason for activating an entire application is simplicity of operation and immediate response to any client request. By having all servers and TUXEDO System components already activated, clients can send service requests without any delays because the required servers will be ready to process these requests. Also, the required network connections between the different machines will be in place, and resource managers, like database management systems, will be ready to process the data received with service requests. Another alternative is activation on demand. Activation on demand adds delays because network connections need to be established and the required application servers need to be started.

15.3.2 Preliminary Setup

Before activating an application, you should follow several preliminary steps. First, you install the application and the TUXEDO software on all the machines involved in the application and adjust the operating system resources to the application requirements. Then, if the application requires distributed transaction management, you need to allocate the disk space necessary for the TUXEDO transaction log (TLOG). Data resources, such as application queues or databases, should also be created. Finally, the TUXEDO listener (**tlisten**) must be started on every machine. This listener controls the network connections established by the TUXEDO software to activate the administrative servers (see Chapter 6, "The Anatomy of a TUXEDO Application").

15.3.3 Application Activation with the Command Line Interface

You can easily control the granularity of application activation: you can activate the entire application or parts of it. For example, you can activate a minimum configuration that includes only the TUXEDO administrative servers on the Master machine and then incrementally activate the other parts of the application, such as other machines, server groups, or servers,—as required by the operation of the application. Listing 15.1 shows how simple it is to load and activate the entire application using the command interface.

```
$ cat activate.script
#Setup environment variables
#Set the location of the TUXEDO software
TUXDIR=/usr/tuxedo
#Set the location of the Application software
APPDIR=/orderapp
#Set the location of the application configuration
TUXCONFIG=${APPDIR}/tuxconfig
export TUXDIR APPDIR TUXCONFIG
#Set the search path
PATH=$PATH:$TUXDIR/bin
export PATH
#go to the application directory
cd $APPDIR
#load the configuration
tmloadcf -y orderconfig
#activate the entire application
tmboot -y
```

Listing 15.1 *Activating an Application with the Command Line Interface*

Although this example assumes a Unix environment, the TUXEDO System also provides the same command interface on other operating system environments. The example illustrates the use of *environment variables* to define the location of the TUXEDO run-time software (TUXDIR), the application software (APPDIR), and the application configuration (TUXCONFIG). The **tmloadcf** command creates a compiled version of the application configuration (${APPDIR}/tuxconfig) from an ASCII file (orderconfig). The **tmloadcf** command is generally used only once to create the compiled configuration file. You can also create a complete configuration from scratch with the **xtuxadm** graphical interface. After the configuration has been created, you can use the facilities of **xtuxadm** or the dynamic reconfiguration utility (**tmconfig**) to change the application attributes.

The **tmboot** command uses the TUXCONFIG environment variable to find the application configuration file. The information in this file contains the persistent part of the TMIB. The **tmboot** command scans the TMIB to find application servers and administrative servers that should be activated. By default, administrative servers are activated first on all the machines defined in the configuration. Then, application servers are booted in the order specified in the configuration.

You can define a specific activation sequence by using the SEQUENCE attribute of a server in the TMIB. This may be important during the activation process if one server requires the services of another server. The TUXEDO System activates servers as follows: servers with the lowest sequence numbers are activated before servers with higher sequence numbers. Then, servers with no sequence order are activated in the order in which they were defined in the TMIB.

15.3.4 Activation of the TUXEDO Basic Administrative Servers

The following TUXEDO basic administrative servers are activated automatically by the activation procedure (see Chapter 6, "The Anatomy of a TUXEDO Application"):

- The **DBBL** administrative server is started on the Master machine; this server synchronizes global updates to the TMIB.

- A **BBL** administrative server is started on every machine defined in the configuration; this server maintains the local copy of the TMIB on the corresponding machine.

- A **BRIDGE** administrative server is also started on every machine; this server provides reliable internode communications with the other machines defined in the configuration.

- Two or more **TMS** administrative servers are started on every group with a transactional resource manager; the **TMS** is a specialized server that performs asynchronous distributed transaction coordination with the transactional resource manager.

Other system supplied servers, such as the EventBroker and application queue manager, are activated only if they are configured in the TMIB.

When an application server is activated, several things happen. First, the server creates the message queues (request and reply queues) specified in the configuration. Then, the server attaches to the TMIB and automatically *advertises* its preconfigured services. Finally, the server initialization routine (**tpsvrinit**) is called to allow the application to perform any other initializations, such as opening a resource manager or dynamically advertising other services. Once this initialization completes, the server is ready to process service requests. Any events generated by the activation procedure are redirected to the TUXEDO event log file (ULOG).

15.3.5 Application Activation with the Graphical Interface

All operations performed by the **tmboot** command can also be issued from the **tmadmin** command interpreter or from the **xtuxadm** graphical interface. Activating the application with **xtuxadm** is very simple: it is just a drag-and-drop operation! We illustrate this mechanism in Figure 15.1. To activate an entire application (for example, the OrderEntry application) on the **xtuxadm** main window, you first select the domain icon—the one that looks like a castle—on the power bar. This selection produces a display of the configured domains in the main window area. Then, you select the OrderEntry domain icon and drag the icon to the light switch activate button. When you depress the mouse button 1, a small pop-up window appears. You can refine your activation criteria on this window. If you select the activate button, the one that looks like a light switch, then the activation procedure starts all application and administrative servers defined in the OrderEntry configuration. You can also apply this activation procedure to machines, groups, or servers. The messages generated by the activation procedure are displayed in another window.

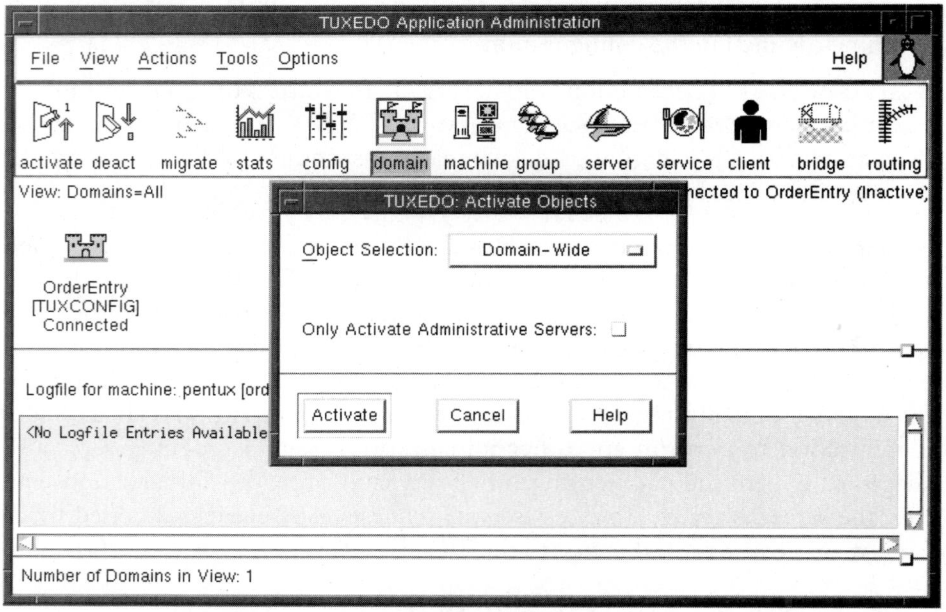

Figure 15.1   **Drag-and-Drop Activation with the xtuxadm Graphical Interface**

15.3.6 Application Activation with the Administrative Programming Interface

Activating an application with the administrative programming interface (see Section 15.7.3) requires more work but allows for a centralized activation command. First, administrative servers on the Master machine must be activated, and then, each one of the other machines defined in the TMIB is activated one by one. Listing 15.2 gives an idea how this is done.

```
/* Allocate input and output Fielded Buffer */
buffer = (FBFR32 *) tpalloc ("FML32", NULL, 4000);
obuffer = (FBFR32 *) tpalloc ("FML32", NULL, 4000);
/* Activate administrative servers on the Master
 * Add parameters to the request buffer */
Fadd32(buffer, TA_OPERATION, "SET", 0);
Fadd32(buffer,TA_CLASS,"T_DOMAIN",0);
Fadd32(buffer, TA_STATE,"ACT",0);    /* change the State to Active */
/*  Issue administrative request */
if(tpadmcall(buffer, &obuffer, 0) == -1) {
        fprintf(stderr, "tpadmcall failed: %s\n", tpstrerror(tperrno));
        ...
}
/* Join the application as an administrator */
tpinfo = (TPINIT *) tpalloc ("TPINIT", NULL, TPINITNEED(0));
strcpy(tpinfo->usrname, "ordadmin");
strcpy(tpinfo->cltname, "tpsysadm");
if(tpinit(tpinfo)== -1){
        fprintf(stderr, "tpinit failed: %s\n", tpstrerror(tperrno));
        ...
}
/* For each machine:
 *        Activate administrative and application servers
 */
...
Fchg32(buffer, TA_OPERATION, 0, "SET", 0);
Fchg32(buffer, TA_CLASS, 0, "T_MACHINE", 0);
Fchg32(buffer, TA_STATE, 0, "ACT", 0); /* Change state of orders01 to Active */
Fchg32(buffer, TA_LMID, 0, "order01",0);
/* Issue administrative request */
if(tpcall(".TMIB", buffer, 0, &obuffer, &olen, 0) == -1) {
        fprintf(stderr, "tpcall failed: %s\n", tpstrerror(tperrno));
        ...
}
...
```

Listing 15.2   *Application Activation with the TMIB Interface*

In Part II, "Overview of the TUXEDO System," we explained how the architecture of the TUXEDO administrative subsystem exploits the basic request/response functionality provided by the TUXEDO System. Hence, the TMIB Interface is the ATMI interface with an extension needed for bootstrapping. Because ATMI requires a running application, this extension—the **tpadmcall** function—is needed to configure a new application or to activate an application. Programs using the **tpadmcall** function must execute on the machine requiring the boostrapping operation—in this case, the Master machine. In Listing 15.2, you can see how **tpadmcall** is used to bootstrap the Master machine. The activation of the Master machine is made by changing the state (TA_STATE) of the domain (represented by the T_DOMAIN class) to active. Once the Master machine is active, the program needs to join the application (**tpinit**) as the administrator to perform any other activations or changes to the TMIB. Other machines are activated (for example, **order01**) by setting their state in the TMIB to "active" (ACT). This state change is done using a request to the ".TMIB" administrative service via a **tpcall** The ".TMIB" administrative service coordinates the activation of the application and administrative servers defined in the TMIB for each machine.

Error management for this type of activation procedure requires careful control of the notification messages generated by the activation process. For example, application servers may fail to boot because the server was built incorrectly or because a resource manager is unavailable. A machine may fail to boot because the **tlisten** program was not running on that machine or because it was started with a different listening network address.

15.3.7 Application Deactivation

The **shutdown** procedure is the reverse of the **booting** procedure. In **xtuxadm**, for example, a machine is deactivated by dragging the machine icon for the active machine to the "deactivate" icon—the light switch in down position. You can also deactivate the application with the **tmshutdown** command. The deactivation procedure deactivates servers in the reverse order: application servers with no sequence attribute, followed by application server with a sequence number (from high to low), and then the TUXEDO administrative servers. You can deactivate the entire application or parts of it—for example, a particular server, a server group, or an entire machine. When you shut down an application, you should not forget the clients still attached to your application. For this reason, the TUXEDO System allows you to specify if you want a quick shutdown or a graceful shutdown. Figure 15.2 shows how you can select the quick shutdown option in the **xtuxadm** deactivation window. A quick shutdown immediately deactivates all administrative and application servers, clients are detached from the application, and the operating system resources used by the TUXEDO System are released. A graceful shutdown allows clients to end their sessions within a certain time. However, services are immediately suspended to prevent clients from issuing new service requests. Service requests in progress will be processed before the servers deactivate.

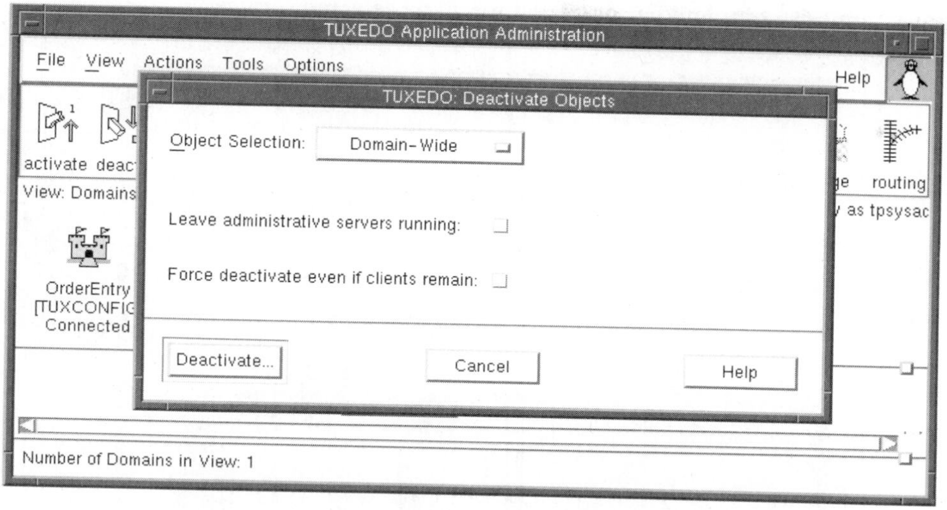

Figure 15.2   **Application Deactivation with xtuxadm**

You can also deactivate an application with the TMIB Interface by setting the state to inactive.

15.4   Monitoring the Application

The TMIB allows administrators to get information about the application configuration, obtain statistics that show the work done by the different components, and watch the events generated by system and the application. It also allows administrators to dynamically reconfigure the application to improve throughput and adapt the behavior of the application to the business needs or to failure conditions.

15.4.1 xtuxadm—The TUXEDO Graphical Interface

The best tool for monitoring a TUXEDO distributed application is the **xtuxadm** graphical interface. Administrators can easily find or change TMIB configuration attributes, find the state of each component, or visualize statistics. The statistics provided by the TUXEDO System allow administrators to find out how much work has been completed on each machine, how much work has been queued on a particular queue, how many requests have been performed by a particular server, what is the relative workload performed by a server, or how many requests have been issued to a particular service. Figure 15.3 shows an example of the statistics reporting tool for the work completed by each service. The bar graph shows requests completed and queued for a few selected services.

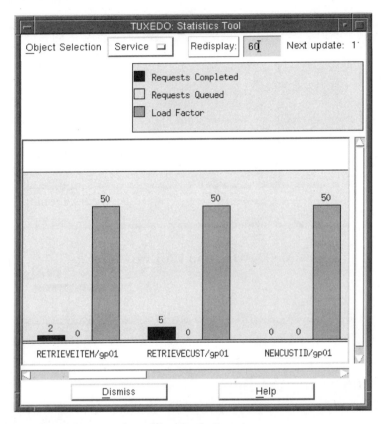

Figure 15.3   Work Completed by Each Service

15.4.2 ULOG—The TUXEDO System Event Log

In addition to these statistics, administrators can use the information stored in the TUXEDO log file to find the cause of system or application failures. The TUXEDO log file is also called the *User Log* file, or ULOG, and has an instance on each machine active in an application. This log contains TUXEDO System error messages, warning messages, debugging messages, or information messages. The ULOG file simplifies finding the errors returned by the TUXEDO ATMI interface and provides a means by which the TUXEDO System and applications can store error information in a central place.

The ULOG is an ASCII file, and a different file is created every day. On POSIX systems, the following default naming convention is used: *ULOG.mmddyy* where *mmddyy* is the date (*mm* = month, *dd* = day, *yy* = year). On file systems with naming constraints (e.g., MSDOS), the default is *ULmmddyy.log*. The file is usually created in the directory specified by the APPDIR environment variable, but administrators can easily change this location. You can replace the file prefix (ULOG) and the location of the file. In general, there is a log file on each active machine defined in the TMIB. However, by using a networked file system, it is possible to have a single log file shared across machines.

You can access the ULOG file with **xtuxadm**, the TMIB Interface, or any text editor. Figure 15.4 shows a section of the ULOG for the "order01" machine in the Mission Critical Control window of **xtuxadm**. You can resize the log area and use the "Commands" button to save, print, or search for messages that satisfy a filter condition. Our example shows a message generated by the TUXEDO Domains administrative server, **DMADM**, indicating that the server is using the default location for the Domains configuration. In Chapter 18, "Getting Applications to Work Together," we explain the TUXEDO Domains facility in more detail.

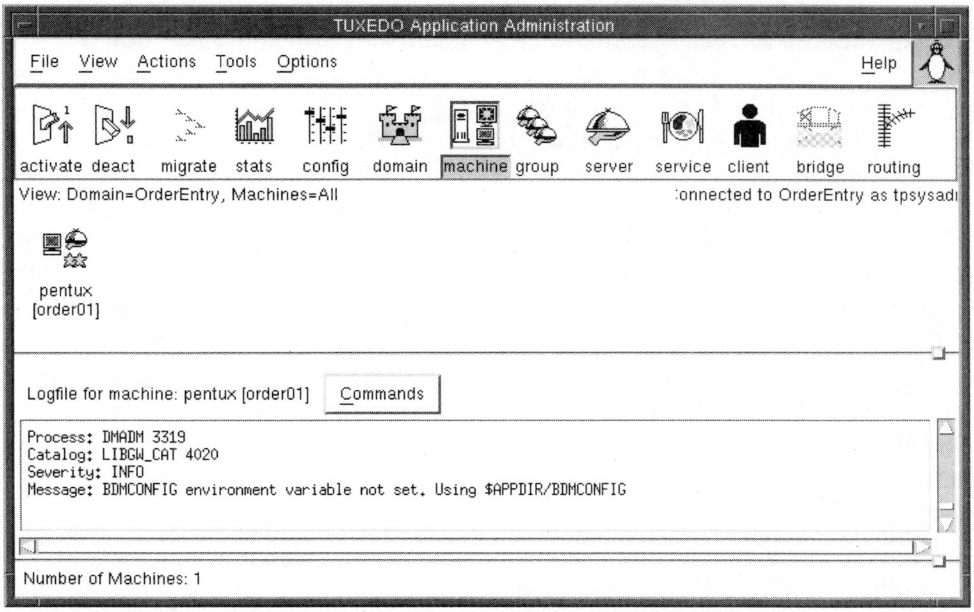

Figure 15.4   **Viewing the User Log File with xtuxadm**

Records in the ULOG have a "tag" and a "text". The tag contains the time of the day, the physical name of the machine where the record is generated, the name and the process identifier of the client or server generating the event, and if the event was produced within a transaction, then the transaction identifier is added to the tag. For system messages, the *text* contains the name of the system message catalog to which this message applies, the message number, and a message with additional information about the nature of the event.

Because fault events have an impact on multiple subsystems and layers of software, administrators may find several messages in the ULOG that relate to the same event. The TUXEDO System Message Manual can be consulted online from the graphical interface to find a complete description of the messages in the ULOG. The description includes the recommended actions that the administrator can take to resolve the problem.

Application designers can also use the ULOG to find the nature of a failure returned by the system. For example, when an ATMI call returns an error, the **tperrno** variable may be set to **TPESYSTEM** or **TPEOS** (that is, a TUXEDO System error or an operating system error has occurred). When this occurs, a message describing the exact nature of the problem can be found in the ULOG. The application can also record messages in the ULOG with the **userlog** function.

15.4.3 The Run–Time Tracing Facility

Besides the ULOG file, the TUXEDO System also provides a run-time tracing facility that allows administrators and application designers to track the execution of the distributed business application. The TUXEDO System run-time has a set of built-in trace points that mark calls to functions in different categories, such as ATMI function calls issued by the application or the XA function calls issued by the TUXEDO System to an X/Open compliant Resource Manager [X/Open-XA]. Administrators and application designers enable tracing by specifying a tracing expression that contains a category, a filtering expression, and an action. The category indicates what type of function call will be traced, for example, ATMI function calls. The filtering expression selects which particular function calls can trigger an action. Several actions are possible. For example, a record can be written to the ULOG, a system command can be executed, or the traced process can be terminated. A client process can also propagate the tracing capability with its service invocations to all the servers involved in the execution of these service requests. This capability is called *dyeing*, and the *trace dye* "colors" all services called by the client.

Application designers enable tracing via the TMTRACE environment variable. The simplest tracing expression consists in defining `TMTRACE=on` in the environment of the client. This expression enables tracing of ATMI function calls on the client and on any server that performs a service on behalf of that client. The trace records will be written to the ULOG file. Application designers can also specify a tracing expression in the environment of a server. For example, the tracing expression `TMTRACE=atmi:/tpservice/ulog`, exported within the environment of the server, generates a record in the ULOG file each time a service is invoked on this server.

Administrators can turn the tracing option on or off with the **changetrace** command of the **tmadmin** utility. This command allows administrators to overwrite tracing expressions on active client and server processes. Administrators can enable global tracing (for all clients and servers) or tracing for a particular machine, group or server. For example, Listing 15.3 shows how an administrator can turn off tracing or turn on tracing on a particular server group (the ORDERS group).

```
$ tmadmin
tmadmin - Copyright   1994 Novell. All rights reserved.
> # turn tracing off
> changetrace -m all off
...
> # turn tracing "on" for the ORDERS group
> changetrace -g ORDERS on
```

Listing 15.3 *Tracing Controlled by the Application Administrator*

15.4.4 Failure Tracking and Handling

Failures occur in a distributed computing environment, and application administrators must be able to detect and correct these failures whenever possible. Failures detected by the TUXEDO System generate events and state changes in the TMIB. These events are recorded in the ULOG file and sent to the EventBroker for subsequent fulfillment. The **xtuxadm** interface subscribes to all TUXEDO System events and represents them visually for the application administrator. For example, a window pops up with a warning message or an icon changes color or starts flashing to get the administrator's attention.

You can handle some failure situations by configuring the application with redundant servers, and the automatic server restart capability. Redundant servers provide high availability, and they can be used to handle large amounts of work, server failures, or even a machine failure. By configuring servers with the automatic restart property, you can handle individual server failures. The TUXEDO System continuously checks the status of active servers, and when it detects that a restartable server has died, then it automatically creates a new instance of that server. You can also specify the maximum number of "lives" of a restartable server. This feature can prevent a recurring application error by limiting the number of times a server is restarted.

A machine failure requires more attention. The TUXEDO System frequently monitors the availability of each active machine. A machine is marked as "partitioned" when the machine cannot be reached by the system. In this situation, a system event is also generated. A partition may happen because of a network failure, a machine failure, or a machine whose performance has degraded so much that you cannot tell if it is alive or dead. We will discuss these failure cases in more detail in Chapter 16, "Failure Handling"

15.4.5 The Application Service Log

TUXEDO application servers can also generate a log of the service requests performed by the server. You can specify this option when a server is activated. The log is redirected to the standard output file (stdout) of the server. Each record contains a service name, start time, and end time. The **txrpt** utility provides a way to analyze the log. This utility produces a summary of the time spent by the server. With this data, you can get a better estimate of the relative workload generated by each service, and then you can use this value to set the workload parameter of the corresponding services in the TMIB.

15.5   Changing the Application Configuration

Distributed applications evolve and change over time. Administrators need to be able to continuously adjust parameters, grow or shrink the application, add or remove users, change access control lists, add or remove application queues, and interact with other domains. The TUXEDO System provides several tools that allow dynamic reconfiguration. For example, you can use the **xtuxadm** configuration tool for graphical control, the **tmconfig** and **tmadmin** utilities for command line (or scripted) control, or the TMIB Interface for programmatic control. The TMIB specification describes what attributes can be changed while the application is active or inactive.

15.5.1 Application Configuration with the Graphical Interface

You can configure new entities or change attributes of existing entities with the **xtuxadm** configuration tool. This tool contains one screen for each configurable class in the TMIB. You can switch to the configuration tool by using the menu bar, the power bar, or by dragging an icon onto the configuration icon (or vice versa). The configuration screen also has a power bar that allows quick switching between the different configurable classes in the TMIB: domains, machines, groups, servers, services, and data-dependent routing.

Figure 15.5 shows the configuration screen in "machine" mode. This screen is divided into two sections: the upper section contains the basic attributes of a machine entity, and the bottom part contains other attribute categories such as networking, security, limits, and the transaction log. When you select one of these categories the related attributes appear on the screen. In the figure, we have selected the networking attributes. Attributes that are not editable look like static text whereas editable attributes are within boxes that support text editing commands. In this way, administrators can easily recognize what attributes can be changed dynamically when an entity is active or inactive.

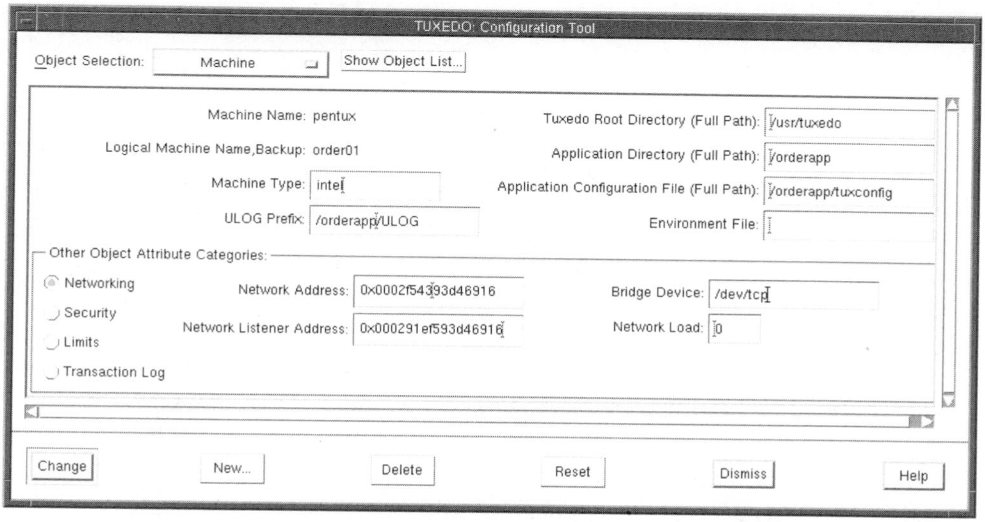

Figure 15.5 **Configuration Screen for the order01 Machine**

15.5.2 Application Configuration with the Command Line Interface

When many changes are needed in the configuration and the application does not need to be active, you can use a text editor on the UBBCONFIG file. This file can be created from the binary configuration file (TUXCONFIG) with the **tmunloadcf** utility. An example of the contents of this file is provided in Listing 15.4.

```
*RESOURCES
IPCKEY          83000
UID             100
GID             200
PERM            0660
MASTER          order01
BLOCKTIME       30
MODEL           MP
*MACHINES
stnj01  LMID=order01 TUXDIR="/tuxedo" APPDIR="/ORDER" TYPE="i386"
stsf01  LMID=order02 TUXDIR="/tuxedo" APPDIR="/home/order" TYPE="HP9x"
*NETWORK
order01 NADDR="0x0002f54393d46916" BRIDGE="/dev/tcp"
        NLSADDR="0x000291ef593d46916"
order02 NADDR="0x000291ef302c137" BRIDGE="/dev/tcp"
        NLSADDR="0x0022fe09302c137"
*GROUPS
ordgrp1 LMID=order01   GRPNO=1
ordgrp2 LMID=order02   GRPNO=2
*SERVERS
DEFAULT: RESTART=Y MAXGEN=5 CLOPT="-A" REPLYQ=N
ordentry        SRVGRP=ordgrp1 SRVID=1 RQADDR=ordqueue1 MIN=3 MAX=5
ordentry        SRVGRP=ordgrp2 SRVID=6 RQADDR=ordqueue2 MIN=2 MAX=4
*SERVICES
Place_Order     ROUTING=orderid
*ROUTING
orderid FIELD=ORDERID BUFTYPE="FML" RANGES="MIN - 999:ordgrp1, *:*"
```

Listing 15.4 *Example of a UBBCONFIG File*

The UBBCONFIG file can be used to preconfigure the TMIB. Entities are defined by specifying attribute-value pairs. For example, in Listing 15.4 the machine "stnj01" has a logical name (LMID=order01), a type (TYPE=i386), and other attributes that specify the location of the TUXEDO software (TUXDIR="/tuxedo") and the application software (APPDIR="/ORDER").

The UBBCONFIG is divided into seven sections:

- The RESOURCES section describes the global parameters for the application; for example, the Master machine is "order01," and the application will be distributed (MODEL = MP for multiple processors).

- The MACHINES section contains the description of the machines used by the application; for example, the first entry specifies that the machine "stnj01" will be known by the TUXEDO System as "order01," and is an Intel-based machine (TYPE = "i386")

- The NETWORK section describes the network addresses used by the **BRIDGE** and the **tlisten** administrative programs; for example, the

tlisten executing in the "order01" machine uses the address specified in the NLSADDR attribute.

- The GROUPS section describes the server groups; for example, the group "ordgrp1" will be executing on machine "order01."

- The SERVICES section contains parameters, such as the data-dependent routing criterion name, the relative workload, and the priority that applies to a particular service.

- The ROUTING section defines the different routing criteria; in our example, we specified a routing criterion called "orderid" on the field "ORDERID" such that, if its value is less or equal to 999, then service requests will go to a server in group "ordgrp1."

Once you create the UBBCONFIG file, you need to compile the file to generate a binary version of the configuration, the TUXCONFIG. The tmloadcf utility performs this compilation. After you create the TUXCONFIG, you can restart your application with the new changes.

15.5.3 Application Configuration with the Administrative Programming Interface

Experienced application designers or application administrators can also build administrative reconfiguration programs with the TMIB Interface. In Listing 15.5, we show how you can add a new machine to the Order Entry application. First, your program joins the application as the Order Entry administrator. Then, it fills the parameters of the administrative request—the operation (SET) is a state change (NEW) of the machine class (T_MACHINE) in the TMIB with the attributes of the new machine (order03). Finally, it sends the request to the administrative service ".TMIB". The attributes that require setting are documented in the TUXEDO Reference Manual [TUXEDO].

15.5.4 The Scripting Facility

You do not always need to write a program to use the TMIB directly. The TUXEDO System provides utilities (**ud** and **ud32**) that read a script stored on an ASCII file, constructs an FML or FML32 buffer, and sends a message to the specified service. The script contains attribute-value pairs, as illustrated in Listing 15.6, which adds a new group to the server group class (T_SRVGRP). Note that the service name that receives the request (the ".TMIB" administrative service) is specified with the attribute SRVCNM.

Thus, the TUXEDO System provides different interfaces or choices depending on your degree of expertise. We certainly recommend the **xtuxadm** graphical

```
...
/* Join the application as the administrator */
strcpy(tpinfo->usrname, "ordadmin");
strcpy(tpinfo->cltname, "tpsysadm");
if(tpinit(tpinfo)== -1) {
        fprintf(stderr, "tpinit failed: %s\n", tpstrerror(tperrno));
        ...

}
/* create FML32 buffers for input and output parameters */
buffer = (FBFR32 *) tpalloc("FML32", NULL, 4000);
obuffer = (FBFR32 *) tpalloc("FML32", NULL, 4000);
/*  Fill the request parameters */
Fadd32(buffer, TA_OPERATION, "SET", 0);  /* change the TMIB */
Fadd32(buffer, TA_CLASS, "T_MACHINE", 0); /* update the T_MACHINE class */
Fadd32(buffer, TA_STATE, "NEW", 0);  /* add new object to the T_MACHINE class*/
/* Fill the machine attributes */
Fadd32(buffer, TA_LMID, "order03", 0);   /* the logical machine name */
Fadd32(buffer, TA_PMID, "stnj02", 0);   /* the physical machine name */
Fadd32(buffer, TA_TUXDIR, "/usr/tuxedo", 0); /*directory with TUXEDO software*/
Fadd32(buffer, TA_APPDIR, "/order", 0); /*directory with the application code*/
Fadd32(buffer, TA_TUXCONFIG, "/order/tuxconfig", 0);  /* configuration */
Fadd32(buffer, TA_BRIDGE, "/dev/tcp", 0); /* network device use by the BRIDGE*/
Fadd32(buffer, TA_NADDR, netaddr, 0); /*network address used by the BRIDGE*/
Fadd32(buffer, TA_NLSADDR, nlsaddr, 0);/* network address used by tlisten */
/* Issue request to the TMIB administrative service */
if(tpcall(".TMIB", buffer,0, &obuffer, &olen, TPNOFLAGS)== -1) {
        fprintf(stderr, "tpcall failed: %s\n", tpstrerror(tperrno));
        ...

}
...
```

Listing 15.5   *Adding a New Machine with the TMIB Interface*

interface for most of the administrative operations, but during the development cycle, you may want to experiment with the other tools and find the tool most suited to your needs.

15.6   Securing Your Application

Security should always be a concern for application administrators. With the TUXEDO System, you can use incremental levels of security that vary from single password for the entire application to an access control facility restricting access to application resources to a set of predefined end users. In this section, we describe how the TUXEDO System leverages the operating system's security and how you can enforce security checking for your application.

```
$cat addmachine.script
# Set the location of the field tables
FLDTBLDIR32 = /usr/tuxedo/udataobj
# Set the field tables used by the TUXEDO administrative service
FIELDTBLS32 =tpadm
export FLDTBLDIR32 FIELDTBLS32
# Invoke the ud scripting program
ud32 -C tpsysadm <<!
SRVCNM          .TMIB
TA_OPERATION    SET
TA_CLASS        T_SRVGRP
TA_STATE        NEW
TA_SRVGRP       ordgrp3
TA_GRPNO        3
TA_LMID         order03

!
```

Listing 15.6 *Adding a New Machine with the ud32 Scripting Utility*

15.6.1 Servers Are Trusted Entities

You can use the operating system security facilities to establish a trusted base for the servers, application services and resources used by the TUXEDO System. On POSIX systems, for example, resources such as shared memory, message queues, and files can be restricted with operating system permissions such that only the administrator can have access to these resources. Once you have established this trusted base, you can use the security facilities provided by the TUXEDO System to protect access to the entire application or to individual application services.

You must provide the identity of the application administrator when you define the application configuration. This identity consists of a user and a group identifier. The user identifier corresponds to the operating system identifier under which someone must log in to perform administrative operations, including application configuration, activation and deactivation of application servers, and run-time application administration. The group identifier relates to an operating system identifier that groups users with common permissions. The TUXEDO System assumes that you can trust the code produced by application service developers—this code should not intentionally perform any security violations. Thus, all servers in the TUXEDO System execute within the administrator's trusted base. That is, all servers run with the administrator's user identifier.

Because a server executes with the administrator's permission, the server is free to access the TUXEDO MIB, private key files, and other operating system resources used in the distributed application. This open access to resources requires careful programming of your application code because invalid access, whether malicious or unintentional, can have a dramatic impact on the business application. For example, the application can be configured so that all or selected servers have restricted access to the memory shared between TUXEDO processes. This protects against accidental scribbling into this memory area. But, the TUXEDO System does not protect you against a programmer out to attack your distributed application by writing code to explicitly attach to and corrupt this memory.

Another impact of running as the administrator is that, if the server is configured, either statically or dynamically, and a user can run as the administrator to activate the server, then the program will be allowed to join the application without any further security checking. So the bottom line is that application server code is trusted and should be thoroughly reviewed and tested to ensure that it works correctly.

15.6.2 Clients Are Not Trusted Entities

Clients, on the other hand, are not required to run as the administrator. Instead, they are started directly by a user and run with the permissions of that user. By default, any program can join a TUXEDO application. But, your application can also be configured to require, from all clients joining the application, a single application password or per user authentication information, such as a per user password or additional information used to verify the identity of the user using the client program. Even when turning on configuration security, the application is vulnerable to attack from client programs.

There are several ways to restrict client access to the application. One approach is to trust the client application software, assuming that you do not have malicious programmers, and to trust a group of users to run the client programs. Resources used by the TUXEDO System would be set up with operating system permissions such that only members of a particular group can access the application. Application security could be configured requiring a password so that someone cannot just walk up to an unattended terminal and start the client program. The limitation of this approach is that a malicious programmer, within the group that has the correct password, can write a rogue program at any time to access the system in an invalid way.

Further security can be gained by setting the operating system permissions so that only the administrator can access the TUXEDO System and other application resources. In this approach, all client programs must be validated and then set to run with the administrator's permissions (on operating systems that support the set-user-identification notion) so that resource access is restricted to a limited set of programs. No other client programs can access the application. When the client joins the application, it can still use the application or per user authentication based on the real user executing the program.

The most secure environment for running application servers is to physically restrict client access. In this configuration, client programs would not be allowed to run on the server computers. Only workstation clients would be allowed access via the network, requiring an application password or user password to join the system.

15.6.3 Security Levels

When you define a new application, you have to specify the security level that you want to assign to your application. You can ignore this attribute if your application needs no such security (for example, if it is in development) or if it runs within a physically secure computing environment.

Figure 15.6 shows the **xtuxadm** Configuration Tool with a selection of the security attributes that apply to the entire application. With this screen, you can set the identity of the administrator and the security type. In our example, the administrator of the Order Entry application has assigned the user and group IDs of the application administrator to be 100 and 200, respectively, the User Authentication level (USER_AUTH), and the name of an authorization service (ORDAUTH) that performs custom authentication checks for the Order Entry application. In the next section, we will discuss how you can customize the TUXEDO administrative subsystem.

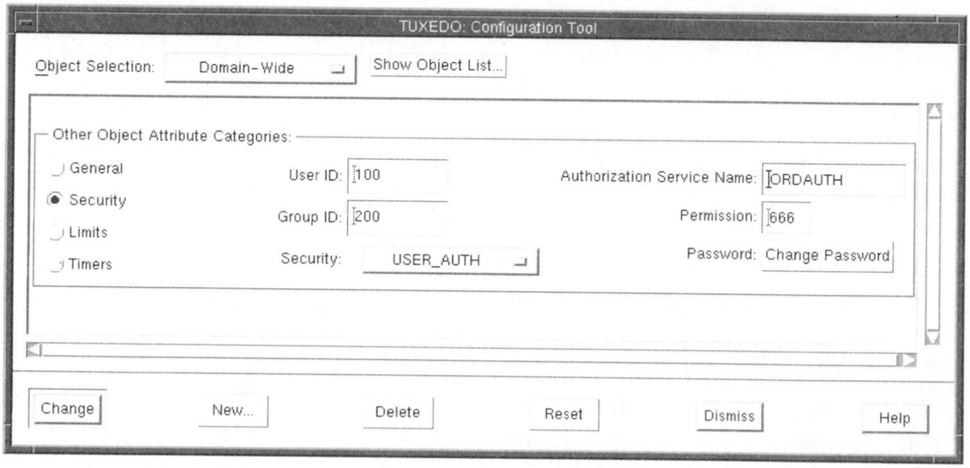

Figure 15.6 Setting the Security Attribute with xtuxadm

The following are the incremental security levels provided by the TUXEDO System:

1. *No authentication* (NONE): Clients do not need to be authenticated when they join the application. Typically, this level might be used in a development environment or in physically secured environments.

2. *Application password* (APP_PW): With this level, you can define a single password for the entire application. Clients must provide this password when they join the application. This level might be used to ensure that a new password is gotten weekly or monthly by users of the application.

3. *End user authentication* (USER_AUTH): In addition to the application password, clients must provide a user name and application-specific data (a password, for example). This level allows application designers to customize the security for their applications.

4. *Optional Access Control* (ACL): Clients must provide the application password, a user name, and a user password. You can control access to services, application queues, and events with *access control lists* (ACLs). This level allows you to configure access only for those resources that need security. For example, you can configure restricted access to a certain set of services while still allowing unprotected access to other services. When a resource has an ACL, access will be denied to end users that are not part of the ACL. Resources without an ACL are accessible to clients which successfully join the application.

5. *Mandatory Access Control* (MANDATORY_ACL): This level is similar to the ACL level. Clients must provide the application password, a user name, and a user password. The main difference from the ACL level is that resources without an ACL are considered restricted—that is, access is not granted to resources that do not have an ACL.

To enable authentication and authorization services, you need to configure the TMIB with

- the identity and passwords of any authorized end users
- the access control lists for services, application queues, and events
- the authorization server (**AUTHSRV**).

You can define these parameters with **xtuxadm** and the TMIB Interface. You can also use the following command line utilities:

- You can define new *principals* with the **tpusradd** command; principals are **end users** or domains that can access your application.

- The **tpgrpadd** command allows you to define new groups of principals —every principal belongs to a particular *principal group*.

- With the **tpacladd** command, you can define a new ACL for a particular resource (service, application queue, or event).

- You can use similar commands to change and delete principals, groups, and ACLs.

15.7 Tuning the Administrative Subsystem to Your Needs

Application designers and administrators can easily adapt the TUXEDO administrative subsystem to the needs of their application. The TUXEDO System allows you to customize parts that are critical to the performance, security, and administration of your application. With the TUXEDO System, you can define custom

- typed buffers

- security

- administrative scripts and programs

We will explore these options in the following sections.

15.7.1 Your Own Typed Buffers

In Chapter 8, "Typed Buffers," we discussed typed buffers and their value in the TUXEDO System. We also discussed the built-in buffer types provided by the TUXEDO System and what is involved in the definition of a custom buffer type. Each buffer type is defined with a name, default size values, and a set of operations that perform special processing on the buffer. The syntax and expected behavior of these operations are defined in greater detail in the TUXEDO System Reference Manual [TUXEDO]. The operations are defined to allow automatic initialization, when the buffer is allocated, and pre- and postprocessing functions when a message is sent or received. Administrators can also define a function that selects a server group based on the contents of the buffer and configuration information. That is, they can write a specialized data-dependent routing function.

The default buffer type switch (the list of buffer types) can be replaced with your own list. This list may include some or all of the default built-in types plus some new types specific to your application. This new buffer type switch is built into the clients and servers that use this information.

15.7.2 Your Own Security

The TUXEDO System allows application designers and administrators to build their own security mechanisms. This feature is available by setting the application security level to *User Level Authentication* (USER_PW) and by defining the name of an application service that performs an application-defined authentication check in the TMIB. Figure 15.6 illustrates how you can set these attributes with the **xtuxadm** interface.

When clients join a TUXEDO application with *User Level Authentication*, they must provide an application password and end-user data. The application password is first validated by the TUXEDO System, and if this check is successful, then the TUXEDO System invokes the application-defined security service. This service receives any data (for example, the end-user password) that may have been sent by the client with the **tpinit** call and returns an application-defined *credential*, called the application key (or **appkey**), in the user return code parameter (**tpurcode**) of the **tpreturn** function. The contents or structure of the data sent by the client and of the certificate computed by the service is not understood by the TUXEDO System. Regardless, the TUXEDO System keeps the certificate hidden from the application code in the client and automatically appends it to every service and queue request issued by the client. The certificate is delivered to application services with their invocation information (**TPSVCINFO**). This allows these services to perform their own security validations.

Application designers can also use the *Access Control* security level to authenticate the end user executing the client program. The TMIB contains the necessary information for this authentication, for example, the end-user name and the password specified for this user. The end-user name can be retrieved from TMIB by using the client identifier received with the invocation. However, you can restrict this capability with the attribute level permissions provided by the TMIB. We will explain this feature in Chapter 17, "A Tour of the TUXEDO Management Information Base."

15.7.3 Your Own Administrative Programs

The primary goal of the TMIB Interface is to allow application designers and administrators to write custom administrative programs. The combination of events with the TMIB Interface is the basis for building self-adapting applications. With this feature you can write administrative services that are invoked when certain events occur, and that then change the TMIB in response to those events.

The administrative programming interface is just an extension of the ATMI programming interface. This extension defines the rules for using the TMIB and the TUXEDO administrative service (".TMIB"). These extensions to ATMI are the following:

- The **tpadmcall** primitive: This function allows changes to the MIB when the application is inactive. It takes three parameters: an input buffer, an output buffer, and special flags. The input and output buffers are FML32 typed buffers. The **tpadmcall** function is typically used to configure an inactive application or to activate the Master machine.

- Two reserved client names: **tpsysadm** and **tpsysop**. The **tpsysadm** client name characterizes users who can administer the application. The **tpsysop** client name characterizes users who can operate the application. Administrators and operators have different permissions in the TMIB. For example, operators cannot create new entities in the TMIB. The TMIB defines attribute level permissions for administrators, operators, and other users. These permissions can be changed by the administrator.

- The ".**TMIB**" service: This service is the TUXEDO administrative service that performs all operations on the TMIB. The ".TMIB" service can be used through standard ATMI functions, such as **tpcall**, **tpacall**, and **tpenqueue**. The ".TMIB" service receives an FML32 buffer with information about the operation on the TMIB and produces an FML32 buffer with the results of the operation. Listing 15.6 show a simple way to use the **ud32** utility to generate ".TMIB" calls without writing any C or COBOL code.

- Operations on the TMIB: "**GET**" and "**SET**." Operations on the TMIB are specified as fields in the input FML32 buffer to the ".TMIB" service. Three fields define each administrative request: the operation field (TA_OPERATION), the class field (TA_CLASS), and the state field (TA_STATE). The operation field specifies the type of operation on the TMIB: obtain (GET) or change (SET) information. The class field defines the class to which the operation is to be applied. The state field is required on SET operations and defines a specific administrative action on a particular object. For example, a SET operation with an **ACTivate** state on the TA_SRVGROUP class will activate all server groups defined in the TMIB. Valid state operations are defined in the TMIB for each class.

In general, programs using **tpadmcall** typically run on the Master machine to change the configuration or to activate the application. Thus, the user running these programs must be the application administrator identified in the TMIB. You should only use **tpadmcall** to bootstrap your application from the TMIB Interface. However, you can also use **tpadmcall** when the application is active, but your program will only have read-only access to information to the TMIB. When the application is active, you will typically use the TMIB Interface as shown in Listing 15.7. Your program joins the application and then uses **tpcall** or **tpacall** to perform operations on the TMIB. These operations are performed via the ".TMIB" administrative service.

```
...
/* Join the application as the administrator  */
strcpy(tpinfo->usrname, "Orderadmin ");
strcpy(tpinfo->cltname, "tpsysadm");
if(tpinit(tpinfo)== -1) {
        fprintf(stderr, "tpinit failed: %s\n", tpstrerror(tperrno));
        ...
}
/* create FML32 buffer */
buffer = (FBFR32 *) tpalloc("FML32", NULL, 4000);
/* fill buffer */
Fadd32(buffer,TA_OPERATION,"GET",0);
Fadd32(buffer,TA_CLASS,"T_MACHINE", 0);
Fadd32(buffer,TA_LMID,"orders01", 0);
/* invoke the administrative service */
if(tpcall(".TMIB",(char *)buffer, 0,(char **)&buffer, &len, TPNOFLAGS)== -1) {
        fprintf(stderr, "tpcall failed: %s\n", tpstrerror(tperrno));
        ...
}
...
```

Listing 15.7   *Client Joins an Application as the Administrator*

Additional authorization permissions are enforced on a per attribute basis, as defined for each class in the TMIB. For example, normal users cannot change any attribute in the TMIB. Replies from the ".TMIB" service can return information about one or more objects. Thus, the reply also contains information about how many objects (TA_OCCURS) are found in the buffer. Multiple occurrences are defined as follows: occurrence 0 of each attribute in the buffer relates to the first object, occurrence 1 to the second, and so on. Errors on calls to ".TMIB" are indicated by a **TPESCVFAIL** error return from **tpcall** or **tpgetrply**.

Services can use the administrative programming interface without having to join the application. This is allowed because servers run within the trusted base of the application and they automatically join the application with the permissions of the administrator. Thus, administrators can write services that are invoked when an application or a system event occurs. Listing 15.8 shows an example of an application administrative service "stoptellers" in a banking application invoked by the "CloseOfBusiness" event. When the "CloseOfBusiness" event is posted, the "stoptellers" service is invoked as a subscription fulfillment. This service calls ".TMIB" to suspend processing of teller services ("Debit", "Credit" and "Balance"). You can also use the TMIB Interface via the **ud32** scripting utility.

```
stoptellers(tpsvcinfo){
...
/* This service is invoked via an application-defined event */
switch(data->event) {
case SUSPEND:
  /* create FML buffer */
  buffer = (FBFR32 *) tpalloc("FML32", NULL, 4000);
  /*  Fill the request parameters */
  Fadd32(buffer, TA_OPERATION, "SET", 0);   /* update the MIB */
  Fadd32(buffer, TA_CLASS, "T_SVCGRP", 0); /* update the T_SVCGRP class */
  Fadd32(buffer, TA_STATE, "SUS", 0);   /* Suspend service */
  /* Fill the service attributes */
  Fadd32(buffer, TA_SERVICENAME,(char *)&data->service[0], 0);
  /* Issue request to the MIB administrative service */
  if(tpcall(".TMIB", buffer, &obuffer, olen, 0) == -1) {
       userlog ("tpcall failed: %s\n", tpstrerror(tperrno));
  ...
  }
  break;
...
tpreturn();
}
```

Listing 15.8 *Suspending a Service with the TMIB Interface*

15.8 Summary

In this chapter, we discussed the basic tasks of an application administrator. We also explained how an administrator can use the tools provided with the TUXEDO System to control the operation of a distributed application. These tools give a lot of flexibility to application administrators and are designed to address different needs of nonexpert to expert administrators. Tools, such as the administrative programming interface, pave the road toward self-adapting applications that change or adapt their environment when certain events occur. There are still two missing pieces that we will discuss in the next chapters: one is failure handling and the other is how to build an application for scalability or interoperability.

16 Failure Handling

PROGRAMMING/
ADMINISTRATION

Now you understand how an application is put together, the features available to an application designer and programmer, and the tools available to an administrator. Hopefully, you understand the ways in which the TUXEDO System eases the job of getting the application up and running. One of the features that distinguishes TUXEDO from other distributed application environments is the management tools for keeping the application running in the face of failures. When an application is in development, programs often behave in unexpected and undesired ways. Even in production, bugs in the application can cause programs to fail. More common are events in the environment that are not directly related to the software: someone turns off their PC that was running part of the application; a network connection is broken; or a computer fails. This chapter will consider a broad range of failure and recovery processing. We will start at the simplest level with abnormal processing in a nontransactional client or server, then move on to computers going down, network failures, and transaction processing errors. First, we will describe some of the philosophy behind the failure handling capabilities of the TUXEDO System.

16.1 Failure Handling Philosophy

There are two basic goals that the TUXEDO failure handling mechanisms try to follow.

The first is that the TUXEDO run-time system tries to cleanup after any failures that can be detected. When servers fail, replacement servers can be started. When communications with remote computer fail, associated services are suspended so that further requests are not sent to that node. There are some failures that cannot be detected without outside help, such as a hardware monitor that tracks computer and network failures. This will be discussed at the end of this chapter.

A second goal is that there be no single point of failure. This can be accomplished through the use of redundant hardware and software. The various administrative components check on each other to ensure aliveness and restart replacements, as needed. Further, fault tolerant hardware can be used to reduce or eliminate down time. Non-Stop TUXEDO running on Tandem hardware is such a configuration [Tandem].

When failures do occur, events are raised and logged. The events are displayed via the administrative GUI in the form of icons indicating failed servers and computers, pop-up windows, and alarm mechanisms. Other clients and servers in the application can subscribe to these events and do even more detailed application processing than is built into the default administration.

Now on to a taxonomy of application failures and failure handling!

16.2 Process Failure

The building blocks for a distributed application are the application clients and servers. By using redundant servers, automatic restarts of servers, and automatic cleanup of abnormally terminated processes, the application can sanely continue in the face of problems at the process level. We will look at handling client and server failures independently.

16.2.1 Client Cleanup

Remember that clients are unstructured programs that join a TUXEDO application and leave under their own choice. While the client is part of the application, it uses resources both from the operating system and the TUXEDO System. When a client exits, its operating system resources, such as open files and memory, are automatically released (in most environments). Client programs that call the **tpterm** routine exit normally and are removed from the system. It is also necessary for the TUXEDO System to keep track of client programs that leave the application abnormally. This includes a client that explicitly exits without leaving the application or a process that aborts due to an uncaught signal (for example, a bug that causes a core dump or an Unrecoverable Application Error).

Figure 16.1 indicates three ways that a client can exit without explicitly calling **tpterm**. The nonsolid client boxes indicate that the client programs have all exited.

For clients running in an ANSI C environment, the TUXEDO runtime system calls **atexit** with **tpterm** as the callback function. The operating system will call the TUXEDO termination primitive **tpterm** when the client exits. This ensures that any resources tied up by the client are released, even if the client fails to leave the application explicitly. This works for both local and /WS clients.

For local clients on a server machine lacking this OS facility or for certain abnormal termination cases that do not automatically clean up, the client's termination is detected by the monitoring done by the **BBL**, and associated resources are

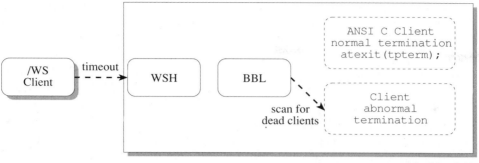

Figure 16.1 Client Termination

released. The time-out period between checks for terminated clients is defined by the administrator. More time between checks means less administrative overhead in checking the viability of clients, but unused resources (including in-flight transactions) stay tied up longer.

Workstation clients are a slightly different story. These processes are connected to the application over a network. In this environment, a workstation client could exit without leaving the application, because the operating system may not support execution of some additional work on exit or, more commonly, because the user turns off the workstation without a chance for **tpterm** to be called. Although the client program is gone, the other end of the network connection may not "feel" the disconnection for a long period, perhaps days. There is no way to interrogate the network software appropriately in a distributed, heterogeneous environment to reliably detect the disconnection.

The protocol between the workstation client and the application could (but does not) support meta-messages to check the viability of the client. For instance, the workstation handler could periodically send a message to the workstation client which is acknowledged without being seen by the application. This would have the disadvantage of more network traffic, significant for applications supporting thousands of workstation clients. It also works only if the application dips into the TUXEDO software so that the message can be received and acknowledged (not all platforms support signals for interrupts). As long as there is a requirement that a client accesses TUXEDO primitives to prove its aliveness, it is more efficient to handle the death of workstation clients by tracking idle time in the workstation handler. The administrator specifies an idle time after which a workstation client will be automatically terminated if it has not done any work. This can lead to unexpected terminations if the client doesn't send or receive any messages for a long period, but does handle freeing up resources and is quite useful if properly configured.

One situation that is not detected is a local client, outside of a transaction, that is looping. There is no process waiting on the client nor does the client go through a gateway into the system that would time it out. In many applications, a human being interacts directly with the client program and would recognize (and abort) a "hung" client. The application administrator, looking at CPU usage or application statistics (if the client was repeatedly doing TUXEDO calls), would also detect the errant client.

The point of this section is that clients need to leave the application to free up resources. If this isn't done explicitly by the application code, one of several methods is used to ensure that the client will eventually leave. In any of the time-out cases, an event is generated to which clients and servers can subscribe and do further processing. These client "obituaries" can be used to delete context, such as nonpersistent events and application data structures associated with the dead clients.

16.2.2 Server Recovery and Cleanup

Remember that servers are primarily under the control of the TUXEDO System. When the administrator activates and deactivates a server, it automatically joins and leaves the application. So, under normal circumstances, a server cleans up after itself. Occasionally, the "last bug" hasn't been found in the server, and it exits abnormally without being deactivated. The same viability check by the **BBL** used for local clients is done to ensure that servers are alive, based on a configured time interval. However, unlike a client, many other processes, both clients and servers, may be dependent on the now defunct server. There are several ways to configure the application to ensure recovery or redundancy will handle this server loss.

Figure 16.2 illustrates some ways that server failure is handled. In the figure, there are three **ACCT** servers configured, each with a different server identifier. Two of them share a queue, ACCTQ. Server 2 has terminated abnormally, and this has been detected by the **BBL**. But those shadows behind Server 2 indicate that it has a few more lives left.

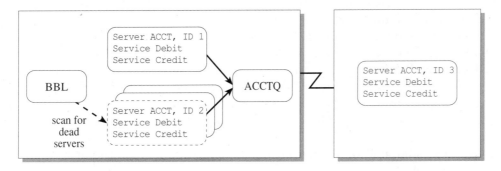

Figure 16.2   **Server Termination**

One approach for recovery from abnormal server termination is to define redundant servers offering the same services. That is, multiple servers are started up, either on the same machine or across multiple machines, to handle the service requests. This not only allows for more concurrent processing of the services, but also handles the case where one of the servers goes down. The dead server is marked as unavailable, and new service requests will be directed to any viable server offering the service. If no other servers are available, the requestor will receive an error indicating that no server can satisfy the request. In Figure 16.2, **ACCT** Server 2 has terminated, but service requests can be routed to one of the remaining **ACCT** servers.

So what happens to messages already sent to the server and waiting on the queue (or already in progress)? If the server was in the midst of processing a request, the request cannot be completed and a failure indication is sent back to the client or server requesting the service. All other service requests sent to the server remain on that server's request queue. All messages on the reply queue and any conversational messages other than the initial request message are considered stale and deleted. The request queue is not deleted just because the server that was reading the queue died. If the server was part of an MSSQ set, then other servers reading the same queue will continue to process the queued messages, even before the system detects the dead server. In Figure 16.2, **ACCT** Servers 1 and 2 share a queue, so the termination of Server 2 will result in all messages currently on the queue being processed by Server 1. No additional forwarding of messages is needed; this is one of the benefits of using MSSQ sets.

If the server was not part of an MSSQ set, then each message in the request queue is processed in one of three ways in the order specified.

1. The server can be restarted to process the messages on the queue.

2. Messages can be read from the queue and forwarded to other servers offering the same services.

3. Failure messages need to be sent back to the originators.

In Figure 16.2, if **ACCT** Server 3 died, then its messages would be forwarded to **ACCT** Server 1. We have not yet discussed network failures, but note that, in this configuration, if a network partition does occur, there is an **ACCT** server on each of the machines, so processing can continue normally.

When a server is configured, the administrator can indicate whether or not a server is to be restarted in the event that it abnormally terminates. For an application where as much automatic recovery as possible is the goal, the server would be configured to be automatically reactivated. Still, if it is an application error that caused the failure, then there is a possibility that the server will continue to get the same input message, will continue to fail, and then will be reactivated again. The administrator also specifies the maximum number of times that a server can be reactivated (up to 256 times) within a period of time (the default being one day). The number of "lives" for the server is called the "maximum generations" for the server, and the period, within which this number is allowed, is called the "grace period." For example, Server 2 in Figure 16.2 could be configured to have three generations (the initial activation and two reactivations) within 3,600 seconds (one hour). Because it has terminated, it will be automatically restarted no more than two more times within the hour.

When the server is reactivated, it reuses the configuration of the server as it was when it went down. That is, if the administrator has dynamically advertised services for the server or set some other options, these are used when the server restarts. The reactivated server reads the same request queue as the prior generation server. Normally, the application server does not behave any differently when it is reactivated and the application need not even know that this is a second or later generation. It is possible for the application to detect a restart condition in **tpsvrinit** by looking for a –R option, indicating that the server is being reactivated and to take special actions.

If a server is not configured to be restarted or has already been activated for the maximum number of generations within the grace period, then the server is not activated again and instead its resources must be cleaned up. Of primary importance is its message queue. The server and its services are taken out of the list of available servers and services. Its queue is drained, one message at a time, and an attempt is made to forward the message to another server offering the desired service. If one does not exist, a message is sent back to the originator of the request indicating that the service is not available.

The approaches above will take care of the case where the server exits abnormally, but won't help in the case where incorrect server logic causes the service code to loop without returning a response to the requesting process. The administrator can configure a service time for each service within a server group, based on an estimated maximum time that the service should take. If the service time is exceeded, then the server is killed. Then the mechanisms described for restarting or cleaning up the server go into effect.

Summing up, failure handling for servers relies mainly on correct application configuration by the administrator. Redundant servers are recommended not only to handle greater volumes of work but also to handle the case when a server goes down. Even if the server is configured to restart, it may take some time for the monitor to recognize that the server has died and reactivate it. The setting of the period between scanning for terminated servers is also important, trading off overhead for shortening the time to find a server that needs reactivating. This time period may be a function of the stability of the application programs. Use of restartable servers is the norm for most applications, and service times should be used for sanity checking if a reasonable value can be determined. TUXEDO System functions are implemented as servers and thus are enabled for the same type of restart.

16.3 Time-Outs

Time-outs are used throughout the TUXEDO System to handle problems that could keep the application hanging for a long time. They are used to recover from many of the failures described in this chapter. At this point, you might be wondering what happens to the requesting process waiting for a server that has died and will either be cleaned up or restarted. Time-outs may be the answer, depending on how long the recovery takes.

There are two types of time-outs that can occur within the application, depending whether or not the application is in a transaction. A time-out in a process that is not in a transaction has an impact only on that process. When in a transaction, any failure requires that the transaction be rolled back, so a time-out within a transaction has more far-reaching effects. Further, a mechanism is needed to terminate the transaction at all infected sites, that is, sites to which the transaction has been propagated if the transaction runs for too long. Rather than sending messages around everywhere to terminate a transaction, it is more efficient to propagate a time-out value when the transaction is propagated to various sites. In this way, each site can time-out independently. Hence the two types of time-outs.

Outside of the transaction demarcation primitives, a client or server can get a *blocking time-out*. This event can occur any time that a client or server is blocked waiting for some TUXEDO action. For example, a blocking time-out can occur in a client program while waiting for a message response, either synchronously or getting a reply to an asynchronous request. The client's software does not know why a time-out has occurred, only that the operation took longer than the period configured. It could have happened because a server failed or was looping, a computer crashed, the network was partitioned, or even a lack of computer resources, such as message queue space. In Figure 16.3, **client1** may time-out on the first call to **tpgetrply** because the **ACCT** server died and has not yet been restarted.

Machine M1

Figure 16.3 **Time-Outs**

Some operations can simply be repeated. An advantage of using the asynchronous request/response over the synchronous is that, if the operation times out, the application can again try to receive the response, in effect getting an additional time-out period. In Figure 16.3, **client1** will try a second **tpgetrply** if the first one fails because of time-out. This will give the operation a second blocking time period to complete before giving up on the operation. With a synchronous operation, such as **tpcall**, the entire operation must be redone. Using time-out values set by the administrator ensures that the application software won't be "hung" forever. In some situations, it will be appropriate to design the application to wait multiple times assuming that the response will come. In other situations, an error will be returned to the end user leaving the retry decision to them.

Although performing a similar function of keeping operations from hanging around too long, *transaction time-outs* are different from blocking time-outs. First, there is an application programming interface to set the time-out on a per transaction basis, a much finer granularity than blocking time-out which is set for the entire application. In Figure 16.3, **client2** set the transaction time-out period to 30 seconds. A transaction time-out always takes precedence over blocking time-outs. Unlike a blocking time-out, if a transaction time-out occurs, then the operation cannot be repeated. Once the transaction is timed out, any asynchronous operation that was made from the process receiving the time-out in transaction mode is automatically timed out. That is, if a client is waiting for a reply to a response sent in transaction mode and it gets a time-out, not only is the descriptor for that response invalidated but other descriptors for replies to asynchronous requests or conversations are also invalid. In Figure 16.3, **client2** will not retry the **tpgetrply** if the first one fails; in fact, doing so will automatically return an error without further processing.

The most important consequence of a transaction time-out is that the entire transaction itself will be rolled back, even if the transaction originator indicates that it should be committed. It is for this reason that all transactional descriptors are invalidated, because the transaction will be rolled back and further work on the transaction is no longer useful. Once a transaction times out, you've had it! In Figure 16.3, **client2** calls **tpabort** if the **tpgetrply** fails and otherwise commits the transaction with **tpcommit**.

In the context of this chapter on failure recovery, time-outs are part of the mix of features that keep the application running in spite of failures. Although the TUXEDO System will clean up after dead processes and restart servers and the administrator has tools to work through machine and network failures, it may not be appropriate for other clients and servers to be held up while this is happening. This is especially true when the use of redundant computers and servers can keep processing going, in most cases, transparent to whatever failures may occur.

16.4   Computer and Network Failure

So far, we have talked about failures that can occur within a single computer. That is, client and server failures can occur even within applications running on a single machine. When you have multiple computers connected by a network in your application, there are more pieces to administer and more things that can go wrong. Fortunately, the TUXEDO System helps you in the job of administering the entire application from a single screen and provides the tools to bring the application back on-line when computers and networks fail.

16.4.1 Detecting and Tracking Down the Failure

When a computer that is part of the application fails, you lose everything on it (except stable resources such as the application queues). If native clients are running there, the associated display hangs. Workstation clients going through that machine also get stuck. Services provided by servers on that machine are no longer available for processing. Depending on how much of the application is dependent on the failed computer, the impact may range from a nuisance to losing major application functionality. This is where careful up-front design of the application is important. It is also a trade-off between how much redundant hardware and associated software are allocated versus additional cost and administration.

Computer and networking problems are discussed together in this section because often it is initially difficult to determine whether a computer or the network is causing the problem. For instance, if a network cable is pulled from the back of a computer, the services and workstation connections to that computer are unavailable to the rest of the application and it might appear that the computer is down when, in fact, servers are still running normally on the machine. Some applications using networking over satellites find that the network availability is quite transient. The difficulty in detecting the problem is particularly bad in the TUXEDO System without some intervention on the part of the administrator. Later in this chapter, we will discuss how this situation can be improved if you have some hardware in place to detect failure.

Earlier, we discussed the notion of configuring one of the computers in the application as a master node. One of the roles of the master is to keep tabs on other computers in the configuration. If the **DBBL** which runs on the master does not hear from a machine within the time period configured by the administrator, the master will try to contact the nonreporting computer. If no reply is received, then that machine and all services advertised by servers on that machine are marked as *partitioned*. Similarly, if an operation that must be broadcast to all machines, such as advertising a new service available, is requested by the master and a nonmaster does not respond within a configured amount of time, that machine is also considered to be partitioned.

A machine is partitioned from another if they are unable to communicate, usually due to network failure or failure of one of the two machines. In a TUXEDO application, it is more common to talk about being partitioned from the machine running as the master because this master node is doing most of the sanity checking and is also necessary for many administrative updates. Although administrative changes may fail, application service processing can continue on a partitioned node, independent of the master for any services that can be reached, that is, services unaffected by the partition. Figure 16.4 shows that Machine M2 is partitioned from the master machine, M1. The **tpcall** made by the client running on M2 to "Credit" will fail because the client is unable to get to the **ACCT** server, running on M1, but the **tpcall** to "Buy" will succeed (assuming no other problems).

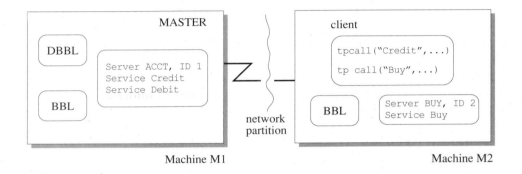

Figure 16.4 Network Partition

When a machine is partitioned, the TUXEDO System does not know what action should be taken to correct the situation, because it could be a transient load problem (the acknowledgment is slow in coming, or operating system queues could be full), a transient network problem, or a more permanent problem, such as a network failure or a dead computer. The result is the same: the master cannot contact a remote machine and a remote machine cannot contact the master. This is where the administrator gets involved to diagnose the problem.

Of course, the first indication of a problem may be calls from users of the application. There are several sources of information available to the administrator from the monitor. The central event log for each machine may have error messages that describe the current problem or at least the symptoms of the problem. Often the system messages will indicate the logical machine name of the computer that cannot be contacted or will indicate an application disconnection of the virtual circuit between the computers. As part of trying to view the event log, you may run into the disconnection problem while trying to read the file, either by doing a remote log in or accessing the file via a networked file system.

A second source for information is the administrative interface (either **xtuxadm** or the **tmadmin** command interpreter). Without looking through files or using operating system commands to access the remote systems individually, it is possible to determine at a glance how many computers are affected, by looking at the available services to see how many are partitioned. The administrative interface also shows information regarding the application network connections and which, if any, are partitioned. If more than one computer is partitioned, then it is probably a network partition because the chances of more than one computer failing simultaneously is small (although a power failure or a more catastrophic event could account for many computers being out of service).

There is one case in which the administrative interface will not indicate a partition. If the master machine goes down, then the machine that normally does the checking for partitioning cannot be doing its job, and no one marks it as partitioned. In this case, you will not be able to join the application as the administrator anyway (assuming you are trying to do so from another machine) until the role of the master is migrated to the backup. It is clear that either the acting master machine is down or the network is partitioned.

Apart from the TUXEDO System, another source of information should be available from diagnostic programs for your network. These may indicate load problems or pinpoint connectivity failures. Finally, you may need to check the partitioned computers themselves to see if they are still running and whether or not they can access the network. This may be as simple as checking another computer in the same room as the configured master computer or may require a phone call to a remote site.

The steps taken for recovering from the failure depend on whether a computer is unavailable or it is a networking problem.

16.4.2 Handling Computer Failure

Normally, administration is done from the configured master machine. This machine is responsible for checking on the other machines in the configuration and broadcasting dynamic changes to the TMIB. It has the best idea of the TMIB without requiring network communications to get it. In an application with heterogeneous machines, the administrator would probably pick the most reliable machine to be the master. Figure 16.5 shows a two machine configuration. Machine M1 is configured as the master machine. When the application is first activated, the **DBBL** will be started on this machine to monitor the other machines and handle configuration updates. The machine where the **DBBL** is running is also called the acting master; as we will discuss shortly, this attribute can change or migrate. Machine M2 is the configured backup computer. That is, it is the machine to which the master control can migrate. Because the **DBBL** is not running on this machine, it is also the acting backup.

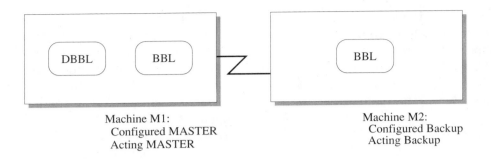

Machine M1:
    Configured MASTER
    Acting MASTER

Machine M2:
    Configured Backup
    Acting Backup

Figure 16.5   Master/Backup

So what happens when the master machine fails? After all, it may be handling an additional administrative load. If the configured master computer fails, the application does not stop running. Clients can still join the application because they register locally on the machine to which they are attached or register where the workstation handlers are for workstation clients. Servers still continue to service requests, and the name serving is still available on each local machine. What is lost is the ability for servers to activate and deactivate, and for the administrator to dynamically reconfigure the system. So although the application can continue to run with the status quo, it is best to get these services, performed by the master, back on-line as soon as possible.

For this to be possible, the administrator must have configured a *backup* computer. This migration of responsibilities is done by simply using the administrative interface to request that the configured backup machine to take over as the acting master machine. This should take only seconds to execute, and the acting master machine is ready to begin monitoring the other machines in the configuration and accepting dynamic reconfiguration changes. Once this migration takes place, all of the administrative operations can be done from the new acting master machine. In Figure 16.6, this reversal of roles is shown. The configured backup machine is now the acting master machine with the **DBBL** running there. The configured master machine, assuming it becomes available, assumes the role of the acting backup computer, which can take over as the acting master again, if necessary. Further, if the acting backup will not be available soon, then the configuration can be dynamically modified to define a new acting backup. The ability to change the backup combined with the continued running during the loss of the master ensures that the **DBBL** is not a single point of failure.

When a computer fails, whether it is the master machine or any other computer in the configuration, the entries for its servers and services remain in the TMIB, even though they are no longer available. They are marked as partitioned so no clients or servers will try to access them. Because the computer is no longer running, the entries need to be cleaned up (for a network partition, they can be reused as we will see below). From the acting master, the administrative interface can be used to remove all information for a partitioned machine. This should only be done if the machine has failed.

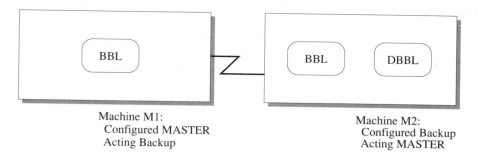

Figure 16.6   **Backup Acting as Master**

At this point, all of the services that had been available on the failed machine are no longer available. It may be desirable to provide these servers on another machine. Even if redundant servers are already running, the load will be greater on the remaining servers. In addition to specifying a backup computer for the master, the administrator can also specify backup computers for each group of servers. Migrating the servers in the case of a failed machine is simply a matter of reactivating the server group from the acting master machine. The activation process will try to start the servers on the configured primary machine for the group. Assuming that the machine is not accessible, the servers will be activated on the configured backup machine automatically. Note that these servers are activated with the original group name, even though they are running on a different machine. This is one reason that data-dependent routing is done by group name instead of a machine name, providing the application with location transparency even when servers fail and are migrating elsewhere.

In Figure 16.7, a single server Group G1 is configured for Machine M1. Machine M2 is configured as the backup machine for this group. Note that after migration, Group G1 is now activated on Machine M2. That means all servers in this group and their associated services are available on Machine M2. Migration is completely transparent to requestors and providers of the services. This is location transparency in action!

16.4.3 Controlled Migration

We have talked about migration of the master node and application servers during a failure. There are times when you need to take a computer out of the application for servicing or upgrading. Similar mechanisms to those described for failure migration can be used, in a controlled way, for this purpose.

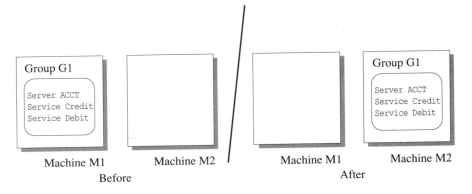

Figure 16.7   Server Group Migration

For a master machine, the role of the master can be migrated to the configured backup machine, and the master computer can be deactivated normally. This leaves the activated configuration in the state described above when the master computer failed and control was migrated to the backup machine. When the configured master computer is available again, either after failure or servicing, it can be reactivated from the acting master machine. At this point, it can regain control as the acting master from the configured backup machine through the administrative interface.

Note that this migration of roles is symmetric: the acting backup can always assume the role of the acting master machine by executing a simple command as the administrator on the acting backup machine. If the master machine will be down for some time, it is recommended that a new backup machine be configured from the acting master machine using dynamic reconfiguration. In this way, there is always an acting backup machine that can take over the job of the master.

Server migration can also be used for application servers when a computer will be off-line for a while. Unlike the failure case, information about the current configuration for servers and services can be preserved and used when activating the servers on the backup machine. When the servers are deactivated on their primary computer, they are deactivated with an indication that migration is being performed. This marks the services as unavailable but retains the entries in the name server instead of deleting them.

Migration can be done for an entire server group or an entire machine. You should think of migrating an entire machine as migrating all groups for that machine to the backup machine. If server groups for a particular machine have multiple backup machines, then the servers must be migrated by group rather than by machine. That is, migration of a machine's servers can only be done en masse if they all migrate to the same target machine. After the servers have been deactivated administratively, it is simply a matter of running a second administrative command to indicate that the servers for a specified server group or machine are to be reactivated on the alternate machine.

Again, this operation is symmetric so that an administrator can deactivate and migrate servers from the acting primary to the acting secondary machine, independent of which was configured as the primary and the secondary. The administrator does not need to specify which servers were running at the time the deactivation was done, which services were advertised by the servers, or even dynamically configured changes, such as new service loads. All of this information is picked up from the configuration of the servers when they were deactivated, and data-dependent routing will continue to work correctly by routing services based on the target group name, not a target machine.

Let's look at an example configuration to review these ideas. In Figure 16.8, the configuration consists of three machines. Machine M1 is configured as the master computer and activated as the acting master. Machine M2 is configured as the backup. A single Group G1 is shown configured with Machine M1 as its primary machine (the default place where the servers are activated) and Machine M3 as its secondary machine. The fact that the backup for the master is different from the group backup site is for illustrative purposes. Many administrators would prefer to keep things simple by having all migration (master plus all servers on a given computer) to a single machine. A single server group offering two services, Credit and Debit, is activated on M1.

Figure 16.8 **Configuration before Migration**

Assume that the administrator is going to service or shut down Machine M1. The steps required would be to migrate the master to Machine M2, deactivate Group G1 indicating that it will be reactivated, and migrate Group G1 to Machine M3. The resulting configuration is shown in Figure 16.9.

At this point, administrative servers on Machine M1 can be deactivated and the computer will no longer be involved in the application. At a later point, it can be reactivated as part of the application and the master role and servers can be migrated back, if desired. There is no urgency in doing this, other than the administrator needing to keep track of where the master role is currently living (of course, if you are looking at the GUI, then the master is obvious). Everything will continue to function as before the migration.

Figure 16.9   Configuration after Migration

There is one more detail to cover regarding migration. Let's say that you deactivate a group or machine indicating that you will reactivate it on the backup, and then decide that you do not want to do that. Commands are available through the administrative interface to cancel a migration. All of the information left in the name server for the deactivated servers and services is deleted. An attempt to reactivate the servers will cause the servers to be activated on the primary machine again with the configured options and services.

16.4.4 Handling Network Failure

Keeping an application running across a network can be a difficult job in an environment where the network is not stable (for example, across satellites dealing with signal fade) or if the network is so heavily loaded that it appears to be inoperable. So that your business can keep working, the TUXEDO System has been designed to continue working in spite of these problems. Some of the recovery mechanisms described in this section require administrator intervention, by default, but can be automated, as we will discuss below.

To understand the detection of network failure, it is necessary to understand the TUXEDO buddy system. The **BRIDGE** and **BBL** programs on each machine, and the **DBBL** and **BBL** programs across machines, in a running application keep track of the viability of each other, recovering from failure in the rare chance that it occurs. Basically, machines check on each other and components within a machine check each other.

Figure 16.10 shows the relationships in the TUXEDO buddy system by dotted lines.

The monitor program for the network traffic, the **BRIDGE**, keeps tabs on the monitor program for servers, the **BBL**, and vice versa, for each machine. If one fails, the other will restart it, retrieving information from the master site as necessary. Loss of the **BRIDGE** will temporarily restrict service access to the local machine. In practice, this rarely, if ever, happens. During its restart, it will reconnect to other **BRIDGE** programs in the application. Loss of the **BBL** will temporarily restrict dynamic reconfiguration and service advertisement, while allowing normal service processing to continue unhampered. Again, this does not happen under normal circumstances (usually only if the process is "accidentally" killed or IPC is removed), but the system has recovery mechanisms to deal with these "accidents." If the **BBL** or **BRIDGE** is restarted, the Bulletin Board is refreshed from the copy at the master site.

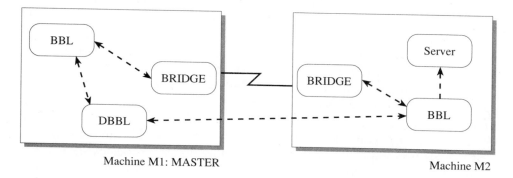

Machine M1: MASTER   Machine M2

Figure 16.10 **The TUXEDO Buddy System**

The **BBL**s keep tabs on the master administrative server, the **DBBL**, and vice versa. The period between checking is configurable by the administrator. Using a short time period shortens the failure detection time; using a longer time period reduces the additional network traffic. Each machine sends an "I'm OK" message to the master periodically. The **DBBL** checks to ensure that it has received a message from each machine periodically (usually a longer period of time than used for the remote machines to send their "I'm OK"). If the master does not receive a message from one of the machines, it sends a status message to the machine. If the machine does not respond shortly, the master marks the remote machine as partitioned and indicates this state to the remaining nonpartitioned machines. It is possible that heavy network load causes the messages to be delayed creating a "false" partition. If the "I'm OK" message finally makes it to the master, then an up-to-date copy of the Bulletin Board is sent to that machine and the machine state is returned to active again. During the time that the machine is considered partitioned, no service requests will be sent to that machine.

Now that we have discussed how important the **DBBL** is, you may be wondering what happens if it goes away. The **BBL** at the master site checks on the **DBBL** process and reboots it, if necessary. If there are multiple failures at the master site, then it is necessary to take over the master responsibilities at the backup site and reactivate the original master. Of course, the backup site can be changed so that, if the original master will be down for an extended period, the master can be migrated to the backup and a new backup can be specified in case of failure at the new master.

It is possible for a transient network failure to occur. That is, the network fails temporarily and recovers, either automatically (as in the case of satellite fade) or with administrator intervention. Assuming that application messages were flowing over the network during the failure, it is likely that one of the transaction monitor programs detected the failure by receiving an error from an operating system call. In this case, the **BRIDGE** monitor programs will be disconnected from each other. If the network failure is short, the **BRIDGE** programs will reconnect and processing will continue as normal. In this case, the recovery is automatic (self-healing) and the application will not notice the temporary failure. If the **BRIDGE** processes are unable to reconnect, then an event is raised and manual intervention is required (the **BRIDGE** programs do not keep trying to reconnect because it could be a long time before the network is available again). The administrator can request reconnection from a site that is not partitioned from the master to the partitioned site using one of the administrative interfaces (for example, the **tmadmin reconnect** command or a few clicks in the GUI).

It may be necessary to deactivate one or more nodes if the network failure is not short in duration. Normally, it is necessary for the **DBBL** to be involved in deactivation. However, a partitioned deactivation can be used to gracefully deactivate the partitioned computers, temporarily starting a **DBBL** to handle the deactivation requests. On the master node, administrative operations must be run to cleanup the corresponding entries in the Bulletin Board. When the network partition is resolved, then the previously partitioned nodes can be activated again. For a long outage, it may be necessary to change a single configuration into two separate configurations and activate the partitioned machines as a separate application. If this failure occurs often, then the best approach is to define two autonomous applications that communicate via the /Domains feature; this is described further in Chapter 18, "Getting Applications to Work Together."

16.5   Failure in Transaction Processing

In Chapter 14, "Transactions in the TUXEDO System," we described how to use transactions in your application and the advantages of being able to undo the work if it cannot be completed. This section will describe how various failures are handled with regard to transactions. These are the mechanisms behind the "all-or-nothing" guarantee, in spite of all of the possible failures that have been described in the earlier part of this chapter.

The general principle followed for any type of failure when involved in a transaction is that the work is rolled back to the state when the transaction started. In some cases, the rollback is immediate. In other situations, the rollback is deferred, waiting for time-out to occur. The reason for taking a more active approach when possible, is that the application may set a large time-out value and resources will continue to be held if the transaction is not rolled back earlier.

When a transaction is started, the application writer must provide a time-out value for the transaction. As communications occur between machines with TUXEDO servers, the time left for the transaction is transmitted so that each machine can handle transaction time-out locally. That is, when a time-out occurs at one site, it isn't necessary to send a time-out message to other sites; it can simply time out on the local machine. Clients and servers waiting for a response or a conversational reply will get an error return immediately. Clients and servers executing application code will get an error return from the next ATMI communications primitive.

Let's consider the failures that were covered earlier with respect to transactions. When an abnormal termination occurs in a client or server that started a transaction, the transaction is immediately timed out. Deferred rollback, via transaction time-out, is used in the following cases:

- when a server, whose service is a participant but not the originator of a transaction, terminates abnormally
- handling computer failure
- handling network failure

Rollback can occur earlier than the transaction time-out in the following cases:

- Another process working on the same transaction may get an error from the resource manager; normally the application would roll back the transaction in this case. For example, a server that encounters an RM error would call **tpreturn** with a **TPSVCFAIL** indication. If an error is returned in the XA interface between the TM and the RM, then the transaction is automatically marked *rollback-only* so that further work cannot be done on the transaction.

- Another process working on the same transaction attempts to call a communications primitive that marks the transaction rollback-only and returns a failure to the application. The communications may fail because the server is no longer available to provide the service, the network layer returned an error, or the computer cannot be contacted.

We have considered what happens before the transaction has completed. It is possible that a failure occurs after the transaction has been decided and a record has been written to the transaction log but before the transaction has been completed at the participant sites. The way this situation is handled is what distinguishes the two-phase commitment protocol from unsuccessful attempts to guarantee consistency without it.

After the participant sites have "voted" and the decision has been logged, the decision is sent to the participant sites. If one (or more) of the participant sites cannot be reached, the coordinator site must keep track of the decision until all sites have been notified and acknowledgments received. The coordinator site will continue to try to notify sites that are unavailable (it waits longer each time that the site is not available). From the other direction, when a site is recovered and the transaction manager server is activated, it will contact the coordinator to find out the status of the transaction.

Handling failure of the coordinator site is more complicated, because the outcome cannot be easily determined without it. If the computer fails before the decision has been sent out, then the transaction will remain in a precommitted state at all participant sites, and the associated resources will remain locked. Depending on what those resources are, an administrator may get involved to free up the resources by taking a *heuristic decision* to commit or roll back the transaction, independent of what decision was taken by the coordinator. If the decisions do not match, then an inconsistency is generated.

To resolve the transaction correctly, it is necessary to gain access to the transaction log. If the failure is short-term, then the transactions will be completed when the application is reactivated on the failed computer. For a long-term failure, it is necessary to get access to the disk, unload the transaction log, and reload the log on a configured backup computer. This is shown in Figure 16.11, indicating the **tmadmin** commands to perform the migration. A transaction manager server is then activated on the backup machine and will act as the coordinator for any transactions contained in the log. It will send the status to any groups involved in the transaction so that they can complete the transaction. If one of the groups no longer "knows" about the transaction, the protocol assumes that the decision already reached that participant and the transaction has been completed correctly; note that this may not be the case if a heuristic decision was taken by the administrator. Summarizing, recovery depends on migrating the transaction log entries and migrating the resource manager group from the failed machine to a backup machine.

You may be wondering how the transaction log is "available" on the backup machine. Assuming that a failure of this kind does not happen often and recovery time need not be "instantaneous," it may mean physically moving the disk between computers. For many business applications that require high availability, hardware support is needed. Mirroring of disks, that is, updating two or more disks for each update, can be used to avoid failure due to the loss of a single disk. In many cases, this will also increase performance because reads can be done from either disk.

Dual ported disks can be used to make a single disk available to more than one computer. When the primary computer using a transaction log fails, the log can be dumped from a second computer and reloaded in the configured log for that computer before migrating the resource manager group to that computer. Note that the databases used by the application would also be stored on the dual ported disks for ease in recovery. Further, some database products support use of the dual ported disks to access the database by multiple computers simultaneously. By replicating the servers and services across more than one computer, visibility of the failure and recovery time can be minimized so that only those clients that were accessing the failed computer notice the failure.

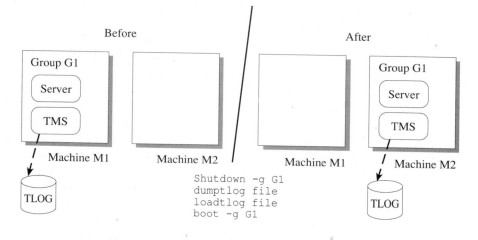

Figure 16.11 **Migration of Transaction Log**

We have not said anything about how deadlocks are handled. A deadlock is the state in which two (or more) parties have resources locked and then wait on each other's resources. In this situation, the parties will wait forever without intervention. Most database systems handle deadlock, either by not allowing the state to occur (not allowing the deadlock to be entered by rejecting one of the requests to wait) or by detecting the deadlock and giving up the resources of one of the parties. In the case of a distributed application that has more than one RM, it is possible to get distributed deadlocks between the RMs that cannot be detected by any one of them. The solution in this case is that a transaction time-out will occur and at least one of the transactions involved in the deadlock will be rolled back. This normally results in an error being returned to the application, indicating that an RM operation (such as a SQL FETCH) failed. The application can later retry the operation, which may succeed if the needed resources are available.

16.6 Automated Application Recovery

Although many of the recovery actions of the TUXEDO System are automatic, some of the more important actions require manual intervention by the administrator. In most if not all of these cases, the reason that the TUXEDO run-time system does not take action is because it cannot determine where the failure is. The tools are there to be used once the failure has been determined.

There are several examples (and more being made available) of hardware configurations with clusters of computers or loosely coupled multiple processor machines that have a "heartbeat monitor" tracking the status of the processors and networks involved. This monitor can take the place of the administrator in determining the cause of a problem when it occurs, and can automatically take the corrective action needed. One of the early ports of the TUXEDO System was to a high availability configuration which had two computers with multiple, loosely coupled processors and a monitor to track processor and network failures. Software was created to take information from the monitor and execute the required actions to keep the application available on one or both of the computers.

At the time this book was written, the TUXEDO System did not contain an abstraction for interfacing with a "heartbeat monitor." However, the administrative API can be used to create one, based on a specific monitor. While you might be tempted to write code for a specific application on a specific configuration, it is worth spending a little more effort to provide a more general approach for ease in administration later on. We would recommend using a table-driven approach, which can easily be updated by the administrator as needed. A simple table, similar to /etc/inittab on UNIX systems, can be used. The first field of each line in the table would contain a state and the remaining field or fields would contain actions to be taken, possibly the processors on which they need to be taken. The state field would correspond to some condition returned by the "heartbeat" monitor. The condition would be mapped to the state value and the table would be searched for actions associated with the state. The actions would be executed in the order in which they are encountered in the table. The actions could include operations such as dumping or loading the transaction log, migrating and restarting the database, migrating and reactivating groups of servers, etc. Some actions would be operating system commands and others would be TUXEDO administrative API operations. As new processors or groups of servers are added, it is simply a matter of adding a few new lines to the table. In this way, the monitor takes over many of the activities that otherwise would require administrator intervention.

16.7 Summary

As more and more components are added to the distributed application, failures are bound to occur. We have discussed how the TUXEDO System deals with failures of programs, processors, and networks with and without transactions. Although many of the failures are handled automatically by the monitor, some require administrator intervention to determine the root cause and take corrective action. It is a good idea to get some practice on using these procedures before an emergency occurs.

Using an external hardware source to monitor the configuration and trigger actions to reconfigure the application around the problem can result in less administrator intervention and greater up-time.

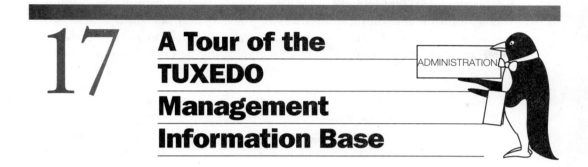

17 A Tour of the TUXEDO Management Information Base

You have finally arrived at the chapter that describes the contents of the TUXEDO Management Information Base (TMIB). We introduced the MIB concept in Chapter 3, "Communication and Administration Paradigms for Distributed Business Applications," and the TMIB basic concepts in Chapter 5, "Application Administration—Overview." In Chapter 6, "The Anatomy of a TUXEDO Application," we discussed the different administrative services provided by the TUXEDO System. In the earlier chapters of this part of the book, we also discussed how you can configure and monitor your applications. In particular, we discussed the TMIB Interface in Chapter 15, "Application Administration and Monitoring." But, to understand how you can exploit the power of the TMIB Interface, you need to know more about the TMIB. In this chapter, we take a look at the different parts of the TMIB, and we explain how these parts fit together.

17.1   What Is the TMIB?

You can think of the TMIB as the knowledge base the TUXEDO System has of your entire application. This knowledge includes the configuration and run-time characteristics of your TUXEDO application. The information stored in the TMIB is presented to you in the form of *classes of objects* (see Figure 17.1). Each class describes the characteristics of a set of similar objects. For example, the server class contains the characteristics of all application and administrative servers defined in your application. These characteristics are called *attributes*. Some of these attributes are used to distinguish one object from another or to relate an object to other objects in other classes. For example, a server in the server class has a name, a unique numeric identifier, and must be associated with a server group. These three attributes are used to identify each server in the server class.

A class can have configuration and run-time attributes. Configuration attributes describe the structure of the objects that define the application. They are persistent and may remain the same across application activations. An example is the attributes identifying the machines in your application. On the other hand, run-time attributes describe characteristics that only apply to an object when the application is active. Run-time attributes generally describe the operation and current status of objects within the application.

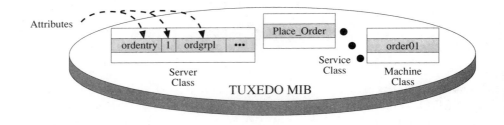

Figure 17.1   **Classes and Attributes in the TUXEDO MIB**

17.1.1 The Structure of a Class

All classes are structured as shown in Figure 17.2. This figure shows a partial view of the class named the T_MACHINE class. This class contains the set of machines that participate in a TUXEDO application. The definition of a class consists of a list of the attributes of the class. These are shown as rows in Figure 17.2. Each attribute has the following characteristics:

- a name,
- a data type,
- a set of permissions that define who can retrieve or update that attribute,
- a range of valid values, and
- a default value.

The name of a class in the TMIB begins with the prefix "T_", and the name of an attribute begins with the prefix "TA_". Each attribute name maps to the name of an FML32 field defined in the **tpadm** field table. When you use the TMIB Interface, you have to include the **tpadm.h** file in your program. These files are supplied with the TUXEDO software.

The permissions associated with an attribute are split into three groups representing (from left to right) the permissions for the administrator, the operator, and other users. Each group has three basic permissions that tell the system if you can

- read the attribute (r)
- write the attribute while the application is inactive (w or U)
- write the attribute while the application is active (w)

T_MACHINE class					
Attributes	Type	Permissions	Values	Defaults	Description
TA_LMID	string	rU-r-r-	string[1...30]	N/A	Logical machine name
TA_PMID	string	rU-r-r-	string[1...30]	N/A	Physical machine name
TA_TUXCONFIG	string	rw-r-r-	string[2...64]	N/A	Configuration file
TA_TUXDIR	string	rw-r-r-	string[2...78]	N/A	TUXEDO software
TA_APPDIR	string	rw-r-r-	string[2...78]	N/A	Application software
TA_STATE	string	rwyr-yr-	G:ACT|INA|PAR S:NEW|INV|ACT |INA|RAC|...	N/A	States changes
...	...	...		...	...

Figure 17.2   The Class T_ Machine

In Figure 17.2, the TA_LMID attribute can be read by administrators, operators, and other users. However, this attribute can only be updated by the administrator when the application is inactive. Some attributes require unique values, and this constraint is specified with the U (unique) value. Attribute values may be restricted to a range of values. In our example, the TA_LMID attribute is a null-terminated string with a maximum of 30 characters. An attribute may also have a default value that is used when a new entity in the class is created and the attribute is not specified.

The TA_STATE attribute exists in all classes. This attribute describes the state of an object in the class. For example, when you retrieve an object from the T_MACHINE class, its state can be active (ACT), inactive (INA), or partitioned (PAR). You can also use the TA_STATE attribute in the TMIB Interface to change the state of an object. For example, when you define a new machine you set TA_STATE to NEW; when you invalidate an existing machine, you set TA_STATE to INV; when you activate or inactivate a machine, you set TA_STATE to ACT or to INA.

The entire TMIB structure is defined by two *metaclasses*: the class of classes (T_CLASS) that contains all the classes in the TMIB, and the class of attributes (T_CLASSATT) that defines the attributes in each class. Hence, it is possible to construct programs that discover the entire TMIB from these classes. The **xtuxadm** graphical interface is an example of such a program. Also, with these two metaclasses, you can change the default attribute permissions delivered with the TUXEDO System. You can find the description of these permissions and all aspects of the TMIB in the TUXEDO Reference Manual (MIB(5) in [TUXEDO]).

17.1.2 How Do I Access the TMIB?

You can access the TMIB via the TMIB Interface, the **ud32** scripting utility, a set of administrative command utilities, and the **xtuxadm** graphical interface. With these interfaces, you can dynamically change the structure of the application by adding or removing objects from the TMIB or by changing the values of the attributes of an object. We have already discussed these interfaces in Chapter 15, "Application Administration and Monitoring."

Direct access to the TMIB is provided via the TMIB Interface and the **ud32** scripting utility. You can use the description of the classes and attributes published in the TUXEDO Reference Manual to customize the administration of your applications from programs or command scripts.

You need a knowledge of FML to use the TMIB Interface or the **ud32** utility. Operations on the TMIB are FML32 buffers sent to the ".TMIB" administrative service. Replies from the ".TMIB" service are also FML32 buffers. Each request must contain the following fields:

- TA_CLASS: the name of the class in the TMIB

- TA_OPERATION: the operation to be performed on the class (GET one or more objects or SET attributes of an object)

- attributes identifying a particular object of the class

- new attribute values for the object (for a SET operation)

You can retrieve one or more objects from a class with a GET operation. Multiple objects are reflected in the reply buffer by multiple field occurrences— occurrence 0 of each field relates to the attribute values of the first object, occurrence 1 to the second object, and so on. The field TA_OCCURS identifies how many objects are in the reply buffer. Errors found by the ".TMIB" administrative service are returned in the TA_ERROR field.

You always access the TMIB in the same way and you do not need to know how the TUXEDO System obtains the information that you need. From your perspective, the MIB gives you centralized access to your applications' administrative information. From the TUXEDO perspective, the information stored in the TMIB is distributed across the machines in your application. The ".TMIB" administrative service provides the centralized image of a particular class by retrieving information from the different machines or TUXEDO subcomponents involved in that class. Each one of the TUXEDO subsystems is in charge of a part of the TMIB. Thus, the TMIB is composed of the following Sub-MIBs (see Fig. 17.3):

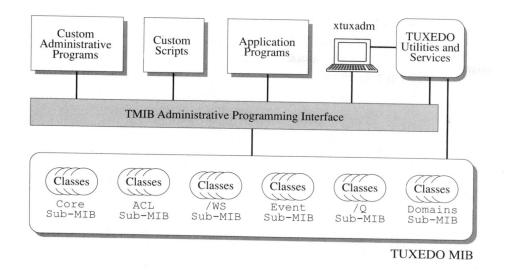

Figure 17.3   The TUXEDO Administrative Architecture

- The Core Sub-MIB (TM_MIB) defines the basic objects of the TUXEDO application.

- The ACL Sub-MIB (ACL_MIB) defines the objects controlled by the TUXEDO Access Control List facility.

- The Workstation Sub-MIB (WS_MIB) defines the objects used by the TUXEDO/WS facility.

- The Application Queues Sub-MIB (APPQ_MIB) defines the objects used by the TUXEDO/Q facility.

- The Event Sub-MIB (EVENT_MIB) defines the objects controlled by the TUXEDO Event Broker facility.

- The Domains Sub-MIB (DM_MIB) defines the objects used by the TUXEDO/Domains facility.

This partitioning of the TMIB into the Sub-MIBs shown in Figure 17.3 is not important to the TMIB programmer. As we explained in Chapter 15, "Administration and Monitoring," TMIB programmers do not see this partitioning, and they access the TMIB with calls to the ".TMIB" administrative service. In the following sections, we will describe all these Sub-MIBs with exception of the Domains Sub-MIB, which had not yet been published as of the writing of this book. In Chapter 18, "Getting Applications to Work Together," we discuss the TUXEDO Domains subsystem in more detail.

17.2   Administering the TUXEDO System— The Core Sub-MIB

The Core MIB defines the basic objects that form a *domain*—a single TUXEDO application. The classes defined in the Core Sub-MIB are presented in Figure 17.4. The classes on the left side of the table have to do with the configuration of an application. The classes on the right side of the table contain information stored or used by the TUXEDO System when an application is active.

Class Name	Description	Class Name	Description
T_DOMAIN	Global attributes	T_CLIENT	Clients
T_MACHINE	Machines	T_BRIDGE	Network Connections
T_GROUP	Server Queues	T_DEVICE	TUXEDO Devices
T_QUEUE	Server Queues	T_MSG	Message Queues
T_SERVER	Servers	T_SVCGRP	Active Services
T_SERVICE	Services	T_TRANSACTION	Transactions
T_ROUTING	Routing Criteria	T_TLISTEN	Active **tlisten** programs
		T_TLOG	Transaction Log
		T_ULOG	Userlog

Figure 17.4   **Classes in the Core Sub-MIB**

17.2.1 The Role of the Core MIB

The Core MIB is the main information repository used by the TUXEDO System to control the operation and configuration of the application. When you configure an application via the UBBCONFIG file or the **xtuxadm** interface, you implicitly define objects in the persistent part of the Core MIB—the classes on the left table in Figure 17.4. The persistent part of the MIB is stored in the TUXCONFIG file, and it changes only when you change your application configuration.

When an application is active, the Core MIB contains classes related to the run-time activity of your application. You can use this information to monitor the behavior of your application. In Chapter 15, "Application Administration and Monitoring," we discussed how you can monitor your application with the different interfaces and utilities provided with the TUXEDO System. In the following sections, we will provide an overview of the classes that deal with the basic structure and activity of your application. Figure 17.5 shows these classes and their relationships. The arrows indicate an "are-associated-with" relationship. For example, a domain is associated with a particular set of machines. The dotted arrows show implicit relationships defined when a server is built and the application server becomes active. We will discuss this in more detail later in this chapter.

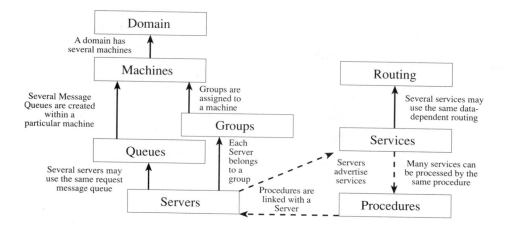

Figure 17.5 **The Persistent Part of the Core Sub-MIB**

17.2.2 Domain and Machines

The TUXEDO application described by the Core Sub-MIB is a domain. A domain represents a collection of machines and resources that you want to administer as a unit. Domains can be set up based on application function, security needs, or geographical location. A bank is a good example of an organization in which several domains may exist: a bank offers many different business services through its branches, loan and mortgage offices, interbank business, and financial investments. The bank also needs a payroll application that may be running independently from the activities at branches and loan offices. These business services typically operate as *federated applications*. Each application in the federation is a domain administered independently from the other domains. In Chapter 18, we will discuss how federated domains can interoperate to form bigger applications.

To define a domain, you first identify the computers required for the execution of the application servers. These machines are usually connected to the same network, and they may be controlled by different operating system environments—for example, Unix, Windows NT, and NetWare. Then, you define the global attributes that apply to the domain. These attributes are defined in the domain class (T_DOMAIN). Figure 17.6 illustrates some of these attributes. For example, the TA_IPCKEY attribute specifies the address of the Bulletin Board. The TA_MASTER attribute is another important attribute. It identifies the Master machine—the machine that is in charge of monitoring the administrative activities of other machines within the domain. We discussed the Master concept in Chapter 16, "Failure Handling."

The other attributes in the T_DOMAIN class specify the domain identifier, the security options used to authenticate clients and authorize access to services, and policies such as the distribution model, the load balancing policy, and the default event notification policy. The T_DOMAIN class also keeps the limits of the domain, such as the maximum number of clients, servers, transactions, buffer types, machines, queues, and services.

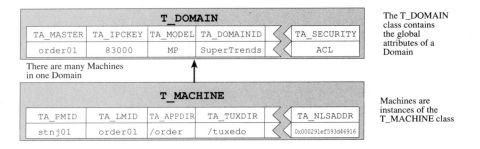

Figure 17.6   Relationship between Domain and Machines

The machine class (T_MACHINE) defines the physical environment within the domain. Each machine in the T_MACHINE class contains a set of attributes that define the TUXEDO environment on that machine (see Figs. 17.6 and 17.7). For example, the TA_PMID attribute contains the name of the machine in the network (for example, "stnj01"). On UNIX systems, this name is often the same as the value returned by the *"uname -n"* command. The TA_LMID attribute contains a logical name that is used as an identifier for this machine in other classes. This logical name allows dynamic changes to the physical environment without impacting the rest of the TMIB. For example, a computer change could result in a new TA_PMID value but, because the TA_LMID remains the same, the rest of the TMIB does not need to change. TA_LMID is also referenced in other TMIB classes.

An Instance of the T_MACHINE Class		
Attribute	Value	Attribute Description
TA_PMID	stnj01	The physical machine name
TA_LMID	order01	The logical machine name
TA_TUXDIR	/usr/tuxedo	The directory with the TUXEDO software
TA_APPDIR	/order	The directory with the application code
TA_TUXCONFIG	/order/tuxconfig	The persistant part of the MIB
TA_BRIDGE	/dev/tcp	Network device used for internode communication
TA_NADDR	0x0002f54393d46916	Network address used for internode communication
TA_NLSADDR	0x000291ef593d46916	Network address used by the TUXEDO listener
...	...	...

Figure 17.7   An Example of an Entity of the Class T_MACHINE

Other attributes define the network addressing, statistics, metrics, boundaries, such as the maximum number of concurrent clients and servers, and the location of the resources within this machine. Examples of these resources are the location of the TUXEDO System software (TA_TUXDIR), and the location of the application code (TA_APPDIR), and the network address (TA_NADDR) and network device (TA_BRIDGE) that define a controlled "entry point" to the machine. This entry point is used by TUXEDO System to establish network connections that channel the service requests between the machines in the domain. Certain attributes that appear in the T_DOMAIN class also appear in the T_MACHINE class. You can define these attributes in the T_MACHINE class to override the global values specified for the same attribute in the T_DOMAIN class. For example, you can use the TA_APPDIR attribute to override the generic location of the application software specified in the T_DOMAIN class.

Once a domain is fully configured (that is, the Core MIB is defined), the administrator can activate the domain. This operation activates all servers defined in the MIB on their corresponding locations. The TUXEDO application is now *active* and client programs can *join* the application and start requesting services.

17.2.3 Servers, Groups, and Queues

Once the physical structure of the domain is defined, you can start deploying the application servers on the different machines in the domain. Deploying servers means assigning machines as the execution environment of these servers and propagating the servers' code to those machines. A general criterion for server deployment is to decrease access time to resources by locating the servers as close as possible to the resources that they will access. Another criterion is to improve throughput by locating servers with heavy loads on machines with more available CPU cycles.

The TUXEDO System allows related servers to be grouped under an entity known as a *Server Group* (or called a *group*). Groups are used as a unit of activation, deactivation, migration, and routing. They also are used to cluster servers around an instance of a resource manager. For example, servers that access the same database should be defined under the same group. By doing so, the application can maximize interaction between the TUXEDO System and the Database System for transaction processing.

A group is defined as an object in the class T_GROUP (see Fig. 17.8) with attributes specifying a group name (TA_SRVGRP), a unique group number (TA_GRPNO), and the logical machine name (TA_LMID) on which the group of servers will run. You can also specify a backup machine that is used to allow group migration across machines. When a group migrates to the backup machine, all servers associated with the group are deactivated and then reactivated on the defined backup machine.

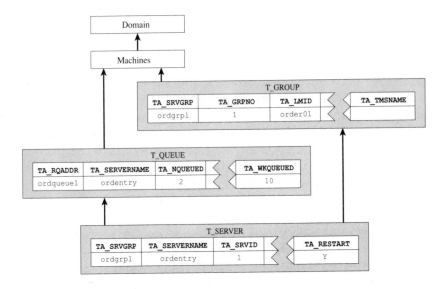

Figure 17.8 **Relationships between Machines, Queues, Groups, and Servers**

Other attributes of the T_GROUP class will be required only if there is a transaction-enabled resource manager used by the servers in the group. These attributes allow a direct association of the server group with a particular resource (for example, a database) that is controlled by the resource manager. In Chapter 14, we discussed the transactional aspect of the TUXEDO System. You may recall that service requests issued within a transaction infect servers associated with a transaction-enabled resource manager. You can control this transaction infection administratively in the following ways:

- By setting the TA_TMSNAME attribute to *NONE*, you can prevent transaction infection—any transactional requests to a service advertised by the group will be rejected.

- By setting the TA_TMSNAME attribute to *NULL*, you allow the transaction infection to be passed through the server to any further service requests. This was called "carrying the transaction infection" in Chapter 14, "Transactions in the TUXEDO System." Remember that transactional service requests to a nontransactional group will fail unless you specify the **TPNOTRAN** flag on **tpcall** or **tpacall**.

- For groups associated with XA-compliant resource managers, you build a customized **TMS** with the XA libraries provided with the resource manager's software. You can use the **buildtms** command to build this customized TMS, and then you specify its name in the TA_TMSNAME attribute of the groups using the resource manager.

Groups are one of the key conceptual elements used by the TUXEDO system to achieve location transparency. Administrators explicitly associate servers with a group. This association creates a transitive association between the servers in the group and the machine associated with the group—servers are associated with a group, and a group is associated with a machine. This transitive association allows an entire set of related servers (the group) to be migrated as a unit to other machines providing, in this way, an important element for fault tolerance and high availability. Although a group cannot span machines, a group can "migrate" between machines. When a group migrates to another machine, all servers associated with the group are shut down and then restarted on the new target machine. Groups are also used in the definition of the data-dependent routing criteria assigned to a service. Therefore, this also creates a transitive association that allows routing criteria specifications to remain unchanged when there is a group migration. Transactions also are associated with groups instead of individual servers. This allows transactional operations like recovery to work even after a group migration.

Servers are defined in the server class (T_SERVER), which contains attributes like the name of the executable code (TA_SERVERNAME) and the name of the group (TA_SRVGRP) to which this server is assigned. Other attributes allow a finer control over the queuing model used by the server, the server's restart characteristics, the command line options for the server, the number of replicas (server instances) for the server, and whether or not the server will provide "conversational services." The rest of the attributes provide run-time statistics and metrics that are used by the TUXEDO System to control the load on each server.

In Chapter 6, "The Anatomy of a TUXEDO Application," we explained how the TUXEDO System uses message queues to deliver service requests to servers. By default, each server has its own message queue (SSSQ), but this model can be overridden to MSSQ. You can do this by using the TA_RQADDR attribute in the T_SERVER class to assign servers to a particular queue. For example, in Figure 17.9, the TA_RQADDR has been set to "ordqueue1"—the logical name given by the administrator to the message queue. This name is used to link together all the servers that use the same MSSQ. These servers must be defined in the same group.

Message queues are run-time implementation entities that are automatically created when a server is activated. They are internal to the TUXEDO System and cannot be accessed directly by the application programmer through the ATMI interface. The T_QUEUE class keeps the attributes of the message queues associated with active servers. The T_QUEUE attributes specify information about the address and location of the queue, the server associated with the queue, and a set of metrics that keeps track of the activity on the queue. Some of these metrics are the workload (TA_WKQUEUED) and the number of service requests (TA_NQUEUED) currently queued. These metrics are used by the load balancing algorithm to assign a particular service request to a server.

An Instance of the T_SERVER Class		
Attribute	Value	Description
TA_SERVERNAME	ordentry	The name of the executable file
TA_SRVID	1	The server identification number
TA_SRVGRP	ordgrpl	The name of the server group
TA_GRPNO	1	The server group number
TA_RQADDR	ordqueue1	The symbolic name of the server's request queue
TA_MIN	2	The minimum number of instances of this server
TA_MAX	4	The maximum number of instances of this server
...	...	...

Figure 17.9   An Example of an Entity of the Class T_SERVER

17.2.4 Services, Procedures, and Routing

Services are defined by application programmers to encapsulate business functions, and they are associated with an application procedure bundled into a server. We have already described the development process involved in the definition of a service and how services are dynamically advertised in the Core MIB when a server becomes active. The association between a service and a server is part of the server itself, and it is normally specified when the server is created or linked. A server may be configured with many services, and a service may be configured in several different servers. Replicated services can be defined in TUXEDO to provide high availability and load balancing across machines. Advertised services are also known as *active services*.

The Core MIB maintains a class of active services (the T_SVCGRP class), as depicted in Figure 17.10. This class maintains an association created at run-time between a service, the server advertising the service, and the corresponding server group. The T_SVCGRP class also maintains a set of metrics that describe the amount of work performed by the service. You can use this class to change the state of the service. For example, you can *suspend* a service or force a server to *activate* (advertise) or *inactivate* (unadvertise) a particular service. You may want to suspend processing of a service to prevent access to the service at certain times of the day.

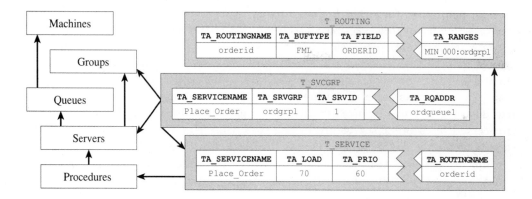

Figure 17.10   Services, Procedures, and Routing

You can also configure the values of some of the attributes of a service. The predefined attributes of a service are kept in the service class (T_SERVICE). You can specify the following attributes: the relative workload of the service, the dequeuing priority, the time limit for processing a request using the service, and the list of buffer types accepted by the service. For example, you may want to give a higher workload to the "Place_Order" service and a higher priority to the "Get_Customer" service. Specifying a higher workload helps the TUXEDO System's load balancing mechanism in making run-time routing decisions. On the other hand, specifying a higher priority attribute results in faster dequeuing for requests to that service.

Other attributes of T_SERVICE class specify the data-dependent routing and transaction control (AUTOTRAN and time-out) characteristics that should be used by the TUXEDO System when requests are issued to the service. The data-dependent routing attribute permits selective routing between a set of replicated services. Routing to a service is done, depending on the contents of the request's data. This feature allows administrators to split application processing across different machines or provide support for different implementations with a behavior dependent on the context in which the corresponding service is invoked. This feature is transparent to requestors (clients) and providers (servers). You can dynamically change the routing attribute assigned to a particular service by updating the TMIB.

The specification of data-dependent routing criteria is done in the routing class (T_ROUTING). The data-dependent routing attribute in the service class (T_SERVICE) is a reference to a routing criterion name in the T_ROUTING class. A routing criterion contains attributes such as a logical name (TA_ROUTINGNAME), the field used for routing TA_FIELDID, and a specification indicating the server groups in charge of processing requests satisfying selected range values for the specified field (TA_RANGES). For example, the service "Place_Order" may be processed differently depending on the item ordered by the customer. The administrator first specifies a routing criterion so that items with product code between 1 and 999 will be processed by server group "ordgrp1," and the rest will be processed by another server group G2. To enable routing, you define a routing attribute for the "Place_Order" service in the service class. When the servers in groups ordgrp1 and G2 become active, they will advertise the "Place_Order" service, and data-dependent routing is then automatically performed by the TUXEDO run-time system.

17.2.5 Clients

In Part II, "Overview of the TUXEDO System," we defined a TUXEDO client and explained the programming environment provided by the TUXEDO System for creating clients. The location of a client is dependent upon the design of the application, but they usually reside very close to where input data is gathered from sources "outside" the application. Clients are run on a workstation or on a machine specified as part of the domain.

Clients running on a server machine in the domain are invoked by a user logged in to that machine. They usually gather input data from a device (such as terminal) connected to this machine. Clients configured in this way require that the machine be an active machine—that is, such a machine already booted by the TUXEDO System administrator. Clients running on a workstation communicate with a workstation handler that is active on a machine in the domain. Workstation handlers are special TUXEDO processes that must be defined in the Core MIB and that act as surrogate local clients for the workstation clients.

When a client joins a TUXEDO application by a successful call to **tpinit** (as described in Chapter 9, "Joining and Leaving the Application"), an object is created in the T_CLIENT class. Figure 17.11 shows an example. Attributes for each client include a system generated identifier for the client, the client name, the user name, the client status, and a complete set of metrics recording the client's activities—for example, the number of transactions and requests that have been performed. You can retrieve these attributes and correlate the clients' activities with the operation of your application.

17.3 Administering TUXEDO Security—The ACL Sub-MIB

In Chapter 9, "Joining and Leaving the Application," and Chaper 15, "Application Administration and Monitoring," we discussed security aspects related to clients and servers that want to join a TUXEDO application. We explained why all server programs are *trusted* and execute on behalf of the TUXEDO administrator. We also explained that clients are nontrusted and that end users running these programs are authenticated when their client programs join the TUXEDO application. In this section, we discuss security from the perspective of the application administrator.

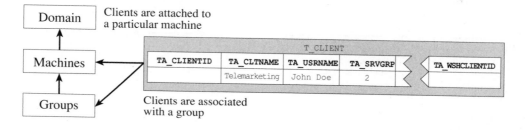

Figure 17.11   Clients

17.3.1 The Role of the ACL Sub-MIB

You can use the operating system security facilities to establish a trusted base for your servers, application services, and the resources used by the TUXEDO System. On POSIX systems, for example, resources such as the shared memory and message queues, can be restricted with operating system permissions, so that only the administrator can have access to these resources. After establishing the trusted base, you can use the security facilities provided by the TUXEDO System to protect client access to the application or to particular services, application queues, and events.

You define your application security options in the T_DOMAIN class. In this class, you can specify your identity and the security type used by your TUXEDO application. The security type attribute (TA_SECURITY) specifies the authentication type and the authorization level enforced by the TUXEDO System when the application is active. For example, you can enable the access control facility by setting the TA_SECURITY attribute to ACL or to ACL_MANDATORY. We explained the meaning of these values in Chapter 15, "Application Administration and Monitoring."

The TUXEDO access control facility is controlled by the ACL Sub-MIB. This sub-MIB specifies *principals* and *access control lists* for application services, application queues, and events. Figure 17.12 shows the relationships between the classes in the ACL MIB and the classes in the Core MIB. Principals are nontrusted entities. They require authentication and authorization. Principals are assigned to a Principal Group. A Principal Group allows administrators to give the same permissions to a set of principals. The permissions specified by an Access Control List defines the access for executing a service, storing a message on an application queue, or posting an event.

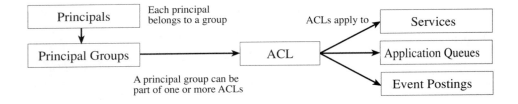

Figure 17.12   The ACL Sub-MIB

17.3.2 Principals and Principal Groups

In practice, principals are the application administrator, application operators, end users, and remote domain names that can access a TUXEDO application. You specify principals in the T_ACLPRINCIPAL class (as shown in Fig. 17.13). A principal has a name, a numeric credential, and is associated with a group of principals (also called an ACL group). For example, the principal with name "John Doe" has credential "101" and belongs to the "OrderTakers" ACL group (see Fig. 17.14). Principals also have a password. When a client joins a TUXEDO application on behalf of a particular principal (end user), it authenticates by providing the application password, the end user's name, and end user's password. Once a client is authenticated, all requests performed by the client will carry the end user's credential. Thus, when "John Doe" is authenticated, all of his requests will carry his identity ("101") for authorization purposes.

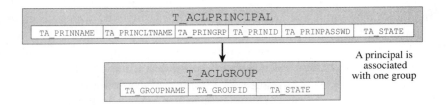

Figure 17.13   Principals and Principal Groups

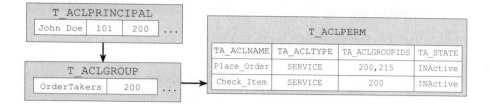

Figure 17.14 **Access Control Lists**

Groups of principals are specified in the T_ACLGROUP class (see Fig. 17.13). A *Principal Group* has two attributes: a name and a group identifier. For example, the "OrderTakers" group might have identifier "200" (see Fig. 17.14). Principal Groups are used in the definition of access control lists. Principal Groups simplify security management by allowing administrators to control authorization with a broader scope than at the individual level. This reduces the amount of administrative work required for ACL entries. For example, if a principal is removed from the T_ACLPRINCIPAL class, then the associations between a Principal Group and an access control list do not need to change. Also, the same set of permissions can be easily enforced for a group of principals. For instance, when a group is included in an access control list, then all principals in that group have the same access permissions to that entity. If your application needs authorization for individuals, then you could assign unique group identifiers to each individual.

17.3.3 Access Control Lists

An *access control list* (ACL) is a list that specifies which Principal Groups are authorized to access TUXEDO System objects. You can define ACLs for service, event, and application queue names. These ACLs are specified in the T_ACLPERM class with the following attributes (see Fig. 17.14): the name of the entity for which authorization is controlled, the type of authorization (execute a service, post an event, dequeue or enqueue a message in an application queue), and the list of Principal Groups that are granted the authorization type.

For example, the "Check_Item" and the "Place_Order" services can have ACLs that grant execution permission to the group "OrderTakers," that is, to all principals that belong to the "OrderTakers" group. The TUXEDO System uses the ACL MIB and the credential information included with every service request to find if the principal has access to the requested service, queue, or event.

17.4   Administering Workstations—The /WS Sub-MIB

For security, convenience, available interfaces, or performance reasons, administrators can require that clients run on a workstation. Administrators define the environment required to control these workstation clients in an extension of the Core MIB called the WS Sub-MIB. This MIB specifies the information required to enable the TUXEDO/WS component to control access to your application from multiple workstations.

17.4.1 The Role of the WS MIB

In Chapter 6, "The Anatomy of a TUXEDO Application," we introduced the workstation handling environment provided by the TUXEDO System. This TUXEDO subsystem is called /WS, and consists of three software elements: the workstation client (WSC) library, the workstation listener (**WSL**) executable, and the workstation handler (**WSH**) executable. Clients using the WSC library can use ATMI to request application services from a TUXEDO application (see Fig. 17.15). The workstation listener acts as the initial point of contact for workstation clients and has the task of assigning workstation handlers to manage the communications with the workstation. The workstation handler acts as surrogate local client for the workstation and manages all the communications with the application.

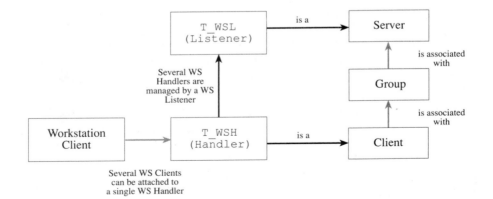

Figure 17.15   The /WS Sub-MIB

The WS MIB specifies information about workstation listeners and workstation handlers. You can specify new workstation listeners in the T_WSL class, and you can retrieve information about active workstation handlers from the T_WSH class. Figure 17.15 depicts the relationships between these classes and the classes in the Core MIB.

17.4.2 Workstation Clients

Workstation clients usually reside on a personal computer (PC), and they act as a "front end" to the application. They are responsible for gathering the data of input requests from end users. For example, a hotel reservations application may use the graphical capabilities of the PC to present rooms available on one window while on a different window it gathers the reservation data to be sent to a TUXEDO server which updates the reservation database.

Workstation clients join a TUXEDO application as any other client. The difference is that a workstation client has to connect to a particular machine within the application domain. This connection is performed transparently by the TUXEDO System when the workstation client calls **tpinit** to join the application. The connection is made to a workstation listener previously assigned by the application administrator. The workstation listener assigns a workstation handler to the workstation, and this handler performs all the necessary authentication and subsequent communications with the application.

The run-time information about workstation clients is kept in the T_CLIENT class of the Core MIB.

17.4.3 Workstation Listeners

You can enable workstation access by defining a workstation listener (**WSL**) in the T_WSL class. The **WSL** listens for connections requested by workstation clients on a network address that you assign. The **WSL** uses the information in the T_WSH class to assign each workstation to a **WSH**.

The T_WSL class is a derivation of the T_SERVER class of the Core MIB. That is, workstation listeners are servers with additional attributes. Because a **WSL** is a server, its attributes are automatically reflected in the T_SERVER class. Each **WSL** must be explicitly associated with a server group. Each **WSL** defined in the T_WSL class contains the following attributes: the network address used for listening for workstation client connections, the minimum and maximum number of allowed handlers, the maximum number of workstation clients supported by each handler (the multiplexing level), and the current number of active handlers associated with this **WSL**. You can also distribute the workstation load by defining several **WSLs** within a domain.

17.4.4 Workstation Handlers

Workstation handlers (**WSH**) manage the communication with a workstation. Each **WSH** acts as a surrogate local client for a set of workstation clients and multiplexes all requests and replies with a particular workstation over a single connection. Handlers are automatically spawned by a **WSL** as the workstation load increases.

The T_WSH class provides information about the run-time activities performed by each **WSH**. The T_WSH class is a derivation of the T_CLIENT class. That is, each **WSH** is a TUXEDO client with additional attributes that specify metrics, such as the current number of clients attached to the handler, information about the network activity, and the amount of work performed by the handler. The **WSL** uses these values to balance workstation assignments to the available handlers. **WSH**s are associated with the same server group as its **WSL**.

17.5   Administering Application Queues—The /Q Sub-MIB

In Chapter 3, "Communication and Administration Paradigms for Distributed Business Applications," and Chapter 4, "Application Development—Overview," we introduced application queuing, and we discussed the advantages of this time-independent communication mechanism. The contents and the use of application queues are entirely under the control of the application designer. In the general case, clients and servers can enqueue and dequeue messages as dictated by the application semantics. However, the structure of an application queue is defined by a TUXEDO administrator. The TUXEDO /Q subsystem provides the administrative environment needed for managing and controlling access to application queues. We already discussed this environment in Chapter 12, "Application Queues," and in this section we discuss the information stored in the /Q Sub-MIB.

17.5.1 The Role of the /Q Sub-MIB

TUXEDO/Q provides the administrative environment required for managing and controlling access to application queues. This environment consists of the /Q Sub-MIB, the QM transaction-based queue manager, the **TMQUEUE** administrative server, and the **TMQFORWARD** administrative server. The /Q Sub-MIB defines the structure of the application queues. The queue manager controls the physical storage assigned to the application queues. The TUXEDO administrative servers use the queue manager to store messages and manage access to a set of application queues.

Figure 17.16 illustrates the different classes in the /Q Sub-MIB. There are four basic classes: queue spaces, queues, messages, and transactions. Messages are stored on a queue, and queues are defined within a particular queue space. Queuing and dequeuing is done within a transaction. We will discuss queue spaces, queues, and messages in more detail in the following sections.

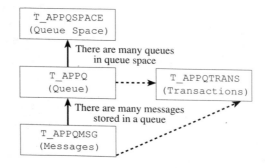

Figure 17.16 **The /Q Sub-MIB**

17.5.2 Queue Spaces

A queue space defines a storage location for queues and messages. Queue spaces are stored as system files on a TUXEDO file-system. TUXEDO file-systems provide a convenient way to arrange disk space and enhance reliability by storing data directly on a disk. A queue space can easily be created by adding a new object to the T_APPQSPACE class. The T_APPQSPACE class defines the attributes associated with a particular queue space, such as the queue space name, configuration information for the queue manager, the maximum number of queues, and the maximum messages allowed in the queue space. Once a queue space exists, you can create application queues.

By grouping queues under a queue space, you can share resources like disk space and reduce the administrative overhead associated with each queue. You can configure access to queue space by defining a server group and a **TMQUEUE** server in the Core MIB. A queue space is attached to a particular machine, and it can be accessed only on that machine. However, you can allow access to the queue space from multiple server groups or even multiple applications, but the corresponding **TMQUEUE** servers must be running on the same machine.

17.5.3 Queues

An application queue is a named data structure that stores messages according to an ordering criterion specified when the queue is created. Application queues are always created within a particular queue space. You can define new application queues by adding objects to the T_APPQ *class*. This class allows you to define a new queue or change the characteristics of an existing queue. Each queue in the class contains the following attributes: a queue name, the name of the queue space storing the *queue*, a queue ordering criterion, an out-of-order enqueuing criterion, *low*- and high-threshold values for the number of messages on the queue, and a command that is executed when a high-threshold value is reached.

You can use the queue ordering attribute to specify the order in which messages are enqueued. For example, "priority, FIFO" specifies that messages are dequeued by priority and that messages of equal priority are dequeued in FIFO order. Sometimes, application programmers may need to control the order of messages in a queue. To use this feature, you must enable the "out-of-order" attribute. When this attribute is defined, programmers can specify an override in **tpenqueue** so that a message is stored at the top of the queue or ahead of another message.

The normal behavior of the /Q queue manager is to put a message back on the queue when the transaction containing the dequeuing operation is rolled back. However, you can control the number of times that this is allowed to happen. This option gives applications an opportunity to retry message processing a limited number of times. Messages that reach the retry limit are automatically moved to an *error queue* that you can specify when you create the queue space.

You can also use the **TMQFORWARD** administrative server to forward messages stored on a queue to a particular application service. The high threshold can be used to automate the administration or error reporting. A simple threshold command might send mail to the administrator. It might also be used to activate a **TMQFORWARD** command. In fact, **TMQFORWARD** has a command line option to deactivate itself when there are no messages to process. The high-threshold command can be used to reactivate **TMQFORWARD** when there are a batch of messages to process. You can also specify if the application service should be invoked outside of a transaction, if it should not send a reply, or if failures should be stored on a specified failure queue.

17.5.4 Messages

Messages are the objects stored within a queue as the result of a call to **tpenqueue**. A message is removed from a queue when the application code dequeues the message with **tpdequeue**. However, at any time, administrators can delete messages, move messages from one queue to another queue, or change the priority or the birth time of a set of messages.

You can perform these operations using the T_APPQMSG class. This class represents all messages stored in /Q queues. Within the T_APPQMSG class, a message is uniquely identified by specifying a message identifier, a queue name, and a queue space name. Other attributes of the message reflect the parameters used by the application when the message was enqueued. These attributes specify the enqueuing priority, the dequeuing time, and the correlation identifier. The T_APPQMSG class also keeps other information, such as the number of current retries attempted on a message and the message length. Note that the actual contents of the message is not an attribute of the class. Thus, you can obtain or override certain attributes, but you cannot alter or retrieve the contents of a message via the TMIB.

17.6   Administering Application and System Events— The Event Sub-MIB

The TUXEDO EventBroker facility allows application designers to write code that reacts to events generated from different parts of the application (a client or a service) or by the TUXEDO System. Events are generated by *posters* and received by *subscribers*. Posters use **tppost** to generate an event and subscribers use **tpsubscribe** to generate a subscription (we introduced these concepts in Chapter 13, "Event-Based Communication"). These event subscriptions are kept in the Event Sub-MIB.

17.6.1 The Role of the Event Sub-MIB

Events come in two "flavors:" application events and systems events. Application designers and administrators can define a set of application events. The semantics of these application events are understood only by the application code. System events are generated by the TUXEDO run-time system when important changes in the TMIB are detected. Systems events are published in the TUXEDO System Manual Pages (see EVENTS(5) in [TUXEDO]). Application programs (clients or services) can subscribe to these system events. To prevent naming conflicts between system and application events, the system event names start with a dot ("."). An example is the event ".SysMachineState" that indicates a state change for a particular machine. Application programs cannot post events that begin with a dot, but they can subscribe to any system events.

The combination of event subscriptions with the ability to change the TMIB via the TMIB Interface allows administrators and application designers to write self-adapting applications. When a failure is detected via a system event notification, an administrative program could perform the corrective measures. For example, the program could activate servers on a backup machine when it detects a failure on the primary machine.

Figure 17.17 illustrates event posters generating events. These events are distributed by the EventBroker as *event notifications* to all subscribers. An optional TUXEDO typed buffer can be included with each event posting and is delivered to the event subscribers. Actions can deliver the event to clients, services, application queues, the TUXEDO log file, and an operating system command. The characteristics of an event subscription are kept in the Event Sub-MIB. You can use the Event Sub-MIB to obtain the characteristics of current event subscriptions, define new subscriptions, or invalidate subscriptions. To enable both system event and application event notification, you need to define the system event broker (**TMSYSEVT**) and the application event broker (**TMUSREVT**) in the Core MIB.

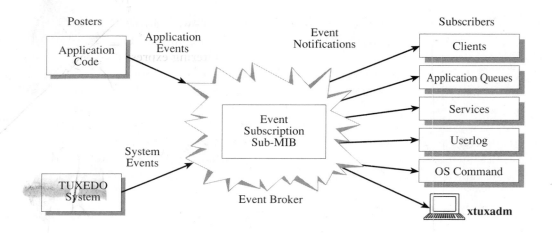

Figure 17.17   Application and System Events

Event subscriptions can be temporary or persistent. Persistent subscriptions survive across application activations and are removed only by a call to **tpunsubscribe** or by the administrator through the Event MIB. Temporary subscriptions are automatically removed by the EventBroker when it detects that the corresponding target is no longer active.

The Event Sub-MIB contains five types of event subscriptions:

- Client Notifications (T_EVENT_CLIENT class) indicate which events trigger an unsolicited message to a client.

- Service Notifications (T_EVENT_SERVICE class) indicate which events trigger a request to an application service.

- Application Queue Notifications (T_EVENT_QUEUE class) indicate which events send a message to an application queue.

- System Command Notifications (T_EVENT_COMMAND class) indicate which events trigger an operating system command.

■ Log File Notifications (T_EVENT_USERLOG class) indicate which events generate a record in the central event log (ULOG).

We will discuss these classes in the following sections.

17.6.2 Client Notification

Event subscriptions generated by clients are kept in the Client Notification class (T_EVENT_CLIENT). Each subscription has the following attributes: the identity of the client, an event subscription expression that controls which events can generate a notification message to this client, and a filtering expression that filters events based upon the contents of the data posted with the event. Clients can be notified of events via unsolicited notification messages.

Client notifications are temporary event subscriptions—they are removed when a client terminates. Clients typically remove these subscriptions by calling **tpunsubscribe**. Temporary event subscriptions are also automatically removed by the EventBroker when it detects that a client has left the application. Administrators can also explicitly remove subscriptions with the TMIB Interface.

17.6.3 Service Notification

Applications can also receive event notifications via the invocation of an application service. These event subscriptions are kept in the service notification class (T_EVENT_SERVICE). The subscriptions in this class contain the following attributes: the event subscription expression, the filtering expression, and the service name.

The service invocation can be done within or outside the poster's transaction. Thus, a service failure can eventually roll back the poster's transaction. Administrators can also force the service invocation to be transactional by enabling the automatic transaction start attribute (TA_AUTOTRAN) in the T_SERVICE class of the Core MIB.

17.6.4 Application Queue Notification

An application can receive event notifications on an application queue. Event subscriptions of this type are kept in the application queue notification class (T_EVENT_QUEUE). The subscriptions in this class contain all attributes necessary to enqueue the event in an application queue. In particular, the queue space name, the queue name, and the queue control parameters (priority, birth time, and correlation identifier) are attributes of this class. The other attributes contain the event subscription expression and the filtering expression.

An advantage of the application queue notification is that event messages are stored on disk and survive system crashes. This is an important feature to be considered when the application is designed: those events that cannot be lost should be sent to an application queue. Note that application queue notifications can be done within the poster's transaction.

17.6.5 Command Notification

An event can trigger the execution of an operating system command. Event subscriptions of this type are kept in the command notification class (T_EVENT_COMMAND). Entities in this class contain an attribute with the system command specification. This command is triggered when an event matches the event subscription expression and a filtering expression specified as attributes of the subscription.

17.6.6 Log File Notification

The TUXEDO System usually writes system events to the ULOG file. System events are automatically written to this log file when the TUXEDO EventBroker is not active. These system events contain detailed information about error conditions, failures, warnings, and system status. Each record written to the log contains a time stamp, the location where the event occurred, and a code identifying the event. Event subscriptions can also explicitly trigger this log-based notification. These event subscriptions are kept in the log notification class (T_EVENT_USERLOG) with attributes that specify the event and filtering expressions and the record that will be written to the log.

17.7   Summary

In this chapter we have reviewed the different parts of a TUXEDO application. We have explained the structure of the TUXEDO MIB, and what you can do with the TMIB. The TMIB Interface can be used to write specialized administrative programs. For example, you can use the TMIB Interface and the event facility to write self-adapting applications that change their structure when important state changes are detected in the TMIB. Otherwise, you can use the administrative tools and utilities provided by the TUXEDO System to create or monitor your application. With these tools, you can tune your application with a fine degree of granularity, and you can control the configuration and monitoring process from a single location.

18 Getting Applications to Work Together

ADMINISTRATION

In previous chapters, we discussed how the TUXEDO client/server model allows client programs to invoke services offered by one or more server programs without having to know where these servers are located in the computer network. This location transparency in the TUXEDO client/server model is the key for distribution control and interoperability. Application programmers always see the same programming interface regardless of where services are offered, and application administrators have complete control over the distribution of servers and services. These characteristics can be extended across multiple applications with the TUXEDO Domains facility. The TUXEDO Domains facility is a family of interoperability solutions that allow administrators to expand the scope of their applications to include access to other TUXEDO or non-TUXEDO applications.

In this chapter, we will discuss how TUXEDO administrators can achieve interapplication cooperation with the TUXEDO client/server model. We will also discuss the functionality provided by the TUXEDO Domains, SNA, OSI TP, and DCE interoperability facilities.

18.1 When to Use Domains

We have already explored how an administrator configures an application in the TUXEDO Core MIB. This MIB defines the basic structure of a TUXEDO application—the collection of machines, servers, and other shared resources that are administered as a unit by the TUXEDO administrator. The TUXEDO application defined by the Core MIB is also called a *domain*. Throughout this section, we use the terms *domain* and *application* interchangeably.

By definition, a TUXEDO domain is *autonomous*—that is, administered independently from other domains. Hence, the scope of the administrative tasks is a primary factor in the definition of a domain. Other factors can be the size of the application, the organizational policies within the enterprise, the secure trusted boundaries, and the groups of users that need access to shared resources and services.

A TUXEDO domain can cooperate with other domains to form large *federated applications*. This cooperation can be easily achieved with the TUXEDO Domains facility. This facility provides a set of administrative tools that allows administrators to specify the services that will be accessible across applications. The Domains facility preserves the characteristics of the TUXEDO programming interface and extends the scope of the model to allow clients to invoke services that are available on other domains. This concept is quite powerful: applications can grow or be partitioned without having to change existing application code.

Figure 18.1 illustrates an example of application cooperation. A catalog order company is growing and wants to organize its computer business operations around two separate applications: the Order Entry application and the Warehouse application. The Order Entry application controls order placement (for example, by telemarketing representatives, phone operators, electronic mail, the World Wide Web, and fax), order status, customer billing, and credit verification. The Warehouse application controls the stock of items in the catalog, updates to the catalog, shipping and delivery of orders to customers, and ordering supplies from different providers.

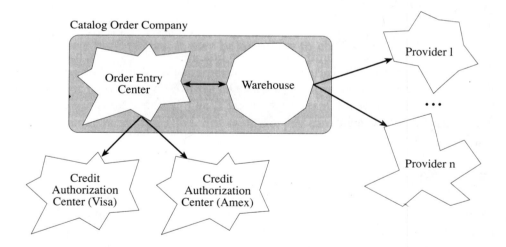

Figure 18.1   A Catalog Order System—An Example of Interapplication Cooperation

The Order Entry application could also interoperate with applications controlled by other companies. For example, a bank or several organizations that provide credit card verification and authorization. The Warehouse application could also interoperate with other companies' applications to purchase catalog items from different suppliers.

With the TUXEDO approach, distributed application cooperation can be endless. For example, the Catalog Order company could have several Order Entry centers and warehouses distributed around the country. Each Order Entry center could route orders to the warehouse closest to the delivery place. Order Entry centers could also share customer information for telemarketing purposes. Warehouses could interoperate to speed delivery so that items not found in one warehouse could be delivered from another warehouse, and so on.

The catalog company example shows different criteria for organizing domains: geographical location, interorganization policy, intercompany cooperation, and scalability. The TUXEDO System approach allows this application interoperability while maintaining location transparency and application independence. The TUXEDO Domains facility manages the data translation, the mapping between naming spaces, the transaction commitment protocols, and the security required for interapplication interoperability. We will explain this further in the following sections.

18.2　Naming Resources Across Domains

The cooperation between two applications cannot be done properly without an agreement between application administrators and programmers. Administrators need to agree on:

- the services that are *exported* or *imported* by each application
- the contracts provided by these services
- the communication protocols between applications (for example, TUXEDO, OSI TP or another)
- what are the required addressing and security parameters

On the other hand, application programmers need only know the contract required by the new services. Recall that a service contract consists of the following:

- the name of the service
- the service's required input parameters
- the specific processing on those inputs
- the output values or list of errors that will be returned to the client as a result of the processing
- the application protocol is the communication is conversation based

To preserve location transparency, client programmers should not know the difference between a service that has been imported from another application and a service offered by a server within the application. Also, programmers do not need to be involved in the negotiation of the cooperation agreement, and they can obtain the service contract from their administrators. Thus, enabling interapplication cooperation is considered to be an administrative task.

18.2.1 Importing and Exporting Services

Domains cooperate by allowing mutual service invocation. Administrators exchange information to define the environment needed for the cooperation of their applications. They *export* and *import* information about their applications. For example, the administrator of the Order Entry application may import the "Check_Item" and "Reorder_Item" services from the Warehouse application (see Fig. 18.2). These services can be used by the "Place_Order" service to find the availability of a particular stock item or to order an item that is not in stock. The Order Entry application administrator may also want to export the "Update_Order" service only to the Warehouse application to allow updates to the status of orders that require items not in stock and that have to be reordered from other providers.

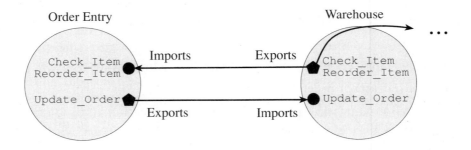

Figure 18.2   Importing and Exporting Services

Figure 18.2 depicts two domains, Order Entry and Warehouse. To each domain, the other is a *remote domain*. Order Entry has one *local service*, "Update_Order." Warehouse has two local services, "Check_Item" and "Reorder_Item." Each domain exports its local services to the other, and each domain imports the other domain's exported services. Thus, in the Order Entry domain, "Check_Item" is a remote service which has been imported into the Order Entry domain.

For a TUXEDO administrator, importing a service means the following:
- The code implementing the service executes in a remote domain.
- The TUXEDO System needs to be configured to obtain access to the remote domain that provides that service.
- The contract of the remote service may need to be normalized to the standards used by the TUXEDO application.
- The service contract for the imported service is made available to application programmers.

Exporting a service has the following meaning:
- The code implementing the service executes within the local domain.
- The TUXEDO System needs to be configured to allow access to the local service.
- The remote domain administrator obtains the contract of the exported service and the addressing information for how to get to the local domain that provides that service.

Once TUXEDO application administrators have reached an agreement on the information exported and imported between their domains, they each define a configuration in their own domain with the control information needed to effect cooperation between these applications.

Note that only application services can be imported or exported. Application queue names, event names, and system service names cannot be used across domains. However, application queue names can be mapped to a remote service. Also, a remote service could be set to receive an event notification.

18.2.2 Domains Configuration

The configuration defined by the TUXEDO administrator captures the information that a TUXEDO domain has about other domains. This information includes services imported from other domains, addressing and security parameters for contacting the known remote domains, services exported to these domains, and parameters for controlling access to exported services. The resources defined in the configuration and their relationships are illustrated in Figure 18.3.

These resources are the following:

- *Remote Domains*: Remote domains are "other" applications that are known by a particular TUXEDO domain; for example, in Figure 18.1, the Order Entry application knows how to access the Warehouse domain and one or more credit card authorization domains.

- *Remote Services*: Remote services are services imported from one or more remote domains; for example, the Order Entry application uses the Check_Item service from the Warehouse application.

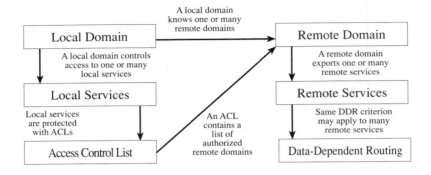

Figure 18.3   Resources in a Domain Configuration

- *Local Domains*: A local domain represents a "view" of a TUXEDO application that is exported by that domain to one or more remote domains; this view includes the set of local services available to remote domains and the control information needed by the remote domains to communicate with the TUXEDO application; a given domain may export different views to remote domains, thus giving separate "appearances" to different remote domains; a local domain also represents the TUXEDO system environment needed to provide access to the remote services imported from one or more remote domains.

- *Local Services*: Local services are services exported to other domains; for example, the Order Entry application exports the Update_Order service to the Warehouse domain—that is, the Update_Order service can be invoked from the Warehouse remote domain.

- *Data Dependent Routing*: Generally, this feature is used by the TUXEDO System to decide where to send requests to a service that is offered in several places, and in the domains context, this feature allows a request to be routed to a remote domain; the decision is made upon the contents of the request's data; for example, the Order Entry application administrator may import a service for credit verification (Verify_Credit) from several credit authorization centers, and by defining a data-dependent routing criterion on an input parameter (credit card type), the administrator instructs the TUXEDO System how to route a Verify_Credit request to the domain providing the authorization for the corresponding credit account.

■ *Access Control Lists*: Access Control Lists (ACLs) define groups of remote domains that can access a TUXEDO application; ACLs are assigned by TUXEDO administrators to one or more local services; for example, the Order Entry application administrator can use an ACL to allow access to the Update_Order local service only from the Warehouse domain.

The relationships between these resources are also illustrated in Figure 18.3. You can define these relationships in the TUXEDO Domains configuration. This configuration defines the "view" that a particular domain has of its "world"—remote services and domains. For example, the Order Entry application administrator defines a configuration with information about how to access the Warehouse and the Credit Authorization domains, and the services imported from and exported to these domains. Likewise, the administrator of the Warehouse application may also want to define a TUXEDO Domains configuration to access services in the Order Entry and the Provider domains. This configuration reflects the view that the Warehouse application has about its "world." Note that in Figure 18.1, the Warehouse domain does not know anything about the Credit Authorization domains, nor does the Order Entry domain know anything about the Provider domains.

We will explore the TUXEDO Domains configuration in more detail in the following section.

18.2.3 Configuring Access to Services in Other Domains

To enable interoperability between two domains, you must create a TUXEDO Domains configuration, and then, you define the TUXEDO administrative servers in the TMIB. In the following sections, we will explain how you can create the TUXEDO Domains configuration and what are the roles of the different administrative servers in the TUXEDO Domains architecture.

18.2.4 Creating a TUXEDO Domains Configuration

You can create a TUXEDO Domains configuration dynamically with **xtuxadm** or statically via an ASCII file, called the *DMCONFIG* file. At the time this book is being written, the **xtuxadm** configuration tool requires that you first configure the TUXEDO Domains administrative servers in the TMIB. Then, before you can specify local and remote domains, you must activate the Domains Administrative Server (**DMADM**). If you define a TUXEDO Domains configuration with the DMCONFIG file static, you need to compile this file with the **dmloadcf** utility. This utility constructs a binary configuration file, BDMCONFIG, that is then used by the **DMADM** server to control the run-time environment needed for interdomain cooperation. Note that to enable domain interoperability, you still need to define the TUXEDO Domains administrative servers in the TMIB.

18.2.5 TUXEDO Domains Administrative Servers

The TUXEDO System uses gateways to provide access to and from remote domains. A *gateway* acts as surrogate server in the TMIB for the services imported from one or more remote domains. That is, the gateway advertises the imported services within the TUXEDO application. Because imported services are advertised locally, they appear to be local services, and become accessible to clients and servers in the local domain. Gateways also control access to the local services exported by a TUXEDO application.

The TUXEDO System provides different types of gateways, each designed for a particular communications protocol. For example, there are gateways for communications with other TUXEDO domains, and for interoperability with other applications that use the OSI TP or the IBM LU6.2 protocols. We will discuss the functionality provided by these gateways later in this chapter.

In addition to gateway servers, the TUXEDO System uses two administrative servers to control dynamic changes to the TUXEDO Domains configuration. Each group of gateways requires an administrative server to control the "view" supported by a local domain. This server, **GWADM**, communicates with the "keeper" of the TUXEDO Domains configuration, the **DMADM** server, to extract or receive updates to the configuration of a local domain. The **DMADM** server automatically propagates any changes made to the TUXEDO Domains configuration to all active **GWADMs**.

We illustrated the TUXEDO Domains administrative environment in Figure 18.4. This figure shows the architecture of Warehouse domain. This application defines a local domain to control access from the Order Entry domain and to a Provider Domain. The assumption is that the Warehouse, Order Entry, and Provider domains use the same communications protocol (for example, the TUXEDO communications protocol).

A local domain also represents the environment needed by the TUXEDO System to provide access to remote domains. This means that a local domain is associated with a particular gateway type and with the server group that defines the gateways in the TMIB. This information must be specified when you define a local domain in the TUXEDO Domains configuration.

18.2.6 Specifying a TUXEDO Domains Configuration with the DMCONFIG File

Imagine that you are the administrator of the Order Entry application. Your task is to provide connectivity with the Warehouse and Credit Authorization applications, but first you need to understand what services are imported and exported by each application. We have illustrated these imported and exported services in Figure 18.5.

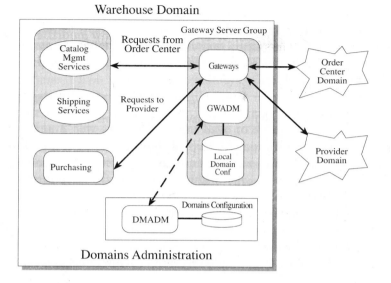

Figure 18.4   TUXEDO Domains Administrative Servers

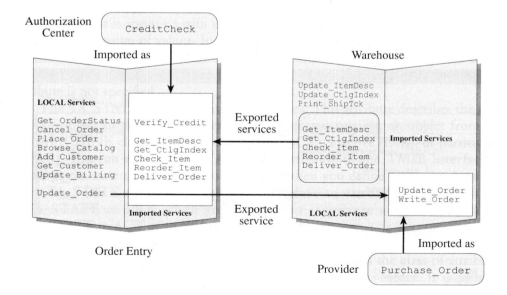

Figure 18.5   Imported and Exported Services

The Warehouse domain exports several services to the Order Entry domain. These services permit the implementation of an on-line catalog browser ("Get_ItemDesc" and "Get_CtlgIndex"), checking if catalog items are available in the warehouse ("Check_Item"), placing an order for items that are not in stock ("Reorder_Item"), and ordering the delivery of a particular catalog order ("Deliver_Order"). Also, the "CreditCheck" service needs to be imported from the Credit Authorization domain to provide credit card verification when new orders are placed by end users. Note that the "CreditCheck" service is imported from the Authorization Center under a different name—Order Entry calls it "Verify_Credit." The Order Entry domain also exports the "Update_Order" service to the Warehouse application. This service provides a notification mechanism when back ordered items have arrived at the warehouse.

With this information, you can now start creating a Domains configuration for the Order Entry domain. Using your preferred text editor, you create the DMCONFIG file as illustrated in Listing 18.1. This configuration file is divided into several sections. Each section identifies the resource types that we defined in Figure 18.2.

```
*DM_LOCAL_DOMAINS
FromToWarehouse  GWGRP=gw01 TYPE=TDOMAIN DOMAINID="SuperTrendsTCP"
ToCredit         GWGRP=gw02 TYPE=OSITP DOMAINID="SuperTrendsOSI"
*DM_REMOTE_DOMAINS
warehouse        TYPE=TDOMAIN DOMAINID="SuperTrendsWarehouse"
visa             TYPE=OSITP DOMAINID="VISA"
amex             TYPE=OSITP DOMAINID="AMEX"
*DM_TDOMAIN
FromToWarehouse  NWADDR="0x0002ff98c00b9d6d"  NWDEVICE="/dev/tcp"
warehouse        NWADDR="0x00020401c00b7d08"  NWDEVICE="/dev/tcp"
*DM_OSITP
# OSI TP addressing for ToCredit, visa-mc, and amex
...
*DM_LOCAL_SERVICES
Update_Order     LDOM=FromToWarehouse
*DM_REMOTE_SERVICES
Get_ItemDesc     LDOM=FromToWarehouse
Get_CtlgIndex    LDOM=FromToWarehouse RDOM=warehouse
Check_Item       LDOM=FromToWarehouse RDOM=warehouse
Reorder_Item     LDOM=FromToWarehouse RDOM=warehouse
Deliver_Order    LDOM=FromToWarehouse RDOM=warehouse
Verify_Credit    LDOM=ToCredit RNAME="CreditCheck" ROUTING=credit-type
*DM_ROUTING
credit-type FIELD=CreditType BUFTYPE="VIEW:credit" RANGES="'AX':amex,*:visa"
```

Listing 18.1 *TUXEDO Domains Configuration for the Order Entry Domain*

The section called *DM_LOCAL_DOMAINS contains the definition of local domains. Local domains can also be visualized as *access points* (or gateways) to and from other domains. Two gateways are defined: one that controls access to the Warehouse domain (called "FromToWarehouse") and another that controls access to the Credit Authorization domains (called "ToCredit"). The parameter GWGRP specifies the corresponding name of the server group in the TMIB to which these gateways belong. Each group of gateways is associated with a particular local domain. For example, the gateway group "gw01" contains a gateway administrative server (**GWADM**) and a TUXEDO gateway server (**TDOMAIN**). The parameter DOMAINID (the local domain identifier) defines a unique name assigned to the gateway. The domain type is an important parameter: the type indicates the protocol used by the gateways. The general rule is that a local domain can handle only communications with remote domains of the same type. A local domain can potentially communicate with all of the defined remote domains that use the same communications type.

Once you define the local domains, you can start defining remote domains in the *DM_REMOTE_DOMAINS section. A remote domain has a local name (e.g., "warehouse"), a type (e.g., TDOMAIN), and a domain identifier (e.g., "SuperTrendsWarehouse"). In our example, there is an entry for the Warehouse domain and two entries for the Credit Authorization centers known by the Order Entry domain ("visa" and "amex").

For each domain, you need to specify addressing information. This information is specified according to the domain type. In our example, we have the *DM_TDOMAIN section that describes addressing for domains of the type TDOMAIN (that is, TUXEDO to TUXEDO) and the *DM_OSITP section that describes the addressing required for domains using the OSI TP protocol. For the *DM_TDOMAIN section, we have two entries: one that specifies the entry point into the Warehouse remote domain and another that specifies the entry point to the Order Entry domain (represented by the "FromToWarehouse" local domain and used by the Warehouse domain to invoke the "Update_Order" service). We have illustrated this addressing information in Figure 18.6. Each entry contains a network address and a device type.

Having the addressing already resolved, you can now start describing the "exported" and "imported" services. Exported services are described in the *DM_LOCAL_SERVICES section, and imported services are described in the *DM_REMOTE_SERVICES section. For example, the Order Entry domain exports the "Update_Order" via the "FromToWarehouse" local domain.

The association between imported and exported services and domains is optional. For example, we choose to restrict access to the "Update_Order" local service via the "FromToWarehouse" local domain. That is, the "Update_Order" service is only exported through the "FromToWarehouse" domain. If this association is not specified, then any local domain can process requests to the

"Update_Order" service. The same applies to the definition of remote services. For example, we choose to specify the "Deliver_Order" remote service as a service associated with the "FromToWarehouse" local domain and the "warehouse" remote domain. If the association with the remote domain is not present, then the assumption is that any remote domain can process requests for this service.

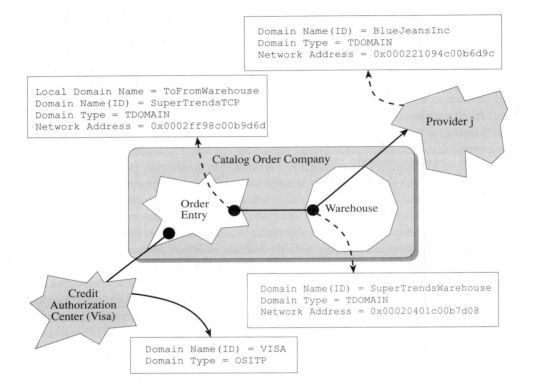

Figure 18.6 Access Points and Domain Naming

You can use the *DM_ROUTING section to specify which remote domain should process a request to a remote service. In our example, the value of the "CreditType" field is used by the system to decide which remote domain should process requests to the "Verify_Credit" service: if the value is "AX," then the service request is processed by the "AMEX" remote domain, and otherwise, the service request is sent to the "VISA" remote domain.

Finally, administrators can use the aliasing capability provided with local and remote services to normalize the service name space across domains. This is illustrated in Listing 18.2. For example, the "Verify_Credit" remote service may have been exported as "CREDCHK" by the "AMEX" domain and as "CREDAUTH" by the "VISA" domain. Although the same service is exported by names, they can be called the same name locally.

```
*DM_REMOTE_SERVICES
...
Verify_Credit    LDOM=ToCredit RDOM=amex   RNAME="CREDCHK" ROUTING=credit-type
Verify_Credit    LDOM=ToCredit RDOM=visa   RNAME="CREDAUTH" ROUTING=credit-type
...
```

Listing 18.2 *Remote Service Aliasing*

18.2.7 Restricting Access to the Services Provided by a Domain

Access to local services can be restricted in several ways:

- by preventing remote domains from accessing local services
- by restricting the set of local services that are exported to remote domains
- by defining an access control list
- by using the TUXEDO security facility

Only remote domains declared in the *DM_REMOTE_DOMAINS section of the TUXEDO Domains configuration file are allowed to access local services. A local domain always controls access from remote domains using the same communications type (for example, TDOMAIN). If a local domain does not provide access to remote domains, then no network addressing would be needed for this local domain. In our example (see Fig. 18.6), the local domain "FromToWarehouse" needs a networking address because it exports the "Update_Order" service. But, if the Order Entry domain only initiates calls into the Warehouse domain (the "Update_Order" service is not exported and not called by the Warehouse), then the entry for "FromToWarehouse" in the *DM_TDOMAIN section can be removed. This would ensure that the gateways implementing the "FromToWarehouse" local domain will not listen for incoming service requests.

A second level of restricted access can be achieved with the Domains security feature available with domains of type TDOMAIN. Administrators can specify that remote domains accessing a particular access point (local domain) should follow an authentication procedure using a password per remote domain. The APP_PW option requires that the administrator specify a compatible security option (i.e., APP_PW, ACL, or ACL_MANDATORY) in the Core MIB. A local domain using these options requires that remote domains provide the application password or their domain password during the network connection setup.

A third level of access restriction comes with the definition of exported services. Local services that can be requested from other domains are declared in the *DM_LOCAL_SERVICES section of the TUXEDO domains configuration file. If the *DM_LOCAL_SERVICES section is not defined and the local domain provides a listening address, then service requests will be accepted for any local services available in the TUXEDO application. In Listing 18.1, there is an entry for the "Update_Order" service in the *DM_LOCAL_SERVICES section restricting incoming access only to this service. Two additional restrictions are possible when an exported service is declared: first, it is possible to control access to exported services via a particular local domain (our example shows that requests to "Update_Order" are allowed only through the "FromToWarehouse" local domain). Second, a Domains-specific access control list can be attached to the exported service. This access control list specifies which remote domains can request the local service.

A fourth level of access restriction comes from the ACL security feature in the TMIB. All accesses from a remote domain happen with that domain as a principal. Administrators can use the remote domain's identifier as a principal name in the ACL MIB. As such, they are subject in the local domain to the local domain's ACLs.

18.3 Domain Types

The concept of domain type is used to encapsulate the protocol used in the communication with remote domains. Access to remote domains that use the same communications and transaction commitment protocol is provided through a group of gateways that implement the configuration defined for a particular local domain (see Fig. 18.5). In our domains configuration example, the Order Entry application requires two gateway groups: one for handling communications with TUXEDO domains (in particular with the Warehouse domain) and another for handling OSI TP communications with the Credit Authorization centers. The administrators of the Order Entry application define these gateway groups in the TMIB.

Currently, three basic communications protocols are supported by the TUXEDO domains feature: bidirectional communications with other TUXEDO-based applications (the TDOMAIN type), applications that use the OSI TP protocol (the OSITP type), and applications that use the IBM LU6.2 protocol (the SNA type). In addition to the domains feature, the TUXEDO System also provides interoperability with DCE applications (the /TxRPC feature). We will discuss the main characteristics of these interoperability solutions in the following sections.

18.3.1 TUXEDO Domains

The TUXEDO /domains feature was especially designed for communications between TUXEDO-based applications. We have already discussed how the domains configuration specifies what services can be shared between TUXEDO applications and the networking addressing required for the communication between TUXEDO domains. We will briefly discuss what additional value is provided in this communications type (also called, TDOMAIN).

TDOMAIN gateways provide connectivity to multiple remote domains over different types of networks. For example, the Warehouse domain could use a TCP/IP network to communicate with the Order Entry domain and another X.25-based network to communicate with Provider domains. TDOMAIN gateways are independent of the transport protocol used for networking.

TDOMAIN gateways also optimize the number of network connections required with other domains. A network connection with a remote domain is established automatically with the first service request to or from that domain and stays up while the local domain is active. Network connections are bidirectional and are reused and multiplexed for requests and replies. Administrators can specify multiple network addresses per remote domain. This feature is used for high availability: the gateway tries to establish a network connection with the backup address before returning a failure to the requestor. Network connection establishment can also be protected with the security feature (see Section 18.3). Local domains using this feature require a password from remote domains during the network connection setup.

The communications between TUXEDO domains are also transaction-enabled. That is, when a request to a service is issued within a transaction, the transaction is propagated to the remote domain that provides the service. Because all transactions are "funneled" through the same network connection, TDOMAIN gateways can reduce the number of transaction branches and reduce the number of messages required for the completion of the distributed transaction.

Finally, TDOMAIN gateways can be used in combination with the TUXEDO Application Queuing facility (/Q) and the administrative API. Administrators just need to define an entry for the enqueuing service in the TUXEDO domains configuration. For example, let us imagine that "Reorder_Item" is a queue space name in the Warehouse application. The Order Entry administrator could define "Reorder_Item" as a remote service within the Order Entry application just by adding the corresponding entry in the *DM_REMOTE_SERVICES section. The Order Entry application can now use **tpenqueue** to store messages in the remote "Reorder_Item" queue space.

18.3.2 OSI TP Domains

The OSI TP Domains facility was designed for bidirectional, transaction-based communication with applications running under non-TUXEDO environments. The OSI TP protocol is currently the only de jure standard protocol available for distributed transaction management. This protocol was specified by the

International Standards Organization (ISO) [ISO IS 10026] and was selected by X/Open as their standard protocol for transaction processing interoperability.

Communications of this type are provided by OSITP gateways. These gateways implement the X/Open XATMI specification that defines how XATMI primitives (XATMI is a subset of the TUXEDO ATMI interface [X/Open-XATMI]) are mapped to the OSI TP protocol and how data is transferred between applications using this specification. OSITP gateways provide all the automated mechanisms required to make the OSI TP protocol totally transparent to TUXEDO applications that use remote services on domains with this protocol.

The OSITP gateway architecture was designed to allow integration with OSI TP protocol stacks provided by different vendors. The interface to such stacks is called the XAP-TP interface [XAP-TP], and it provides a low-level event-driven interface to the OSI TP protocol stack.

Application administrators using this feature configure the OSI TP stack with the tools provided by the vendor of this stack. Then, they use the Domains configuration to define exported and imported services, and the OSI addressing required for the communications with the remote domains. Security with OSI TP applications is enforced by restricting the set of exported services and by using Access Control lists.

18.3.3 Access to SNA Domains

The TUXEDO SNA Domains feature provides interoperability with applications that use the IBM LU6.2 protocol. This feature is bidirectional—it allows TUXEDO clients to invoke remote services that run as an application under MVS/CICS and CICS applications to invoke services running within a TUXEDO application. Using SNA Domains, TUXEDO applications can use ATMI to communicate with applications executing under the IBM CICS system, and CICS applications can use interfaces, such as CPIC or APPC (that map to the LU6.2 protocol) to communicate with TUXEDO applications. The SNA Domains feature replaces the TUXEDO /Host feature provided in earlier releases of the product.

Figure 18.7 illustrates the flow of a request to the "Verify_Credit" remote service. This service is actually a CICS application, the "CREDCHK" application. The SNA Domains gateway establishes a conversation with this application when a request to the "Verify_Credit" service arrives at the gateway. The gateway converts the data received with the request and sends it to the CICS application. The "CREDCHK" application performs the credit check, sends a reply back to gateway, and ends the conversation. The SNA gateway converts the data from EBCDIC to ASCII and then returns the reply to the program that invoked the "Verify_Credit" service.

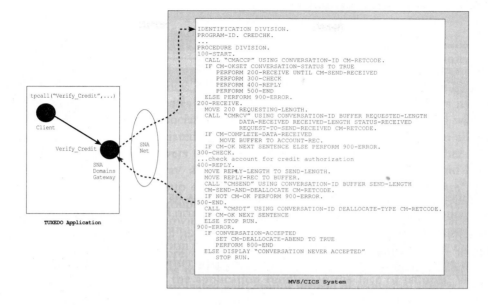

Figure 18.7   An SNA Application Acting as a TUXEDO Service

To enable communications with remote SNA domains, you must configure the gateway environment in the TMIB. First, you define a server group for the gateways and the TUXEDO Domains administrative servers in the TMIB. Then, you create a TUXEDO Domains configuration, with the services imported from and exported to the remote applications and with the communications and security parameters needed to access these remote applications.

SNA gateways provide support for request/response and conversational communication with multiple remote applications. This communication requires a set of rules that define how the conversation is established (or terminated) with the remote application and how information is transferred between the two applications. The TUXEDO System uses a communications model that is compatible with the X/Open XATMI specification [X/Open-XATMI] and that replaces the OSI TP mappings with LU6.2 mappings. This model defines the rules required for the conversation between the TUXEDO System and an LU6.2-based application.

Finally, you must be aware that there are a few constraints imposed by the SNA environment. For example, messages can have a maximum of only 32k bytes, and SNA sessions must be preestablished. Also, at the time this book was written, the SNA Domains feature provides support only for LU6.2 mapped conversations with CM_SYNC_LEVEL 0. That is, the TUXEDO SNA gateway did not yet support transactional requests with CICS applications (CM_SYNC_LEVEL 2).

18.3.4 DCE Interoperability

As described in Chapter 10, "Request/Response Communication," the TUXEDO System TxRPC feature supports a remote procedure call (RPC) interface, so that a client can call a remote procedure using a local procedure syntax. Application programmers specify the remote routines via an Interface Definition Language (IDL). An IDL compiler is used to generate proxy procedures, called stubs, that provide the code to enable remote procedure calls. The IDL interface provided by the TxRPC feature is the same as the X/Open specification [X/Open-TxRPC], which is a superset of the OSF DCE IDL interface. However, the generated stubs do not use the same communications protocol. Thus, a TUXEDO TxRPC stub cannot communicate directly with a stub generated by an OSF IDL compiler.

Application programmers can build their own gateways by mixing the code generated by the OSF and TUXEDO. For example, a client program can use both DCE client stubs and TUXEDO client stubs. The application code in a TUXEDO remote procedure can call DCE RPCs using DCE client stubs. The application code in a DCE remote procedure can call a TUXEDO RPC. The TUXEDO System also provides a built-in approach (a gateway) that automates interoperability between DCE and TUXEDO applications. This approach is illustrated in Figure 18.8. This figure shows a gateway built to allow TUXEDO clients to invoke a DCE remote procedure. A similar approach can be used to allow DCE clients to invoke TUXEDO remote procedures. We will explain only the first approach.

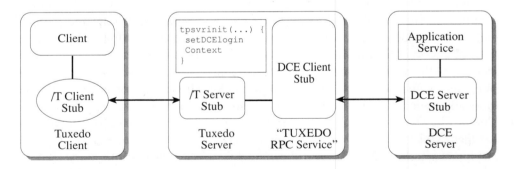

Figure 18.8 **Interoperability with DCE Applications**

The TUXEDO client depicted in Figure 18.8 is built as any normal TUXEDO client (or server) invoking remote procedures. Similarly, the DCE server is built using the normal DCE tools. TUXEDO administrators build the gateway using the **builds_dce** gateway command provided by the TUXEDO TxRPC feature. This tool simplifies the process of running the two IDL compilers and linking the resulting files to build a TUXEDO server with DCE client stubs linked in. Note that the resulting gateway has a dual personality. To the TUXEDO System, it is a server which is the target of RPC requests. To the DCE application, it is a client generating RPC requests.

DCE clients are usually required to run as some DCE authenticated principal. Two alternatives can be used to obtain the DCE login context. One approach is to run the "dce_login" before activating the TUXEDO application, but all gateways will be running on behalf of the same principal. Another approach is to use the TUXEDO server initialization procedure (**tpsvrinit**) to set the login context of the gateway and start a thread that refreshes DCE credentials before they expire. Finally, OSF DCE does not support transactions. That means that the gateway is not able to perform transaction-based remote procedures with DCE.

18.4 Summary

The TUXEDO System interoperability solutions extend the client/server model across multiple heterogeneous applications. These solutions preserve the characteristics of ATMI and allow clients to invoke services that are available on other domains. Total location transparency is offered to application programmers—they always see the same programming interface regardless of where services are offered. Administrators are the main users of the TUXEDO interoperability solutions. They can use the administrative capabilities to federate applications according to different criteria. For example, administrators can define different domains because of the geographical location of the computer systems or to enforce interorganizational boundaries. They can also use the Domains facility to connect to applications provided by other companies. Structuring applications as federated applications has the advantage that the administration of a federated application remains independent of the administration of the other applications.

In this chapter we have presented the different interoperability solutions provided by the TUXEDO System. We discussed the TUXEDO Domains facility that provides transaction-based cooperation between TUXEDO applications and applications that use the OSI TP protocol. We also discussed the TUXEDO solution for interconnectivity with applications that the IBM LU6.2 protocol. Finally, we discussed different approaches for remote procedure call interoperability with the OSF DCE environment.

19   Epilogue

ONWARD!

The Journey You've Taken . . .

You have come a long way since the preface of this book. You have covered many concepts, a lot of terminology, and even some code. Like you, the TUXEDO System has come a long way. From "Client/Server in a Box" it has grown to a system capable of very large-scale, distributed business processing. That growth did not come all at once. Likewise, we expect that understanding what the TUXEDO System might mean for you will take a while to sink in. Many system designers have found in the TUXEDO System just the right tool to help them distribute their business applications. Its simple but powerful programming and administrative facilities have allowed them to concentrate on their business problems. Many, in fact, have become TUXEDO enthusiasts—in time you might be one too!

. . . The Road Ahead . . .

In reading this book, we hope that you have gained some insight into how the TUXEDO System might help you solve *your* distribution problems. If so, the next thing for you to do is to learn more about the TUXEDO System. You may wish to talk to current users, to read case studies, to take a course, or even to get an evaluation copy and "Try on a TUX." Below we provide you with a list of resources to consider, should you wish to continue along the TUXEDO path. *Our* plan is to continue to work on the TUXEDO System and to move it along its journey of innovation. We look forward to a journey together.

—*Juan, Mark, Terry, and Steve*

Additional Material About the TUXEDO System

If you want the next level of detail about the TUXEDO System, you can purchase the TUXEDO System documentation [TUXEDO].

If you want to purchase the documentation or software, contact the BEA sales office at

BEA Systems
385 Moffett Park Drive
Sunnyvale, CA 94089-1208
408-743-4000

or visit BEA Systems' home page at http://www.beasys.com. You can do your own search on the Internet by going to http://lycos.cs.cmu.edu/ and searching on TUXEDO. Ignore the sites having to do with clothing. Happy surfing!

TUXTALK is a moderated discussion of transaction processing topics relating to the TUXEDO and associated connectivity tools. Discussions include client/server architecture, distributed transaction processing, X/Open and OSI transaction processing standards, connecting heterogeneous environments, TPC benchmarking, Integrating Resource Managers (DBMS), and "How to" advice and experience.

To subscribe to TUXTALK, send the following command to listserv@beasys.com in the BODY of E-mail:

SUBSCRIBE TUXTALK yourfirstname yourlastname

For example: SUBSCRIBE TUXTALK Stephen Felts

A Appendix A— Example

This chapter contains a working example that you can compile and run to see the TUXEDO System in action. However, you will need a TUXEDO System development environment to compile, link, and run it. The Epilogue provided some pointers on how to get an evaluation copy of the software.

A.1 Downloading the Files

In case you were worried that you would have to type it all in, don't worry. If you have Internet access, you can download all of the files. They are available via anonymous FTP from `ftp.aw.com` in the directory `cp/amdrade`. You can also access the files via the World Wide Web at URL `http://www.aw.com/cp/andrade.html`.

A.2 Overview

The sample application is an order entry system. The client program allows for you to enter customer information, select a single item (one of several Widgets), and enter an associated credit authorization number (the credit authorization is assumed to be done using separate hardware/software). The order is enqueued in a TUXEDO /Q queue base. Further downstream processing for the orders (for example, order filling, shipping, accounting processing) is not part of this sample; a menu entry is available to clear the queue.

The sample programs include three of the four TUXEDO communication paradigms:

1. Request response communications are used for most of the client/server interactions. Services are provided to get a customer identifier, to add a new customer record, to retrieve a customer record, and to retrieve an item record.

2. A conversational service is used to scan the item records retrieving one batch of five at a time until the desired record is found.

3. Queued communications are used to enqueue the order to stable storage until it can be processed. Because the order processing is not part of this sample, a menu option is provided to clear the queue of all messages; this also uses queued communications.

The process and file architecture is shown in Figure A.1. There are two application servers: one to demonstrate request/response and a second for conversations. The enqueueing is done to the **TMQUEUE** server and **TMS_QM** is used during two-phase commit. A TUXEDO /Q queue base named "SAMPLE" is used to store the orders in the queue "ORDERS." Regular files are used to store the customer identifier counter, the customer records, and the list of items that can be ordered.

Besides having some simplifying assumptions, this sample has several limitations that a production application would not have:

1. As we mentioned earlier in the book, many applications rely on a database management system, for example, an RDBMS. So that you can run this application as is, we chose not to depend on a database. Instead, we used regular files with simple file locking, where we needed tables of information (the item and customer records), and we depend on the TUXEDO /Q queue base to hold the orders until they are processed. The file accesses could be replaced by SQL statements with your favorite database manager.

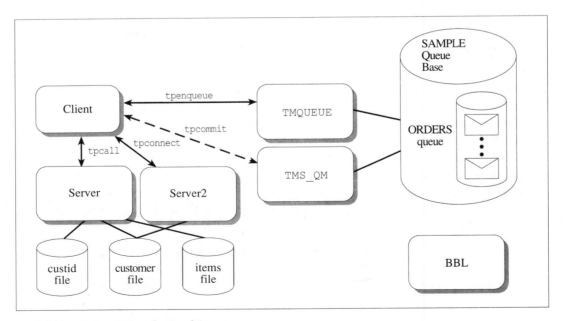

Figure A.1   Sample Architecture

2. These days, it is quite common to have a Graphical User Interface (GUI), or, if not, at least a full screen interface that allows for moving backward and forward between fields. For portability and simplicity, the sample was written using a line-at-a-time interface. One shortcoming of the interface in this example is that, if you make a mistake on an earlier field, you need to go back and start the order processing from the beginning. The client code could be replaced with code using X Windows in a UNIX environment or written using a rapid application development environment like Delphi or Visual Basic in a Windows environment (or more portably in JAVA).

3. Although smaller applications like the one in the sample may be run on a single machine, many TUXEDO applications span multiple computers using either workstation clients, multiple server machines, and/or multiple domains. The sample has a single client and two application server programs, all of which run on a single computer. A workstation client could be built using the same code with a simple change to include the -w option on the **buildclient** command line and by configuring a Workstation Listener. Additional server machines or computers in other domains could also be configured. These larger configurations are left as an "exercise for the reader" (network addresses need to be assigned and configured—this is beyond the scope of this example).

4. Some simplications are taken in the C source code. A maximum input line length of 1024 characters is assumed and typed buffers are also allocated based on this maximum size. **gets** is used instead of **fgets** for reading the standard input. There are some places where error checking is ignored (indicated by a (**void**) function cast) and some of the error messages could provide more details.

The following sections list the source code for the sample application. The source is intended, for the most part, to be self-documenting. Some additional comments are provided to guide you through the pieces. Calls to the ATMI and FML interface are shown in **bold**.

A.3   Header Files

As you saw in Chapter 9, the following is an FML field table for the application. The makefile shown in Listing A.8 will generate a C header file, appflds.h, with field identifiers for the application fields.

```
# Sample Application Fields
# name                   number       type         flags     comments
CUSTID                   1110         string       -         -
NAME                     1111         string       -         -
ADDRESS                  1112         string       -         -
```

CITY	1113	string	—	—
STATE	1114	string	—	—
ZIP	1115	string	—	—
PHONE	1116	string	—	—
OCCURS	1117	long	—	—
ITEMID	1118	string	—	—
ITEMNAME	1119	string	—	—
ITEMPRICE	1120	string	—	—.
AUTHID	1121	string	—	—

Listing A.1 *Example appflds Field Table*

```
#ifndef APP_H
#define APP_H

/* Maximum Line in the Data Files */
#define MAXLINE 1024

/* Maximum Number of Fields Per Line */
#define MAXFLDS 10

/* Data Files and Associated Lock Files */
#define CUSTFILE "customer"
#define CUSTLOCK "custlock"
#define ITEMFILE "items"
#define CUSTIDFILE "custid"
#define CUSTIDLOCK "custidlk"

/* Functions Called by Servers */
int addcust(FBFR *fbfr);
int retrievecust(FBFR *fbfr);
int newcustid(FBFR *fbfr);
int getline(char buffer[MAXLINE], FILE *fp, char *flds[MAXFLDS]);
#endif
```

Listing A.2 *Example app.h Header File*

The app.h header file has the names of the data files and the associated lock files. As configured, the application will only have one server updating the files but multiple copies of the server could easily be configured, hence, the lock files.

A.4 Server Source Code

The request/response server code simply has the four entry points which implement advertised services and call functions in another file. In each case, the input and output buffers are FML, **TPFAIL** is returned on failure, and **TPSUCCESS** when the action completes successfully.

```
#include <atmi.h>
#include <fml.h>
#include "app.h"
#include "appflds.h"          /* this header file is generated from the
                                 field table */

/*
 * REQUEST/RESPONSE SERVICES
 */

/*
 * NEWCUSTID - service to assign the next available customer identifier.
 */
void
NEWCUSTID(TPSVCINFO *tpsvcinfo)
{
        if (newcustid((FBFR *)tpsvcinfo->data) < 0)
                tpreturn(TPFAIL, 0, tpsvcinfo->data, 0L, 0);
        else
                tpreturn(TPSUCCESS, 0, tpsvcinfo->data, 0L, 0);
}

/*
 * NEWCUST - service to add a customer record to the database.
 */
void
NEWCUST(TPSVCINFO *tpsvcinfo)
{
        if (addcust((FBFR *)tpsvcinfo->data) < 0)
                tpreturn(TPFAIL, 0, tpsvcinfo->data, 0L, 0);
        else
                tpreturn(TPSUCCESS, 0, tpsvcinfo->data, 0L, 0);
}

/*
 * RETRIEVECUST - service to retrieve an existing customer record.
 */
void
RETRIEVECUST(TPSVCINFO *tpsvcinfo)
{
        if (retrievecust((FBFR *)tpsvcinfo->data) < 0)
                tpreturn(TPFAIL, 0, tpsvcinfo->data, 0L, 0);
        else
                tpreturn(TPSUCCESS, 0, tpsvcinfo->data, 0L, 0);
}

/*
 * RETRIEVEITEM - service to retrieve an existing item record.
 */
void
RETRIEVEITEM(TPSVCINFO *tpsvcinfo)
{
        if (retrieveitem((FBFR *)tpsvcinfo->data) < 0)
                tpreturn(TPFAIL, 0, tpsvcinfo->data, 0L, 0);
        else
                tpreturn(TPSUCCESS, 0, tpsvcinfo->data, 0L, 0);
}
```

Listing A.3   *Example server.c File*

The file util.c has the functions that implement the request/response service operations. In addition to implementing the four service operations, code is included to create and destroy the lock files, and to read input lines from the data files and parse them into fields. The customer and item data files each have multiple fields with colon separators. The customer file has NAME, ADDRESS, CITY, STATE, ZIP, and PHONE fields. The item file has ITEMID, ITEM-NAME, and ITEMPRICE fields.

This code uses a minimal number of FML functions. They are as follows:

Fvals: Get the value of a field occurrence and return it as a string (or the empty string if it does not exist)

Fvall: Get the value of a field occurrence and return it as a long integer

Fchg: Change the value of a field occurrence

Finit: Initialize the buffer so that it has no fields

Fdel: Deletes a field occurrence from the buffer

```c
#include <stdio.h>
#include <errno.h>
#include <sys/stat.h>
#include <userlog.h>
#include <Uunix.h>
#include <atmi.h>
#include <fml.h>
#include "app.h"
#include "appflds.h"

/* Internal Functions */
static int filelock(char *lockfile);
static int fileunlock(char *lockfile);

int
addcust(FBFR *fbfr)
{
        FILE *fp;

        /* Serialize Access */
        if (filelock(CUSTLOCK) < 0) {
                userlog("Failed to lock %s", CUSTLOCK);
                return(-1);
        }

/* Open Customer File for Appending */
        fp = fopen(CUSTFILE, "a");
        if (fp == NULL) {
                (void) fileunlock(CUSTLOCK);
                userlog("Failed to open %s", CUSTFILE);
                return(-1);
        }
```

```
        /* Fetch fields from the input buffer and append the record */
        if (fprintf(fp, "%s:%s:%s:%s:%s:%s:%s\n",
                        Fvals(fbfr, CUSTID, 0),
                        Fvals(fbfr, NAME, 0),
                        Fvals(fbfr, ADDRESS, 0),
                        Fvals(fbfr, CITY, 0),
                        Fvals(fbfr, STATE, 0),
                        Fvals(fbfr, ZIP, 0),
                        Fvals(fbfr, PHONE, 0)) <= 0) {
                (void) fileunlock(CUSTLOCK);
                userlog("Failed to write to %s", CUSTFILE);
                (void) fpclose(fp);
                return(-1);
        }

        /* Close File and Unlock */
        (void) fclose(fp);
        (void) fileunlock(CUSTLOCK);
        return(0);
}

int
retrievecust(FBFR *fbfr)        /* input buffer should contain CUSTID or
                                   NAME field */

{
        int cnt;
        FILE *fp;
        char line[MAXLINE];
        char *flds[MAXFLDS];
        char *val;              /* pointer to either CUSTID or NAME */
        int custid;

        /* Check if custid or name specified */
        val = Fvals(fbfr, CUSTID, 0);
        if (val[0] == '\0') {
                val = Fvals(fbfr, NAME, 0);
                if (val[0] == '\0') {
                        userlog("No CUSTID specified");
                        return(-1);
                }
                custid = 0;
        }
        else
                custid = 1;

        fp = fopen(CUSTFILE, "r");
        if (fp == NULL) {
                userlog("Failed to open %s", CUSTFILE);
                return(-1);
        }

        for (;;) {
                cnt = getline(line, fp, flds);
                if (cnt < 0) {
                        if (custid)
                                userlog("Failed to find CUSTID %s", val);
                        else
                                userlog("Failed to find NAME %s", val);
                        (void) fclose(fp);
                        return(-1);
                }
```

```
                    if (cnt == 0)
                            continue;
                    if (custid) {
                            if (strcmp(val, flds[0]) != 0)
                                    continue;
                    }
                    else {
                            if (strcmp(val, flds[1]) != 0)
                                    continue;
                    }

                    /* populate FML buffer with customer fields */
                    (void) Fchg(fbfr, CUSTID, 0,flds[0], 0),
                    (void) Fchg(fbfr, NAME, 0,flds[1], 0),
                    (void) Fchg(fbfr, ADDRESS, 0, flds[2], 0),
                    (void) Fchg(fbfr, CITY, 0, flds[3], 0),
                    (void) Fchg(fbfr, STATE, 0, flds[4], 0),
                    (void) Fchg(fbfr, ZIP, 0, flds[5], 0),
                    (void) Fchg(fbfr, PHONE, 0, flds[6], 0);
                    (void) fclose(fp);
                    return(1);
            }
    }

    int
    retrieveitem(FBFR *fbfr)         /* input is either ITEMID or ITEMNAME -
                                        output is ITEM fields */

    {
            int cnt;
            FILE *fp;
            char line[MAXLINE];
            char *flds[MAXFLDS];
            char *val;
            int itemid;

            /* Check if itemid or item name specified */
            val = Fvals(fbfr, ITEMID, 0);
            if (*val == '\0') {
                    val = Fvals(fbfr, ITEMNAME, 0);
                    if (*val == '\0') {
                            userlog("No ITEMID specified");
                            return(-1);
                    }
                    itemid = 0;
            }
            else
                    itemid = 1;

            fp = fopen(ITEMFILE, "r");
            if (fp == NULL) {
                    userlog("Failed to open %s", ITEMFILE);
                    return(-1);
            }

            for (;;) {
                    cnt = getline(line, fp, flds);
                    if (cnt < 0) {
                            if (itemid)
                                    userlog("Failed to find ITEMID %s", val);
                            else
                                    userlog("Failed to find ITEMNAME %s", val);
                            (void) fclose(fp);
```

```
                              return(-1);
                   }
              if (cnt == 0)
                     continue;
              if (itemid) {
                     if (strcmp(val, flds[0]) != 0)
                            continue;
              }
              else {
                     if (strcmp(val, flds[1]) != 0)
                            continue;
              }

              (void) Fchg(fbfr, ITEMID, 0,flds[0], 0),
              (void) Fchg(fbfr, ITEMNAME, 0,flds[1], 0),
              (void) Fchg(fbfr, ITEMPRICE, 0,flds[2], 0),
              (void) fclose(fp);
              return(1);
       }
}
int
newcustid(FBFR *fbfr) /* generate a new customer identifier */
{
       char line[1024];
       FILE *fp;
       char *p;
       int i;
       int ret;
       int len;
       long custid;

       if (filelock(CUSTIDLOCK) < 0) {
              userlog("Failed to lock %s", CUSTIDLOCK);
              return(-1);
       }
       fp = fopen(CUSTIDFILE, "r+");

       custid = 0;
       if (fp != (FILE *) NULL) {           /* get and update last
                                               identifier stored on first
                                               record */
              if (fgets(line, sizeof(line), fp) != NULL) {
                     len = strlen(line);
                     if (line[len-1] == '\n') {
                            line[len-1] = '\0';
                            len—;
                     }
                     if (len == 7) {
                            p = line;
                            for (i = 0; i < 7; i++) {
                                   if (*p < '0' || *p > '9') {
                                          custid = 0;
                                          break;
                                   }
                                   custid = (custid * 10) + (*p++ - '0');
                            }
                     }
              }
              if (custid && fseek(fp, 0L, SEEK_SET) == 0) {
                     custid++;
                     (void) fprintf(fp, "%7.7ld\n", custid);
```

```
                              (void) fclose(fp);
                              /* don't set fp to NULL */
                              ret = 1;
                      }
                      else {
                              (void) fclose(fp);
                              fp = NULL;
                              (void) unlink(CUSTIDFILE);
                      }
              }
              if (fp == NULL) {
                      custid++;
                      fp = fopen(CUSTIDFILE, "a");
                      if (fp == NULL) {
                              userlog("Failed to create %s", CUSTIDFILE);
                              custid = 0;
                              ret = -1;
                      }
                      else {
                              (void) fprintf(fp, "%7.7ld\n", custid);
                              (void) fclose(fp);
                              ret = 1;
                      }
              }
              (void) fileunlock(CUSTIDLOCK);
              if (custid) {
                      (void) sprintf(line, "%7.7ld", custid);
                      (void) Fchg(fbfr, CUSTID, 0, line, 0);
              }
              return(ret);
      }

      /*
       * filelock - create a lockfile - assumes atomic creat()
       */
      static int
      filelock(char *lockfile)
      {
              long    oldmtime;
              int     fd;
              int     ret;
              int     count;
              pid_t   pid;
              pid_t   oldpid;
              struct stat sbuf;
              static char tempfile[512];

              pid = getpid();
              (void)sprintf(tempfile, "%8.8lx", (long)pid);

              for (count=10; count--; (void)sleep(4)) {
                      if ((fd = creat(tempfile,0666)) >= 0) {
                              (void)write(fd, (char *)&pid,
                                      (unsigned)sizeof(pid));
                              (void)close(fd);
                              if (link(tempfile,lockfile) >= 0) {
                                      (void)unlink(tempfile);
                                      return(0);
                              }
                              (void)unlink(tempfile);
                      }
```

```
                        else {
                                (void) unlink(tempfile);
                        }
                        if (stat(lockfile, &sbuf) < 0)
                                continue;
                        oldmtime = sbuf.st_mtime;
                        if ((fd = open(lockfile, O_RDONLY)) < 0)
                                continue;
                        ret = read(fd,(char *)&oldpid,(unsigned int)sizeof
                                (oldpid));
                        (void)close(fd);
                        if (ret != sizeof(pid) || ret != sbuf.st_size) {
                                (void)unlink(lockfile);
                                continue;
                        }
                        if (pid == oldpid)
                                return(0);
                        if (kill((pid_t)oldpid,0) == -1 && errno == ESRCH) {
                                if (stat(lockfile, &sbuf) == 0
                                 && oldmtime == sbuf.st_mtime) {
                                        (void)unlink(lockfile);
                                }
                        }
                }
        return(-1);
}

/*
 * fileunlock - delete the lock file.
 */
static int
fileunlock(char *lockfile)
{
        register int fd;
        long    n;
        pid_t   pid;
        pid_t   oldpid;

        pid = getpid();
        if ((fd = open(lockfile, O_RDONLY)) == -1) {
                return(-1);
        }
        n = read(fd, (char *)&oldpid, (unsigned int)sizeof(oldpid));
        (void)close(fd);
        if (n == sizeof(oldpid) && oldpid == pid) {
                (void)unlink(lockfile);
                return(0);
        }
        else {
                return(-1);
        }
}

/*
 * getline - Get the next input line and parse into fields.
 */
int
getline(char line[MAXLINE], FILE *fp, char *flds[MAXFLDS])
{
        int     len;
        char    *p;
```

```
char    *q;
int     cnt;

for (;;) {
        if (fgets(line, (int) MAXLINE, fp) == NULL) {
                return(-1);
        }

        len = strlen(line);
        if (line[len-1] == '\n') {
                line[—len] = '\0';
        }

        p = line;
        if ((*p == '#') || (*p == '\n') || (*p == '\0')) {
                /* Ignore line */
                continue;
        }
        break;
}

for(cnt = 0; (q = strchr(p, ':')) != NULL; cnt++) {
        *q++ = '\0';
        if (cnt >= MAXFLDS)     /* shouldn't happen */
                return(cnt);

        flds[cnt] = p;          /* save beginning of field */

        p = q;
}
flds[cnt++] = p;                /* save last/only field */
return(cnt);
}
```

Listing A.4   *Example util.c File*

server2 is a conversational server that implements the scan on the items data file. The client sends data with its connect in the form of a fielded buffer. Upon connection, the server has send control and sends back the first set of records, giving control to the client. Then it waits for a response from the client. The client can then request more records, request 0 records which will cause an orderly termination (the server will return), or can disconnect immediately. Multiple records are returned in a single FML buffer by using multiple occurrences of each field. The number of occurrences is returned in the OCCURS field.

```
#include <atmi.h>
#include <fml.h>
#include <userlog.h>
#include "app.h"
#include "appflds.h"
```

```
/*
 * SEARCHITEM - conversational service to scan item records, as
 *      needed.
 */
void
SEARCHITEM(TPSVCINFO *tpsvcinfo)
{
        FILE *fp;                       /* input file pointer */
        char buffer[MAXLINE];           /* input buffer */
        char *flds[MAXFLDS];            /* fields in input buffer */
        int cnt;                        /* Count of field found */
        long occurs, found;             /* Occurrences desired, retrieved */
        long len;                       /* Length of reply data */
        FBFR *fbfr;                     /* Local pointer to data */
        long revent;                    /* Returned Event */

        fbfr = (FBFR *)tpsvcinfo->data;       /* input/output buffer */

        fp = fopen(ITEMFILE, "r");
        if (fp == NULL) {
                userlog("Failed to open %s", ITEMFILE);
                tpreturn(TPFAIL, 0, (char *)fbfr, 0L, 0);
        }

        /* Find Out How Many Occurrences Are Desired */
        occurs = Fvall(fbfr, OCCURS, 0);
        if (occurs <= 0)
                occurs = 1;             /* by default, return 1 entry */

        /* Reinitialize the Buffer */
        Finit(fbfr, Fsizeof(fbfr));

        for (found = 0;;) {
                /* Read the Next Line */
                cnt = getline(buffer, fp, flds);
                if (cnt < 0) {
                        /* No More Records */
                        (void) fclose(fp);
                        Fchg(fbfr, OCCURS, 0, (char *)&found, 0);
                        tpreturn(TPSUCCESS, 0, (char *)fbfr, 0L, 0);
                }
                if (cnt == 0)  /* Empty Line */
                        continue;

                /* Store the Next Occurrence */
                (void) Fchg(fbfr, ITEMID, (FLDID)found, flds[0], 0),
                (void) Fchg(fbfr, ITEMNAME, (FLDID)found, flds[1], 0),
                (void) Fchg(fbfr, ITEMPRICE, (FLDID)found, flds[2], 0),
                found++;

                if (found == occurs) {
                        /* Got the Requested Number - Send it Back */
                        Fchg(fbfr, OCCURS, 0, (char *)&found, 0);

                        if (tpsend(tpsvcinfo->cd, (char *)fbfr, 0,
                                TPRECVONLY|TPSIGRSTRT, &revent) == -1) {
                                /* transfer send control */
                                (void) fclose(fp);
                                tpreturn(TPFAIL, 0, (char *)fbfr, 0L, 0);
                        }

                        /* See if the Requestor Wants More - check for
                         * failure or disconnect from partner
```

```
        */
        if (tprecv(tpsvcinfo->cd, (char **)&fbfr, &len,
                TPSIGRSTRT, &revent) == -1 &&
                tperrno != TPEEVENT &&
                revent != TPEV_SENDONLY) {
                (void) fclose(fp);
                tpreturn(TPFAIL, 0, (char *)fbfr, 0L, 0);
        }

        /* See How Many More are Desired */
        occurs = Fvall(fbfr, OCCURS, 0);
        if (occurs <= 0) {
                /* Orderly Termination */
                occurs = 0;
                Fchg(fbfr, OCCURS, 0, (char *)&occurs, 0);
                (void) fclose(fp);
                tpreturn(TPSUCCESS, 0, (char *)fbfr, 0L, 0);
        }

        /* Get the Next Batch */
        found = 0;
        }
    }
}
```

Listing A.5 *Example server2.c File*

A.5 Client Source Code

The client manages it all. It prints the line-at-a-time menu, prompts for customer and item information, and calls the appropriate services.

```
/*
 * Sample Client Program
 */
#include <stdio.h>
#include <ctype.h>
#include <Uunix.h>
#include <atmi.h>
#include <fml.h>
#include "app.h"
#include "appflds.h"

/* Internal Functions */
static void Order_Item(void);
static int Get_Cust(FBFR **fbfr);
static int New_Cust(FBFR **fbfr);
static int Get_Item(FBFR **fbfr);
static int Enqueue_Order(FBFR *cust, FBFR *item);
static int Search_Item(FBFR **fbfr);
static void Print_Cust(FBFR *fbfr);
static void Print_Item(FBFR *fbfr);
```

```
static int Clear_Queue(void);

/* Internal Data */
static char line[1024];          /* Input Line */

/*
 * main()
 *      print the high level menu and execute the procedures
 */
main(int argc, char *argv[])
{
        int item;
        int done = 0;

        argc = argc;             /* unused */
        argv = argv;             /* unused */

        for (;!done;) {

                /* First Level Menu */
                (void) printf("1. Order item\n");
                (void) printf("2. Clear the Enqueue\n");
                (void) printf("3. Quit\n");
                (void) printf("Enter desired menu selection: ");
                (void) gets(line);
                if (*line == 'q' || *line == 'Q')
                        break;

                if (!isdigit(*line))
                        continue;        /* Invalid Entry */

                item = atoi(line);
                switch(item) {
                case 1:
                        Order_Item();
                        break;
                case 2:
                        (void) Clear_Queue();
                        break;
                case 3:
                        done = 1;
                        break;
                }
        }
        (void) tpterm();
        return(0);
}

/*
 * Order_Item - Get the customer, item, and authorization
 *      information and enqueue an order.
 */
static void
Order_Item(void)
{
        FBFR *fbfr_cust;
        FBFR *fbfr_item;

        (void) printf("\nORDER ITEM\n\n");

        /* Get FML Buffers for Customer and Item Information */
        fbfr_cust = (FBFR *)tpalloc("FML", NULL, 1024);
        if (fbfr_cust == NULL) {
                (void) printf("Memory allocation failed: %s\n",
```

```
                            tpstrerror(tperrno));
                    return;
        }
        fbfr_item = (FBFR *)tpalloc("FML", NULL, 1024);
        if (fbfr_item == NULL) {
                    tpfree((char *)fbfr_cust);
                    (void) printf("Memory allocation failed: %s\n",
                            tpstrerror(tperrno));
                    return;
        }

        /* Get the Customer Record */
        if (Get_Cust(&fbfr_cust) < 0) {
                    tpfree((char *)fbfr_cust);
                    tpfree((char *)fbfr_item);
                    return;
        }

        /* Have the Customer Record - Get the Item Number */
        if (Get_Item(&fbfr_item) < 0) {
                    tpfree((char *)fbfr_cust);
                    tpfree((char *)fbfr_item);
                    return;
        }

        /* Get the Credit Card Authorization and Enqueue the Order */
        if (Enqueue_Order(fbfr_cust,fbfr_item) < 0) {
                    tpfree((char *)fbfr_cust);
                    tpfree((char *)fbfr_item);
                    return;
        }

        tpfree((char *)fbfr_cust);
        tpfree((char *)fbfr_item);
        return;
}

/*
 * Get_Cust - Get the customer information from the database or
 *      prompt for it and create a new record.
 */
static int
Get_Cust(FBFR **inoutfbfr)
{
        char *namep;            /* Pointer to customer name */
        long len;               /* Length of reply data */
        FBFR *fbfr;             /* Local pointer to data */
        int ret;                /* Return value from ATMI */

        /* Get the Customer Record, if One Exists */

        fbfr = *inoutfbfr;      /* local copy for ease of use */

        for (;;) {
                namep = NULL;   /* Haven't found it yet */

                (void) printf
                ("Customer Number or Name (or return for New): ");
                line[0] = '\0';
                (void) gets(line);
                if (*line == '\0')
                        break;  /* Create One */
```

```
                        /* Retrieve Existing Customer Record */
                        if (isdigit(*line))
                                Fchg(fbfr, CUSTID, 0, line, 0); /* Lookup CUSTID */
                        else
                                Fchg(fbfr, NAME, 0, line, 0); /* Lookup NAME */

                        ret = tpcall("RETRIEVECUST", (char *)fbfr, 0, (char **)&fbfr,
                                &len, 0);
                        *inoutfbfr = fbfr;                      /* pass back new buffer */

                        if (ret == -1) {
                                if (tperrno == TPESVCFAIL)
                                        (void) printf("Failed to find customer.\n");
                                else
                                        (void) printf(
                                        "Failed to find customer.\n"); %s\n",
                                                tpstrerror(tperrno));
                                break;                 /* Create One */
                        }

                        namep = Fvals(fbfr, NAME, 0);
                        if (*namep == '\0') {
                                /* Customer Record not Found */
                                (void) printf("Customer not found\n");
                                Finit(fbfr, Fsizeof(fbfr));
                                /* Try again */
                        }
                        else {
                                /* Check if this is the Right Customer */
                                Print_Cust(fbfr);
                                (void) printf("Is this the correct customer: ");
                                (void) gets(line);

                                if (*line != 'n' && *line != 'N')
                                        break;                 /* Found It - Stop search */

                                Finit(fbfr, Fsizeof(fbfr));
                                /* Try again */
                        }
                }

                if (namep == NULL) {     /* Don't Have Customer - Create One */
                        if (New_Cust(inoutfbfr) < 0) {
                                (void) printf("Order aborted\n");
                                ret = -1;
                        }
                        else
                                ret = 0;
                }
                else
                        ret = 0;
                return(ret);
}

/*
 * Print_Cust - Print the current customer information.
 */
static void
Print_Cust(FBFR *fbfr)
{
        (void) printf("CUSTID: %s\n", Fvals(fbfr, CUSTID, 0));
        (void) printf("NAME: %s\n", Fvals(fbfr, NAME, 0));
        (void) printf("ADDRESS: %s\n", Fvals(fbfr, ADDRESS, 0));
```

```
        (void) printf("CITY: %s\n", Fvals(fbfr, CITY, 0));
        (void) printf("STATE: %s\n", Fvals(fbfr, STATE, 0));
        (void) printf("ZIP: %s\n", Fvals(fbfr, ZIP, 0));
        (void) printf("PHONE: %s\n", Fvals(fbfr, PHONE, 0));
}

/*
 * Print_Item - Print the current item information.
 */
static void
Print_Item(FBFR *fbfr)
{
        (void) printf("ID: %s\n", Fvals(fbfr, ITEMID, 0));
        (void) printf("NAME: %s\n", Fvals(fbfr, ITEMNAME, 0));
        (void) printf("PRICE: $%s\n", Fvals(fbfr, ITEMPRICE, 0));
}

/*
 * New_Cust - prompt for new customer information and create database
 * record.
 */
int
New_Cust(FBFR **inoutfbfr)
{
        char *custidp;                  /* Pointer to customer id data */
        long len;                       /* Length of reply data */
        FBFR *fbfr;                     /* Local pointer to data */
        int ret;                        /* Return value from ATMI */

        fbfr = *inoutfbfr;              /* local copy for ease of use */

        /* Prompt for each Field and Add to FML Buffer */

        (void) printf("NAME: ");
        line[0] = '\0'; (void) gets(line);
        if (*line == '\0') {
                return(-1);
        }
        (void) Fchg(fbfr, NAME, 0, line, 0);

        (void) printf("ADDRESS: ");
        line[0] = '\0'; (void) gets(line);
        if (*line == '\0') {
                return(-1);
        }
        (void) Fchg(fbfr, ADDRESS, 0, line, 0);

        (void) printf("CITY: ");
        line[0] = '\0'; (void) gets(line);
        if (*line == '\0') {
                return(-1);
        }
        (void) Fchg(fbfr, CITY, 0, line, 0);

        (void) printf("STATE: ");
        line[0] = '\0'; (void) gets(line);
        if (*line == '\0') {
                return(-1);
        }
        (void) Fchg(fbfr, STATE, 0, line, 0);

        (void) printf("ZIP: ");
        line[0] = '\0'; (void) gets(line);
```

```
        if (*line == '\0') {
                return(-1);
        }
        (void) Fchg(fbfr, ZIP, 0, line, 0);

        (void) printf("PHONE: ");
        line[0] = '\0'; (void) gets(line);
        if (*line == '\0') {
                return(-1);
        }
        (void) Fchg(fbfr, PHONE, 0, line, 0);

        (void) printf("Add customer to database?: ");
        if (gets(line) == NULL || (*line != 'y' && *line != 'Y' &&
                *line != '\0')) {
                return(-1);
        }

        /* Call Service to Assign a Customer Identifier */
        ret = tpcall("NEWCUSTID", (char *)fbfr, 0, (char **)&fbfr, &len, 0);
        *inoutfbfr = fbfr;      /* pass back new buffer */

        if (ret == -1) {
                (void) printf("Failed to get new customer id: %s\n",
                        tpstrerror(tperrno));
                *inoutfbfr = fbfr;
                return(-1);
        }

        /* Print the Assigned Customer ID */
        custidp = Fvals(fbfr, CUSTID, 0);
        (void) printf("CUSTID: %s\n", custidp);

        /* Call Service to Add Customer Record to Database */
        ret = tpcall("NEWCUST", (char *)fbfr, 0, (char **)&fbfr, &len, 0);
        *inoutfbfr = fbfr;      /* pass back new buffer */

        if (ret == -1) {
                (void) printf("Failed to add new customer: %s\n",
                        tpstrerror(tperrno));
                *inoutfbfr = fbfr;
                return(-1);
        }
        return(0);
}

/*
 * Get_Item - Get item record from database
 */
static int
Get_Item(FBFR **inoutfbfr)
{
        char *namep;            /* Pointer to item name */
        long len;               /* Length of reply data */
        FBFR *fbfr;             /* Local pointer to data */
        int ret;                /* Return value from ATMI */

        /* Get the Item Record */

        fbfr = *inoutfbfr;      /* local copy for ease of use */

        for (;;) {
                namep = NULL;

                (void) printf("Item Name or Number (or return for Search): ");
```

```
            line[0] = '\0';
            (void) gets(line);
            if (*line == '\0')
                    break; /* Search */

            /* Get Item Record */
            if (isdigit(*line))
                    Fchg(fbfr, ITEMID, 0, line, 0); /* Lookup ITEMID */
            else
                    Fchg(fbfr, ITEMNAME, 0, line, 0); /* Lookup ITEMNAME */

            ret = tpcall("RETRIEVEITEM", (char *)fbfr, 0, (char **)&fbfr,
                    &len, 0);
            *inoutfbfr = fbfr;      /* pass back new buffer */

            if (ret == -1) {
                    if (tperrno == TPESVCFAIL)
                            (void) printf("Failed to find item\n");
                    else
                            (void) printf("Failed to lookup item: %s\n",
                                    tpstrerror(tperrno));
                    break; /* Search */
            }

            namep = Fvals(fbfr, ITEMNAME, 0);
            if (*namep == '\0') {
                    /* Item Record not Found */
                    (void) printf("Failed to find item\n");
                    Finit(fbfr, Fsizeof(fbfr));
            }
            else {
                    /* Check if this is the Right Item */
                    Print_Item(fbfr);
                    (void) printf("Is this the correct item: ");
                    (void) gets(line);

                    if (*line != 'n' && *line != 'N')
                            break; /* Found It - Stop search */

                    Finit(fbfr, Fsizeof(fbfr));
            }
    }

    if (namep == NULL) {            /* Don't Have Item - Search */
            if (Search_Item(inoutfbfr) < 0) {
                    (void) printf("Order aborted\n");
                    ret = -1;
            }
            else
                    ret = 0;
    }
    else
            ret = 0;
    return(ret);
}

/*
 * Search_Item - Scan and print all item records until desired entry
 * found.
 */
static int
Search_Item(FBFR **inoutfbfr)
{
```

```
        long len;               /* Length of reply data */
        FBFR *fbfr;             /* Local pointer to data */
        int ret;                /* Return value from ATMI */
        int i, j;               /* Indices */
        FLDOCC occ;             /* Field Occurrence */
        long occurs;            /* Total Occurrences */
        int cd;                 /* Connection Descriptor */
        long revent;            /* Returned Event */

        fbfr = *inoutfbfr;      /* local copy for ease of use */

again:
        occurs = 5;
        Fchg(fbfr, OCCURS, 0, (char *)&occurs, 0);
        cd = tpconnect("SEARCHITEM", (char *)fbfr, 0, TPRECVONLY);
        *inoutfbfr = fbfr;      /* pass back new buffer */

        if (cd == -1) {
                (void) printf("Failed to get item information: %s\n",
                        tpstrerror(tperrno));
                return(-1);
        }

        for (;;) {
                ret = tprecv(cd, (char **)&fbfr, &len, 0, &revent);
                *inoutfbfr = fbfr;      /* pass back new buffer */

                if (ret == -1 && (tperrno != TPEEVENT ||
                        (revent != TPEV_SVCSUCC && revent != TPEV_SENDONLY))){
                        (void) printf("Failed to retrieve items: %s\n",
                                tpstrerror(tperrno));
                        (void) tpdiscon(cd);
                        return(-1);
                }
                occurs = Fvall(fbfr, OCCURS, 0);
                for (i = 0; i < occurs; i++) {
                        (void) printf("%d: %s\t%s\t$%s\n", i+1,
                                Fvals(fbfr, ITEMID, i),
                                Fvals(fbfr, ITEMNAME, i),
                                Fvals(fbfr, ITEMPRICE, i));
                }
                (void) printf("Enter menu number or return for more: ");
                line[0] = '\0';
                (void) gets(line);
                if (isdigit(line[0]) && line[1] == '\0' &&
                        (i = line[0] - '0' - 1) < occurs) {
                        tpdiscon(cd);

                        /* Delete all occurrences but the one we want */
                        occ = 0;
                        for (j = 0; j < occurs; j++) {
                                if (j == i) {
                                        occ = 1;
                                        continue;
                                }
                                Fdel(fbfr, ITEMID, occ);
                                Fdel(fbfr, ITEMNAME, occ);
                                Fdel(fbfr, ITEMPRICE, occ);
                        }
                        return(0);
                }
                if (occurs < 5) {
```

```
                          /* Got a TPEV_SVCSUCC */

                          (void) printf(
                                  "No more entries; do you{want to search again? ");
                          line[0] = '\0';
                          (void) gets(line);
                          if (*line == 'Y' || *line == 'y' || *line == '\0')
                                  goto again;
                          return(-1);
                  }
              Finit(fbfr, Fsizeof(fbfr));
              occurs = 5;
              Fchg(fbfr, OCCURS, 0, (char *)&occurs, 0);
              ret = tpsend(cd, (char *)fbfr, 0, TPRECVONLY, &revent);
              if (ret == -1) {
                      (void) printf("Failed to retrieve items: %s\n",
                              tpstrerror(tperrno));
                      (void) tpdiscon(cd);
                      return(-1);
              }
          }
    }
}

/*
 * Enqueue_Order - Combine customer, item, and credit authorization
 *      information into order record - enqueue it to stable
 *      storage.
 */
static int
Enqueue_Order(FBFR *cust, FBFR *item)
{
        TPQCTL tpqctl;          /* Enqueuing control information */

        (void)printf("Enter credit card authorization or return to cancel: ");
        line[0] = '\0';
        (void)gets(line);

        if (*line == '\0') {
                (void)printf("Order aborted\n");
                return(-1);
        }

        Fchg(cust, AUTHID, 0, line, 0);
        Fchg(cust, ITEMID, 0, Fvals(item, ITEMID, 0), 0);
        Fchg(cust, ITEMNAME, 0, Fvals(item, ITEMNAME, 0), 0);
        Fchg(cust, ITEMPRICE, 0, Fvals(item, ITEMPRICE, 0), 0);

        /* Store the Item Name in the Correlation Identifier */
        (void) memset(tpqctl.corrid, 0, sizeof(tpqctl.corrid));
        (void) strcpy(tpqctl.corrid, Fvals(cust, ITEMNAME, 0));
        tpqctl.flags = TPQCORRID;

        /* Start Transaction Bracket */
        if (tpbegin(20,0) == -1) {
                (void)printf("Transaction initiation failed: %s\n",
                        tpstrerror(tperrno));
                return(-1);
        }

        /* Enqueue to Stable Storage */
        if (tpenqueue("SAMPLE", "ORDERS", &tpqctl, (char *)cust, 0,
```

```
                    TPSIGRSTRT) == -1) {
                    (void)printf("Enqueueing failed: %s\n",
                            tpstrerror(tperrno));
                    (void) tpabort(0);
                    return(-1);
            }

    /* Finish Up the Transaction */
    if (tpcommit(0) == -1) {
            (void)printf("Transaction commit failed: %s\n",
                    tpstrerror(tperrno));
            return(-1);
    }
    (void)printf("Order queued for processing\n");
    return(0);
}

/*
 * Clear_Queue - dequeue all messages from the queue.
 */
static int
Clear_Queue()
{
    int cnt;                    /* Count of deleted messages */
    long len;                   /* Length of reply data */
    FBFR *fbfr;                 /* Local pointer to data */
    TPQCTL tpqctl;              /* Dequeuing control information */

    (void)printf("Are you sure you want to clear the queue: ");
    line[0] = '\0';
    (void)gets(line);

    if (*line != 'y' && *line != 'Y') {
            (void)printf("Enqueue not cleared\n");
            return(-1);
    }

    fbfr = (FBFR *)tpalloc("FML", NULL, 1024);
    if (fbfr == NULL) {
            (void) printf(
            "Enqueue not cleared - memory allocation failed: %s\n",
                    tpstrerror(tperrno));
            return(-1);
    }

    tpqctl.flags = TPNOFLAGS;

    /* Start Transaction Bracket */
    if (tpbegin(20,0) == -1) {
            (void)printf("Transaction initiation failed: %s\n",
                    tpstrerror(tperrno));
            tpfree((char *)fbfr);
            return(-1);
    }

    /* Dequeue All Messages Until No More */
    cnt = 0;
    while (tpdequeue("SAMPLE", "ORDERS", &tpqctl, (char **)&fbfr, &len,
            TPSIGRSTRT) != -1) {
            cnt++;
            tpqctl.flags = TPNOFLAGS;
    }
    if (tperrno != TPEDIAGNOSTIC ||
```

```
                  (tpqctl.diagnostic != QMENOMSG &&
                  tpqctl.diagnostic != QMEINUSE)) {
                  if (tperrno == TPEDIAGNOSTIC)
                          (void)printf("Enqueueing failed: diagnostic %ld\n",
                                  tpqctl.diagnostic);
                  else
                          (void)printf("Enqueueing failed: %s\n",
                                  tpstrerror(tperrno));
                  tpabort(0);
                  tpfree((char *)fbfr);
                  return(-1);
            }

      /* Finish Up the Transaction */
      if (tpcommit(0) == -1) {
                  (void)printf("Transaction commit failed: %s\n",
                          tpstrerror(tperrno));
                  tpfree((char *)fbfr);
                  return(-1);
            }

      /* Print Count Deleted */
      if (cnt == 1)
                  (void)printf("1 Message Deleted\n");
      else
                  (void)printf("%d Messages Deleted\n", cnt);
      tpfree((char *)fbfr);
      return(0);
}
```

Listing A.6 *Example client.c File*

A.6   Generating the Application

That's it for the source code. Now it's time to put it all together. To do that, it is necessary to set the environment variables for TUXDIR, TUXCONFIG, FLDTBLDIR, and FIELDTBLS. TUXDIR/bin must also be in the PATH. On some platforms, the shared objects are found via other environment variables. The "env" file can be "dotted" in on UNIX platforms to set the environment. For Windows it will be necessary to modify this file to the proper format for setting the environment or type in the commands manually.

```
# Set the Environment

# Make Sure that TUXDIR is set
if [ "$TUXDIR" = "" ]
then
        if [ "$ROOTDIR" = "" ]
        then
                TUXDIR=/home/units/r60
```

```
                echo "WARNING: TUXDIR not set - defaults to $TUXDIR"
        else
                TUXDIR=$ROOTDIR
        fi
        export TUXDIR
fi

# Set APPDIR, TUXCONFIG, QMCONFIG
APPDIR=`pwd`
TUXCONFIG=$APPDIR/TUXCONFIG
QMCONFIG=$APPDIR/queuebase
export TUXDIR APPDIR TUXCONFIG QMCONFIG

# Set FML environment
FLDTBLDIR=${TUXDIR}/udataobj:${APPDIR}
FIELDTBLS=Usysflds,appflds
export FIELDTBLS FLDTBLDIR

# Set PATH, paths to find shared objects
a="`echo $PATH | grep ${TUXDIR}/bin`"
if [ x"$a" = x ]
then
        PATH=:${TUXDIR}/bin:${PATH}
        export PATH
fi
#
a="`echo $LD_LIBRARY_PATH | grep ${TUXDIR}/lib`"
if [ x"$a" = x ]
then
        LD_LIBRARY_PATH=${TUXDIR}/lib:${LD_LIBRARY_PATH}
        export LD_LIBRARY_PATH
fi
a="`echo $SHLIB_PATH | grep ${TUXDIR}/lib`"
if [ x"$a" = x ]
then
        SHLIB_PATH=${TUXDIR}/lib:${SHLIB_PATH}
        export SHLIB_PATH
fi
a="`echo $LIBPATH | grep ${TUXDIR}/lib`"
if [ x"$a" = x ]
then
        LIBPATH=${TUXDIR}/lib:${LIBPATH}
        export LIBPATH
fi
```

Listing A.7   *Example UNIX env File (shell script)*

Once the environment is set, the client and server programs can be built by executing **make**, using the following makefile. This makefile is for UNIX platforms. It will need some modifications for Windows. It may also need some additional arguments in the CFLAGS for various platforms.

```
# Sample Makefile for Unix
CFLAGS=-I$(TUXDIR)/include -g
SRC = \
                UBBCONFIG\
                app.h\
                appflds\
                client.c\
                createq\
                crtlog\
                env\
                ipclean\
                items\
                makefile\
                server.c\
                server2.c\
                util.c

all: server server2 client

server:         server.o util.o
                buildserver
                    -s NEWCUSTID,NEWCUST,RETRIEVECUST,RETRIEVEITEM
                    -o server -f server.o -f util.o

server2:        server2.o util.o
                buildserver -s SEARCHITEM -o server2 -f server2.o
                -f util.o

client:         client.o
                buildclient -o client -f client.o

util.o:         util.c appflds.h app.h
                $(CC) $(CFLAGS) -c util.c

client.o:       client.c appflds.h app.h
                $(CC) $(CFLAGS) -c client.c

server.o:       server.c appflds.h app.h
                $(CC) $(CFLAGS) -c server.c

server2.o:      server2.c appflds.h app.h
                $(CC) $(CFLAGS) -c server2.c

appflds.h:      appflds
                mkfldhdr appflds

save::
                cp $(SRC) save

print::
                pr $(SRC)

clean::
                rm -f *.o client server server2 appflds.h ULOG* stderr stdout

clobber::
                rm -f *.o client server server2 appflds.h ULOG* stderr stdout
                rm -f TLOG TUXCONFIG custid customer queuebase
```

Listing A.8   *Example makefile*

Once the executables are built, the TUXEDO configuration must be set up before running the application. The UBBCONFIG file must be edited to set the <uname> for the machine name, <TUXDIR> and <APPDIR>.

```
# Sample Single Machine Configuration File
# Change <uname>, <TUXDIR>, <APPDIR> values appropriately
*RESOURCES
IPCKEY          67890
MAXACCESSERS    40
MAXSERVERS      35
MAXSERVICES     75
MAXCONV         10
MASTER          SITE1
SCANUNIT        10
MODEL           SHM
LDBAL           Y
*MACHINES
<uname> LMID=SITE1
                TUXDIR="<TUXDIR>"
                APPDIR="<APPDIR>"
                TLOGDEVICE="<APPDIR>/TLOG"
                TLOGNAME=TLOG
                TUXCONFIG="<APPDIR>/TUXCONFIG"
                ULOGPFX="<APPDIR>/ULOG"

*GROUPS
APPG1           LMID=SITE1 GRPNO=1
APPG2           LMID=SITE1 GRPNO=2 TMSNAME=TMS_QM
        OPENINFO="TUXEDO/QM:<APPDIR>/queuebase:SAMPLE"
*SERVERS
DEFAULT: RESTART=Y MAXGEN=5 REPLYQ=Y CLOPT="-A"
TMQUEUE         SRVGRP=APPG2   SRVID=1 CLOPT="-s SAMPLE:TMQUEUE — "
                GRACE=0

server          SRVGRP=APPG1   SRVID=1
server2         SRVGRP=APPG1   SRVID=2 CONV=Y

*SERVICES
```

Listing A.9   *Example UBBCONFIG*

The configuration is loaded by executing

tmloadcf -y UBBCONFIG.

The transaction log can be created by running the following **crtlog** script. Note that these commands must be entered manually on Windows without a shell.

```
# Create the Transaction Log
tmadmin -c <<!
```

```
echo
crdl -b 500 -z ${APPDIR}/TLOG
q
!
```

Listing A.10 *Example crtlog File*

The queue base can be created by running the following **createq** script. Again, this script will need to be manually entered on Windows.

```
# Set the QMCONFIG and Q IPC key
QMCONFIG=`pwd`/queuebase
QIPCKEY=67891

# Create the Device List, "SAMPLE" Queue Space, and "ORDERS" Queue
qmadmin <<!
crdl $QMCONFIG 0 1000
echo on
# name ipckey pages queues
qspacecreate SAMPLE $QIPCKEY 900 20 30 30 100 "" n 32
qopen SAMPLE
qcreate ORDERS fifo top 2 0 "" "" ""
q
!
```

Listing A.11 *Example createq File*

A.7   Running the Application

To boot the application at this point, you would simply run **tmboot** as in the following listing.

```
tmboot -y
Booting all admin and server processes in /tuxedo/TUXCONFIG

Booting admin processes ...

exec BBL -A :
    process id=27861 ... Started.

Booting server processes ...

exec TMS_QM -A :
    process id=27862 ... Started.
```

```
exec TMS_QM -A :
    process id=27863 ... Started.
exec TMS_QM -A :
    process id=27864 ... Started.
exec TMQUEUE -s SAMPLE:TMQUEUE — :
    process id=27865 ... Started.
exec server -A :
    process id=27866 ... Started.
exec server2 -A :
    process id=27867 ... Started.
7 processes started.
```

Listing A.12 *Example Activation*

You can see what servers and services are available by running the command interpretor, **tmadmin**, or the GUI, **xtuxadm**.

```
tmadmin
# print services
> psc
Service Name    Routine Name    a.out Name Grp Name   ID      Machine   # Done   Status

RETRIEVEITEM    RETRIEVEITEM    server     APPG1       1       SITE1     0        AVAIL
RETRIEVECUST    RETRIEVECUST    server     APPG1       1       SITE1     0        AVAIL
NEWCUSTID       NEWCUSTID       server     APPG1       1       SITE1     0        AVAIL
NEWCUST         NEWCUST         server     APPG1       1       SITE1     0        AVAIL
SAMPLE          TMQUEUE         TMQUEUE    APPG2       1       SITE1     0        AVAIL
SEARCHITEM      SEARCHITEM      server2    APPG1       2       SITE1     0        AVAIL
TMS             TMS             TMS_QM     APPG2       30001   SITE1     0        AVAIL
TMS             TMS             TMS_QM     APPG2       30002   SITE1     0        AVAIL
TMS             TMS             TMS_QM     APPG2       30003   SITE1     0        AVAIL

# print servers
>psr
a.out Name      Queue Name      Grp Name   ID      RqDone   Load Done Current Service

BBL             67890           SITE1       0       1        50       (IDLE)
server          00001.00001     APPG1       1       0        0        (IDLE)
TMQUEUE         00002.00001     APPG2       1       0        0        (IDLE)
server2         00001.00002     APPG1       2       0        0        (IDLE)
TMS_QM          APPG2_TMS       APPG2       30001   0        0        (IDLE)
TMS_QM          APPG2_TMS       APPG2       30002   0        0        (IDLE)
TMS_QM          APPG2_TMS       APPG2       30003   0        0        (IDLE)

>q
```

Listing A.13 *Example tmadmin Session*

Use the client to enter customer and item information. The following is a sample run.

```
> client
1. Order item
2. Clear the Enqueue
3. Quit
Enter desired menu selection: 1

ORDER ITEM

Customer Number or Name (or return for New):
NAME: John Doe
ADDRESS: 10 Main Street
CITY: Anytown
STATE: NJ
ZIP: 07866
PHONE: 201-555-1212
Add customer to database?: y
CUSTID: 0000001
Item Name or Number (or return for Search):
1: 1000 Widget 0   $20.00
2: 1001 Widget 1   $21.00
3: 1002 Widget 2   $22.00
4: 1003 Widget 3   $23.00
5: 1004 Widget 4   $24.00
Enter menu number or return for more: 3
Enter credit card authorization or return to cancel: 101010
Order queued for processing
1. Order item
2. Clear the Enqueue
3. Quit
Enter desired menu selection: 3
>
```

Listing A.14   *Example Client Run*

To shutdown the application, simply execute

tmshutdown -y.

A.8   Summary

This chapter provides a sample application that includes many of the communication paradigms and features described throughout the book. Download it and run it yourself! You can use this as the basis for an application that you want to write and extend as needed.

B Appendix B— Glossary

The following acronyms, terms, and phrases appear within the text. Some of the terms have more general definitions, but the terms are defined here more narrowly with the meanings implied by their use with respect to the TUXEDO System.

2P-CPA see *Two-phase commit, presumed abort.*

abort see *rollback.*

abort-only see *rollback-only.*

ACL see *Access Control List.*

Access Control List (ACL) a list of groups permitted access to services, application queues, and events used for authorization checking.

activate to move an entity (computer, server, etc.) from an inactive state to and an active state.

Administrative API see *TMIB API.*

advertisement the process of indicating to all participants in an application that a service is active.

agent a software module which carries out the instructions of another module, usually on a remote site from the controlling module.

API see *Application Programming Interface.*

application the software and permanent resources (databases, files, RMs, etc.) used to computerize a business function; in the TUXEDO System, it is defined by a TMIB, and is synonymous with a domain.

application function shipping function shipping among application components. See *function shipping.*

application key a 32-bit identifier associated with each client when it joins a TUXEDO application; passed to each service and used for application authorization.

application password   a string, assigned by the administrator, required for all clients to join an application when security is configured.

application protocol   a predefined sequence of bits and bytes or messages communicated between application entities in the ISO model.

application queue   a stable storage area in a queue base used for queued communications.

application resources   data accessed via a Resource Manager.

Application Programming Interface (API)   definition of the calling formats to a set of procedures that perform a set of related tasks.

Application-to-Transaction Monitor Interface (ATMI)   the TUXEDO communications application programming interface.

asynchronous communications   communications in which the requestor does not wait for the response but will poll for it at a later time.

asynchronous request/response   see *asynchronous communications*.

ATMI   see *Application-to-Transaction Monitor Interface*.

atomicity   the "all-or-nothing" property of a transaction. This property ensures that ALL of the transactional-aware resources participating in the transaction either make any updates permanent at the end of a transaction or roll them back to their state at the beginning of the transaction.

auditing   the recording of accesses to a system and its data.

authentication   the security mechanism by which the TUXEDO System ensures that a client is who it says it is and is allowed to join the application.

authorization   the granting of permission to access an entity or perform an action; in the TUXEDO System, access is controlled by ACLs on services, queues, and events.

AUTHSVR   an administrative server that provides the authentication service.

AUTOTRAN   a configured option such that a service will automatically be started in transaction mode if the incoming request is not in transaction mode.

backup   a redundant component (computer, server, etc.) that takes over the work of the primary during a failure situation to provide high availability.

batch-oriented   an application characterized by *queued communications* (contrast with *on-line access*).

BB   see *Bulletin Board*.

BBL   see *Bulletin Board Liaison*.

BDMCONFIG   the TUXEDO binary configuration file for the definition of local and remote domains.

birth time   a future time, specified in either absolute or relative terms, before which a message enqueued in an application queue cannot be dequeued.

blocking condition   a condition in an application where a module is waiting for something to happen, such as sending a request or receiving a reply.

boot   see *activate*.

bracket   programmatic instructions used to indicate the beginning and end of a transaction.

BRIDGE   an administrative server that manages network communications between computers within an application.

Bulletin Board   a distributed, partially replicated, memory data structure used to maintain information in the TUXEDO System for name serving, transaction management, and run-time information; the dynamic part of the TMIB.

Bulletin Board Liaison (BBL)   an administrative server on each computer in the application that manages application servers.

business objects   the essential items of a business around which an application's service routines should be designed to manipulate them.

byte-stream file system   a file system in which all files are merely a sequence of bytes.

call descriptor   see *handle*.

CARRAY   a typed buffer format in which the data is an array of uninterpreted bytes; it always requires an associated length value.

centralized administration   control of a distributed application from a single site or "console."

client   a software module that gathers and presents data to an application; it generates requests for services and receives replies. This term can also be used to indicate the requesting role that a software module assumes by either a client or server process.

client name   the name supplied by the application client when joining the application, used for identifying and notifying a client.

client identifier   the identifier assigned to a client when joining the application.

client stub   a module generated by the IDL compiler to take the place of local routines for use with TxRPC; these routines send their arguments to the associated server for processing and handle the return data.

client/server   a means of distributing applications into cooperating software modules, some of which are called clients and others servers. Clients request work of servers. See also *request/response*.

commit   to terminate a transaction, making changes to the associated resources permanent.

Common Object Request Broker Architecture (CORBA)   the specification of an Object Request Broker (ORB) and associated software by the Object Management Group (OMG).

Communications API   an interface to a set of procedures that may be used to communicate with other software modules.

communications stack   a set of software which effects communication among software modules.

compensating transaction   application logic used to complete a transaction that has been left in an inconsistent state as a result of the interruption of the business logic.

component   part of an application.

consistency   the property of a transaction which ensures that data is presented to an application in an unchanging manner except for modifications made during the transaction.

contract   the agreement of the input and output parameters and processing between a client and server.

conversation   a communications paradigm involving a dialogue between the initiator and another module, consisting of multiple interactions with implied or explicit state or context.

conversational service   a service offered by a server that can be used with the conversational paradigm.

coordinator role   the role played by a TM during commitment. The coordinator directs the execution of the commitment algorithm.

correlation identifier   an identifier assigned by the application to be associated with a message when doing queued communications.

CORBA   see *Common Object Request Broker Architecture*.

custom typed buffer   an application-provided message format, with an associated type and subtype, that has been configured by the administrator.

daemon   a process that runs and does processing in the background.

data-dependent routing   assignment of a request to a server offering the requested service, based on the values of the data within the message.

data independence the ability to access and update data without knowing the underlying storage format or offset.

data shipping processing in an application whereby data is shipped back to the requestor to compute the result (contrast function shipping).

data translation the conversion of data for transfer between machines of different types; see also presentation service.

DBBL see *Distinguished Bulletin Board Liaison*.

DCE see *Distributed Computing Environment*.

decryption the rendering of an encrypted message into an intelligible form.

default initialization a client joining the application implicitly by calling an ATMI routine without a preceding call to **tpinit**.

deferred communications communications between modules which do not execute simultaneously. Typically deferred communications are performed via queues. See also queued communications.

descriptor see *handle*.

dip-in notification the unsolicited event notification mechanism by which a client receives notification when it calls any of the ATMI routines.

Distinguished Bulletin Board Liaison (DBBL) an administrative server that runs on the master machine and manages the distribution of the Bulletin Board and global updates thereto.

Distributed Computing Environment (DCE) middleware software, developed by the OSF, that includes communications, security, time, and file system services.

distribution, distributed computing, distributed application processing of application logic across more than one computer.

domain an autonomously administered application; particularly used in a situation where multiple applications intercommunicate.

DMADM an administrative server that manages updates to the TUXEDO Domains configuration.

DMCONFIG the ASCII definition of the local and remote domains known by the TUXEDO Domains feature.

drag-and-drop within the TUXEDO GUI (**xtuxadm**), the process of depressing a mouse button to select an icon associated with an object and moving it to another icon associated with an action to perform that action on the object; for example, dragging machine icon to the activate icon to boot a computer.

durability   the property of a transaction which guarantees the permanence of modified data upon commit.

dynamic reconfiguration   changing the definition of the application while the application is active.

encryption   the act of converting a message into a form which renders its contents unintelligible to unauthorized parties.

event   the occurrence of a condition, state change, or the availability of some information, usually of interest to one or more modules.

EventBroker™   module that forwards posted events to interested (registered) targets.

event data   information accompanying an event.

event generator   a module which indicates the occurrence of an event.

event identifiers   the method of naming an event.

event notification   signaling an interested party that a condition or state change has occurred.

event posting   sending an event to the EventBroker that will be forwarded to interested targets.

event target   a module which is notified of an event.

exception   when using TxRPC, an exception is a way of capturing errors raised by servers, without altering the remote procedure's definition.

executable   a program that can be run on an operating system.

fan-out parallelism   a programming paradigm in which multiple asynchronous communications calls are made so that parallel application processing is achieved.

fastpath   the mode in which an application client or server operates always attached to the Bulletin Board (contrast with *protected mode*).

fat-client/skinny-server   an application where most processing is done in the client module (contrast with *skinny-client/fat-server*).

fault tolerance   the ability of the application to continue running despite failures.

federated application   an application that is made up of a collection of other applications, called domains, that are intercommunicating.

field identifier   a numeric identifier associated with a data value in an FML buffer.

Field Manipulation Language   generically, an interface for maintaining buffers with field/value pairs; specifically, the 16-bit version of this interface (contrast with *FML32*).

field table   a mapping between FML field identifiers and field names.

FIFO   first-In, first-Out.

FML   see *Field Manipulation Language*.

FML32   the 32-bit version of FML.

forwarding   the mechanism by which pipelined parallelism is implemented, where processing of a request is sent on to another service that will complete the work and reply to the original requestor.

forwarding agent   an administrative server whose role is to dequeue messages in application queues, send them to request/response service routines for processing, and enqueue any replies to reply queues. All three operations are done as part of a single global transaction to guarantee atomicity of request forwarding.

function   see *procedure*.

function shipping   processing in an application whereby the operation is processed near the data and only the result is sent back to the requestor (contrast with *data shipping*).

gateway   a communications module between different environments (for example, between domains).

GET Operations   operations which retrieve data from the TMIB (contrast with *SET Operation*).

global transaction   a transaction that may span more than one resource manager.

global transaction identifier (GTRID)   a data structure which names a transaction created by a *Transaction Manager* (contrast with *local transaction identifier*).

group   see *server group*.

GTRID   see *global transaction identifier*.

GUI   Graphical User Interface.

GWADM   a server that provides administrative operations for maintaining the configuration needed to support access from/to remote domains.

heterogeneous (nodes)   computers running with different data formats, different operating systems, etc.

handle   in ATMI, a token returned to the application for further reference to an asynchronous request/response call or a conversational call.

heuristic decision   the unilateral commit or rollback of a transaction by a resource manager, independent of the decision taken for the global transaction of which it was a part.

IDL   see *Interface Definition Language*.

implementation transparency   see *information hiding*.

infection   the passing of a property from one module to another. Two types of infections occur in the TUXEDO System, timer and transaction.

information hiding   processing of a request by a service so that the requestor is not aware of how the processing occurs, allowing for reimplementation of the service without impacting the requestor.

Interface Definition Language (IDL)   the language used to describe data types and functions used for Remote Procedure Calls.

Interprocess Communication   the mechanisms by which modules in separate address spaces communicate within a computer—typically includes shared memory, semaphores, and message queues.

IPC   see *Interprocess Communication*.

ISO   International Standards Organization.

isolation   the property of a transaction which ensures that concurrent operations on the underlying data do not interfere with each other.

joining the application   the process of a client making itself known to the application.

language-based   an interface whereby calls are made to subfunctions (contrast with *library-based*).

LAN   Local Area Network.

LAN partition   partition where the network is a LAN; see partition.

library   a collection of modules.

library-based   an interface based on calling routines from a programming language (contrast with *language-based*).

load balancing   assignment of requests to queues for servers offering the requested service in a manner to optimize throughput and/or response time.

local client   a client program that runs on a computer where the TUXEDO System administrative programs and application servers run (contrast with *workstation client*).

local transaction   a transaction that is active in a single resource manager.

local transaction identifier   a data structure which names a transaction created by a resource manager.

location transparency   the ability to define a resource so that its name implies no particular network address or physical location.

lock   a data structure used to control access to data items by a resource manager.

Logical Machine IDentifier (LMID)   the logical machine name given to a computer in a TUXEDO application.

LMID   see *Logical Machine IDentifier*.

machine   in this context, a computer that is part of the TUXEDO application.

managed entities   resources that can be managed by the application administrator.

management framework   a software system that enables the management of a distributed system. Typically, the framework provides an architecture in which managed entities report their status and are controlled.

marshaling   the packing up of arguments and return values for transfer between machines.

master node   in the TUXEDO System, the computer configured as the master for an application; it contains the master copy of the configuration and is the computer where the **DBBL** runs.

message   data exchanged between communicating executables.

message catalog   a file containing strings printed by the programs and libraries that are translated into different languages for internationalization.

message identifier   a unique identifier returned to the application when enqueing a message for queued communications.

method   one of an object's processing functions.

MIB   see *TMIB*.

migration   the deactivation of servers on one computer and reactivation of the same servers on a backup computer.

module   a collection of procedures.

MP model   an application configuration that uses more than one computer..

MSSQ   see *Multiple Servers Single Queue*.

multiple-program broadcasting   communication mechanism used by a client or server to send an unsolicited notification, along with any data, to one or more client programs.

Multiple Servers Single Queue (MSSQ)   A queue servicing arrangement whereby multiple servers, all of which provide the same services, read requests from a single queue (contrast with *SSSQ*).

mutual authentication a procedure whereby both parties become assured of the identities of each other.

named rendezvous the string upon which two modules in an application agree to communicate. In the TUXEDO System this service name includes application queue names, or event names.

NetWare™ a network operating system developed by Novell.

network address a unique identifier by which a process on a remote computer may be contacted across a network.

node a computer that is part of a TUXEDO application.

object a data item and associated processing functions.

object reference a data structure which identifies an object to be manipulated.

Object Request Broker (ORB) a specification of OMG for a system which enables objects to communicate.

Object Transaction Service (OTS) the specification of transaction interfaces for an Object Request Broker (ORB) by the Object Management Group (OMG).

on-line access an application characterized by *on-line communications*. An application where a request needs to be satisfied in the immediate future, usually because a person awaits the result (contrast with *batch-oriented*).

on-line communications communications between two modules that are both concurrently executing (contrast with *queued communications*).

Open System Interconnect Transaction Processing the standard for transaction processing services and protocol.

operation the syntax and parameter definitions for a function contained within a TxRPC interface definition.

operating system the system software that controls a computer.

ORB see *Object Request Broker*.

orphanage see *transaction orphanage*.

OSF Open Software Foundation.

OSI TP see *Open System Interconnect Transaction Processing*.

OTS see *Object Transaction Service*.

outsourcing hiring another company to perform your computer operations.

paradigm a style or form of doing something.

participant relating to transactions, a resource manager whose access is to be part of the transaction.

partition decomposition of an application into modules that can be split onto more than one node; network partition—part of the application cannot communicate with another part of the application, usually due to a network failure.

phase one the first phase of commit. In this phase, the resources modified during the transaction are prepared for phase two. Phase one culminates with the recording of the transaction decision on a log.

phase two the second phase of commit. In this phase, the transaction decision is announced to the participants. Resource managers typically release locks held during the course of the transaction. This makes the results of the transaction visible to other accessors.

pipelined parallelism a programming paradigm in which processing occurs serially by more than one module, so that each stage in the pipeline performs some fraction of the total operation and passes its results off to the next stage, with the final stage responding to the requestor.

Physical Machine Identifier the physical name of a computer in a TUXEDO application.

PMID see *Physical Machine Identifier*.

POSIX an IEEE for an operating system interface, based heavily on UNIX (an earlier operating system interface).

post an event indicate that a condition occurred, so that the EventBroker can notify modules that have "subscribed" for the named event.

prenatal message a message which is put into a queue, but which cannot be dequeued until an application indicated birth time has arrived; see also *birth time*.

prepare notice a request from a TM to a resource manager for it to complete phase one of the 2PCPA algorithm. The RM answers the request with an indication that it is prepared for commitment or does not wish to commit.

prepare phase see *phase one*.

prioritized message a message which is inserted into a queue according to a priority scheme. Typically, this overrides the default FIFO ordering of a queue.

prepare to commit notify all participants in a transaction that they should get ready to complete the transaction; normally, this involves writing updates to stable storage.

presentation service a layer in a communication stack that converts data when it is transmitted between computers with differing binary representation.

primitive   see *procedure*.

principals   users and remote domains in an application that need authentication and authorization.

principal groups   collections of principals that may be assigned access rights using Access Control Lists.

priority   processing of messages based on an urgency factor assigned by the application.

privacy   the prevention of messages from being read by unauthorized people or programs. See also *encryption*.

procedure   a callable set of instructions.

procedural language   a programming language, such as C or COBOL, in which the programmer indicates what and how the operations are to be done.

protected mode   the mode in which an application client or server operates so that it detaches from the Bulletin Board when not in one of the ATMI routines (contrast with *fastpath*).

protocol, communications protocol   the sequence of bits and bytes or messages communicated between two or more components.

protocol violation   an ill-formed message or an attempt to issue a message in an appropriate context.

proxy   see *stub*.

/Q   the TUXEDO subsystem that provides reliable, application queues.

queue   a memory data structure to hold messages for processing (contrast with *application queue*).

queue base   a storage mechanism for holding messages, during queued communications, until they are processed.

queued communications   deferred communications between two modules, both of which may not be executing concurrently, so that the message is stored in a queue until the communications can be completed (contrast with *on-line communications*).

queue space   a collection of one or more application queues, used for doing queued communications.

Queuing API   an interface to a set of procedures that may be used to communicate between modules using queued communications.

RDBMS   Relational Database Management System.

recovery   processing to restore an application to a coherent state after a transaction, server, network, or computer has failed.

recovery procedure   see *recovery*.

reliable queuing   the storage of requests and replies using stable storage that survives computer failure.

RPC   see *Remote Procedure Call*.

Remote Procedure Call (RPC)   a procedure call that is executed in a nonlocal program or address space.

request buffer   a typed buffer containing a request for a service from a client or server.

request queue   the memory data structure that holds incoming requests for services.

reply buffer   a typed buffer containing a response for a request.

reply queue   the memory data structure that holds responses to requests.

request/response   a communications paradigm in which the client sends a request and the server responds with a reply.

requestor   a module which asks another to perform a task. See *client*.

requestee   a module asked to perform a task. See *server*.

Resource Manager (RM)   a module or collection of modules, the most common of which are databases, that maintain the state of the application.

response queue   see *reply queue*.

return event   an event that ATMI returns during conversational communication. The return event is the means by which both normal and abrupt disconnect and transfer of send-control events are reported.

RM   see *Resource Manager*.

RM API   the interface provided by a resource manager (for example, SQL for an RDBMS).

rollback   terminate a transaction such that all resources updated within a transaction revert to the original state before the transaction started.

rollback-only   an indication by a software module which is participating in a transaction that the transaction must not be committed.

routine   see *procedure*.

schema   the organization of a database system.

self-describing buffer   a data buffer that contains a description of its own format and contents; a message format in which the data type(s) and length(s) are known or can be determined without additional external information.

send control   in conversational communications, the right process that is allowed to call **tpsend** in the half-duplex (one-way) communications protocol.

server   a software module that accepts requests from clients and other servers and returns replies.

server adaptor   see *standard main*.

server group   a collection of servers that can be activated, deactivated, and migrated as a unit.

server initialization   the one-time application processing that is done when a server is activated.

server termination   the one-time application processing that is done when a server is deactivated.

server stub   a module generated by the IDL compiler on the server side for use with TxRPC; these routines unpack the input data, call the associated routine, and handle the returned data.

service   the name given to an application routine available for request by a client in the system with well-defined inputs, outputs, and processing.

service dispatch   execution of the routine associated with a requested service.

service layering   constructing new services from one or more existing services.

Service Request Broker (SRB)   a system which enables software modules to communicate via service requests.

service suspension   the administrative operation of marking a service temporarily unavailable for processing new requests.

SET Operation   an operation that modifies an object in the TMIB. Such operations may change the observable behavior of the system.

signal-based notification   the unsolicited event notification mechanism by which a client is interrupted to receive the notification.

single-program notification   communication mechanism used by a client or server to send an unsolicited notification, along with any data, to a single client program.

Single Server Single Queue (SSSQ)   a queue servicing arrangement whereby a single-memory queue is associated with a single server (contrast with *MSSQ*).

skinny-client/fat-server   an application where most processing is done in the server module (contrast with *fat-client/skinny-server*).

software pipeline   a sequence of software modules. Each member of the sequence, except the first module, receives its input from the output of its predecessor. Once a module has produced output, it is available to process another input. The terminal member of the sequence returns a result to the requestor.

specially ordered message   a message which is inserted into a queue in a place determined by application logic related to that specific message.

SQL   see *Structured Query Language*.

SRB   see *Service Request Broker*.

SSSQ   see *Single Server Single Queue*.

standard main   the processing done by the TUXEDO System for all application servers; it includes processing command line options, advertising services, and dispatching requests to the associated services. Also called the server adaptor.

stale messages   messages that are no longer valid for processing, either because of time-out or because the application has explicitly indicated it is no longer interested in the message.

stateless interaction   an interaction between a client and a server where the service neither uses nor maintains any extra information about the client to process its request; all the information necessary to complete the work is in the client's request buffer. Stateless interactions are usually associated with the request/response paradigm.

stateful interaction   an interaction is stateful when client and server keep track of where they are in a conversation by code position and the data kept in local variables. Stateful interactions are usually associated with the conversational paradigm.

status codes   an argument of a special type added to a TxRPC procedure definition through which errors are reported.

stored procedure   a set of instructions that is defined, named, saved and executed within a database system.

STRING   a typed buffer format in which the data is composed of non-0 characters followed by a 0 character.

Structured Query Language (SQL)   a standard language for accessing relational database management systems.

stub   a routine generated by the TxRPC compiler based on the interface definition of the RPC. For each RPC definition, two stubs are generated: a client-side stub and a server-side stub. A stub contains the data marshaling and unmarshaling logic as well as the communication logic allowing clients and servers to exchange data.

subordinate role   the actions performed by all participants, except the coordinator, in the 2PC-PA protocol. Subordinates are instructed by the coordinator to prepare for commitment and are informed by the coordinator as to the outcome of the transaction.

subroutine   see *procedure*.

subscription   a request to the EventBroker for notification of the occurrence of an event.

subtype   the name of a specific format for a specified buffer type; for example, a specific structure definition for the VIEW type.

synchronous communications   communications in which the requestor waits for the reply.

synchronous to the client   see synchronous communications.

thread   a unit of execution or an execution context. An executing sequence of instructions and the memory they manipulate.

time-out   an event that occurs when processing takes longer than expected or configured; time-outs can occur either when blocking for an operation or due to a transaction taking longer than specified by the application.

time-independent communication   see *deferred communication*.

TCP   see *Transmission Control Protocol*.

TLI   see *Transport Level Interface*.

tlisten   TUXEDO Listener—an administrative program that provides an entry point to all computers within the application; it is used primarily to propagate files and activate servers.

TLOG   see *transaction log*.

TM   see *Transaction Manager*.

TMIB   see *TUXEDO Management Information Base*.

TMIB API   see *TUXEDO Management Information Base Application Programming Interface*.

tmloadcf   the administrative command line program for loading an ASCII configuration definition into a binary representation.

TMQFORWARD   an administrative server that provides forwarding of enqueued messages for a TUXEDO queue base.

TMQUEUE   an administrative server that provides enqueuing and dequeueing access to a TUXEDO queue base.

TMS   see *Transaction Manager Server*.

TMSYSEVT   the TUXEDO System EventBroker and monitor. This server handles subscriptions to events generated by the TUXEDO System.

tmunloadcf   the administrative command line program for unloading the binary configuration file into an ASCII configuration definition; see also **tmloadcf**.

TMUSREVT   the TUXEDO System User EventBroker. This server handles subscriptions to events generated by the application.

transaction   a bracket around application work such that all or none of the operations are done.

transaction coordinator   see *coordinator*.

transaction identifier   see *global transaction identifier* and *local transaction identifier*.

transactional infection   see *infection*.

transaction initiator   the application software module that begins a transaction.

transaction log   a stable storage area where the completion of global transactions is logged.

Transaction Manager or Monitor   the software that manages global transactions across multiple computers and resource managers.

Transaction Manager Server (TMS)   an administrative server that manages the two-phase commit protocol and recovery for global transactions.

transaction orphanage   a collection of transactions which are not active in any executable.

transaction terminator   the application software module that ends a transaction.

transaction-aware resources   resources which "understand" the transaction notion within their execution. Such resources are subject to commit or rollback processing, as directed by a Transaction Manager.

Transmission Control Protocol (TCP)   the de facto standard transport level protocol used on LANs.

Transport Level Interface   a standard operating system interface to networking services.

TUXCONFIG   the TUXEDO binary configuration file for an application definition.

TUXEDO File System Management of TUXEDO System data in the form of a directory with files, stored either on raw disk or within a single file on the operating system file system.

TUXEDO Management Information Base (TMIB) a set of classes of objects with attributes within an application (for example, the class of servers with a name, identifier, command line arguments, etc.).

TUXEDO Management Information Base Application Programming Interface (TMIB API) an interface to a set of procedures to GET and SET information in the TMIB using TUXEDO ATMI and FML32.

Two-phase commit (2PC), presumed abort (PA) algorithm to ensure the atomicity of a committing transaction.

two-way alternate a form of conversational communication where either party is able to send a message, but only one party at a time is permitted to do so.

TX an X/OPEN interface for transaction demarcation; based on ATMI.

TxRPC Transactional Remote Procedure Call, the X/OPEN standard for transactional RPCs.

type the name of a data format for a typed buffer.

typed buffer a memory area, allocated from the TUXEDO System, that has an associated data type and subtype or format.

UBBCONFIG the ASCII file where TUXEDO administrators can define an application configuration; this file is compiled by **tmloadcf** to generate the static TMIB.

ULOG USERLOG—the name given to the log file where events are recorded.

unmarshaling the unpacking of arguments and return values after transfer.

unsolicited notification or communication an event where a module receives information that it did not request.

Universal Unique Identifier (UUID) A unique identifier that defines a TxRPC interface definition across all applications and all networks. Every IDL must have a UUID. The program **uuidgen** generates uuids.

UUID see *Universal Unique Identifier*.

VIEW a typed buffer format in which the data is composed of one or more fields similar to a C structure or a COBOL record.

view file a description of the layout of fields in a VIEW.

view compiler The TUXEDO **viewc** command which parses a view file and generates a binary file used at run-time to interpret VIEW typed buffers.

workflow the processing of a business operation using several steps, each of which must wait until the previous step completes successfully.

workload the relative amount of work associated with a service or with all service requests waiting on a request queue.

Workstation feature of the TUXEDO System that provides access to servers from clients executing on workstations.

Workstation Client (WSC) a client that accesses the TUXEDO System via the network (contrast with *local client*).

Workstation Handler (WSH) a surrogate client that executes operations on behalf of work station clients.

Workstation Listener (WSL) a TUXEDO server that listens for connection requests from work station clients and assigns them to Workstation Handler processes.

/WS see *Workstation*.

WSC see *Workstation Client*.

WSH see *Workstation Handler*.

WSL see *Workstation Listener*.

XA the X/Open Transaction Manager to Resource Manager interface.

XAP-TP an X/Open interface to the OSI TP protocol.

XATMI an X/Open interface based on ATMI.

X/OPEN a standards organization which merged with the OSF.

xtuxadm the TUXEDO graphical user interface for administration; it runs using the X Windows graphical interface.

C

Appendix C—References

[ANSIX3159] American National Standard X3.159.1989. *ANSI SQL.*

[CORBA] Object Management Group (OMG), July 1995. *The Common Object Request Broker: Architecture and Specification, Revision 2.0.*

[Date] Date, C.J., 1987. *Relational Database: Selected Writings.* Reading, MA: Addison-Wesley.

[Date2] Date, C.J., 1988. *A guide to the SQL Standard, 2nd ed.* Reading, MA: Addison-Wesley.

[Gray–Reuter] Gray, Jim, and Andreas Reuter, 1993. *Transaction Processing: Concepts and Techniques.* San Mateo, CA: Morgan Kaufmann Publishers, Inc.

[IBM-CICS] IBM, 1991. *Customer Information Control System/Enterprise Systems Architecture (CICS/ESA): General Information,* GC 33-0155: *Application Programming Guide,* SC 33-0675: *Distributed Transaction Programming,* SC 33-0783. Hursley Park, Hampshire, UK.

[IBM-LU6.2] IBM, 1991. *System Network Architecture (SNA) Logical Unit 6.2 (LU6.2) Transaction Programmer's Reference for LU6.2,* GC 30-3084. Research Triangle Park, NC.

[IBM-R*] Mohan, C., B. Lindsay, and R. Obermarck, (December) 1986. *Transaction Management in the R* Distributed Database System,* ACM TODS, Vol. 11, No. 4, pp. 378–396.

[Kernighan] Kernighan, B.W. and D.M. Ritchie, 1978 (classic C) and 1988 (ANSI C). *The C Programming Language.* Englewood Cliffs, NJ: Prentice-Hall.

[LMOS] Bergeron, R.F., and M.J. Rochkind, 1982. *Automated Repair Service Bureau Software— Tools and Components.* The Bell System Technical Journal, Vol. 61, No. 6 (July–August), pp. 1177.

[NETWARE] Novell, 1994. *Netware 4.0 Architecture.* Part Number 100-001900-002, Provo, Utah.

[NFS] Sun Microsystems, 1989. NFS: *Network File System Protocol Specification.*

[Ousterhout] Ousterhout, J.K., 1995. *Tcl and the Tk Toolkit.* Reading, MA: Addison-Wesley.

[OSF DCE] Open Software Foundation, 1992, *Introduction to DCE,* Open Software Foundation.

[OSF DCE RPC] Open Software Foundation, 1992. *DCE Application Development Reference.* Open Software Foundation. Englewood Cliffs, NJ: Prentice-Hall.

[OSI] ISO 7498, 1984. *Information Processing Systems—Open System Interconnection—Basic Reference Model.*

[OSI-TP] ISO/IEC 10026-1, 1992. *Information Technology—Open Systems Interconnection— Distributed Transaction Processing, Part 1: OSI TP Model.*
ISO/IEC 10026-2, *Information Technology—Open Systems Interconnection—Distributed Transaction Processing, Part 2: OSI TP Service.*
ISO/IEC 10026-3, *Information Technology_Open Systems Interconnection—Distributed Transaction Processing, Part 3: OSI TP Protocol Specification.*

[Pendergrast] Pendergrast, Jr., J.S. 1995. *Desktop Korn Shell Graphical Programming.* Reading, MA: Addison-Wesley.

[SNMP] Stallings, William, 1993. SNMP, SNMPV2, andCMIP, Reading, MA: Addison-Wesley.

[Tandem] Tandem Corp., 1995. *Technical Brief—NonStop TUXEDO: Open TP Monitor for Distributed Transaction Processing.*

[TUXEDO] Novell, TUXEDO System 6.1, 1995.
  Product Overview; Reference Manual; Message Manual; Programmer's Guide; Administrator's Guide; Application Development Guide; COBOL Guide; /Domain Guide; FML Guide; XTUX-ADM Guide; /Q Guide; TxRPC Guide; Workstation Guide.

[uucp] Nowitz, D.A. and M.E. Lesk, 1980. *Implementation of a Dial-Up Network on UNIX Systems,* Fall COMPCON, pp. 483–486, Washington, D.C. (September 1980).

[X/Open-TX] X/Open CAE Specification, 1995. *Distributed TP: The TX Specification,* X/Open Company Limited. Reading, Berkshire, UK

[X/Open-TxRPC] X/Open CAE Specification, 1995. *Distributed TP: The TxRPC Specification,* X/Open Company Limited.

[X/Open-CPIC] X/Open CAE Specification, 1995. *Distributed TP: The XCPI-C Specification,* Version 2, X/Open Company Limited.

[X/Open-DTP] X/Open, November 1993. *X/Open Guide, Distributed Transaction Processing: Reference Model,* ISBN 1-8512-019-9, X/Open Pub G307.

[X/Open-XA] X/Open CAE Specification, December 1991. *Distributed Transaction Processing: The XA Specification,* ISBN 1-872630-24-3, X/Open Pub C300.

[X/Open-XATMI] X/Open CAE Specification, November 1995. *Distributed Transaction Processing: The XATMI Specification,* ISBN 1-85912-130-6, X/Open Pub C506.

[X/Open-XAP-TP] X/Open CAE Specification, April 1995. ASCE/*Presentation: Transaction Processing (XAP-TP),* ISBN 1-85912-091-1, X/Open Pub C409

[X-Window] Quercia, V. and T. O'Reilly, 1990. *X Window System User's guide.* Sebastopol, CA: O'Reilly Associates, Inc.

Index

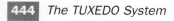